NEBUCHADNEZZAR'S
DREAM

Prophecy, Empires, and the End of History

Dr. Maxwell Shimba

Printed by Shimba Publishing LLC
Printed in the United States of America

TABLE OF CONTENTS

INTRODUCTION

Nebuchadnezzar's Dream: Prophecy, Empires, and the End of History by Dr. Maxwell Shimba offers an in-depth exploration of one of the most significant prophetic visions in human history—Nebuchadnezzar's dream, as recorded in the Book of Daniel. This prophetic account, which describes the rise and fall of a series of empires symbolized by a great statue of varying metals, has fascinated theologians, historians, and political thinkers for centuries. Dr. Shimba delves into the symbolism, historical significance, and theological implications of the dream, exploring how it has shaped perceptions of world history, modern geopolitical events, and the ultimate end of human civilization.

Through meticulous research, theological insight, and a broad interdisciplinary approach, Dr. Shimba examines how this ancient prophecy has been interpreted throughout history and how it continues to resonate in contemporary religious thought, political ideology, and social activism. This book brings together a wide range of perspectives from Christianity, Judaism, and Islam, as well as from secular thinkers who view prophecy as a tool for understanding the cyclical nature of human empires and the forces that shape the rise and fall of nations.

The Core of Nebuchadnezzar's Dream

At the heart of this work is the enigmatic vision revealed to King Nebuchadnezzar of Babylon in the Book of Daniel, Chapter 2. In the dream, Nebuchadnezzar sees a massive statue made of different metals—each representing a different empire. The head of gold represents his own empire, Babylon; the chest and arms of silver signify the Medo-Persian Empire; the belly and thighs of bronze symbolize Greece; and the legs of iron point to Rome. The final part of the statue, the feet of iron mixed with clay, represents the divided kingdoms that follow Rome, which many interpret as the modern nations of today.

However, the dream doesn't end with the vision of empires. A stone not cut by human hands strikes the statue, shattering it, and grows into a great mountain that fills the earth. This stone symbolizes the Kingdom of God, a divine reign that will replace all human systems and endure forever. It is this rock that holds the ultimate significance in Nebuchadnezzar's dream: the prophetic promise of a kingdom beyond human control that will establish God's final victory over the powers of the world.

Dr. Shimba examines the symbolic power of each element in the dream and connects these prophetic elements to historical realities and the future expectations of religious traditions. He argues that Nebuchadnezzar's dream offers not just a timeline of empires but a theological vision of history's ultimate purpose, one that still holds relevance today.

The Role of Empires in the Divine Plan

One of the major themes of Nebuchadnezzar's Dream is how this prophecy has historically been interpreted as a divine commentary on the nature of human power and its inherent fragility. Each metal in the statue symbolizes the material strength of the corresponding empire, but also its ultimate weakness. While Babylon is represented by gold, the most precious and stable of metals, it is soon succeeded by empires of lesser value, culminating in the feet of iron mixed with clay, which are both strong and brittle.

Dr. Shimba analyzes how each empire—Babylon, Medo-Persia, Greece, and Rome—played a pivotal role not just in world history but in the unfolding of God's plan. He traces how theologians across the centuries have understood these empires as part of a divinely ordained cycle, with each kingdom fulfilling its purpose before being swept away by a greater power.

Furthermore, he argues that these prophetic symbols are not confined to ancient history. The concept of the feet of iron and clay has often been applied to the modern world, where nations and political alliances, though powerful, are marked by division, instability, and fragility. Dr. Shimba suggests that this final phase of the statue symbolizes the post-Roman era and points to the fragmented political landscape we see today, marked by the rise and fall of nations, economic crises, and global instability.

Prophecy and the End of History

The climax of Nebuchadnezzar's dream, the destruction of the statue by the stone not cut by human hands, has been interpreted by many as the ultimate end of human history. In this act, the prophecy reveals the temporary nature of all human empires and the inevitable triumph of God's kingdom. This aspect of the dream has inspired centuries of eschatological thought, particularly within Christian and Jewish traditions, which see this as the Messianic age where God's justice will be fully realized on earth.

Dr. Shimba delves into the various interpretations of this divine intervention, exploring how different religious traditions view the final kingdom that will replace the earthly empires. He explores the Christian interpretation of this stone as Jesus Christ, whose return will bring about the Millennial Kingdom, and the Jewish understanding of this kingdom as the Messianic Age, a time of peace and justice led by a future descendant of David.

In addition, Dr. Shimba looks at how Islamic eschatology views this prophetic destruction as part of the end-time events involving the Mahdi and the return of Isa (Jesus), who will defeat the Dajjal (the Antichrist) and establish a kingdom of divine justice. He provides a comparative analysis, showing how these religious traditions share a common hope for a divine intervention that will bring an end to human systems of oppression and establish God's eternal reign.

The Relevance of Nebuchadnezzar's Dream in the Modern World

One of the key contributions of Dr. Shimba's book is his exploration of how Nebuchadnezzar's dream continues to influence modern religious thought and political movements. In particular, he looks at how this prophetic vision has shaped Christian Zionism, premillennial dispensationalism, and Islamic eschatology, all of which see current world events—especially the Middle Eastern conflict and the status of Jerusalem—as directly tied to the fulfillment of this ancient prophecy.

- Christian Zionism: Dr. Shimba explores how many Christian Zionists view the modern State of Israel as the fulfillment of biblical prophecy, specifically connecting it to the restoration of the Jewish people prophesied in the Old Testament. The belief in the end-times significance of

Jerusalem, the rebuilding of the Third Temple, and the geopolitical events surrounding Israel are deeply tied to the vision of the divine stone that will establish God's kingdom.

- Premillennial Dispensationalism: This movement interprets modern events through the lens of Revelation and Daniel's prophecy, seeing the current global instability—economic crises, wars, and political fragmentation—as part of the final stage represented by the feet of iron and clay. Dr. Shimba analyzes how this belief influences political engagement in Western nations, particularly in the United States, where evangelical Christians are key players in supporting pro-Israel policies and other end-times-related political stances.

- Islamic Eschatology: Dr. Shimba also provides insights into how Islamic movements interpret Nebuchadnezzar's dream within their own apocalyptic traditions. Many see the modern conflicts in the Middle East as precursors to the final battle between good and evil, where Isa (Jesus) and the Mahdi will defeat the forces of Dajjal and establish God's eternal kingdom on earth.

Structure of the Book

Nebuchadnezzar's Dream: Prophecy, Empires, and the End of History is divided into several chapters that guide the reader through both the historical and theological aspects of the prophecy:

1. The Vision: A detailed recounting of Nebuchadnezzar's dream and Daniel's interpretation.

2. Empires in Prophecy: A historical analysis of the empires symbolized by the metals in the statue.

3. Theological Progression: How the prophecy has been interpreted across various religious traditions.

4. The Modern World: How Nebuchadnezzar's dream continues to influence religious and political movements today.

5. Eschatological Implications: The ultimate meaning of the stone and the establishment of God's kingdom.

In Nebuchadnezzar's Dream: Prophecy, Empires, and the End of History, Dr. Maxwell Shimba offers a comprehensive and compelling analysis of one of the Bible's most important prophetic visions. By connecting this ancient dream to both historical events and modern geopolitics, Dr. Shimba demonstrates the enduring relevance of prophetic thought in shaping how we understand the world around us—and what we expect for the future.

This book invites readers to reflect on the divine plan woven through history, the fragility of human power, and the hope for a future where God's kingdom will bring lasting justice, peace, and restoration

DR. MAXWELL SHIMBA

CHAPTER 01

THE BOOK OF ACTS

In the annals of biblical prophecy, few visions carry the apocalyptic weight and far-reaching influence of Nebuchadnezzar's dream, as recounted in the book of Daniel (Daniel 2:31-45). This dream, given to the powerful Babylonian king during his reign in the 6th century BCE, serves as a profound prophecy that has captured the imagination of theologians, historians, and believers for millennia. Its vivid symbolism and cryptic imagery have been interpreted as a roadmap of human history, one that charts the rise and fall of great empires, the fragility of human kingdoms, and ultimately, the divine establishment of God's eternal kingdom.

Nebuchadnezzar's dream features a grand statue composed of various metals, each representing a different kingdom, with a mysterious and powerful stone that strikes the statue and ushers in the final, indestructible kingdom. The interpretation of this dream, delivered by the prophet Daniel, outlines the course of world empires and conveys a powerful message about the sovereignty of God over human history.

This introductory chapter will present an overview of Nebuchadnezzar's dream, its key symbols, and the prophetic meaning as laid out in Daniel 2:31-45. It will also lay the foundation for how this prophecy connects with the broader themes of apocalyptic thought, particularly in relation to historical events like the Crusades and interpretations of the end of history.

Nebuchadnezzar's Dream (Daniel 2:31-35)

Nebuchadnezzar's dream begins with a magnificent image of a statue that dominates the vision. The statue is composed of four distinct metals, arranged in descending order of value but increasing in strength, symbolizing a progression through different kingdoms. The vision is described in Daniel 2:31-35:

The Statue:

1. Head of Gold – The head of the statue is made of pure gold, representing the pinnacle of human civilization and power. This golden head is identified by Daniel as the Babylonian Empire, led by Nebuchadnezzar himself.

2. Chest and Arms of Silver – The upper torso and arms are crafted from silver. This symbolizes a kingdom inferior to Babylon but still of great strength and wealth,

commonly identified as the Medo-Persian Empire, which succeeded Babylon.

3. Belly and Thighs of Bronze – The midsection of the statue is made of bronze, representing another kingdom that would rise after the Medo-Persians. Historically, this is understood to be the Greek Empire, known for its widespread influence under Alexander the Great.

4. Legs of Iron – The lower part of the statue, particularly the legs, is made of iron, symbolizing a kingdom characterized by its military might and indomitable power. This has traditionally been identified as the Roman Empire, whose dominion stretched across vast territories and whose influence endured for centuries.

5. Feet of Iron and Clay – The statue's feet are composed of a mixture of iron and clay, symbolizing a divided kingdom that is both strong and fragile. Many interpreters see this as representing the fractured state of post-Roman kingdoms, particularly in Europe, with some kingdoms possessing great strength (iron) while others are weak and brittle (clay). The mix of iron and clay also suggests an inability for these kingdoms to fully unify.

The Stone:

After the description of the statue, the vision culminates in the appearance of a stone "cut out without hands." This stone strikes the feet of the statue, causing the entire structure to collapse and be shattered into dust, which is blown away by the wind. The stone then grows into a great mountain that fills the whole earth, symbolizing a kingdom that will never be destroyed—a divine kingdom established by God, transcending all human powers and empires.

Daniel's Interpretation (Daniel 2:36-45)

Following the recounting of Nebuchadnezzar's dream, Daniel provides the interpretation of the vision. In verses 36-45, Daniel reveals the symbolic meaning behind the statue's different parts, identifying the sequence of world empires that would follow Babylon. Each of the metals represents a kingdom that would rise, dominate the known world, and eventually fall, succeeded by the next.

- The Golden Head is explicitly identified as the Babylonian Empire, with Nebuchadnezzar as its supreme ruler. Daniel says to the king: "You, O king, are the king of kings. The God of heaven has given you dominion and power and might and glory." However, this kingdom, though glorious, is not eternal and will be followed by successive empires.

- The Silver Chest and Arms represent the kingdom that will succeed Babylon, commonly understood as the Medo-Persian Empire, which conquered Babylon in 539 BCE.

- The Bronze Belly and Thighs refer to the third kingdom, historically associated with the Greek Empire, which emerged after the Medo-Persians and spread Greek culture and governance through the conquests of Alexander the Great.

- The Iron Legs symbolize the Roman Empire, which followed the Greeks and ruled with an iron fist, bringing unparalleled strength, legal structures, and military discipline to the known world.

- The Iron and Clay Feet represent a divided kingdom, often interpreted as the various kingdoms that arose from the ruins of the Roman Empire. These kingdoms are a mixture of strength (iron) and weakness (clay), symbolizing their inability to unite into a single enduring empire.

The prophecy, however, does not end with the succession of these earthly kingdoms. Daniel concludes with the striking image of the stone that destroys the statue. This stone, cut "without hands," represents the divine kingdom that God will establish. Unlike the previous kingdoms, which were transient and built on human power, this kingdom is eternal and will fill the whole earth. It is often interpreted as the messianic kingdom of Christ, which brings an end to human rule and establishes God's reign over all.

Apocalyptic Significance of Nebuchadnezzar's Dream

Nebuchadnezzar's dream has long been seen as a key piece of biblical apocalyptic prophecy, outlining the divine plan for the course of world history. Each kingdom in the dream represents not only a specific historical empire but also a broader spiritual truth about the limitations of human power and the ultimate sovereignty of God.

- Historical Progression: The succession of empires demonstrates the transient nature of human rule. Despite their power and glory, each kingdom falls in turn, giving way to the next. This reflects a common theme in apocalyptic literature: that human attempts to dominate the world are ultimately futile in the face of divine power.

- The Divine Kingdom: The final aspect of the prophecy—the stone that destroys the statue and becomes a mountain—points to the establishment of a divine kingdom that will endure forever. This is seen by many Christian interpreters as a foreshadowing of the coming of Christ and the eventual realization of God's Kingdom on earth.

- Prophecy and History: Throughout the centuries, theologians, historians, and religious leaders have applied this vision to their own times, seeing in the successive kingdoms a blueprint for understanding the rise and fall of empires throughout history. From the fall of Rome to the divided kingdoms of Europe, from the Crusades to modern times, Nebuchadnezzar's dream has served as a lens through which to interpret the unfolding of history and the ultimate fulfillment of God's plan.

In this book, we will explore how Nebuchadnezzar's dream has been interpreted through various lenses—historically, theologically, and apocalyptically. The dream's progression from gold to clay, and the ultimate intervention of divine power, offers a profound meditation on the limits of human empire and the hope of a coming age where justice, peace, and divine rule are realized. As we delve deeper into each symbol and its prophetic meaning, we will also examine how this vision connects to significant historical events, such as the Crusades, and how it continues to shape eschatological thought about the end of history.

Explanation of Symbols within Nebuchadnezzar's Vision

In the biblical book of Daniel (Daniel 2:31-45), Nebuchadnezzar's dream features a statue composed of different metals, each part symbolizing a kingdom or empire. The dream reveals a progression of human history, from the reign of Nebuchadnezzar's Babylon to the establishment of God's eternal kingdom. Each material of the statue carries deep prophetic significance, and these symbols have been interpreted as representing key empires that shaped ancient and medieval history. Below is a detailed explanation of the symbols and their apocalyptic meanings.

1. The Head of Gold – Babylon

- Symbolism: Gold is a symbol of supreme wealth, grandeur, and authority. The head of gold represents the Babylonian Empire, which was at the height of its power during Nebuchadnezzar's reign.

- Prophetic Meaning: Babylon is described by Daniel as "the king of kings" (Daniel 2:37-38), a dominant world empire marked by immense splendor and sophistication. The use of gold highlights the empire's supremacy over the ancient world. Historically, Babylon's rule lasted from around 605 to 539 BCE, known for its impressive architectural achievements (like the Hanging Gardens) and for centralizing power in the Near East. The head of gold thus symbolizes the apex of human civilization in its era, but it is also transient, as Babylon eventually falls to the Medo-Persian Empire.

- Spiritual Meaning: Babylon is often depicted in the Bible as a symbol of pride, excess, and rebellion against God's authority. The fall of Babylon foreshadows the collapse of human powers that seek to glorify themselves above divine rule. It also represents the start of a sequence of kingdoms that are ultimately inferior to the divine order.

2. The Chest and Arms of Silver – Medo-Persia

- Symbolism: Silver, though valuable, is inferior to gold, signifying a kingdom of lesser splendor but great strength and durability. The statue's chest and arms, symbolizing the Medo-Persian Empire, suggest a dual kingdom—hence the two arms.

- Prophetic Meaning: The Medo-Persian Empire followed the Babylonian empire, conquering Babylon in 539 BCE. Under kings like Cyrus the Great and Darius, this empire expanded across a vast territory, incorporating peoples from Egypt to India. However, despite its strength, the Medo-Persians did not possess the cultural or architectural grandeur of Babylon. Daniel's prophecy aligns this empire with silver to indicate its notable, but inferior, status compared to Babylon.

- Spiritual Meaning: The Medo-Persian Empire is often associated with the theme of divine justice. Cyrus the Great, for example, is seen in the Bible as an instrument of God's will, particularly for his role in allowing the Jews to return to Jerusalem and rebuild the temple (Isaiah 45:1). This aspect of prophecy reflects the notion that even pagan empires can be used by God to fulfill His purposes in history.

3. The Belly and Thighs of Bronze – Greece

- Symbolism: Bronze is stronger than silver but less precious, symbolizing a kingdom known for military prowess and philosophical influence rather than wealth or grandiosity. The belly and thighs represent the Greek Empire, which succeeded the Medo-Persian rule.

- Prophetic Meaning: The Greek Empire, led initially by Alexander the Great, conquered much of the known world by the 4th century BCE. Alexander's empire extended from Greece to India, creating a vast Hellenistic culture that influenced language, philosophy, science, and politics across multiple regions. Bronze, a common material in ancient weaponry, is an apt symbol for the Greek Empire, reflecting its focus on conquest and intellectual achievement. The belly and thighs correspond to the geographical spread of the empire, with Greece as its cultural center.

- Spiritual Meaning: The Greek influence marked a profound cultural shift in the ancient world. Hellenistic philosophy and culture played a significant role in shaping later religious thought, including early Christian theology. However, despite its intellectual brilliance and military success, the Greek Empire was not eternal. Like the other kingdoms in the vision, it was part of the broader historical progression that would eventually give way to divine rule.

4. The Legs of Iron – Rome

- Symbolism: Iron is a symbol of strength, rigidity, and dominance, representing the unyielding military and political power of the Roman Empire. The two legs signify the division of the empire into the Western Roman Empire and the Eastern (Byzantine) Empire.

- Prophetic Meaning: The Roman Empire was one of the most powerful empires in human history, dominating the Mediterranean world and beyond from around 27 BCE to the eventual fall of its Western half in 476 CE. The Eastern Roman Empire (Byzantium) continued until 1453 CE. Iron, known for its use in weapons and tools, symbolizes Rome's unparalleled military and administrative strength. Its empire was marked by a long period of political stability and control through law, with its legacy still influencing modern legal and governmental systems.

- Spiritual Meaning: The Roman Empire, despite its strength, is not portrayed as invincible. While Rome's influence is immense, Daniel's vision suggests that even the most powerful human structures will eventually give way to God's eternal kingdom. Rome's role in biblical prophecy is often linked to its persecution of early Christians, the crucifixion of Christ under Roman governance, and its eventual Christianization under Constantine. The empire's dual nature (Western and Eastern) also symbolizes the divided yet enduring legacy of Rome.

5. The Feet of Iron and Clay – Divided Kingdoms

- Symbolism: The mixture of iron and clay represents a kingdom that is partly strong and partly fragile. Clay, unlike iron, is brittle and easily shattered, suggesting instability and division within this future kingdom.

- Prophetic Meaning: Historically, many interpreters associate the feet of iron and clay with the various kingdoms and empires that rose after the fall of Rome. These could include the fragmented European kingdoms during the Middle Ages, the Holy Roman Empire, and even more modern alliances and coalitions of nations. The image of iron mixed with clay signifies the difficulties these kingdoms would face in maintaining unity and strength. While some of these post-Roman states retained the military strength (iron) of Rome, their inherent divisions (clay) made them weaker and more susceptible to internal collapse.

- Spiritual Meaning: The feet of iron and clay symbolize the fragility of human governance, particularly when human kingdoms are divided by conflicting ideologies, interests, and values. It represents the vulnerability of human institutions that, despite their military or political strength, are ultimately fragile and unable to endure indefinitely. The inability of these kingdoms to fully unify suggests that human attempts to create lasting peace or unity will fail in the absence of divine authority.

6. The Stone Not Cut by Human Hands – God's Kingdom

- Symbolism: The stone, cut without hands, represents a divine intervention, a kingdom established by God rather than by human effort. It is not part of the statue (human empires) but comes from outside, symbolizing its divine origin.

- Prophetic Meaning: The stone strikes the feet of the statue, causing the entire structure to crumble, symbolizing the ultimate destruction of all human empires. After this, the stone grows into a great mountain that fills the whole earth, representing the establishment of God's eternal kingdom. This kingdom is often interpreted as the messianic rule of Christ, which will endure forever and replace all earthly powers. The mountain is symbolic of strength, stability, and eternal dominion.

- Spiritual Meaning: The stone symbolizes the ultimate sovereignty of God over history. It represents the divine kingdom that will outlast all human empires, characterized by justice, peace, and righteousness. In Christian theology, the stone is often linked to Christ, who is described as the "cornerstone" and the one who will establish God's eternal reign on earth. This eternal kingdom will not be like the transient kingdoms of the world; it will endure forever, signaling the culmination of history and the realization of God's divine plan.

Summary of the Symbolism in Nebuchadnezzar's Dream

Nebuchadnezzar's vision presents a prophetic outline of human history, depicting the rise and fall of successive world empires. Each material of the statue symbolizes the varying strength, wealth, and durability of these kingdoms, but all are ultimately impermanent. The stone, which destroys the statue and grows into a mountain, represents God's kingdom, the only eternal dominion that will replace all human authority.

In the context of apocalyptic prophecy, the dream serves as a powerful reminder of the fragility of human power and the ultimate sovereignty of God over the course of history. While human kingdoms rise in glory and strength, they are temporary and vulnerable, but God's kingdom will endure forever, bringing history to its divine fulfillment.

Historical Relevance of Apocalyptic Prophecy in Religious and World History

Apocalyptic prophecy has played a powerful and often dramatic role in shaping religious beliefs, social movements, and historical events throughout world history. Rooted in a deep conviction that the current world order is temporary and destined for divine intervention, apocalyptic thought has influenced how people understand their present circumstances, their expectations for the future, and their roles within this cosmic narrative.

Apocalyptic prophecies generally describe a future scenario where divine forces intervene to overthrow existing worldly powers and establish a new, eternal order—typically characterized by peace, justice, and the direct rule of God or a messianic figure. These prophecies are often accompanied by catastrophic events, the final judgment of humanity, and the fulfillment of a divine plan. Such narratives are present in many religious traditions, including Judaism, Christianity, Islam, and Zoroastrianism, each with their own distinct prophetic frameworks.

The influence of apocalyptic prophecy extends far beyond religious thought; it has impacted political movements, inspired wars, and shaped societies, particularly during periods of crisis or uncertainty. Below is a survey of key moments in religious and world history where apocalyptic prophecy has played a central role.

1. Apocalyptic Prophecy in Ancient Jewish Thought

The origins of apocalyptic prophecy in the Abrahamic traditions can be traced back to the Hebrew Bible, particularly in books like Daniel, Isaiah, and Ezekiel, which contain visions of the end times and the eventual triumph of God over evil. The Jewish people, especially during times of exile and oppression, were deeply influenced by apocalyptic promises of deliverance. These prophecies offered hope during periods of suffering, especially during the Babylonian captivity (circa 586 BCE) and the later Seleucid persecutions under Antiochus IV (2nd century BCE).

Key Examples:

- The Book of Daniel: As discussed in relation to Nebuchadnezzar's dream, Daniel's vision of the rise and fall of kingdoms is a seminal example of apocalyptic prophecy. It provided a framework for understanding historical events as part of a divine plan, encouraging Jews to remain faithful as they awaited God's intervention.

- Messianic Expectations: In times of political instability, such as during the Roman occupation of Judea, Jewish apocalyptic writings anticipated the coming of a Messiah who would restore Israel and establish God's kingdom on earth. This expectation was a major factor during the revolts against Roman rule, such as the Jewish-Roman Wars (66-70 CE) and the Bar Kokhba Revolt (132-135 CE).

2. Christian Apocalyptic Thought: The Book of Revelation and Early Christianity

Christianity emerged in the context of Jewish apocalyptic thought, with Jesus' ministry being viewed by many of his followers as the fulfillment of messianic prophecies. The New Testament, particularly the Book of Revelation (also known as the Apocalypse of John), presents a highly symbolic and detailed vision of the end times. Revelation describes a final battle between good and evil, culminating in the defeat of Satan and the establishment of God's kingdom on a renewed earth. This prophetic vision became central to early Christian eschatology and has continued to influence Christian theology throughout history.

Key Themes in Christian Apocalypticism:

- The Second Coming of Christ: The belief that Christ will return to judge the living and the dead is a cornerstone of Christian apocalyptic thought. Early Christians believed they were living in the "end times," a belief that persisted through various eras of crisis, such as during the persecution of Christians under the Roman Empire.

- The Antichrist and Final Tribulation: The figure of the Antichrist, a false messianic leader who will deceive the world before being overthrown by Christ, is a key character in Christian apocalyptic literature. Many periods of history, including the Protestant Reformation and modern times, have seen individuals accused of being the Antichrist.

Historical Relevance:

- Fall of Rome: The collapse of the Western Roman Empire in 476 CE was interpreted by many early Christians as a sign of the impending apocalypse. Church fathers like Augustine of Hippo grappled with these events in works like The City of God, emphasizing the transient nature of earthly empires in contrast to the eternal city of God.

- Medieval Millennialism: Throughout the Middle Ages, apocalyptic expectation flared during periods of crisis such as famines, plagues, and wars. The year 1000 CE, in particular, saw widespread millennial expectations, as many believed that the end of the first millennium would mark the end of the world.

3. The Crusades and Apocalyptic Prophecy

The Crusades (11th–13th centuries) were deeply influenced by apocalyptic expectations within both Christianity and Islam. For many medieval Christians, the call to reclaim Jerusalem from Muslim rule was seen as a fulfillment of apocalyptic prophecy, with Jerusalem playing a central role in both biblical and contemporary end-times speculation. Pope Urban II's call for the First Crusade in 1095 framed the mission as not only a defense of Christendom but as part of a divine mandate.

Christian Apocalypticism and the Crusades:

- Holy War and Eschatology: The Crusades were perceived as part of the cosmic struggle between good and evil, with many believing that the conquest of the Holy Land would hasten the return of Christ. Preachers such as Bernard of Clairvaux used apocalyptic imagery to inspire Crusaders, portraying the Muslim forces as agents of the Antichrist.

- Jerusalem and the End Times: The city of Jerusalem held deep apocalyptic significance, with prophecies suggesting that it would play a key role in the final events leading to the Second Coming. The capture of Jerusalem by Crusaders in 1099 was seen as a divinely ordained victory.

Islamic Apocalypticism and Jihad:

- Muslim Views of the Crusades: In response to the Christian Crusades, many Muslim scholars and leaders framed the conflict in apocalyptic terms as well. Islamic eschatology contains its own prophecies about a final confrontation between the forces of Islam and unbelievers. Leaders like Saladin were viewed as defenders of the Islamic faith, with the Crusaders being seen as part of the apocalyptic conflict predicted in Islamic texts.

4. Reformation and Apocalyptic Movements

The Protestant Reformation in the 16th century was heavily influenced by apocalyptic themes. Reformers such as Martin Luther and John Calvin saw the Roman Catholic Church as corrupt and identified the papacy with the Antichrist. This interpretation was supported by a long tradition of viewing the Church as part of the prophetic narrative found in the Book of Revelation.

Apocalyptic Movements during the Reformation:

- Luther and the Papacy: Martin Luther's denunciation of the Catholic Church included the belief that the Pope represented the Antichrist, and that the Church's power was a sign of the end times. Apocalyptic language fueled the zeal of reformers, who saw their mission as part of a divine effort to restore the true Christian faith.

- Radical Reformation: Various radical movements, such as the Anabaptists, took apocalypticism further, believing that the final judgment was imminent. In some cases, this led to violent uprisings, such as the Münster Rebellion (1534-1535), where apocalyptic fervor drove radical Anabaptists to seize control of the German city of Münster and establish what they believed to be a new "Kingdom of God."

5. Modern Apocalypticism: 19th and 20th Centuries

In more recent history, apocalyptic themes have persisted in both religious and secular contexts. The 19th century saw the rise of new apocalyptic movements, such as the Millerites, who believed that Christ would return in 1844, a movement that eventually gave rise to the Seventh-day Adventist Church. The 20th century, meanwhile, witnessed the widespread fear of nuclear apocalypse during the Cold War era, a period in which both religious and secular narratives about the end of the world converged.

Key Examples:

- The Adventist Movements: Following the failed prediction of Christ's return in 1844 (known as the "Great Disappointment"), Adventist groups continued to interpret current events through an apocalyptic lens. Today, denominations such as the Seventh-day Adventist Church emphasize apocalyptic prophecy in their teachings.

- Cold War and Nuclear Apocalypse: The threat of nuclear war during the Cold War led to a secular form of apocalyptic anxiety. Many believed that humanity was on the brink of a man-made apocalypse, with films, literature, and political rhetoric reflecting these fears.

- 21st Century Apocalypticism: Apocalyptic expectations continue to influence religious movements, particularly within evangelical Christianity. Events like the establishment of the state of Israel in 1948 have been seen by some as the fulfillment of biblical prophecy. Additionally, contemporary geopolitical conflicts in the Middle East are often framed within an apocalyptic narrative by certain religious groups.

Apocalyptic Prophecy and World History

Apocalyptic prophecy has been a powerful force throughout world history, influencing religious movements, political actions, and social upheavals. From the visions of

Daniel and Revelation to the apocalyptic fervor of the Crusades and the Reformation, believers have looked to prophecy as a way to make sense of historical events and their place within a divine plan. Even in modern times, apocalyptic expectations continue to shape religious beliefs and inspire both hope and fear regarding the future. The recurring pattern of prophecy influencing human history serves as a reminder of the profound and enduring impact that visions of the end have on the course of human civilization.

Expanded Discussion on the Historical Relevance of Apocalyptic Prophecy in Religious and World History

Apocalyptic prophecy, with its promise of divine intervention, cataclysmic events, and the eventual establishment of a perfect and just kingdom, has profoundly shaped human history across cultures, religions, and epochs. These prophecies have not only been sources of spiritual guidance but have also influenced political movements, social revolutions, and conflicts. To understand the full scope of their impact, we will examine several additional examples of how apocalyptic ideas have shaped different historical periods, movements, and key events.

1. Apocalypticism in Second Temple Judaism and the Intertestamental Period

The period between the Hebrew Bible and the New Testament, often referred to as the Intertestamental Period (circa 400 BCE – 1st century CE), was one of intense political turmoil and cultural exchange. During this time, apocalyptic prophecy became particularly prominent in Jewish thought, largely in response to foreign domination and persecution, notably by the Seleucid Empire and later by Rome.

Second Temple Apocalyptic Texts:

- The Book of Enoch: This non-canonical text, written during the Second Temple period, contains detailed apocalyptic visions that include angelic battles, divine judgment, and the ultimate triumph of righteousness. The Book of Enoch had a profound influence on Jewish apocalyptic thought and later Christian eschatology. It describes the coming of a messianic figure, judgment of the wicked, and the establishment of a new divine order, themes that would deeply resonate with early Christians.

- The Maccabean Revolt (167–160 BCE): This Jewish uprising against the Seleucid Empire, led by the Maccabees, was steeped in apocalyptic imagery. The desecration of the Jewish Temple by Antiochus IV Epiphanes was seen as a sign of the end times, as prophesied in the Book of Daniel. The successful revolt, celebrated during Hanukkah, was interpreted as a temporary victory against the forces of evil, with full deliverance yet to come.

The Role of the Roman Occupation:

- Eschatological Expectations Under Roman Rule: By the time of Roman rule over Judea, Jewish expectations of an imminent messianic kingdom were at a peak. The oppression by Roman governors and the defilement of the Holy Land contributed to an increasing focus on apocalyptic prophecy. Many Jewish sects, such as the Essenes (authors of the Dead Sea Scrolls), believed that they were living in the last days and that a divine warrior would soon come to deliver them from the Roman Empire.

- Messianic Movements: Several messianic claimants arose during this period, each invoking apocalyptic visions to rally support. Leaders such as Simon bar Kokhba, who led a major revolt against Rome (132–135 CE), were viewed by many as fulfilling the prophecies of the coming messiah who would overthrow the Romans and establish God's kingdom. These movements highlight how apocalyptic prophecy often intersected with political resistance and nationalism.

2. Apocalyptic Prophecy in Early Christianity and the Roman Empire

The apocalyptic visions of the New Testament, particularly the Book of Revelation, played a central role in shaping early Christian identity and their view of history. Christians in the first few centuries CE lived under the shadow of the Roman Empire, which not only persecuted them but also dominated the political and cultural landscape.

In this context, apocalyptic prophecy was not just a source of hope for future deliverance but also a powerful critique of imperial power.

Revelation and the Roman Empire:

- Symbolism of the Beast: The Book of Revelation's imagery of the "Beast" (Revelation 13) was often interpreted as a symbol of the Roman Empire. The Beast, which enforces worship of itself and persecutes the faithful, is identified with the emperors who demanded divine honors, such as Nero and Domitian. Early Christians believed that the fall of the Roman Empire, foretold in the visions of Revelation, was imminent and would be brought about by divine judgment.

- The Martyrdom of Early Christians: The persecution of Christians under Roman emperors like Nero and Diocletian was seen by the early Church as part of the tribulations preceding the final judgment. Martyrdom, in particular, was interpreted through an apocalyptic lens, with those who died for their faith being seen as participants in the ultimate victory of Christ at the end of days.

Constantinian Shift:

- Christianity Becomes the State Religion: The Roman Emperor Constantine's conversion to Christianity and the subsequent establishment of Christianity as the official religion of the Roman Empire in the early 4th century marked a dramatic shift. Many Christians saw Constantine's rise as a fulfillment of apocalyptic prophecies regarding the establishment of Christ's kingdom on earth. Some even viewed Constantine as a messianic figure who was preparing the world for the Second Coming of Christ.

- Augustine's Interpretation: As the Roman Empire began to decline, Augustine of Hippo addressed apocalyptic fears in his monumental work The City of God. Augustine rejected the idea that the fall of Rome was necessarily a sign of the imminent end of the world. Instead, he proposed that the true "City of God" was spiritual and eternal, transcending the rise and fall of earthly empires. His work helped temper apocalyptic expectations in the West, emphasizing that the ultimate fulfillment of prophecy would come in God's own time.

3. The Medieval Period and the Crusades: Apocalyptic Warfare

During the Middle Ages, apocalyptic prophecy became intertwined with the concept of Holy War, particularly during the Crusades (1096–1291). The Crusades were military campaigns launched by European Christians to reclaim Jerusalem and other holy sites from Muslim control. For many medieval Christians, these wars were seen as part of an apocalyptic struggle that would lead to the final establishment of God's kingdom on earth.

Apocalyptic Rhetoric in the Crusades:

- Pope Urban II's Call for the First Crusade (1095): In his famous speech at the Council of Clermont, Pope Urban II framed the Crusade as a divinely sanctioned mission to reclaim the Holy Land and prepare the way for Christ's return. He invoked apocalyptic imagery, describing the liberation of Jerusalem as necessary for the fulfillment of end-times prophecy. Thousands of European knights and peasants took up the cross, inspired by the belief that they were participating in a cosmic battle between good and evil.

- The Role of Jerusalem in Apocalyptic Thought: Jerusalem held a central place in medieval Christian eschatology. The city was seen as the focal point of divine history and the future site of Christ's millennial reign, as described in the Book of Revelation. The capture of Jerusalem by the Crusaders in 1099 was celebrated as a significant apocalyptic event, though this victory proved temporary as Muslim forces eventually recaptured the city.

Islamic Apocalypticism in Response to the Crusades:

- Jihad and the Apocalyptic Struggle: In response to the Crusades, many Muslim leaders and theologians also framed the conflict in apocalyptic terms. Saladin, the Muslim leader who recaptured Jerusalem in 1187, was viewed as a champion of Islam in the apocalyptic struggle against the

Crusaders. Islamic eschatology, like its Christian counterpart, included prophecies about the final confrontation between Muslims and non-believers, and the Crusades were often interpreted as part of this cosmic conflict.

- Prophecies of the Mahdi: In Islamic apocalyptic thought, the Mahdi is a messianic figure who will appear before the Day of Judgment to restore justice and fight against the forces of evil. Some Muslims believed that the Crusader invasions were a sign that the Mahdi's appearance was imminent, further intensifying the apocalyptic fervor of the era.

4. The Protestant Reformation and Apocalyptic Interpretations

The Protestant Reformation (16th century) was not only a theological revolt against the Catholic Church but also a period of intense apocalyptic expectation. Many of the leading reformers, including Martin Luther and John Calvin, interpreted their struggle against the papacy in apocalyptic terms, identifying the Pope as the Antichrist and the Catholic Church as the "whore of Babylon" described in the Book of Revelation.

Luther and the Papacy as Antichrist:

- Apocalyptic Critique of the Church: Martin Luther's writings were filled with apocalyptic imagery, depicting the Reformation as part of a final struggle between Christ and the forces of evil. Luther believed that the corruption of the Catholic Church was a sign that the end times were near and that God was using the Reformation to cleanse the Church in preparation for Christ's return. His identification of the papacy with the Antichrist became a central theme in Protestant apocalyptic thought.

- The Printing Press and Apocalyptic Literature: The invention of the printing press in the 15th century allowed for the widespread dissemination of apocalyptic literature, including Luther's writings and other Protestant tracts that used the Book of Revelation to argue for reform. This created a widespread sense of eschatological urgency among the laity, further fueling the spread of the Reformation.

Radical Apocalyptic Movements:

- Anabaptists and the Münster Rebellion (1534–1535): Among the more radical branches of the Reformation, the Anabaptists took apocalyptic expectations to extreme levels. In the city of Münster, a group of Anabaptists, led by Jan Matthys and John of Leiden, seized control and declared the establishment of a new Kingdom of God. They believed that Münster was destined to be the New Jerusalem where Christ would return to reign. The rebellion ended in violent suppression, but it remains one of the most dramatic examples of apocalyptic movements in the Reformation era.

5. Apocalyptic Thought in the Modern Era

The rise of modern apocalyptic movements, especially in the 19th and 20th centuries, reflects a continued fascination with prophetic visions of the end times. From religious sects predicting the imminent return of Christ to secular fears of nuclear annihilation during the Cold War, apocalypticism has remained a powerful force in shaping both religious belief and political action.

The Millerites and the Great Disappointment (1844):

- William Miller's Prophecies: In the early 19th century, a Baptist preacher named William Miller predicted that Christ would return to earth in 1844, based on his interpretation of biblical prophecy. His predictions garnered a large following, known as the Millerites, who believed that the Second Coming was imminent. When the predicted date came and went without Christ's return, it became known as the "Great Disappointment."

- Legacy of Adventist Movements: Although Miller's prediction failed, the movement gave rise to several new religious denominations, including the Seventh-day Adventist Church, which continues to emphasize apocalyptic prophecy and the imminent return of Christ.

Cold War Apocalypticism:

- Secular Apocalypse: Nuclear War: The threat of nuclear war during the Cold War created a secular form of apocalyptic fear. The possibility of global annihilation through human-made weapons gave rise to apocalyptic imagery in political discourse, popular culture, and literature. Books like Nevil Shute's On the Beach and films like Dr. Strangelove depicted a world on the brink of destruction, reflecting the widespread anxiety of the era.

- Religious Apocalyptic Movements: In parallel, religious apocalyptic movements also thrived during the Cold War. Some Christian evangelicals believed that the geopolitical tensions between the United States and the Soviet Union were a fulfillment of biblical prophecy, with the final battle of Armageddon potentially being fought with nuclear weapons. The establishment of the state of Israel in 1948 further fueled apocalyptic expectations, with many interpreting it as the fulfillment of biblical prophecies about the return of the Jews to the Holy Land before the end times.

The Enduring Power of Apocalyptic Prophecy

Throughout history, apocalyptic prophecy has played a central role in shaping not only religious belief but also political movements, social revolutions, and wars. From the Jewish apocalyptic texts of the Second Temple period to the radical millennialism of the Reformation and the modern fear of nuclear apocalypse, visions of the end of the world have been a constant companion to humanity. These prophecies serve both as warnings of impending catastrophe and as promises of ultimate deliverance, offering hope in times of crisis and guiding the faithful through the uncertainties of history.

As we move further into the 21st century, the enduring relevance of apocalyptic thought remains evident. Whether through religious movements anticipating the return of Christ, secular concerns about climate change and global instability, or cultural expressions of dystopian futures, the human fascination with the end times continues to shape our understanding of history and our place within it.

The Connection Between Prophecy, the Crusades, and Interpretations of the End of History

The Crusades, a series of religious and military campaigns fought between Christian Europe and the Muslim world from the late 11th to the late 13th centuries, were deeply intertwined with apocalyptic prophecy and eschatological interpretations. Both Christian and Islamic participants viewed these conflicts not merely as political or territorial struggles but as battles with profound spiritual and cosmic significance. The Crusades were seen as part of a larger divine narrative concerning the end of history, where the fate of Jerusalem and the Holy Land held central importance in the apocalyptic visions of both religious traditions.

Now, let us explores the connection between apocalyptic prophecy, the Crusades, and broader interpretations of the end of history in both Christian and Muslim contexts. By examining the religious motivations, prophetic interpretations, and historical events surrounding the Crusades, we can better understand how both sides perceived the conflict as part of a divine plan that would ultimately bring about the end of the world and the establishment of God's eternal kingdom.

1. The Crusades and Christian Apocalyptic Prophecy

For many medieval Christians, the Crusades were seen as a direct fulfillment of biblical prophecies about the end times. The reclamation of Jerusalem and other holy sites from Muslim control was not simply a political or religious duty but an eschatological mission to prepare the way for Christ's return and the establishment of the Kingdom of God on earth.

Jerusalem in Christian Eschatology:

The city of Jerusalem held enormous spiritual significance in Christian theology, particularly in apocalyptic prophecy. In the Book of Revelation (21:2), Jerusalem is described as the site of the New Jerusalem, where God's kingdom will descend to earth at the end of time. Therefore, controlling the physical city was seen as essential to fulfilling the prophecies of the Second Coming of Christ and the establishment of His millennial reign.

Pope Urban II's Call for the First Crusade (1095):

The First Crusade was launched in 1095 when Pope Urban II delivered a stirring call to arms at the Council of Clermont. Urban's speech framed the Crusade as a divinely sanctioned mission to liberate the Holy Land from Muslim control. In his rhetoric, Urban used apocalyptic imagery to motivate Christian knights and peasants, portraying the battle as a cosmic struggle between the forces of Christendom and the forces of evil. He suggested that participating in the Crusade would not only bring honor but also eternal reward, including the remission of sins.

Urban's call was deeply rooted in eschatological thinking. Many believed that the liberation of Jerusalem was a necessary precursor to the events described in the Book of Revelation. The capture of Jerusalem in 1099 was hailed as a miraculous victory, and for some, it seemed to confirm that the end times were drawing near.

Theological Justifications for the Crusades:

Throughout the Crusades, Christian preachers and theologians drew on apocalyptic prophecy to justify and inspire participation in the campaigns. Bernard of Clairvaux, one of the most influential preachers of the Second Crusade (1147–1149), used the language of prophecy and divine mandate to stir up support. Bernard framed the Crusades as part of God's plan to purify the world and prepare for the final battle between good and evil. He even invoked the imagery of the Antichrist, suggesting that the Muslim forces in the Holy Land were agents of the ultimate enemy that Christ would defeat at His return.

Jerusalem as the Focal Point of the End Times:

The Christian obsession with Jerusalem during the Crusades was not just a matter of reclaiming sacred land; it was deeply tied to apocalyptic beliefs about the end of history. Many medieval Christians believed that Christ could not return to establish His kingdom until Jerusalem was in Christian hands. This belief intensified the apocalyptic fervor surrounding the Crusades, as each campaign was seen as hastening the fulfillment of prophecy. As such, the Crusades were framed as both a defensive war for Christendom and an active participation in the unfolding of God's divine plan for the end of history.

2. The Crusades and Islamic Apocalyptic Prophecy

On the other side of the conflict, many Muslims also interpreted the Crusades through the lens of apocalyptic prophecy. Islamic eschatology, like its Christian counterpart, contains prophecies about a final battle between the forces of good and evil, culminating in the Day of Judgment. For many

Muslims, the arrival of Christian Crusaders in the Holy Land was seen as a sign that these prophesied events were unfolding.

Islamic Eschatology and the End of History:

Islamic apocalyptic prophecy, as found in the Hadith and other sources, includes the belief in a final confrontation between the forces of Islam and non-believers, particularly in the region of the Levant (modern-day Syria, Lebanon, Jordan, and Israel). This region, which includes Jerusalem, holds special significance in Islamic end-times prophecy. The Dome of the Rock in Jerusalem, for example, is traditionally believed to be the site from which the Prophet Muhammad ascended to heaven during the Night Journey, and it is seen as a key location in the unfolding of apocalyptic events.

The Role of Jihad in Islamic Apocalyptic Thought:

The concept of jihad (struggle) has always had both a spiritual and a military dimension in Islam. During the Crusades, Muslim leaders framed the defense of Jerusalem and the Holy Land as part of a divinely mandated jihad against the invading Crusaders. This struggle was not just about defending territory but was understood as part of the larger cosmic battle between the forces of truth (Islam) and the forces of falsehood (the Crusaders). In this context, many Muslims believed that their participation in the jihad was a fulfillment of prophetic tradition and that the defeat of the Crusaders would be a sign of God's favor.

Saladin and the Recapture of Jerusalem (1187):

The figure of Saladin (Salah al-Din), who successfully recaptured Jerusalem from the Crusaders in 1187, is deeply connected to Islamic apocalyptic prophecy. Saladin was portrayed by both his contemporaries and later generations as a divinely guided leader who fulfilled the prophecy of a Muslim victory in the Holy Land. His victory at the Battle of Hattin and the subsequent recapture of Jerusalem were seen by many as a sign that God was on the side of the Muslims and that the final apocalyptic battle against the Crusaders was nearing its conclusion.

In Islamic eschatology, there is also the figure of the Mahdi, a messianic leader who will appear before the Day of Judgment to restore justice and defeat the enemies of Islam. Some Muslims during the Crusades believed that the arrival of the Crusaders signaled the imminent arrival of the Mahdi and that the final battle between the forces of good and evil was about to begin.

3. The Crusades and the End of History

Both Christians and Muslims during the Crusades saw the conflict as part of a larger narrative concerning the end of history. For Christians, the Crusades were part of the apocalyptic drama foretold in the Bible, where Jerusalem would be reclaimed, and Christ would return to establish His kingdom. For Muslims, the Crusades were seen as part of the prophesied final jihad, where Islam would triumph over unbelievers before the Day of Judgment.

This shared apocalyptic framework shaped the way both sides viewed not only the Crusades themselves but also the course of history as a whole. The Crusades were not merely a political or military conflict; they were understood as events that carried cosmic significance and were directly connected to the divine plan for the end of history.

Theological Interpretations of the Crusades in Later History:

In the centuries following the Crusades, both Christian and Islamic theologians continued to interpret the events of the Crusades in apocalyptic terms. For many Christians, the failure of the later Crusades and the eventual fall of Jerusalem to Muslim forces in 1244 was seen as a sign that the end times had not yet arrived but were still imminent. The memory of the Crusades continued to influence Christian eschatology, especially in the context of later conflicts between Christian Europe and the Ottoman Empire.

In the Islamic world, the victory of Saladin and the eventual defeat of the Crusaders became a symbol of God's favor and the ultimate victory of Islam. The idea that the

Crusades were part of the larger jihad against unbelievers continued to resonate in Islamic thought, influencing later generations of Muslim rulers and scholars.

Apocalyptic Prophecy and Modern Interpretations of History:

Even in modern times, the legacy of the Crusades continues to shape interpretations of prophecy and the end of history. Some contemporary Christian apocalyptic movements, particularly within evangelical Christianity, continue to view the Middle East as the stage upon which the final events of biblical prophecy will unfold. The establishment of the state of Israel in 1948 and ongoing conflicts in the region are often framed in terms of apocalyptic prophecy, with many seeing these events as signs that the end of history is approaching.

Similarly, some Islamic movements today draw on the legacy of the Crusades and apocalyptic prophecy to frame contemporary conflicts in the Middle East as part of the final jihad before the Day of Judgment. The struggle for control of Jerusalem remains a potent symbol in both Christian and Islamic eschatological thought, reflecting the deep connections between prophecy, historical events, and interpretations of the end of history.

Conclusion: The End of History Through the Lens of the Crusades

The Crusades were more than just a series of wars between Christian and Muslim forces; they were seen by both sides as part of a larger cosmic struggle that would ultimately determine the fate of the world. Apocalyptic prophecy played a central role in shaping how both Christians and Muslims understood the Crusades and their place in the divine plan for history. For Christians, the Crusades were a key step in the fulfillment of biblical prophecy, while for Muslims, they were part of the prophesied final jihad. In both traditions, the events of the Crusades were deeply connected to eschatological expectations about the end of history and the coming of God's kingdom.

This enduring connection between prophecy, the Crusades, and the end of history continues to shape religious thought and political action even today, as both Christian and Muslim apocalyptic traditions grapple with the legacy of these historic conflicts and the ongoing significance of Jerusalem in eschatological narratives.

Delving Deeper into Theological Arguments Used During the Crusades and Modern Apocalyptic Movements Related to These Events

The Crusades were not merely political or military campaigns but were driven by deeply rooted theological arguments that framed them as part of a divine plan. The apocalyptic expectations associated with the Crusades were shaped by religious leaders and theologians who used scripture and prophecy to inspire participation and justify the violence. Similarly, modern apocalyptic movements have drawn on the legacy of the Crusades and the religious symbolism surrounding Jerusalem and the Holy Land, interpreting current events in the Middle East as part of the end-times narrative.

In this section, we will delve deeper into the theological justifications for the Crusades, the role of prophecy in those justifications, and how these apocalyptic themes continue to influence modern religious and political movements.

1. Theological Arguments for the Crusades: Holy War as Divine Mandate

The Crusades were presented by their proponents as more than just military expeditions; they were seen as holy wars, sanctioned by God, with profound spiritual significance. This framing was crucial for convincing knights, nobility, and commoners alike to take up the cross and embark on perilous campaigns to the Holy Land. Several theological arguments were central to this justification, many of which drew on apocalyptic prophecy and eschatological expectations.

A. The Concept of Holy War and Just War Doctrine

The idea of holy war was not new to medieval Christianity, but the Crusades represented a significant development in the way Christians understood the relationship between warfare and religious duty. Traditionally, Christian doctrine had emphasized the concept of just war, a set of ethical guidelines for determining when war could be morally justified. This idea was developed by theologians like Augustine of Hippo, who argued that war could be just if it met certain criteria, such as being waged by a legitimate authority, for a righteous cause, and with the right intention (to restore peace and justice).

However, the Crusades went beyond the concept of just war to embrace the idea of holy war—a divinely sanctioned conflict in which the participants were not only justified in their actions but were promised spiritual rewards, including the remission of sins. Pope Urban II, in his call for the First Crusade, famously promised that anyone who took up the cross and fought to liberate Jerusalem would receive a plenary indulgence, meaning the forgiveness of all sins and direct entry into heaven if they died in battle.

This theological shift framed the Crusades as part of a divine mandate, a war ordained by God to reclaim Christian holy sites and defend Christendom against Muslim forces. The remission of sins was a powerful motivator, particularly in an era when the fear of eternal damnation loomed large in the minds of believers. By participating in the Crusades, Christians could secure their eternal salvation and fulfill what was perceived as God's will.

B. Apocalyptic Rhetoric and the Role of Jerusalem

Jerusalem, as the focal point of Christian apocalyptic prophecy, played a central role in the theological justification for the Crusades. In the medieval Christian imagination, Jerusalem was not just a city; it was the center of the world, the place where Christ had been crucified, and the site where He would return at the end of days to establish His kingdom.

The Book of Revelation (Revelation 21:2) describes the coming of the New Jerusalem, a heavenly city that would descend from the sky after the final defeat of Satan and the forces of evil. Many medieval Christians believed that reclaiming the earthly city of Jerusalem was a necessary step in preparing for the fulfillment of this prophecy. By restoring Christian control over the city, they were participating in the divine plan for the end of history and the Second Coming of Christ.

Pope Urban II's speech at Clermont (1095) invoked this apocalyptic vision, encouraging Christians to see the liberation of Jerusalem as part of the cosmic struggle between good and evil. Urban's rhetoric suggested that the forces of

Islam, who controlled Jerusalem at the time, were agents of the Antichrist or other demonic powers, and that by defeating them, Christians were helping to hasten the arrival of God's kingdom.

C. Theological Figures and Crusade Preaching

Theological figures such as Bernard of Clairvaux, a leading proponent of the Second Crusade (1147–1149), played a crucial role in shaping the theological arguments for the Crusades. Bernard's sermons were filled with apocalyptic imagery and emphasized the spiritual rewards of participating in the Crusade. He framed the Crusades as a divine battle in which Christians could prove their faith and courage, portraying the Muslim forces as agents of Satan who were standing in the way of Christ's kingdom.

In his letters and sermons, Bernard wrote that the Crusade was not just a political struggle but a cosmic war between the forces of Christ and the forces of evil. He urged knights to take up arms, not out of worldly ambition, but to secure their place in heaven. Bernard's influence was so profound that he was able to rally a large number of European nobles to the cause, though the Second Crusade ultimately ended in failure.

The Franciscan and Dominican Orders, which emerged during the later Crusades, also played a role in spreading apocalyptic interpretations of the conflict. These orders, particularly in their missionary work in the Holy Land, often viewed their efforts as part of the eschatological mission to convert non-Christians and prepare for Christ's return.

2. Modern Apocalyptic Movements and the Legacy of the Crusades

The theological and apocalyptic themes that drove the Crusades have continued to influence religious thought and political movements in the modern era. While the historical Crusades ended in the 13th century, their legacy has persisted, particularly in how both Christians and Muslims interpret the significance of Jerusalem and the broader Middle East in the context of the end of history.

A. Christian Zionism and the Role of Israel in Apocalyptic Prophecy

One of the most significant modern apocalyptic movements that draws on the legacy of the Crusades is Christian Zionism. This movement, which emerged in the 19th century and gained significant traction in the 20th century, holds that the return of the Jewish people to the Holy Land and the establishment of the state of Israel in 1948 are fulfillments of biblical prophecy.

Many Christian Zionists believe that the reestablishment of Israel is a necessary precursor to the Second Coming of Christ. This belief is rooted in apocalyptic interpretations of passages from the Old Testament (such as Ezekiel 37, which describes the "dry bones" of Israel being restored to life) and the New Testament (particularly the Book of Revelation). For these Christians, the modern state of Israel is seen as playing a key role in the final events of history, including the Battle of Armageddon, the appearance of the Antichrist, and the ultimate victory of Christ.

Jerusalem remains central to these apocalyptic expectations. Christian Zionists often emphasize the importance of maintaining Jewish control over the city, particularly the Temple Mount, where the ancient Jewish temple once stood. Some believe that the rebuilding of the temple is necessary for the fulfillment of prophecy and the return of Christ. This has led to significant political and religious support for Israel, particularly from evangelical Christians in the United States.

B. Islamic Apocalyptic Movements and the Crusade Legacy

In the Muslim world, the memory of the Crusades has continued to shape apocalyptic thought, particularly in response to Western interventions in the Middle East. The Crusades are often invoked in Islamic rhetoric as a symbol of Western aggression and the historical struggle between Islam and Christianity. This historical memory has been particularly influential in the formation of modern jihadist movements.

Islamic apocalyptic prophecies, found in the Hadith and other sources, describe a final battle between Muslims and non-believers, often in the region of the Levant (modern-day Syria, Lebanon, Jordan, and Israel). Some modern Islamist movements, particularly groups like ISIS (Islamic State) and Al-Qaeda, have drawn on these prophecies to frame their actions as part of the final apocalyptic struggle. For example, ISIS has frequently invoked the Hadith of Dabiq, which predicts that a final battle between Muslim and Christian forces will take place in the town of Dabiq in northern Syria, signaling the beginning of the end times.

These groups have also used the legacy of the Crusades to frame their struggle as a continuation of the medieval conflict between Islam and the Christian West. Western military interventions in the Middle East, including the U.S.-led invasions of Afghanistan and Iraq, are often depicted as modern-day Crusades, with jihadist leaders portraying themselves as defenders of Islam in an apocalyptic struggle.

C. Apocalypticism and Geopolitical Conflicts in the Middle East

The ongoing geopolitical conflicts in the Middle East, particularly the Israeli-Palestinian conflict, continue to be framed in apocalyptic terms by both Christian and Islamic movements. For many evangelical Christians, the conflict over Jerusalem is seen as a fulfillment of biblical prophecy, with the restoration of Jewish sovereignty over the city being a key event in the end-times narrative.

Similarly, many Islamist movements see the conflict as part of the broader eschatological struggle between Muslims and non-believers. The religious significance of Jerusalem in both Christian and Islamic apocalyptic thought ensures that the city remains a focal point of tension and conflict, with both sides viewing the control of the city as central to the fulfillment of divine prophecy.

The Lasting Legacy of Apocalyptic Thought in the Crusades and Beyond

The theological arguments used during the Crusades, rooted in apocalyptic prophecy and the belief in a divinely mandated holy war, continue to resonate in modern apocalyptic movements. Whether through the Christian Zionist belief in the prophetic significance of Israel and Jerusalem or the use of Crusade imagery by Islamist movements, the legacy of the Crusades remains a powerful force in shaping religious and political conflicts.

Both Christians and Muslims continue to interpret the events in the Middle East through the lens of apocalyptic prophecy, drawing on centuries-old theological arguments that frame the struggle for Jerusalem as a key part of the end of history. As these movements evolve, the connection between prophecy, holy war, and the end of history remains as relevant as ever, influencing both religious belief and geopolitical realities.

Further Exploration: Modern Apocalyptic Movements and Theological Texts Related to the Crusades

The theological arguments and apocalyptic expectations surrounding the Crusades have left a profound legacy in both Christian and Islamic traditions. Modern apocalyptic movements, particularly within evangelical Christianity and radical Islamist groups, continue to draw on these historical themes, seeing the events of today as the fulfillment of prophecies foretold centuries ago. In this section, we will explore specific modern apocalyptic movements, examine their theological underpinnings, and analyze the historical texts that continue to influence them.

1. Modern Apocalyptic Movements in Christianity

Several modern Christian movements, particularly those within evangelical and dispensationalist circles, interpret contemporary events—especially those concerning the Middle East—as part of a larger eschatological plan that ties back to biblical prophecy and the Crusades. These movements often view the Crusades as part of a long historical struggle between Christianity and Islam, which they believe will culminate in the fulfillment of end-times prophecy.

A. Christian Zionism and Dispensationalism

Christian Zionism is one of the most influential modern apocalyptic movements within evangelical Christianity. At its core, Christian Zionism is the belief that the modern state of Israel, established in 1948, is the fulfillment of biblical prophecies concerning the return of the Jewish people to the Holy Land. Many Christian Zionists believe that this event sets the stage for the Second Coming of Christ.

Dispensationalism is a theological framework that supports Christian Zionist beliefs. This system of thought divides history into distinct "dispensations" or periods, during which God interacts with humanity in different ways. According to dispensationalist eschatology, we are currently living in the final dispensation, known as the "Church Age," which will end with the Rapture (the sudden removal of believers from the earth), the rise of the Antichrist, and the Battle of Armageddon.

Key Texts and Beliefs:

- The Scofield Reference Bible (1909), edited by Cyrus Scofield, popularized dispensationalism in the United States. This annotated Bible provided a clear eschatological framework that connected biblical prophecy with contemporary events, especially regarding Israel and the Middle East.

- Hal Lindsey's The Late Great Planet Earth (1970): This book was one of the best-selling apocalyptic works of the 20th century. Lindsey interpreted events such as the Six-Day War (1967) and the re-establishment of Israel as signs of the imminent fulfillment of biblical prophecy. He argued that the Crusades were part of the ongoing eschatological struggle between Christianity and Islam.

- John Hagee: A prominent Christian Zionist pastor, Hagee's books and sermons often focus on the prophetic significance of Israel and the Middle East. He leads Christians United for Israel (CUFI), one of the largest Christian pro-Israel organizations in the world. Hagee teaches that modern conflicts over Jerusalem are part of the biblical timeline leading to the return of Christ.

Apocalyptic Expectations:

- Christian Zionists see the re-establishment of Israel as a precursor to key end-time events, including the rebuilding of the Third Temple in Jerusalem and the appearance of the Antichrist.

- Jerusalem is central to these beliefs, as it is seen as the place where Christ will return to defeat the forces of evil in the Battle of Armageddon, as described in the Book of Revelation.

B. Theological Justifications for Holy War and the Legacy of the Crusades

The Crusades were often justified through theological texts that framed them as part of God's will for the purification of Christendom and the reclamation of holy sites. These justifications, rooted in a combination of just war theory and apocalyptic prophecy, continue to influence certain Christian apocalyptic movements today.

Key Theological Texts:

- Augustine of Hippo's The City of God (5th century): Augustine's work laid the groundwork for Christian just war theory. While Augustine himself did not advocate for holy war in the way the Crusaders would later interpret it, his ideas about the relationship between the earthly city (human governments) and the heavenly city (God's kingdom) were foundational for later theological justifications of the Crusades. His assertion that earthly kingdoms were temporary compared to the eternal City of God helped shape medieval apocalyptic thought.

- Bernard of Clairvaux's Crusade Sermons: As one of the most influential theologians of the 12th century, Bernard preached extensively in favor of the Second Crusade. He used apocalyptic imagery, suggesting that participation in the

Crusade would bring about spiritual rewards and help hasten the fulfillment of divine prophecy. Bernard's vision of the Crusades as a cosmic battle between good (Christians) and evil (Muslims) continues to resonate in certain modern Christian apocalyptic movements.

Connection to Modern Movements:

- Modern evangelical leaders sometimes invoke the language of spiritual warfare, echoing the theological arguments of the Crusades. They see the ongoing conflict in the Middle East, particularly the struggles over Jerusalem, as a continuation of this apocalyptic battle between the forces of Christendom and its enemies.

- Spiritual Warfare: The concept of spiritual warfare, popular in evangelical circles, often parallels the apocalyptic themes of the Crusades. For example, modern Christian movements may frame conflicts like the War on Terror or the Israeli-Palestinian conflict in terms of a spiritual and apocalyptic battle between Christianity and Islam.

2. Islamic Apocalyptic Movements and the Crusade Legacy

The memory of the Crusades has continued to influence modern Islamic apocalyptic movements, particularly in the way certain groups frame Western interventions in the Middle East as a continuation of the

Crusader legacy. Islamic apocalypticism, like its Christian counterpart, includes prophecies about a final battle between Muslims and non-believers, often centered around the region of the Levant and Jerusalem.

A. Jihadist Movements and the Return of the Mahdi

Many radical Islamist groups have drawn on apocalyptic prophecies to justify their actions, presenting themselves as participants in the final battles between Islam and its enemies. These groups often invoke the Crusades as part of a larger narrative of Western aggression against Islam.

Key Groups:

- ISIS (Islamic State): One of the most prominent jihadist groups to embrace apocalyptic prophecy, ISIS often framed its actions in terms of the final battle between Islam and the "Crusader" West. The group specifically invoked the Hadith of Dabiq, a prophecy that foretells a great battle between Muslims and "Rome" (interpreted as the West) in the town of Dabiq in northern Syria. ISIS's magazine was even named Dabiq, emphasizing its belief in the imminent fulfillment of this apocalyptic prophecy.

- Al-Qaeda: While less explicitly focused on apocalypticism than ISIS, Al-Qaeda has frequently invoked the memory of the Crusades to justify its attacks on Western targets. Osama bin Laden's rhetoric often portrayed the United States and its allies as "Crusaders" continuing the medieval wars against Islam. In his 1998 fatwa, bin Laden framed the Western presence in the Middle East as part of a new Crusade, calling on Muslims to defend Islam in a struggle that he suggested had apocalyptic significance.

Key Texts and Prophecies:

- The Hadith of Dabiq: This is a key prophetic tradition in Islamic eschatology that describes a final battle between the forces of Islam and their enemies in the Levant. The prophecy is often interpreted as part of the larger apocalyptic narrative in which the Mahdi (a messianic figure) will appear to lead Muslims to victory.

- Sayyid Qutb's Milestones (1964): Qutb, an influential Islamist thinker, laid the ideological groundwork for many modern jihadist movements. While not explicitly apocalyptic, his writings emphasized the need for Muslims to engage in jihad against Western "Crusaders" and secular Muslim regimes. His vision of Islam as being in a constant struggle against external and internal enemies has been interpreted by some radical groups as part of an apocalyptic narrative.

Apocalyptic Expectations:

- Many jihadist movements believe that the appearance of the Mahdi is imminent and that their actions are helping to prepare the world for his arrival. The Mahdi is expected to lead Muslims in the final battle against the enemies of Islam, after which there will be a period of peace and justice before the Day of Judgment.

- Jerusalem remains central to Islamic apocalypticism, much as it does in Christian prophecy. Control of the city, especially the Al-Aqsa Mosque and the Dome of the Rock, is seen as a key element in the final eschatological struggle. Islamist groups often frame their attacks on Israel and their opposition to Western involvement in the region as part of this broader apocalyptic conflict.

3. Theological Texts and Apocalyptic Literature from the Crusades

The legacy of theological texts produced during the Crusades continues to influence both Christian and Islamic apocalyptic movements today. These texts provided the intellectual and spiritual framework for understanding the Crusades as part of a larger divine plan for the end of history.

A. Christian Apocalyptic Literature

During the Crusades, many Christian theologians and preachers produced apocalyptic literature that framed the conflict as part of the cosmic battle between good and evil. These texts often interpreted the Crusades as a fulfillment of prophecies from the Book of Daniel and the Book of Revelation, which describe the rise and fall of empires and the eventual establishment of God's kingdom.

Key Texts:

- The Song of Roland: This epic poem, written around the time of the

First Crusade, mythologizes the Christian-Muslim conflict, portraying it as part of the larger struggle between Christendom and Islam. While not explicitly apocalyptic, the poem reflects the medieval view of Muslims as agents of Satan, a theme that would later influence apocalyptic rhetoric during the Crusades.

- Peter the Hermit's Preaching: A charismatic preacher of the First Crusade, Peter the Hermit's sermons were filled with apocalyptic imagery. He framed the Crusades as part of the divine mission to reclaim Jerusalem and prepare for the end of days.

B. Islamic Apocalyptic Texts

Islamic apocalyptic literature from the Crusades era often focused on the concept of jihad as part of the eschatological struggle against the enemies of Islam. These texts were deeply influenced by the Hadith traditions concerning the final battle in the Levant and the appearance of the Mahdi.

Key Texts:

- Ibn al-Athir's The Complete History: A 13th-century historian, Ibn al-Athir chronicled the Crusades from an Islamic perspective. While his work is primarily historical, it reflects the broader apocalyptic expectations of the time, particularly the belief that the Muslim victories over the Crusaders were a sign of divine favor and the approaching end times.

- The Kitab al-Fitan (Book of Tribulations): This early Islamic text, attributed to various authors, contains a collection of Hadiths concerning the end times. It describes the signs of the Day of Judgment, including the rise of false prophets, the appearance of the Mahdi, and the final battle between Muslims and non-believers.

The Enduring Influence of Apocalyptic Texts and Movements

The apocalyptic themes that shaped the Crusades continue to resonate in modern religious and political movements, both Christian and Islamic. The theological texts and prophecies that justified the Crusades have left a lasting legacy, influencing how contemporary movements interpret their roles in the unfolding of history. Whether through the Christian Zionist focus on Israel and the return of Christ or the jihadist emphasis on the final battle between Islam and the West, the connection between prophecy, holy war, and the end of history remains a powerful force in shaping global conflicts and religious expectations today.

CHAPTER 02

NEBUCHADNEZZAR'S DREAM AND ITS INTERPRETATION

Nebuchadnezzar's dream, as recorded in the Book of Daniel (Daniel 2:31-45), is one of the most famous and symbolically rich visions in biblical prophecy. The dream is a cornerstone of apocalyptic literature, providing a prophetic overview of world empires and the eventual establishment of God's eternal kingdom. This chapter will provide a detailed recounting of Nebuchadnezzar's dream and explore Daniel's interpretation of the vision, offering insights into its symbolic meanings and its lasting significance in both religious and historical contexts.

1. Nebuchadnezzar's Dream: A Vision of the Statue (Daniel 2:31-35)

Nebuchadnezzar, the king of Babylon, had a troubling dream that he could neither understand nor remember. Disturbed by the vision, he summoned his court of wise men, magicians, and astrologers, demanding that they not only interpret the dream but also recount it to him—an impossible task for any human. Daniel, a Jewish exile in the Babylonian court, was granted wisdom from God to fulfill the king's request. With divine insight, Daniel revealed the content of the dream and provided its interpretation.

In the dream, Nebuchadnezzar saw a massive statue, which was awe-inspiring in size and appearance. The statue was made of different materials, with each part representing a different kingdom in human history.

A. The Statue: Composition and Symbolism

The statue in Nebuchadnezzar's dream was composed of various metals, each decreasing in value but increasing in strength. Each section of the statue represented a different empire, symbolizing the rise and fall of world powers.

1. The Head of Gold: The head of the statue was made of pure gold. This section symbolized the Babylonian Empire, with Nebuchadnezzar himself as the embodiment of its glory and authority.

2. The Chest and Arms of Silver: The next section of the statue, the chest and arms, was made of silver. This represented an empire inferior to Babylon, commonly

understood as the Medo-Persian Empire, which succeeded Babylon in ruling the known world.

3. The Belly and Thighs of Bronze: Below the silver chest, the belly and thighs of the statue were made of bronze, representing the rise of the Greek Empire, which followed the Medo-Persians. The bronze symbolized a kingdom of vast cultural and military influence, though less majestic than its predecessors.

4. The Legs of Iron: The statue's legs were made of iron, symbolizing a strong and militarily dominant empire. This section is widely interpreted as the Roman Empire, known for its military prowess and political domination over vast territories.

5. The Feet of Iron and Clay: Finally, the feet of the statue were a mixture of iron and clay, symbolizing a divided and fragile kingdom. Many scholars interpret this as representing the fragmented states that arose from the ruins of the Roman Empire. The combination of iron and clay symbolizes a kingdom with both strength and inherent weakness, unable to fully unite or maintain its power.

B. The Stone Not Cut by Human Hands

After describing the statue, Daniel recounted a dramatic and mysterious event: a stone, cut out without human hands, appeared and struck the statue on its feet. The impact shattered the entire statue, causing the gold, silver, bronze, iron, and clay to disintegrate into dust, which was blown away by the wind. The stone then grew into a great mountain that filled the whole earth.

This stone, divine in origin, represents a kingdom established by God—one that will destroy all human empires and endure forever. The stone growing into a mountain symbolizes the eternal reign of God's kingdom, which will surpass and replace all worldly powers.

2. Daniel's Interpretation of the Dream (Daniel 2:36-45)

After recounting the dream, Daniel proceeded to interpret its meaning, providing King Nebuchadnezzar with a prophetic vision of the future. Each section of the statue represents a different kingdom, and the entire dream illustrates the progression of world empires leading to the establishment of God's eternal kingdom.

A. The Head of Gold – The Babylonian Empire

Daniel began his interpretation by directly addressing Nebuchadnezzar, explaining that the head of gold represented the Babylonian Empire. He said:

"You, O king, are the king of kings. The God of heaven has given you dominion and power and might and glory; into your hands he has placed all mankind and the beasts of the field and the birds of the air. Wherever they live, he has made you ruler over them all. You are that head of gold." (Daniel 2:37-38)

Nebuchadnezzar's Babylon was a majestic and powerful kingdom, symbolized by the precious and radiant gold. The kingdom's wealth, grandeur, and influence over the ancient Near East made it the most illustrious of the empires represented in the dream. However, despite its power, Babylon's reign would be temporary, as another kingdom would rise to take its place.

B. The Chest and Arms of Silver – The Medo-Persian Empire

Daniel then explained that after Babylon, an inferior kingdom would arise, represented by the chest and arms of silver:

"After you, another kingdom will arise, inferior to yours." (Daniel 2:39)

This kingdom is widely understood to be the Medo-Persian Empire, which conquered Babylon in 539 BCE under the leadership of Cyrus the Great. Although silver is less valuable than gold, it is still a precious metal, reflecting the strength and stability of the Medo-Persian rule. The dual arms of the statue likely symbolize the dual nature of the empire, which was composed of the Medes and the Persians.

C. The Belly and Thighs of Bronze – The Greek Empire

Following the Medo-Persian Empire, a third kingdom would emerge, represented by the belly and thighs of bronze:

"Next, a third kingdom, one of bronze, will rule over the whole earth." (Daniel 2:39)

This kingdom is commonly interpreted as the Greek Empire, which, under Alexander the Great, conquered vast territories across Europe, Asia, and Africa in the 4th century BCE. Bronze, a metal associated with weaponry and military strength, is an appropriate symbol for the Greek Empire, which was renowned for its military conquests and the spread of Hellenistic culture throughout the known world. Alexander's empire did indeed rule over much of the world known to the ancient Greeks, from Greece to India.

D. The Legs of Iron – The Roman Empire

The fourth kingdom, represented by the legs of iron, would be different from the previous empires, marked by its unparalleled strength and power:

"Finally, there will be a fourth kingdom, strong as iron—for iron breaks and smashes everything—and as iron breaks things to pieces, so it will crush and break all the others." (Daniel 2:40)

This fourth kingdom is generally recognized as the Roman Empire, which followed the Greek Empire and became one of the most powerful and influential empires in history. Iron, a metal known for its durability and strength, symbolizes Rome's military might and capacity for conquest. The Roman Empire, which began as a republic and expanded into a vast imperial dominion, "crushed" many nations and brought them under its control through both military force and legal authority.

The fact that the statue has two legs likely represents the division of the Roman Empire into the Western Roman Empire and the Eastern Roman Empire (Byzantine Empire), which occurred in 395 CE. Despite its strength, the Roman Empire was eventually weakened and divided, laying the groundwork for the next phase of history.

E. The Feet of Iron and Clay – Divided Kingdoms

The feet of the statue, composed of a mixture of iron and clay, represented a divided and unstable kingdom:

"Just as you saw that the feet and toes were partly of baked clay and partly of iron, so this will be a divided kingdom; yet it will have some of the strength of iron in it, even as you saw iron mixed with clay. As the toes were partly iron and partly clay, so this kingdom will be partly strong and partly brittle." (Daniel 2:41-42)

This part of the statue symbolizes the divided kingdoms that followed the collapse of the Roman Empire, particularly in Europe. The mixture of iron and clay represents the fragility and instability of these kingdoms, which were often powerful in certain respects but unable to achieve the cohesion or strength of the previous empires. The feet of iron and clay are often interpreted as representing the post-Roman kingdoms of Europe, including the Holy Roman Empire and other medieval states, which were fractured and prone to internal conflict.

The weakness of the clay symbolizes the vulnerability of these kingdoms, despite their attempts to maintain strength through military and political alliances. Daniel's interpretation suggests that these kingdoms would never fully unify or achieve the durability of previous empires.

F. The Stone Not Cut by Human Hands – God's Eternal Kingdom

The climax of Nebuchadnezzar's dream comes with the appearance of the stone "cut out without hands," which struck the statue and destroyed it entirely:

"In the time of those kings, the God of heaven will set up a kingdom that will never be destroyed, nor will it be left to another people. It will crush all those kingdoms and bring them to an end, but it will itself endure forever." (Daniel 2:44)

This stone represents the kingdom of God, which will be established not by human hands but by divine intervention. The destruction of the statue signifies the end of human rule and the collapse of worldly empires. The stone's growth into a great mountain symbolizes the eternal and all-encompassing nature of God's kingdom, which will fill the whole earth and last forever.

Christians often interpret this as a prophecy of the Messianic Kingdom, inaugurated by Jesus Christ and to be fully realized at His Second Coming. In Christian eschatology, this kingdom will overthrow all earthly powers and establish God's perfect reign of peace, justice, and righteousness.

3. Significance of the Dream in Apocalyptic Prophecy

Nebuchadnezzar's dream offers a broad prophetic vision of world history, from the Babylonian Empire to the ultimate establishment of God's eternal kingdom. Each successive empire, despite its power, is destined to fall, showing the temporary nature of human authority compared to the everlasting kingdom of God.

The dream's prophetic relevance extends beyond the ancient world, as theologians and scholars throughout history have interpreted the vision in light of contemporary events. The dream emphasizes the sovereignty of God over history, illustrating that despite the rise and fall of empires, divine purposes will ultimately prevail.

In Christian thought, this vision also serves as a foundation for apocalyptic expectations regarding the end of history. Many view the dream as a symbolic representation of the struggle between human powers and the divine kingdom, with the stone symbolizing Christ's return and the final triumph of God's rule over all creation.

Nebuchadnezzar's dream, as interpreted by Daniel, offers a powerful prophetic overview of world history, symbolizing the rise and fall of empires and the ultimate victory of God's eternal kingdom. The dream's symbolic imagery of the statue and the stone serves as a reminder that all human kingdoms are temporary and subject to divine authority. While Babylon, Persia, Greece, and Rome each had their time of dominance, they would all be superseded by a kingdom "not made by human hands," a kingdom that will endure forever. This vision continues to shape apocalyptic thought and serves as a source of hope for those who believe in the ultimate triumph of God's kingdom over all earthly powers.

Exploration of the Empires Mentioned in Nebuchadnezzar's Dream

Nebuchadnezzar's dream, as interpreted by Daniel, depicts a succession of world empires, each represented by a different section of the statue in his vision. These empires are described in detail through the symbolic use of metals, with each empire's influence, power, and ultimate fall forming part of the broader narrative of human history leading to the establishment of God's eternal kingdom. This section explores each of these empires—their historical context, their rise to power, and how they align with Daniel's prophetic vision.

1. The Head of Gold: The Babylonian Empire

Historical Context

The Babylonian Empire, represented by the head of gold, was at the height of its power during Nebuchadnezzar's reign (605-562 BCE). The empire, based in Mesopotamia, was renowned for its wealth, grandeur, and cultural achievements. The city of Babylon was one of the most magnificent cities of the ancient world, known for its stunning architecture, including the famous Hanging Gardens of Babylon—one of the Seven Wonders of the Ancient World.

The Babylonian Empire reached its peak under Nebuchadnezzar II, who expanded its territories through military conquests and brought much of the ancient Near East under Babylonian control, including the kingdom of Judah. The Babylonians famously destroyed Jerusalem and the First Temple in 586 BCE, leading to the exile of the Jewish people—a significant event in Jewish history.

Symbolism of the Gold Head

- Gold symbolizes the grandeur and wealth of the Babylonian Empire, as well as its supremacy as the dominant power of its time.

- Nebuchadnezzar's empire is described as being given power and dominion over all, fitting the description of a golden age of Babylonian rule, characterized by a centralized and absolute monarchy.

Downfall

Despite its glory, the Babylonian Empire was short-lived. In 539 BCE, it was conquered by the Persian Empire under Cyrus the Great, marking the end of Babylon's dominance. This transition aligns with the prophetic vision of the statue, where the head of gold is replaced by the next empire represented by the chest and arms of silver.

2. The Chest and Arms of Silver: The Medo-Persian Empire

Historical Context

The Medo-Persian Empire (also known as the Achaemenid Empire) succeeded the Babylonians and is symbolized by the chest and arms of silver in the statue. The empire began when Cyrus the Great of Persia overthrew the Babylonian Empire in 539 BCE and established a vast empire that stretched from Asia Minor to India.

The Medo-Persian Empire was unique in its organization and governance. Cyrus the Great is noted for his relatively benevolent rule, especially in his policies toward conquered peoples. For example, after defeating Babylon, he allowed the Jewish exiles to return to Jerusalem and rebuild their temple, as described in the biblical books of Ezra and Nehemiah. The Medo-Persians were also known for creating the Satrapy system, a method of provincial administration that enabled efficient governance across their vast territories.

Symbolism of the Silver Chest and Arms

- Silver is a valuable metal, though inferior to gold, symbolizing an empire that was powerful but not as glorious as Babylon. It also suggests that the Medo-Persians were less centralized than the Babylonians.

- The two arms of the statue represent the dual nature of the empire, which was composed of the Medes and the Persians. While the Persians were the dominant force, the Medes played a significant role in the early formation of the empire.

Downfall

The Medo-Persian Empire continued to expand and prosper under leaders such as Darius the Great and Xerxes, but its dominance came to an end in 330 BCE when it was conquered by Alexander the Great, the leader of the next empire in the prophecy.

3. The Belly and Thighs of Bronze: The Greek Empire

Historical Context

The Greek Empire, represented by the belly and thighs of bronze, refers primarily to the conquests of Alexander the Great (356-323 BCE). Alexander, the king of Macedonia, embarked on one of the most ambitious military campaigns in history, conquering the entire Persian Empire and extending his territory from Greece to Egypt, Persia, and even parts of India.

The Greek Empire brought about the spread of Hellenistic culture, blending Greek ideas, language, and art with the customs of the many lands Alexander conquered. This cultural diffusion had a profound impact on the ancient world, shaping the development of cities, art, science, and philosophy for centuries.

After Alexander's untimely death in 323 BCE, his vast empire was divided among his generals, leading to the creation of several Hellenistic kingdoms, such as the Ptolemaic Kingdom in Egypt and the Seleucid Empire in the Near East.

Symbolism of the Bronze Belly and Thighs

- Bronze, a common metal for weapons and armor, symbolizes the military prowess of the Greek Empire. The Greeks were renowned for their advanced military strategies and effective use of phalanx formations and cavalry.

- The belly and thighs represent the empire's vast cultural influence and geographical expanse. The use of thighs may suggest the mobility and spread of Hellenistic culture across many regions after Alexander's conquests.

Downfall

While the Greek Empire flourished under Alexander, it fragmented after his death. The Greek kingdoms persisted for a time but were gradually absorbed into the Roman Empire by the 1st century BCE, marking the rise of the next empire in Daniel's vision.

4. The Legs of Iron: The Roman Empire

Historical Context

The Roman Empire, symbolized by the legs of iron, was one of the most powerful and long-lasting empires in world history. Rome began as a republic and later expanded into a vast empire that dominated the Mediterranean world and beyond.

Rome's success was built on its strong military discipline, extensive road networks, advanced engineering, and administrative efficiency. The Roman legions were highly effective in expanding and maintaining control over the empire's far-flung territories, from Britain in the west to the Near East in the east.

The Roman Empire also had a significant influence on the development of law, politics, architecture, and language in Western civilization. The Pax Romana, or Roman Peace, was a period of relative stability and prosperity that lasted for over 200 years, from the reign of Augustus to the beginning of the empire's decline.

Symbolism of the Iron Legs

- Iron is a strong, durable metal, symbolizing the military strength and unyielding nature of the Roman Empire. The Roman legions were known for their discipline, effectiveness, and ability to crush opposition.

- The two legs are often interpreted as representing the division of the Roman Empire into two parts: the Western Roman Empire, which fell in 476 CE, and the Eastern Roman Empire, or Byzantine Empire, which persisted until 1453 CE.

Downfall

The Western Roman Empire fell in 476 CE due to internal decay, invasions by Germanic tribes, and economic instability. However, the Eastern Roman Empire, centered in Constantinople, continued for nearly another thousand years until its conquest by the Ottoman Turks in 1453.

5. The Feet of Iron and Clay: The Divided Kingdoms of Europe

Historical Context

The feet of iron and clay represent a kingdom or series of kingdoms that are partly strong and partly weak. Many interpreters see this as a symbol of the post-Roman world, particularly the divided kingdoms of medieval Europe. After the fall of the Roman Empire, Europe fragmented into numerous smaller states and kingdoms, including the Holy Roman Empire, the Franks, and various feudal realms.

These kingdoms were often powerful in certain respects, such as military strength or political influence (iron), but they were also plagued by internal divisions, instability, and weak governance (clay). The mixture of iron and clay suggests that these kingdoms lacked the cohesion and durability of the previous empires.

Symbolism of the Feet of Iron and Clay

- The iron in the feet suggests that these kingdoms still possessed some degree of strength, particularly in terms of military power or remnants of Roman infrastructure.

- The clay represents the inherent fragility of these kingdoms, which were frequently divided by competing interests, internal conflicts, and shifting alliances.

The Holy Roman Empire and Other Medieval Kingdoms

The Holy Roman Empire (800–1806 CE), for instance, is often cited as an example of a state that sought to revive the glory of Rome but remained fragmented due to the competing interests of local rulers. This empire, along with other European powers, was never able to fully reunify the territories of the former Roman Empire, leading to a period of political fragmentation and feudalism.

6. The Stone Not Cut by Human Hands: The Kingdom of God

Symbolism of the Stone

The final element in Nebuchadnezzar's dream is the stone cut without human hands, which strikes the statue and causes it to crumble. This stone represents the Kingdom of God, which is divine in origin and not established through human effort.

- The stone's destruction of the statue symbolizes the ultimate overthrow of human empires by God's eternal kingdom.

- The stone growing into a mountain that fills the whole earth represents the universal and everlasting reign of God, which will replace all worldly kingdoms and last forever.

Historical and Theological Interpretation

In Christian theology, the stone is often seen as a symbol of Jesus Christ, whose kingdom is not of this world but will be established through divine intervention. The prophecy is interpreted as predicting the ultimate triumph of

God's kingdom over all earthly powers, culminating in the Second Coming of Christ and the end of history.

In a broader eschatological sense, the stone symbolizes the idea that all human attempts to establish lasting political or social order will ultimately fail, as God's kingdom will be the final and eternal authority.

The Prophetic Sequence of World Empires

Nebuchadnezzar's dream, as interpreted by Daniel, outlines a sequence of world empires, each representing a different phase in human history. From the glorious Babylonian Empire to the divided kingdoms of Europe, the prophecy emphasizes the transience of human power and the ultimate sovereignty of God. The final kingdom, symbolized by the stone, represents the hope of an eternal, divine kingdom that will replace all earthly authorities.

This prophetic vision has shaped not only religious thought but also historical interpretations of empire and politics. Each of the empires mentioned in the dream—Babylon, Medo-Persia, Greece, Rome, and the divided kingdoms—played a significant role in shaping world history, but their eventual downfall serves as a reminder of the fragility of human institutions compared to the enduring reign of God's kingdom.

Each Part of the Statue: Head of Gold, Chest of Silver, Belly of Bronze, Legs of Iron, Feet of Iron and Clay

Nebuchadnezzar's dream, as recorded in the Book of Daniel (Daniel 2:31-45), features a striking statue that serves as a prophetic representation of world empires. Each part of the statue, from the head of gold to the feet of iron and clay, represents different kingdoms that would rise and fall, leading to the ultimate establishment of God's eternal kingdom. The dream is a vivid symbol of the transient nature of human power and the sovereignty of divine authority over history.

In this chapter, we will examine each part of the statue—the head of gold, the chest of silver, the belly of bronze, the legs of iron, and the feet of iron and clay—analyzing the empires they represent, the symbolic meaning of the metals, and how these empires contributed to the grand narrative of world history.

1. The Head of Gold: The Babylonian Empire

Description

The head of the statue was made of pure gold, the most precious of all the materials in the dream. This section of the statue represented the Babylonian Empire and its king, Nebuchadnezzar II.

Historical Significance

The Babylonian Empire, especially during Nebuchadnezzar's reign (605-562 BCE), was one of the most powerful and opulent kingdoms of the ancient Near East. Babylon was known for its incredible wealth, architectural wonders (such as the Hanging Gardens), and military might. The empire extended its influence over vast territories, including Judah, and famously destroyed Jerusalem in 586 BCE, exiling its inhabitants.

Nebuchadnezzar himself was a towering figure, responsible for building Babylon into one of the most magnificent cities of the ancient world. His kingdom symbolized wealth, power, and splendor—qualities fittingly represented by the gold in the vision.

Symbolism of Gold

- Gold is the most valuable of the metals, symbolizing great wealth, majesty, and splendor. In the context of the dream, it represents Babylon's position as the greatest of the ancient empires.

- Gold also implies impermanence in worldly terms. Despite its brilliance, even the head of gold would not endure forever, as human empires are subject to the forces of time and divine will.

End of the Empire

Despite its grandeur, the Babylonian Empire fell to the Medo-Persian Empire in 539 BCE, marking the transition to the next part of the statue—the chest and arms of silver.

2. The Chest and Arms of Silver: The Medo-Persian Empire

Description

The chest and arms of the statue were made of silver, a metal less valuable than gold but still precious. This section symbolized the Medo-Persian Empire, which followed Babylon in dominance.

Historical Significance

The Medo-Persian Empire, also known as the Achaemenid Empire, arose under the leadership of Cyrus the Great, who conquered Babylon in 539 BCE. This empire was unique for its vast territorial expanse and relatively progressive policies, such as religious tolerance and centralized administration.

Cyrus is particularly noted in the Bible for allowing the Jewish exiles to return to Jerusalem and rebuild the Temple, an event of great significance in Jewish history. The Medo-Persians extended their influence from India to the Mediterranean, becoming one of the largest empires of the ancient world.

Symbolism of Silver

- Silver symbolizes a kingdom that is valuable but inferior to Babylon, reflecting the Medo-Persian Empire's political power but lesser cultural brilliance compared to Babylon's golden era.

- The two arms of the statue represent the dual nature of the empire, composed of the Medes and the Persians, two distinct peoples who ruled together, with Persia eventually becoming the dominant force.

End of the Empire

The Medo-Persian Empire thrived until it was conquered by Alexander the Great in 330 BCE, signaling the rise of the next empire—the belly and thighs of bronze.

3. The Belly and Thighs of Bronze: The Greek Empire

Description

The belly and thighs of the statue were made of bronze, symbolizing the third great empire in Nebuchadnezzar's vision, widely understood to be the Greek Empire under Alexander the Great.

Historical Significance

The Greek Empire, led by Alexander, was one of the most influential empires in history, spreading Hellenistic culture across the ancient world. Alexander's conquests were unprecedented, stretching from Greece to Egypt, through Persia, and as far as India. His empire, though short-lived, left a lasting legacy in terms of language, culture, and governance, blending Greek ideas with those of the conquered regions.

After Alexander's death in 323 BCE, his empire fragmented into several Hellenistic kingdoms, ruled by his generals, such as the Ptolemaic Kingdom in Egypt and the Seleucid Empire in the Near East.

Symbolism of Bronze

- Bronze is associated with strength, military power, and the widespread influence of Greek civilization. It reflects the dominance of Greek culture and warfare during this period.

- The belly and thighs suggest the geographic spread of Hellenistic culture across multiple regions, particularly highlighting the division of Alexander's empire into various successor states after his death.

End of the Empire

While the Greek Empire significantly shaped the ancient world, it was eventually absorbed by the rising Roman Empire, which came to dominate the Mediterranean and beyond.

4. The Legs of Iron: The Roman Empire

Description

The legs of the statue were made of iron, the strongest of all the metals in the vision. This section of the statue represents the Roman Empire, known for its military might and political dominance.

Historical Significance

The Roman Empire began as the Roman Republic, expanding rapidly through military conquest and political alliances. By the time of the emperors, Rome controlled vast territories around the Mediterranean, including Europe, North Africa, and the Middle East. The Romans built extensive road networks, advanced legal systems, and impressive architectural structures, many of which still stand today.

The Pax Romana (Roman Peace) was a period of relative stability and prosperity in the empire, lasting over two centuries. The empire eventually split into the Western Roman Empire and the Eastern Roman Empire (later known as the Byzantine Empire), with each half developing distinct characteristics.

Symbolism of Iron

- Iron is a symbol of strength, power, and the ability to crush opposition. The Roman Empire was known for its military discipline and its unyielding control over its territories.

- The two legs of the statue represent the eventual division of the Roman Empire into the Western Roman

Empire, which fell in 476 CE, and the Eastern Roman Empire, which lasted until the fall of Constantinople in 1453 CE.

End of the Empire

The Western Roman Empire fell due to internal corruption, economic decline, and invasions by various barbarian tribes, while the Eastern Roman Empire continued as the Byzantine Empire for nearly another thousand years before being conquered by the Ottoman Turks.

5. The Feet of Iron and Clay: The Divided Kingdoms of Europe

Description

The feet of the statue were made of a mixture of iron and clay, symbolizing a kingdom or kingdoms that would be both strong and weak. This section is widely interpreted as representing the divided kingdoms that arose after the fall of the Roman Empire, particularly in medieval Europe.

Historical Significance

After the collapse of the Roman Empire, Europe fragmented into numerous smaller kingdoms and states, including the Holy Roman Empire, Franks, Byzantines, and various feudal territories. These kingdoms were often strong in certain areas, such as military power or regional control, but they were also plagued by internal divisions, weak governance, and a lack of cohesion.

The Holy Roman Empire (800-1806 CE) is often cited as an example of a state that sought to revive the glory of Rome but was constantly weakened by political fragmentation and struggles for power between local rulers and the central authority.

Symbolism of Iron and Clay

- The iron represents strength—the remnants of Roman infrastructure, military power, and political authority that persisted in some of these kingdoms.

- The clay represents weakness—the fragility of the kingdoms, their inability to unify, and their susceptibility to internal conflict and instability.

- The combination of iron and clay suggests a kingdom that is inherently unstable and unable to achieve the durability of previous empires.

End of the Divided Kingdoms

The European kingdoms continued to evolve, but they never fully unified into a cohesive empire like their predecessors. The mixture of iron and clay illustrates the ongoing tension between strength and division that has characterized much of European history, particularly in the medieval period.

6. The Stone Not Cut by Human Hands: God's Eternal Kingdom

Description

In the dream, a stone cut out without hands strikes the feet of the statue, causing the entire structure to collapse. The stone then grows into a mountain that fills the whole earth. This stone represents the Kingdom of God, which will destroy all earthly kingdoms and endure forever.

Symbolism of the Stone

- The stone, which is not made by human hands, symbolizes the divine nature of God's kingdom. It is not a human creation but a manifestation of God's will.

- The destruction of the statue signifies the end of human empires and the beginning of God's eternal reign.

- The stone growing into a mountain represents the universal and everlasting kingdom of God, which will replace all worldly powers and fill the earth with justice and righteousness.

Theological Interpretation

For Christians, the stone is often seen as representing Jesus Christ and the establishment of His kingdom through the Messianic reign. Christ is referred to as the cornerstone (Psalm 118:22; Ephesians 2:20), and His return is seen as the fulfillment of the prophecy of the stone striking the statue and inaugurating the final, eternal kingdom.

In Christian eschatology, this vision points to the Second Coming of Christ, the final judgment, and the creation of a new heaven and earth where God's kingdom reigns supreme, as described in the Book of Revelation.

The Symbolism of Nebuchadnezzar's Statue and the Rise and Fall of Empires

Each part of the statue in Nebuchadnezzar's dream represents a different phase in world history, illustrating the rise and fall of great empires. The head of gold symbolizes the splendor of Babylon, while the chest of silver, belly of bronze, and legs of iron represent successive empires that each played a crucial role in shaping the ancient world. The feet of iron and clay reflect the fragmented and unstable nature of post-Roman Europe.

Ultimately, the stone not cut by human hands symbolizes the Kingdom of God, which will surpass and replace all human kingdoms. The vision reveals the transience of human power and the sovereignty of God over the course of history, offering hope for a future in which divine justice and peace will prevail forever.

This prophetic vision has deeply influenced theological thought and historical interpretation, serving as a reminder that while human empires may rise and fall, God's eternal kingdom is the ultimate fulfillment of history.

Delving Deeper into the Theological Implications of the Stone and God's Kingdom

The final element of Nebuchadnezzar's dream—the stone not cut by human hands—is a profoundly significant symbol with deep theological implications. In Daniel's interpretation, the stone strikes the statue's feet, causing the entire structure to collapse, symbolizing the ultimate downfall of all human kingdoms. The stone then grows into a great mountain that fills the earth, representing the eternal Kingdom of God. This stone is distinct from the statue, as it is not a product of human effort but of divine origin.

In this section, we will delve into the theological implications of the stone, focusing on its role as a symbol of God's sovereignty, its connections to messianic prophecies, and its place in Christian eschatology regarding the Second Coming of Christ and the Kingdom of God.

1. The Divine Origin of the Stone: A Kingdom Not Made by Human Hands

One of the key theological implications of the stone is its divine origin. Daniel explicitly describes the stone as being "cut out, but not by human hands" (Daniel 2:34), indicating that it was not crafted through human effort or ingenuity. This phrase emphasizes the supernatural nature of the stone and its role in establishing a kingdom that is not subject to the limitations or failures of human empires.

A. Human Effort vs. Divine Intervention

- The previous empires represented by the statue (Babylon, Medo-Persia, Greece, Rome) were all built by human power, military conquest, and political strategy. However, despite their strength and glory, they are ultimately temporary and flawed, subject to decay, division, and destruction.

- In contrast, the Kingdom of God, symbolized by the stone, is not dependent on human rulers, armies, or governments. It is eternal, unshakable, and divinely ordained. This highlights the sovereignty of God over human history, illustrating that no matter how powerful an empire may appear, it cannot stand against the divine will.

B. A New Kind of Kingdom

- The fact that the stone grows into a mountain that fills the whole earth (Daniel 2:35) signifies that God's kingdom is not confined to a particular time, place, or people, but is universal and will eventually encompass all of creation.

- This image also contrasts the temporary nature of human kingdoms, which rise and fall, with the eternal nature of God's kingdom, which will endure forever. The stone's ability to shatter the statue reflects the idea that all human attempts to create lasting political or social order will ultimately fail, as only God's kingdom can stand the test of time.

2. The Stone as a Messianic Symbol: Jesus Christ as the Cornerstone

In Christian theology, the stone is often interpreted as a symbol of Jesus Christ, the cornerstone of God's eternal kingdom. This interpretation draws on a rich tradition of messianic prophecies in both the Old and New Testaments that refer to the Messiah as a stone or rock, which serves as both a foundation and a source of judgment for those who reject God's kingdom.

A. Old Testament Foundations: The Stone as a Messianic Image

Several Old Testament passages refer to the stone as a messianic symbol, and these texts are often seen as foreshadowing the coming of Christ:

- Psalm 118:22: "The stone the builders rejected has become the cornerstone." This verse is frequently cited in the New Testament to refer to Christ (Matthew 21:42; Acts 4:11; 1 Peter 2:7). The image of the rejected stone becoming the cornerstone suggests that Christ, though initially rejected by many, will ultimately become the foundation of God's kingdom.

- Isaiah 28:16: "So this is what the Sovereign LORD says: 'See, I lay a stone in Zion, a tested stone, a precious cornerstone for a sure foundation; the one who relies on it will never be stricken with panic.'" This prophecy speaks of a cornerstone that will provide a firm foundation for God's people, another image frequently associated with Christ in the New Testament.

- Daniel 2:44: In Daniel's interpretation of Nebuchadnezzar's dream, the stone represents the kingdom of God that will never be destroyed. Christian theologians have historically seen this as a reference to Christ's reign, which will supersede all earthly powers.

B. Jesus as the Stone that Shatters the Kingdoms

In the New Testament, Jesus explicitly applies the imagery of the stone to Himself, particularly in the context of judgment and the establishment of His kingdom:

- Matthew 21:42-44: Jesus refers to Himself as the stone the builders rejected and adds: "Anyone who falls on this stone will be broken to pieces; anyone on whom it falls will be crushed." This echoes the imagery of the stone in Nebuchadnezzar's dream, which crushes the statue, symbolizing the end of all worldly powers and the establishment of God's kingdom.

- Acts 4:11: The apostle Peter, in his sermon before the Sanhedrin, declares that Jesus is "the stone you builders rejected, which has become the cornerstone." This reinforces the idea that Christ is the foundation of God's kingdom, and His rejection by the religious and political authorities of His time mirrors the broader rejection of God's rule by human kingdoms.

In this interpretation, the stone not cut by human hands represents Christ's kingdom, which is not established through human means but through divine power. His kingdom is destined to grow and fill the earth, and all human attempts to oppose it will ultimately be crushed.

3. The Kingdom of God: Present Reality and Future Fulfillment

Theologically, the Kingdom of God has been interpreted in Christian thought in both present and future terms. Jesus often spoke of the Kingdom of God as something that had already begun with His coming, but that would only reach its full realization in the future when God's reign is fully established on earth. This tension between the "already" and the "not yet" of the kingdom is key to understanding the role of the stone in Nebuchadnezzar's dream.

A. The Present Reality of God's Kingdom

- Inaugurated Eschatology: Jesus' ministry, death, and resurrection are seen as the inauguration of the Kingdom of God. In this sense, the stone in Nebuchadnezzar's dream has already struck the statue, signifying that Christ's coming has initiated the overthrow of worldly powers. Although the full collapse of human kingdoms has not yet occurred, the spiritual foundation of God's kingdom has been laid.

- Jesus' Teachings on the Kingdom: Throughout the Gospels, Jesus teaches that the Kingdom of God is already breaking into the world. In Luke 17:21, Jesus says, "The kingdom of God is in your midst," indicating that His presence on earth is the beginning of the kingdom's establishment. However, the fullness of the kingdom is yet to come.

- The Church as a Foretaste of the Kingdom: In Christian theology, the Church is often seen as a sign and foretaste of the Kingdom of God. Although the full realization of God's reign will only occur at the end of time, the Church is called to live out the values of the kingdom—justice, peace, love, and mercy—here and now, anticipating the final fulfillment of the prophecy.

B. The Future Fulfillment of the Kingdom

- The Second Coming of Christ: Christian eschatology teaches that the ultimate fulfillment of the Kingdom of God will occur at the Second Coming of Christ, when He will return to judge the world and establish His reign over all creation. This corresponds to the stone in Nebuchadnezzar's dream growing into a mountain that fills the earth, symbolizing the universal and eternal reign of God.

- Revelation 11:15: "The kingdom of the world has become the kingdom of our Lord and of His Messiah, and He will reign forever and ever." This passage reflects the ultimate triumph of God's kingdom over all earthly powers, echoing the prophecy in Daniel 2.

- The Defeat of All Earthly Powers: At Christ's return, the kingdoms of this world will be judged, and all human authority will give way to the authority of God. This is the final overthrow of the statue in Nebuchadnezzar's dream, where human empires are reduced to dust, and only God's kingdom remains.

4. The Mountain that Fills the Earth: The Universal and Eternal Kingdom of God

The stone in Nebuchadnezzar's dream does not simply destroy the statue; it grows into a mountain that fills the entire earth (Daniel 2:35). This image carries profound theological meaning, representing the universal and eternal nature of God's kingdom.

A. The Universal Scope of God's Kingdom

- The mountain that fills the earth symbolizes the idea that God's kingdom will extend over all creation, encompassing every nation, culture, and people. Unlike the previous empires, which were confined to specific regions or peoples, God's kingdom is for everyone and will bring all of creation under divine authority.

- This universal scope of the kingdom is reflected in the Great Commission (Matthew 28:19), where Jesus commands His disciples to "go and make disciples of all nations." The spread of the Gospel to every corner of the world is seen as part of the expansion of God's kingdom, just as the stone in the dream grows into a mountain.

B. The Eternal Nature of God's Kingdom

- Unlike the human empires represented by the statue, which rise and fall, God's kingdom is described as eternal: "It will never be destroyed, nor will it be left to another people" (Daniel 2:44). This underscores the permanence and indestructibility of God's rule, in contrast to the transient nature of worldly powers.

- Revelation 21:1-3 provides a vision of the final fulfillment of God's kingdom, where there will be "a new heaven and a new earth" and where God will dwell with His people forever. The imagery of a mountain growing to fill the earth echoes this future vision of a renewed creation under the perfect rule of God.

5. The Final Judgment: The Collapse of Human Kingdoms

The stone's impact on the statue signifies the final judgment of all human empires. This is a key eschatological theme in both Jewish and Christian traditions. In Nebuchadnezzar's dream, the destruction of the statue represents the collapse of all worldly systems—political, military, economic, and cultural—when they are confronted with the ultimate authority of God.

A. The Transience of Human Power

- One of the central messages of the dream is the temporary nature of human authority. Despite the power and grandeur of kingdoms like Babylon, Persia, Greece, and Rome, they are ultimately fleeting in the grand scheme of history. The iron and clay mixture in the feet of the statue especially highlights the weakness and instability of human attempts to maintain power.

- The stone's destruction of the statue reflects the biblical theme that only God's kingdom will endure, and that all human power is subject to divine judgment.

B. The Eschatological Hope of Justice

- In Christian eschatology, the destruction of human kingdoms is seen as the fulfillment of the promise that God will bring about justice and righteousness on earth. The Kingdom of God is not merely about political rule but about the establishment of divine justice, where evil is judged, and peace is restored.

- Revelation 19:11-16 depicts Christ's return as a time of final judgment, where He will "strike down the nations" and establish His righteous reign. This corresponds to the stone in Nebuchadnezzar's dream, which brings an end to the flawed and sinful systems of human governance.

The Theological Significance of the Stone and God's Kingdom

The stone not cut by human hands in Nebuchadnezzar's dream is a rich symbol of the Kingdom of God, representing its divine origin, universal scope, and eternal reign. In Christian theology, the stone is identified with Jesus Christ, the cornerstone of God's kingdom, whose coming signifies the end of human rule and the beginning of a new, divine order.

The dream serves as a profound reminder that all human kingdoms are temporary, and only God's kingdom will endure forever. For believers, this vision provides hope in the ultimate victory of justice and righteousness, as God's kingdom will grow to fill the earth and bring about the fulfillment of history. It also highlights the tension between the present reality of God's kingdom, inaugurated through Christ, and its future fulfillment at His return, when all things will be made new.

This powerful image continues to resonate in Christian eschatology, offering a vision of hope, justice, and the final establishment of God's eternal reign over all creation.

Exploring the Symbolism of the Stone and Its Relation to Eschatological Beliefs

The symbolism of the stone in Nebuchadnezzar's dream (Daniel 2:31-45) is a profound and multi-faceted image that resonates deeply with eschatological beliefs—theological interpretations concerning the end of history and the ultimate fulfillment of God's plan. The stone, "not cut by human hands," grows into a mountain that fills the whole earth, symbolizing the Kingdom of God. This imagery holds significant meaning in the context of apocalyptic prophecy, messianic expectations, and the Second Coming of Christ.

In this section, we will further explore the symbolism of the stone as it relates to eschatology, examining key themes such as the judgment of nations, the inauguration of God's kingdom, and its connections to biblical prophecies about the Messiah, the Second Coming, and the final judgment.

1. The Stone and the Inauguration of God's Kingdom

One of the central themes of the stone's symbolism is the inauguration of God's kingdom—a kingdom distinct from human empires in both its origin and nature. The stone is not created by human hands, emphasizing that the Kingdom of God is established through divine intervention, not human effort. This directly contrasts with the empires symbolized by the statue, which were built on human power, conquest, and political strategy.

A. The Divine Origin of the Kingdom

- The phrase "not cut by human hands" implies that the stone, and thus the kingdom it represents, is supernatural. This emphasizes the idea that God's kingdom is not a human creation but is initiated by divine authority.

- In eschatological terms, the Kingdom of God is often seen as something that breaks into human history through a dramatic intervention—whether that be the coming of the Messiah, the return of Christ, or the final judgment. This parallels the stone's sudden appearance in Nebuchadnezzar's dream, which signifies the unexpected and decisive nature of God's actions in world affairs.

- The inauguration of God's kingdom is central to Christian eschatology, where it is believed that Jesus' ministry marked the beginning of this kingdom. However, its full realization will only occur at the Second Coming when Christ returns to establish His eternal rule.

B. Present and Future Dimensions of the Kingdom

- Inaugurated eschatology refers to the belief that the Kingdom of God has already begun but has not yet been fully realized. In Christian theology, this tension is often expressed through the "already, but not yet" framework: the kingdom is "already" present through Christ's work and the activity of the Holy Spirit, but it is "not yet" fully realized until the end of the age.

- The stone's role in shattering the statue and growing into a mountain that fills the whole earth symbolizes this future fullness of God's kingdom. The kingdom is already breaking into the world, but its complete establishment is tied to the end of history, when all human powers will be overthrown, and God's rule will be all-encompassing.

C. The Church as a Foretaste of the Kingdom

- In Christian eschatology, the Church is often understood as a foretaste or sign of the Kingdom of God. Although the final kingdom has not yet been established, the Church is called to live according to the principles of that kingdom—promoting justice, peace, and righteousness.

- The growth of the stone into a mountain that fills the earth can also be interpreted as representing the spread of the Gospel and the gradual expansion of God's reign through the Church's mission. However, the ultimate fulfillment of this vision will occur when Christ returns, bringing an end to all human systems of governance.

2. The Stone as a Symbol of Judgment

In Nebuchadnezzar's dream, the stone strikes the feet of the statue, causing the entire structure to collapse into dust.

This act represents the judgment of nations and the destruction of all human kingdoms. The idea of God intervening in history to judge the nations and establish His kingdom is a central theme in both Jewish and Christian eschatology.

A. Judgment of Human Kingdoms

- The collapse of the statue reflects the impermanence of human empires and the ultimate futility of human attempts to build lasting political power. Each empire, represented by a different metal, is part of a succession of kingdoms that eventually fall, showing that no human power is eternal.

- In eschatological terms, the destruction of the statue represents the final judgment of all earthly powers, a common theme in apocalyptic literature. Daniel 7:9-14 offers a similar vision, where the Ancient of Days (God) judges the nations and establishes the eternal kingdom of the Son of Man (often identified with the Messiah).

- The Book of Revelation also echoes this theme. In Revelation 19:11-16, Christ returns as a warrior-king, striking down the nations and establishing His reign. This corresponds to the stone in Daniel 2 that crushes the statue, symbolizing the final overthrow of all human authorities and the establishment of God's perfect justice.

B. The Stone as a Stumbling Block and Source of Judgment

- In the New Testament, Jesus often refers to Himself as a stone that brings both salvation and judgment. In Matthew 21:42-44, He identifies Himself as the cornerstone (drawing from Psalm 118:22) and adds: "Anyone who falls on this stone will be broken to pieces; anyone on whom it falls will be crushed." This echoes the image of the stone in Nebuchadnezzar's dream, which shatters the statue.

- This dual aspect of the stone—as both a foundation for the kingdom and an instrument of judgment—highlights the eschatological reality that Christ's return will bring salvation to the faithful but judgment to those who oppose God's kingdom. The Second Coming is seen as a moment of vindication for the righteous and condemnation for the wicked.

- 1 Peter 2:7-8 reinforces this idea, describing Christ as a "stone that causes people to stumble and a rock that makes them fall." The rejection of Christ by the powers of the world parallels the rejection of God's kingdom by earthly rulers in Daniel's vision.

3. The Stone and Messianic Prophecies

The image of the stone in Daniel's dream has strong connections to messianic prophecies in the Old Testament, which foretell the coming of a divine ruler who will establish

God's kingdom on earth. In Christian eschatology, these prophecies are seen as being fulfilled in the person of Jesus Christ, who is identified as both the Messiah and the cornerstone of God's kingdom.

A. The Messianic Role of the Stone

- As mentioned earlier, several Old Testament passages describe the Messiah as a stone or rock. Isaiah 28:16 speaks of a "precious cornerstone for a sure foundation," which is interpreted by Christians as a prophecy of Christ. The cornerstone represents the foundation of God's kingdom, which is built upon the Messiah's authority.

- The stone in Daniel 2 is often understood as another messianic symbol, representing the coming of the Messiah who will establish an everlasting kingdom. The destruction of the statue signifies the Messiah's victory over all earthly powers, while the stone growing into a mountain symbolizes the universal scope of His reign.

B. The Kingdom of the Son of Man

- In Daniel 7:13-14, another apocalyptic vision features the Son of Man coming on the clouds of heaven to receive an eternal kingdom. This figure is often identified with the Messiah in both Jewish and Christian interpretations. The Son of Man's kingdom is described as one that "will never be destroyed," similar to the stone that grows into a mountain in Daniel 2.

- Jesus frequently referred to Himself as the Son of Man, connecting His mission to the messianic expectations in Daniel 7. In Christian eschatology, the Second Coming of Christ is seen as the fulfillment of this prophecy, where Jesus returns to establish His kingdom, overthrowing all worldly authorities and inaugurating the new creation.

C. The Universal and Eternal Reign of the Messiah

- The mountain that fills the earth in Daniel 2:35 symbolizes the universal nature of God's kingdom. This aligns with messianic prophecies that describe the Messiah's reign as extending over all nations. Isaiah 2:2-4 speaks of a time when "the mountain of the LORD's temple will be established as the highest of the mountains" and all nations will stream to it. This imagery is directly echoed in the vision of the stone growing into a mountain that encompasses the whole world.

- The eternal nature of the Messiah's reign is also emphasized in passages like Isaiah 9:7: "Of the greatness of his government and peace there will be no end. He will reign on David's throne and over his kingdom, establishing and upholding it with justice and righteousness." This is reflected in Daniel's prophecy that the kingdom represented by the stone will "never be destroyed" (Daniel 2:44).

4. The Stone and the Second Coming of Christ

In Christian eschatology

, the Second Coming of Christ is the event in which Jesus returns to earth to judge the nations, defeat evil, and establish God's kingdom in its fullness. The stone in Nebuchadnezzar's dream is often seen as a symbol of this future event, where Christ's return brings an end to all human governments and inaugurates the eternal reign of God.

A. Christ as the Returning King

- The stone's destruction of the statue in Daniel 2 is frequently interpreted as a symbol of Christ's return, when He will overthrow the kingdoms of this world and establish His reign. This is a central theme in the Book of Revelation, where Christ is depicted as a victorious king who defeats the forces of evil and ushers in the new creation (Revelation 19:11-16; Revelation 21).

- Revelation 11:15 proclaims, "The kingdom of the world has become the kingdom of our Lord and of his Messiah, and he will reign forever and ever." This reflects the same idea as Daniel's vision, where the stone represents the final victory of God's kingdom over all earthly powers.

B. The Final Judgment and the End of History

- The stone's role in destroying the statue also symbolizes the final judgment of all nations. In Christian eschatology, the Second Coming is not only about the establishment of God's kingdom but also about the judgment of the wicked and the vindication of the righteous.

- Revelation 20:11-15 describes the Great White Throne Judgment, where all people are judged according to their deeds. This parallels the stone in Daniel 2, which represents the destruction of sinful human systems and the establishment of divine justice.

C. The New Creation and the Fulfillment of Prophecy

- The stone growing into a mountain that fills the earth can also be interpreted as a symbol of the new heaven and new earth described in Revelation 21. In this vision, God's kingdom is fully realized, and there is no longer any separation between heaven and earth. The stone's growth represents the transformation of creation as God's kingdom comes in its fullness.

- The final establishment of God's kingdom fulfills the prophetic vision of Daniel 2, where all human empires are replaced by an eternal, just, and universal kingdom that will never be destroyed.

The Stone's Symbolism in Eschatological Context

The stone in Nebuchadnezzar's dream is a powerful symbol of the Kingdom of God and its role in human history and eschatology. It represents the divine intervention that will overthrow all human powers, the establishment of a kingdom that is both universal and eternal, and the coming of the Messiah who will rule over all nations. In Christian theology, the stone is often identified with Jesus Christ, the cornerstone of God's kingdom, whose return will bring about the final judgment and the renewal of creation.

This vision serves as a reminder that while human kingdoms may rise and fall, only God's kingdom will endure forever. The stone's ability to shatter the statue reflects the reality that all human power is ultimately subject to divine judgment, and the growth of the stone into a mountain signifies the hope of a future in which God's reign will encompass the entire world.

The stone's symbolism continues to resonate deeply in Christian eschatology, offering both a warning to those who oppose God's rule and a promise of eternal peace and justice to those who belong to His kingdom.

Exploring the Connection Between Nebuchadnezzar's Dream and Other Eschatological Themes in the Bible

Nebuchadnezzar's dream in Daniel 2 connects deeply with other eschatological themes in the Bible, providing a prophetic vision of the future that resonates across both the Old and New Testaments. This vision of the rise and fall of world empires, culminating in the establishment of God's eternal kingdom, mirrors broader biblical themes related to judgment, the Messiah, and the final establishment of God's reign. Additionally, the historical implications of the kingdoms represented by the statue provide important context for how this prophecy unfolded and its relevance in understanding the movement of world history.

In this section, we will explore the connection between Nebuchadnezzar's dream and other major eschatological passages in the Bible, while also delving deeper into the historical significance of each empire mentioned in the dream.

1. Connection to Other Eschatological Themes in the Old Testament

The Book of Daniel is filled with visions that share themes with other prophetic writings in the Old Testament. The concept of the kingdom of God replacing human rule and the final judgment of nations runs through various books of the Bible, reinforcing Daniel's vision of history moving toward a divine culmination.

A. The Book of Isaiah: The Coming Kingdom and Judgment

The Book of Isaiah contains several passages that parallel the vision in Daniel 2, especially concerning the future kingdom of God, the role of the Messiah, and the ultimate triumph of righteousness over wickedness.

- Isaiah 2:2-4 speaks of a time when the mountain of the Lord's house will be established as the highest of the mountains, and all nations will stream to it. This vision of God's mountain echoes the imagery of the stone in Daniel growing into a great mountain that fills the earth. Both passages symbolize the universal reign of God over all nations, with people seeking justice and peace under divine rule.

- Isaiah 9:6-7 prophesies the birth of a Messianic King, whose government and peace will have no end, and who will establish justice and righteousness. This passage is often seen as foretelling the coming of Jesus Christ, whose kingdom will be eternal, just as the stone in Daniel's vision represents an eternal kingdom that will never be destroyed.

- Isaiah 11:1-10 further develops this messianic vision, describing a time of universal peace and righteousness under the reign of the Branch from the stump of Jesse (a reference to the Davidic Messiah). Like the stone that replaces the statue, this future king will bring about a transformation of the world, ending war and injustice.

B. The Book of Ezekiel: Judgment on the Nations

The Book of Ezekiel is rich in apocalyptic imagery and shares Daniel's emphasis on the judgment of nations and the establishment of God's kingdom. Several passages reflect the themes of divine sovereignty and the futility of human power.

- Ezekiel 38-39 speaks of the battle of Gog and Magog, a prophetic battle that mirrors the apocalyptic conflict between the forces of good and evil. This is connected to the final judgment described in Daniel, where human kingdoms are destroyed by the stone. Both Ezekiel and Daniel share the eschatological theme that God will defeat the enemies of His people and establish His eternal rule.

- Ezekiel 40-48 presents a vision of the restored Temple and the renewal of Israel under God's direct rule. This concept of restoration ties into Daniel's vision of the eternal kingdom that replaces all earthly empires.

C. The Book of Joel: The Day of the Lord

In the Book of Joel, the Day of the Lord is described as a day of judgment and salvation, where God will judge the nations and restore His people. Joel's prophecy emphasizes the cosmic scope of God's intervention in history, much like the stone in Daniel's vision, which brings about the collapse of human power structures.

- Joel 3:12-14 speaks of the Valley of Decision, where the nations will be judged. This parallels the destruction of the statue in Nebuchadnezzar's dream, symbolizing the judgment of all human kingdoms at the end of history.

2. Connection to Eschatological Themes in the New Testament

The eschatological themes in Daniel, particularly the imagery of the stone and the establishment of God's kingdom, resonate strongly with the New Testament, especially in the teachings of Jesus, the writings of Paul, and the Book of Revelation. The New Testament presents a unified vision of the Kingdom of God, the Second Coming of Christ, and the final judgment, all of which align with the prophetic message in Daniel 2.

A. The Teachings of Jesus on the Kingdom of God

Jesus frequently spoke about the Kingdom of God, portraying it as both a present reality and a future hope. His teachings echo the themes found in Daniel's vision, where the stone symbolizes a kingdom that will ultimately replace all earthly powers.

- Luke 17:20-21: Jesus teaches that the Kingdom of God is not something that can be observed by outward signs but is already present "in your midst." This reflects the inaugurated nature of the kingdom, which is present through Christ but will only be fully realized in the future. Just as the stone in Daniel begins small and grows into a mountain, the kingdom starts quietly and will grow to encompass the whole world.

- Matthew 13:31-32: In the parable of the mustard seed, Jesus likens the Kingdom of God to a small seed that grows into a large tree. This parallels the stone growing into a mountain, symbolizing the expansion and growth of God's rule until it covers all the earth.

B. The Second Coming and the Final Judgment

The New Testament also develops the theme of the Second Coming of Christ and the final judgment, where Christ will return to overthrow all human powers and establish God's kingdom in its fullness. This imagery directly corresponds to the stone in Daniel that destroys the statue, signifying the end of human rule.

- Revelation 11:15: "The kingdom of the world has become the kingdom of our Lord and of his Messiah, and he will reign forever and ever." This passage mirrors the imagery in Daniel 2, where the stone represents the kingdom that will last forever, replacing all human kingdoms.

- Revelation 19:11-16: This vision of Christ returning as a conquering king who defeats the nations aligns with the stone shattering the statue in Nebuchadnezzar's dream. In both cases, the coming of God's kingdom means the end of worldly powers and the establishment of divine justice.

- 2 Thessalonians 2:8: Paul speaks of Christ's return as the moment when He will overthrow the lawless one (often interpreted as the Antichrist) "with the breath of his mouth and destroy by the splendor of his coming." This imagery echoes the idea of Christ as the stone that will crush all opposition and bring about the fulfillment of God's kingdom.

C. The Cornerstone and the Kingdom

In the New Testament, the stone is also associated with Jesus Christ, particularly in terms of His role as the cornerstone of God's kingdom. The metaphor of the cornerstone emphasizes both salvation and judgment, reinforcing the dual role of Christ in bringing grace to the faithful and judgment to those who oppose God's kingdom.

- Matthew 21:42-44: Jesus refers to Himself as the cornerstone that the builders rejected, drawing from Psalm 118:22. He adds that "anyone who falls on this stone will be broken to pieces; anyone on whom it falls will be crushed," echoing the imagery of the stone in Daniel's vision. The rejection of Christ by the world's powers leads to their ultimate destruction, just as the statue in Nebuchadnezzar's dream is shattered by the stone.

- 1 Peter 2:6-8: Peter quotes from Isaiah and Psalms to describe Jesus as the cornerstone chosen by God, but also as a stone that causes many to stumble. This reinforces the idea that Christ is the foundation of the new kingdom, but also the instrument of judgment for those who reject Him.

3. Historical Implications of the Kingdoms Represented by the Statue

Nebuchadnezzar's dream is not just a prophetic vision but also a depiction of actual historical empires that played pivotal roles in shaping the ancient and medieval world. The succession of empires represented by the statue—Babylon, Medo-Persia, Greece, and Rome—mirrors the rise and fall of these powers, providing a theological framework for understanding world history in light of divine sovereignty.

A. The Head of Gold: The Babylonian Empire

The Babylonian Empire, represented by the head of gold, reached its peak under Nebuchadnezzar II, who ruled from 605 to 562 BCE. Babylon was renowned for its wealth, architectural marvels (including the Hanging Gardens), and military power. Nebuchadnezzar's conquest of Judah and the destruction of the First Temple in Jerusalem were pivotal events in Jewish history, leading to the Babylonian Exile.

- Historically, the Babylonians were seen as a glorious empire, but their dominance was relatively short-lived, lasting less than a century before being conquered by the Persians

. The "gold" in the statue reflects the splendor of Babylon, but also its impermanence.

B. The Chest and Arms of Silver: The Medo-Persian Empire

The Medo-Persian Empire (also known as the Achaemenid Empire) succeeded Babylon and expanded its territory across the Near East, becoming one of the largest empires in history. Under Cyrus the Great, the Medo-Persians allowed the Jewish exiles to return to Jerusalem and rebuild the temple, as recorded in the books of Ezra and Nehemiah.

- The silver in the statue represents the inferior majesty of this empire compared to Babylon but emphasizes its strength in governance and administration. The Medo-Persians ruled for over two centuries before their defeat by Alexander the Great.

C. The Belly and Thighs of Bronze: The Greek Empire

The Greek Empire, particularly under Alexander the Great, is symbolized by the belly and thighs of bronze. Alexander's conquests spread Hellenistic culture across the Mediterranean, the Near East, and parts of Asia, leaving a lasting legacy in philosophy, art, science, and politics.

- The bronze reflects the military strength and cultural influence of Greece. Though Alexander's empire fragmented after his death, the Hellenistic world continued to shape the development of Western civilization for centuries.

D. The Legs of Iron: The Roman Empire

The Roman Empire, represented by the legs of iron, was known for its military might, legal systems, and extensive infrastructure. Rome dominated the Mediterranean world for centuries and profoundly influenced the development of Western civilization.

- The iron symbolizes the strength and durability of Rome, which crushed its enemies and built an empire that endured for nearly a thousand years in the West and even longer in the East as the Byzantine Empire. However, the division into two legs likely symbolizes the eventual split of the empire into the Western and Eastern Roman Empires.

E. The Feet of Iron and Clay: The Divided Kingdoms of Europe

The feet of iron and clay represent a divided kingdom, commonly understood to symbolize the fragmentation of the Roman Empire and the rise of medieval Europe. The mixture of iron and clay reflects both the strength (remnants of Roman power) and the fragility (internal divisions) of these post-Roman kingdoms.

- The Holy Roman Empire is often seen as part of this symbolism, as it sought to revive the glory of Rome but remained fragmented and weak, divided among local rulers and feudal lords.

Prophecy, History, and Eschatology

Nebuchadnezzar's dream in Daniel 2 presents a profound connection between world history and eschatology, illustrating the rise and fall of human empires and the ultimate establishment of God's eternal kingdom. This vision finds strong parallels throughout both the Old and New Testaments, where the themes of judgment, the Messiah, and the final triumph of God's reign are central to the biblical narrative.

Historically, the kingdoms represented by the statue played crucial roles in shaping the ancient world, but the dream also serves as a reminder of the transient nature of human power. In contrast, the Kingdom of God, symbolized by the stone, is eternal and unstoppable, representing the final fulfillment of God's plan for creation.

Theologically, the dream points toward the Second Coming of Christ, where all human rule will be replaced by the righteous reign of God. The connections to other eschatological passages in the Bible reinforce the message that human history is moving toward a divine climax, where God's kingdom will be established forever, bringing justice, peace, and salvation to all who belong to it.

Symbolic Meaning of the Metals and Their Prophetic Associations with Historical Empires

In Nebuchadnezzar's dream, as interpreted by Daniel (Daniel 2:31-45), the statue made of different metals serves as a prophetic symbol for the rise and fall of successive world empires. Each metal represents an empire and carries with it symbolic meanings relating to the character, strength, and ultimate fate of that empire. This chapter explores the symbolic significance of each metal—gold, silver, bronze, iron, and the combination of iron and clay—and how these symbols align with the historical empires they represent.

The metals in the statue not only reflect the glory, strength, and power of each kingdom but also their weaknesses and eventual fall, leading to the establishment of God's eternal kingdom, symbolized by the stone "cut without human hands." The chapter delves into the historical background of each empire and the prophetic meanings behind the choice of each metal.

1. The Head of Gold: The Babylonian Empire

A. Symbolic Meaning of Gold

Gold, as the most precious and valuable of all the metals in the statue, symbolizes wealth, glory, and splendor. It was traditionally associated with royalty, divinity, and enduring grandeur. In Nebuchadnezzar's dream, the head of gold represents the Babylonian Empire, which under Nebuchadnezzar II (605-562 BCE) was one of the most magnificent and prosperous empires of the ancient world.

Gold also carries the connotation of absolute authority and dominion, attributes that characterize Nebuchadnezzar's reign. His kingdom was unmatched in its time, with the city of Babylon standing as a symbol of power, opulence, and architectural achievement. The grandeur of the city, including its famed Hanging Gardens and monumental temples, reflected the imperial glory of Babylon.

B. Prophetic Association with the Babylonian Empire

- The Babylonian Empire, centered in the ancient city of Babylon in Mesopotamia, was renowned for its military might, cultural achievements, and wealth. Nebuchadnezzar II expanded the empire's reach, conquering Jerusalem in 586 BCE, destroying the First Temple, and initiating the Babylonian Exile of the Jewish people.

- Babylon was considered the jewel of the ancient world, and its leadership under Nebuchadnezzar was seen as divinely sanctioned. In Daniel's prophecy, Babylon is the head of gold, the greatest of the empires in terms of wealth and glory.

However, gold, while beautiful and valuable, is also malleable and can be easily corrupted, symbolizing the eventual fall of Babylon. Despite its grandeur, Babylon's reign was not eternal, as the prophecy foretold that it would be replaced by a lesser but stronger empire, the Medo-Persian Empire.

2. The Chest and Arms of Silver: The Medo-Persian Empire

A. Symbolic Meaning of Silver

Silver, a metal of considerable value though not as precious as gold, symbolizes wealth, strength, and governance. It reflects an empire that is powerful and rich but not as glorious or centralized as the Babylonian Empire. The choice of silver for the chest and arms suggests a kingdom that is organized and durable, with strong administrative capabilities, but also one that lacks the same splendor and brilliance of Babylon.

Silver was often associated with mediation and justice, which aligns with the administrative policies of the Medo-Persian Empire. This empire is often regarded as fairer and more systematized in its governance than Babylon, particularly under Cyrus the Great, who was known for his policies of religious tolerance and administrative reforms.

B. Prophetic Association with the Medo-Persian Empire

- The Medo-Persian Empire (also known as the Achaemenid Empire) succeeded the Babylonian Empire in 539 BCE after Cyrus the Great conquered Babylon. The empire extended from Egypt to India, becoming the largest empire the world had ever seen at the time.

- The two arms of silver likely symbolize the dual nature of the Medo-Persian Empire, which was composed of two major peoples: the Medes and the Persians. Initially, the Medes were more dominant, but eventually, the Persians, under Cyrus, became the leading force in the empire.

Silver also carries the idea of inferiority in terms of cultural grandeur when compared to Babylon's gold, signifying that while the Medo-Persian Empire was powerful and expansive, it did not achieve the same cultural or architectural heights as Babylon. The transition from gold to silver reflects the gradual decline in imperial glory as history progresses, though the strength of governance and military power remains formidable.

3. The Belly and Thighs of Bronze: The Greek Empire

A. Symbolic Meaning of Bronze

Bronze is a metal associated with strength, durability, and military power, making it an appropriate symbol for the Greek Empire, especially under Alexander the Great. Bronze was widely used for weaponry and armor in the ancient world, signifying an empire built on military conquest and strategic prowess.

Bronze also represents cultural influence and expansion. The Greek Empire was notable for spreading Hellenistic culture across the known world, blending Greek ideas with local traditions in the areas it conquered. This cultural diffusion had a lasting impact on art, philosophy, language, and governance across Europe, the Near East, and Asia.

B. Prophetic Association with the Greek Empire

- The Greek Empire, led by Alexander the Great, succeeded the Medo-Persian Empire in 330 BCE. Alexander's conquests created one of the largest empires in history, spreading from Greece to Egypt, Persia, and India. Though Alexander's empire was short-lived due to his untimely death in 323 BCE, the Hellenistic influence endured for centuries.

- The belly and thighs of bronze likely symbolize the vast territorial and cultural expanse of the Greek Empire, with the thighs representing the division of Alexander's empire after his death into several Hellenistic kingdoms, such as the Ptolemaic Kingdom in Egypt and the Seleucid Empire in the Near East.

Bronze, while strong and durable, is inferior to gold and silver in terms of value, reflecting the Greek Empire's relative lack of political cohesion and cultural grandeur compared to Babylon and Persia. Despite its vast influence, the Greek Empire was ultimately fragmented and unable to maintain a lasting centralized rule, leading to its eventual absorption by the Roman Empire.

4. The Legs of Iron: The Roman Empire

A. Symbolic Meaning of Iron

Iron, the strongest of the metals in the statue, symbolizes military might, political dominance, and unbreakable strength. Iron is a metal associated with power and conquest, qualities that are fitting for the Roman Empire, which dominated much of the known world for centuries.

Iron's properties reflect the Roman Empire's ability to crush opposition and enforce its rule across vast territories. The Roman legions, disciplined and effective, were key to the empire's expansion and maintenance of control over its territories. Iron is also cold and unyielding, symbolizing the efficiency and often brutal methods through which Rome maintained its dominance.

B. Prophetic Association with the Roman Empire

- The Roman Empire succeeded the Greek Empire and became one of the most powerful and long-lasting empires in world history. It began as the Roman Republic, growing into a vast imperial power that ruled over much of Europe, North Africa, and the Near East.

- The two legs of iron are often interpreted as symbolizing the eventual division of the Roman Empire into the Western Roman Empire (which fell in 476 CE) and the Eastern Roman Empire (which continued as the Byzantine Empire until 1453 CE).

Iron also reflects the militaristic nature of Roman rule. The Roman Empire was known for its extensive use of legions to control its territories and for its ability to adapt and reform its military strategies to maintain its dominance. However, iron, while strong, is not a precious metal, symbolizing that despite Rome's strength, it lacked the cultural grandeur and legacy of earlier empires like Babylon and Persia.

5. The Feet of Iron and Clay: The Divided Kingdoms of Europe

A. Symbolic Meaning of Iron and Clay

The feet of the statue, made of a mixture of iron and clay, symbolize a kingdom that is partly strong and partly brittle. Iron represents continued strength, likely the remnants of the Roman Empire, while clay symbolizes weakness, division, and fragility. The combination of these two materials suggests an empire or series of kingdoms that retain some elements of Roman strength but are fundamentally unstable and prone to internal conflict.

The inability of iron and clay to mix highlights the inherent tension between strength and fragility, symbolizing the fractured nature of the kingdoms that arose after the fall of Rome. These kingdoms were often powerful in some respects but weak in others, divided by internal strife and unable to achieve the cohesion of the empires that preceded them.

B. Prophetic Association with the Divided Kingdoms of Europe

- The feet of iron and clay are often interpreted as representing the fragmented kingdoms that emerged after the fall of the Roman Empire, particularly in medieval Europe. The Holy Roman Empire (800–1806 CE) is often seen as part of this prophecy, as it attempted to revive the glory of Rome but was constantly weakened by political fragmentation and internal divisions.

- This period of European history was marked by the rise of feudalism, the formation of various kingdoms, and the continued influence of the Roman legacy in governance and law. However, the inherent weakness of these kingdoms—symbolized by the clay—made them unstable and vulnerable to conflict and invasion.

The mixture of iron and clay represents the enduring legacy of Rome in European history, with elements of Roman governance, law, and military structure persisting in medieval and early modern Europe. However, the inability to fully unify under a single strong authority reflects the limitations of these kingdoms, which were constantly divided by internal conflicts, weak alliances, and shifting political loyalties.

6. The Stone Not Cut by Human Hands: God's Eternal Kingdom

While not a metal, the stone in Nebuchadnezzar's dream plays a crucial role in the prophecy, representing the Kingdom of God that will destroy all human empires and endure forever. The stone, "cut without human hands," signifies that this kingdom is divine in origin, not the result of human effort or conquest. It strikes the statue at its feet, causing the entire structure to collapse, symbolizing the end of human rule and the establishment of God's eternal reign.

The stone then grows into a mountain that fills the whole earth, representing the universal scope and eternal nature of God's kingdom. In Christian theology, this stone is often identified with Jesus Christ, the Messiah, who will return to judge the nations and establish God's kingdom in its fullness.

The Prophetic Meaning of the Metals and the Rise and Fall of Empires

Nebuchadnezzar's dream offers a symbolic overview of world history, where the metals of the statue represent the transience of human power and the ultimate sovereignty of God. Each metal—gold, silver, bronze, iron, and the mixture of iron and clay—carries prophetic meaning related to the empires they symbolize, illustrating both their strengths and their inherent weaknesses. The dream reveals that all human kingdoms, no matter how powerful, will eventually be replaced by the Kingdom of God, which is eternal and unshakable.

The prophecy presents a powerful reminder of the temporary nature of human authority and the inevitability of divine judgment. The rise and fall of the Babylonian, Medo-Persian, Greek, and Roman empires all point to the fulfillment of this vision, while the divided kingdoms of Europe reflect the fragile nature of human governance in the post-Roman world. Ultimately, the stone in the dream serves as a symbol of hope for believers, pointing to the final triumph of God's kingdom over all earthly powers.

Exploring the Role of the Roman Empire in Christian Eschatology and the Theological Implications of the Stone

The Roman Empire, symbolized by the legs of iron in Nebuchadnezzar's dream, plays a pivotal role in Christian eschatology. In the New Testament and early Christian writings, Rome is often seen as both a symbol of worldly power and as a key player in the unfolding of the divine plan, particularly regarding the Second Coming of Christ and the final judgment. The theological implications of the stone that strikes and destroys the statue at its feet also carry profound eschatological meaning, representing the ultimate victory of God's kingdom over all human empires.

This section explores the deeper significance of the Roman Empire in Christian eschatology and delves further into the theological symbolism of the stone, especially its connection to messianic prophecy, the final judgment, and the establishment of God's eternal kingdom.

1. The Roman Empire in Christian Eschatology

In the context of Nebuchadnezzar's dream, the Roman Empire, represented by the legs of iron, is portrayed as the last great empire before the establishment of God's kingdom. Its role in history and prophecy has been extensively analyzed in both the New Testament and later Christian writings, where it is often depicted as the empire under which significant eschatological events unfold.

A. The Roman Empire and the First Coming of Christ

The Roman Empire was the dominant power during the time of Jesus' birth, ministry, and crucifixion. This historical context is crucial for understanding the eschatological significance of Rome in the Christian narrative. Several key events related to the fulfillment of prophecy occurred during the reign of Rome:

- The Birth of Jesus: According to Luke 2:1-7, Jesus was born in Bethlehem during the reign of the Roman

Emperor Caesar Augustus. The decree for a census issued by Augustus led to Joseph and Mary traveling to Bethlehem, fulfilling the prophecy of Micah 5:2, which stated that the Messiah would be born in Bethlehem.

- Jesus' Crucifixion under Roman Rule: The Roman Empire, through its governor Pontius Pilate, played a direct role in the crucifixion of Jesus. The crucifixion, which took place under Roman authority, is seen as a fulfillment of prophecies such as Isaiah 53, where the Suffering Servant dies for the sins of the world. This event is central to Christian theology, marking the atonement and the beginning of the new covenant.

- Rome as the Setting for the Inauguration of the Kingdom: Jesus proclaimed the Kingdom of God in the midst of Roman rule, declaring that His kingdom was "not of this world" (John 18:36). The contrast between the worldly power of Rome and the spiritual kingdom of Christ sets the stage for eschatological expectations. The Roman Empire, with its vast reach and centralized power, is seen as the last great human kingdom before God's kingdom begins to unfold through Christ's ministry and, ultimately, through His Second Coming.

B. The Roman Empire and the Book of Revelation

The Book of Revelation is rich in apocalyptic imagery related to the Roman Empire, often presenting Rome as a symbol of oppressive worldly power. This symbolism reflects the early Christian experience of persecution under Roman rule and the belief that God would bring about Rome's downfall as part of the final judgment.

- Rome as Babylon: In Revelation 17-18, Rome is symbolically referred to as Babylon the Great, a city of great wealth and wickedness that opposes God and persecutes His people. Babylon, representing Rome, is destined for destruction. The portrayal of Rome as the "harlot" sitting on many waters (Revelation 17:1) emphasizes its political dominance and moral corruption, drawing a parallel to Nebuchadnezzar's Babylon as the embodiment of human arrogance and rebellion against God.

- The Beast and the Roman Empire: In Revelation 13, the beast with ten horns is often interpreted as a symbol of the Roman Empire, with the ten horns representing Roman emperors or client kings. The beast is described as a political and military power that opposes God's people, demanding worship and allegiance. Many early Christians saw the Roman emperors, particularly those like Nero and Domitian, as embodiments of this beast, persecuting the Church and opposing God's kingdom.

- The Fall of Rome as a Sign of the End Times: The eventual fall of the Roman Empire in the West in 476 CE was interpreted by many early Christians as a significant event in the unfolding of eschatological prophecy. Some believed that the collapse of Rome would herald the Second Coming of Christ and the final establishment of God's kingdom. The imagery of the stone in Daniel's vision striking the feet of the statue reflects this belief that Rome's fall would mark the beginning of God's eternal reign.

C. Rome's Role in the Development of Christian Eschatology

Rome's role in Christian eschatology is twofold: it represents the culmination of human empires and serves as a backdrop for the fulfillment of messianic prophecy. The Roman Empire is viewed as the final worldly power before the establishment of God's kingdom, symbolizing the strength and fragility of human systems of governance. As the empire that controlled much of the known world during the early Christian period, Rome serves as a historical and prophetic reference point for the return of Christ and the ultimate judgment of the nations.

2. The Theological Implications of the Stone in Nebuchadnezzar's Dream

The stone "cut without human hands" in Nebuchadnezzar's dream is one of the most profound symbols in biblical prophecy, representing the Kingdom of God that will ultimately destroy all human kingdoms and grow into a mountain that fills the entire earth. The theological implications of the stone are deeply connected to messianic prophecy, the final judgment, and the eternal reign of Christ.

A. The Stone as the Messiah

In Christian theology, the stone is frequently associated with Jesus Christ, the Messiah. Several passages in both the Old and New Testaments support the idea that the stone represents Christ, who is both the cornerstone of the new covenant and the agent of judgment against the powers of the world.

- Isaiah 28:16: "See, I lay a stone in Zion, a tested stone, a precious cornerstone for a sure foundation; the one who trusts in it will never be stricken with panic." This prophecy is often interpreted as referring to the coming of Christ, who is the cornerstone of God's kingdom.

- Psalm 118:22: "The stone the builders rejected has become the cornerstone." Jesus refers to this verse in Matthew 21:42, identifying Himself as the rejected stone that becomes the foundation of God's kingdom. This rejection by the religious and political leaders of His time mirrors the broader rejection of divine authority by human kingdoms.

- 1 Peter 2:6-8: Peter applies the imagery of the stone to Jesus, describing Him as the cornerstone chosen by God but rejected by men. This passage emphasizes both the salvific and judgmental roles of Christ. For believers, Jesus is the cornerstone of salvation, but for those who reject Him, He becomes a stone of stumbling and rock of offense.

B. The Stone as the Instrument of Divine Judgment

The stone's action in Nebuchadnezzar's dream—striking the feet of the statue and causing the entire structure to collapse—carries profound eschatological significance. It symbolizes the final judgment of all human kingdoms and the establishment of God's eternal reign.

- Divine Sovereignty Over Human History: The stone's destruction of the statue reflects the sovereignty of God over all human history. No matter how powerful or long-lasting a kingdom may appear, it is ultimately subject to God's judgment. The feet of iron and clay, representing the fragility of human attempts to maintain power through force or alliances, are destroyed by the stone, showing that only God's kingdom is eternal.

- Judgment and the End of Worldly Powers: The Book of Revelation and other eschatological texts describe the final judgment as the moment when all earthly powers are overthrown and Christ establishes His reign. The stone in Daniel's vision serves as a precursor to this event, foreshadowing the Second Coming of Christ, when He will return as both a judge and king to destroy the systems of human oppression and rebellion.

- Revelation 19:11-16 depicts Christ returning as a warrior-king, bringing judgment upon the nations. This mirrors the image of the stone shattering the statue, representing the complete overthrow of human kingdoms in favor of God's eternal rule.

C. The Growth of the Stone into a Mountain: The Universal and Eternal Kingdom

After destroying the statue, the stone in Nebuchadnezzar's dream grows into a great mountain that fills the whole earth. This imagery points to the universal and eternal nature of God's kingdom, which will ultimately encompass all nations and peoples.

- The Mountain as God's Kingdom: In biblical symbolism, a mountain often represents the presence and authority of God. Isa iah 2:2-4 describes a vision in which the mountain of the Lord's temple is exalted above all other mountains, and all nations stream to it. This reflects the universal reign of God, where His law and justice extend over all creation.

- The Eternal Kingdom of Christ: The growth of the stone into a mountain represents the final fulfillment of Christ's reign. In Christian eschatology, Christ's kingdom will not only replace all human kingdoms but will endure forever, as described in Revelation 21-22, where the new heaven and new earth are established, and God dwells with His people for eternity.

D. The Already and Not Yet of God's Kingdom

In Christian theology, the concept of the "already and not yet" describes the tension between the present reality of God's kingdom, inaugurated by Christ's first coming, and its future fulfillment at His return. The stone's destruction of the statue represents both the inauguration and consummation of the kingdom.

- The Already: Jesus' life, death, and resurrection are seen as the inauguration of God's kingdom. Christ's victory over sin and death begins the process of the overthrow of worldly powers, though the final judgment has not yet occurred.

- The Not Yet: The full realization of God's kingdom will only occur at the Second Coming when Christ returns to judge the world and establish His eternal reign. The stone in

Nebuchadnezzar's dream symbolizes this future moment when all human kingdoms will be destroyed, and God's kingdom will be fully established, growing into a mountain that fills the earth.

The Role of Rome and the Stone in Christian Eschatology

The Roman Empire plays a central role in Christian eschatology as the final human empire before the establishment of God's kingdom. Rome's rule during the time of Christ, its role in the crucifixion, and its symbolic representation in the Book of Revelation as a persecutor of the Church, all contribute to its eschatological significance. Rome represents both the culmination of human power and the opposition to God's kingdom, but it is ultimately destined for destruction, as symbolized by the legs of iron in Nebuchadnezzar's dream.

The stone, representing the Kingdom of God and the Messiah, plays a pivotal role in the final judgment and the establishment of the eternal kingdom. Theologically, the stone points to Jesus Christ, the cornerstone of God's new covenant, who will return to overthrow all human kingdoms and establish a reign of justice, peace, and righteousness. The growth of the stone into a mountain that fills the earth symbolizes the universal and eternal nature of Christ's kingdom, which will ultimately encompass all creation.

The dream of the statue and the stone provides a prophetic framework for understanding the movement of history from human empires to the eschatological fulfillment of God's plan, culminating in the Second Coming of Christ and the final judgment of the nations.

The Final Judgment and the Stone's Role in Christian Eschatology

Continuing from our earlier exploration, the concept of final judgment is a pivotal element of Christian eschatology. This theme is intricately tied to the image of the stone in Nebuchadnezzar's dream, which symbolizes the ultimate destruction of human kingdoms and the establishment of God's eternal reign. The final judgment is portrayed as the climactic event in biblical prophecy where human history reaches its conclusion, and the Kingdom of God is fully realized. Below, we will delve further into the final judgment in Christian eschatology, the role of Christ as judge, and the messianic prophecies connected to the stone.

1. The Final Judgment: Destruction of Earthly Kingdoms and the Establishment of God's Kingdom

In Nebuchadnezzar's dream, the stone strikes the feet of the statue, representing the destruction of all human kingdoms. This act of destruction corresponds to the biblical theme of the final judgment, where God decisively intervenes in history to judge the nations, destroy all forms of human rebellion, and establish His eternal kingdom. The stone's impact is a vivid representation of the moment when worldly powers are brought to an end, and God's sovereign rule is inaugurated in its fullness.

A. The Judgment of Nations in the Old Testament

In the Old Testament, the final judgment is often depicted as the Day of the Lord, a time when God will judge the nations and establish His righteous rule.

- Isaiah 24:21-23: "In that day the Lord will punish the powers in the heavens above and the kings on the earth below. They will be herded together like prisoners bound in a dungeon; they will be shut up in prison and be punished after many days. The moon will be dismayed, the sun ashamed; for the Lord Almighty will reign on Mount Zion and in Jerusalem, and before its elders—with great glory."

In this passage, the judgment of nations is described as a time when earthly powers, symbolized by kings and rulers, are brought low and punished by God. This parallels the stone's destruction of the statue in Daniel's vision, where the culmination of human empires leads to their ultimate judgment and overthrow.

- Joel 3:12-14: "Let the nations be roused; let them advance into the Valley of Jehoshaphat, for there I will sit to judge all the nations on every side. Swing the sickle, for the harvest is ripe. Come, trample the grapes, for the winepress is full and the vats overflow—so great is their wickedness! Multitudes, multitudes in the valley of decision! For the day of the Lord is near in the valley of decision."

The Valley of Jehoshaphat is often interpreted as the symbolic site of the final judgment. In Joel's prophecy, God calls the nations to account for their wickedness and rebellion. This imagery echoes Daniel's vision of the stone bringing judgment upon the statue, symbolizing the defeat of all human opposition to God's rule.

B. The Final Judgment in the New Testament

The New Testament develops the theme of final judgment further, with a focus on the return of Jesus Christ as the one who will judge the living and the dead. This judgment is often portrayed as the moment when worldly systems of power are overturned, and God's kingdom is fully established.

- Matthew 25:31-46: In the parable of the sheep and the goats, Jesus describes the final judgment as a time when the Son of Man will separate the righteous from the unrighteous. The righteous, symbolized by the sheep, are welcomed into the kingdom, while the unrighteous, symbolized by the goats, are cast into eternal punishment.

- Revelation 20:11-15: The Great White Throne Judgment describes the final judgment where the dead are judged according to their deeds. The Book of Life is opened, and those not found in it are cast into the lake of fire. This imagery aligns with the destruction of human kingdoms in Daniel's vision, where the empires of the world are judged and destroyed by the stone.

The stone in Nebuchadnezzar's dream symbolizes this moment of final judgment, where Christ returns as the judge to destroy all human powers and inaugurate His eternal reign.

2. Christ as the Divine Judge: The Role of the Stone in Messianic Prophecy

In Christian eschatology, Jesus Christ is not only the Savior but also the judge who will return to execute God's justice upon the world. The image of the stone in Daniel's vision is deeply connected to messianic prophecies that foretell the coming of the Messiah as both a foundation for salvation and an instrument of divine judgment. The stone's dual role as both cornerstone and stone of stumbling highlights the dual aspects of Christ's messianic mission: to establish God's kingdom and to judge the nations.

A. The Stone as the Cornerstone

In biblical prophecy, the Messiah is frequently referred to as a stone or rock, emphasizing His role as the foundation of God's redemptive work and the cornerstone of the new covenant. This image is used throughout both the Old and New Testaments to highlight the Messiah's significance in establishing God's kingdom.

- Psalm 118:22: "The stone the builders rejected has become the cornerstone." This passage is applied to Jesus multiple times in the New Testament (e.g., Matthew 21:42, Acts 4:11), emphasizing that although He was rejected by the leaders of His time, He has become the foundation of God's kingdom.

- Isaiah 28:16: "So this is what the Sovereign Lord says: 'See, I lay a stone in Zion, a tested stone, a precious cornerstone for a sure foundation; the one who relies on it will never be stricken with panic.'" Jesus is seen as this cornerstone, the secure foundation upon which God's eternal kingdom is built.

In this sense, the stone in Nebuchadnezzar's dream represents the Messiah's arrival to inaugurate God's kingdom. The stone's growth into a mountain that fills the earth symbolizes the expansion of Christ's kingdom, which will encompass all nations and peoples.

B. The Stone as the Stone of Stumbling

In addition to being the cornerstone, Jesus is also referred to as a stone of stumbling and rock of offense for those who reject Him. This aspect of the stone's symbolism emphasizes the role of the Messiah in bringing judgment upon the world.

- Isaiah 8:14-15: "He will be a holy place; for both Israel and Judah he will be a stone that causes people to stumble and a rock that makes them fall. And for the people of Jerusalem he will be a trap and a snare. Many of them will stumble; they will fall and be broken, they will be snared and captured."

- 1 Peter 2:7-8: Peter applies this passage to Jesus, describing Him as the stone that causes people to stumble: "They stumble because they disobey the message—which is also what they were destined for."

In this context, the stone in Daniel's vision represents both salvation for those who accept God's rule and judgment for those who reject it. The stone's destruction of the statue signifies the defeat of all opposition to God's kingdom, fulfilling the messianic prophecies of the Day of the Lord, where the nations will be judged and Christ's reign will be fully established.

C. Christ's Return and the Final Judgment

In Christian eschatology, the Second Coming of Christ is the moment when the stone strikes the statue, so to speak—when Christ returns to judge the nations, destroy the powers of this world, and establish His eternal reign.

- 2 Thessalonians 2:8: Paul speaks of Christ's return as the moment when He will overthrow the lawless one with the breath of His mouth and destroy him by the splendor of His coming. This mirrors the action of the stone in Daniel's vision, which shatters the statue and brings an end to human rule.

- Revelation 19:11-16: In this passage, Christ returns as a victorious warrior, riding a white horse and bringing judgment upon the nations. He defeats the beast and the kings of the earth, establishing His rule over all creation.

The final judgment is the culmination of this process, where Christ, as the divine judge, separates the righteous from the wicked, rewards His faithful servants, and casts down the powers of the world that have opposed His kingdom. The stone's destruction of the statue is a vivid symbol of this eschatological moment, where human history gives way to the eternal kingdom of God.

3. The Stone as a Symbol of Hope and Renewal

While the stone in Daniel's dream represents judgment for those who oppose God's kingdom, it also carries profound meaning for believers, symbolizing hope, renewal, and the ultimate victory of righteousness. The stone's growth into a mountain that fills the earth signifies the establishment of a new creation, where God's justice and peace reign eternally.

A. The Mountain of the Lord's House

The imagery of a mountain that fills the earth is closely connected to Old Testament prophecies about the mountain of the

Lord, which represents God's presence and authority over all creation.

- Isaiah 2:2-4: "In the last days, the mountain of the Lord's temple will be established as the highest of the mountains; it will be exalted above the hills, and all nations will stream to it. Many peoples will come and say, 'Come, let us go up to the mountain of the Lord, to the temple of the God of Jacob. He will teach us His ways, so that we may walk in His paths.'"

This vision of the mountain of the Lord represents the universal reign of God, where His law and peace are extended to all nations. It is a vision of hope for the renewal of creation and the restoration of justice.

B. The New Heaven and New Earth

In the Book of Revelation, the final vision of the new heaven and new earth represents the culmination of God's plan for creation. The stone's growth into a mountain in Daniel's dream foreshadows this eschatological hope, where

God's kingdom is fully established, and all things are made new.

- Revelation 21:1-3: "Then I saw 'a new heaven and a new earth,' for the first heaven and the first earth had passed away, and there was no longer any sea. I saw the Holy City, the new Jerusalem, coming down out of heaven from God, prepared as a bride beautifully dressed for her husband. And I heard a loud voice from the throne saying, 'Look! God's dwelling place is now among the people, and He will dwell with them. They will be His people, and God Himself will be with them and be their God.'"

The new creation is the final result of the stone's action in Daniel's vision. Once human empires have been destroyed, and God's kingdom has been established, the new Jerusalem comes down from heaven, symbolizing the eternal dwelling of God with His people. The mountain that fills the earth represents the universal reign of Christ, where there is no more death, mourning, or pain, and God's justice prevails forever.

The Stone, the Roman Empire, and the Final Fulfillment of Prophecy

The Roman Empire, symbolized by the legs of iron in Nebuchadnezzar's dream, plays a crucial role in Christian eschatology as the last great human kingdom before the

Second Coming of Christ and the final judgment. The stone in the dream represents Jesus Christ, the Messiah, who will return to judge the nations and establish God's eternal kingdom. The destruction of the statue by the stone symbolizes the end of all human rule and the ultimate victory of God's kingdom, which will grow into a mountain and fill the whole earth.

The theological implications of the stone go beyond mere judgment, offering believers a message of hope and renewal. The stone not only destroys but also builds—growing into a mountain that represents the new creation and the eternal reign of God. This vision points toward the final fulfillment of messianic prophecy, where Christ returns as both judge and king, bringing an end to sin and establishing a kingdom of justice, peace, and righteousness that will last forever.

CHAPTER 03

THE GOLD HEAD - BABYLON

In Nebuchadnezzar's dream, the head of gold represents the Babylonian Empire under the reign of Nebuchadnezzar II (605–562 BCE). Babylon, known for its immense wealth, grandeur, and cultural achievements, occupies a significant place in both biblical prophecy and world history. The choice of gold to symbolize Babylon highlights its unique role as the greatest and most magnificent of the ancient empires, but it also foreshadows its eventual fall as part of the broader narrative of human kingdoms giving way to God's eternal kingdom.

This chapter will explore the symbolism of Babylon as the head of gold, examining its historical and theological significance, its role in biblical prophecy, and how it serves as a representation of the epitome of human power and pride destined to fall under divine judgment.

1. The Symbolism of Gold and Babylon's Grandeur

The use of gold to symbolize the Babylonian Empire is no accident. Gold, the most precious of all metals, has long been associated with wealth, beauty, splendor, and power. In biblical literature, gold is often used to describe the majesty of kings, the wealth of temples, and the opulence of empires. Babylon's association with gold signifies the empire's economic prosperity, political dominance, and architectural brilliance.

A. Babylon's Wealth and Opulence

Babylon during Nebuchadnezzar's reign was the center of the ancient world, renowned for its vast wealth and monumental architecture. The city of Babylon itself was a marvel, home to some of the greatest wonders of the ancient world:

- The Hanging Gardens of Babylon, one of the Seven Wonders of the Ancient World, are traditionally attributed to Nebuchadnezzar's reign. Though their actual existence remains debated, the gardens symbolize Babylon's luxury and cultural sophistication.

- The Ishtar Gate, an elaborate entrance adorned with blue-glazed bricks and depictions of lions, bulls, and dragons, was a testament to Babylon's architectural grandeur. The gate, dedicated to the goddess Ishtar, symbolized the power and prestige of the empire.

- Babylon's extensive city walls and palaces, built with advanced engineering techniques, reflected the empire's wealth and desire to project its might and invulnerability.

Gold, therefore, represents not only the wealth of the empire but also the extravagant lifestyle and the heights of human achievement in art, architecture, and governance. Babylon was seen as a kingdom that had reached the pinnacle of what human effort could achieve—yet, despite this splendor, it was ultimately transient, subject to the judgment of God.

B. Political and Military Power

Under Nebuchadnezzar, Babylon reached the height of its political and military power. The empire expanded through military conquests, subjugating surrounding regions and peoples, including Judah. Babylon's dominance over the ancient Near East during this period is unparalleled, and its reputation as a center of political and military strength is well-documented.

- Conquest of Jerusalem (586 BCE): Nebuchadnezzar is perhaps most famously remembered for his conquest of Jerusalem, the destruction of the First Temple, and the

Babylonian Exile of the Jewish people. This event had a profound theological impact on the Jewish understanding of history and divine judgment. In the biblical narrative, Babylon is portrayed not just as a political power but as an instrument of God's judgment against the unfaithfulness of His people (Jeremiah 25:9).

- Babylon's military strength and dominance are symbolized by gold, which, though beautiful, can also be associated with the power to oppress and subjugate others.

2. Babylon as the Epitome of Human Pride and Rebellion

While Babylon's splendor and power are reflected in the symbolism of gold, the empire is also characterized in biblical prophecy as the epitome of human pride, arrogance, and rebellion against God. Babylon becomes a symbol of a kingdom that, despite its wealth and power, defies divine authority and is therefore doomed to fall under God's judgment.

A. Babylon in Biblical Prophecy

Throughout the Bible, Babylon is often used as a symbol of human pride and the hubris of kingdoms that attempt to exalt themselves above God. This association begins as early as the story of the Tower of Babel in Genesis 11, where humanity's attempt to build a tower that reaches the heavens is thwarted by God, resulting in the scattering of people and the confusion of languages.

- Isaiah 14:12-15 speaks of the fall of Lucifer, using Babylon as a metaphor for pride and rebellion. The king of Babylon is portrayed as one who seeks to exalt himself above God, only to be brought low: "You said in your heart, 'I will ascend to the heavens; I will raise my throne above the stars of God…' But you are brought down to the realm of the dead, to the depths of the pit."

- Jeremiah 50-51 contains oracles against Babylon, predicting its eventual destruction as a result of its arrogance and oppression of God's people. Though Babylon is portrayed as a great empire, it is also shown to be fleeting, destined for divine judgment.

B. Nebuchadnezzar's Pride and Humbling

Nebuchadnezzar himself becomes a symbolic figure of human pride and eventual humbling before God. In Daniel 4, Nebuchadnezzar has another dream, this time foretelling his temporary fall from power. Daniel interprets the dream as a warning that Nebuchadnezzar's pride will lead to his downfall unless he acknowledges the sovereignty of God.

- Daniel 4:30-32 records Nebuchadnezzar's boast: "Is not this the great Babylon I have built as the royal residence, by my mighty power and for the glory of my majesty?"

Immediately after this declaration of pride, Nebuchadnezzar is struck down, losing his sanity and living like an animal for seven years, until he recognizes that God is the true ruler over all kingdoms of men.

- This story illustrates the biblical theme that human kingdoms, no matter how great, are ultimately subject to God's judgment and control. Nebuchadnezzar's eventual repentance symbolizes the need for humility before God's sovereignty.

Babylon's gold head in the statue represents not only its greatness but also its temporal nature. The dream foretells that despite Babylon's splendor, it would be replaced by another empire. In Christian eschatology, Babylon becomes a symbol of worldly powers that oppose God and are ultimately destroyed.

3. Babylon as a Symbol in Apocalyptic Literature

In apocalyptic literature, particularly in the Book of Revelation, Babylon becomes a symbol for the final rebellious world system that opposes God in the last days. This symbolic use of Babylon connects to its historical role as the epitome of human pride and rebellion, but it is expanded to represent the forces of evil in the cosmic struggle between God and the kingdoms of the world.

A. Babylon the Great in Revelation

In Revelation 17-18, Babylon is depicted as Babylon the Great, the Mother of Prostitutes and the abominations of the earth. This Babylon symbolizes the corrupt and oppressive systems of the world that lead people away from God and exploit the vulnerable.

- Revelation 17:3-6 describes a woman (Babylon) sitting on a scarlet beast, adorned with gold and precious stones, yet filled with abominations. She represents both worldly wealth and power but also moral corruption and idolatry. Her eventual destruction by the beast represents the inevitable fall of the systems that oppose God.

- Revelation 18 describes the fall of Babylon as a catastrophic event, where the merchants and kings of the earth mourn the loss of their wealth and luxury, symbolizing the sudden and total collapse of worldly systems based on materialism and oppression.

This portrayal of Babylon in apocalyptic literature draws directly from the historical and prophetic symbolism associated with the Babylonian Empire. Just as historical Babylon fell despite its grandeur, so too will the worldly powers represented by Babylon the Great fall when Christ returns to establish His eternal kingdom.

B. Babylon's Fall as a Precursor to God's Kingdom

In both the Old Testament and New Testament, the fall of Babylon serves as a precursor to the establishment of God's kingdom. Babylon's collapse symbolizes the overthrow of human pride and rebellion, making way for the reign of God.

- In Isaiah 13:19, Babylon is described as being overthrown by God in the same way as Sodom and Gomorrah, symbolizing the total destruction of a corrupt and rebellious society.

- In Revelation 19, following the fall of Babylon the Great, the scene shifts to the coming of Christ and the marriage supper of the Lamb, where the final victory over evil is celebrated and Christ's reign is fully established.

In this eschatological framework, Babylon, as the head of gold, represents the ultimate human empire that is rich in wealth and power but hollow in righteousness. Its fall is the first step toward the final triumph of God's kingdom.

4. The Fall of Babylon and Its Prophetic Significance

While the gold head represents Babylon's immense power and influence, the prophecy foretells that Babylon will not last forever.

Despite being the most glorious of the empires symbolized by the metals, Babylon is destined to fall and be succeeded by the Medo-Persian Empire, represented by the chest and arms of silver.

A. The Historical Fall of Babylon

Historically, Babylon fell in 539 BCE when it was conquered by Cyrus the Great of the Persian Empire. The fall of Babylon was relatively peaceful, with Cyrus entering the city without significant resistance. This event is significant in biblical prophecy, as it not only marked the end of the Babylonian Empire but also led to the return of the Jewish exiles to Jerusalem and the rebuilding of the Temple, as prophesied in Isaiah 44:28 and Jeremiah 29:10.

- Daniel 5 describes the dramatic end of the Babylonian Empire under Belshazzar, Nebuchadnezzar's successor. During a great feast, a mysterious hand writes a message on the wall: "Mene, Mene, Tekel, Parsin." Daniel interprets the message, declaring that Babylon's days are numbered, its king has been weighed and found wanting, and its kingdom will be divided and given to the Medes and Persians. That very night, Babylon falls to the Persians.

B. Prophetic Significance of Babylon's Fall

The fall of Babylon is a fulfillment of prophecy and serves as a model for understanding the transience of human power. No matter how powerful or glorious a kingdom may appear, it is ultimately subject to God's sovereignty.

- The prophecy of Babylon's fall is a reminder that human kingdoms are temporary and will eventually give way to the eternal kingdom of God, symbolized by the stone in Nebuchadnezzar's dream that grows into a mountain and fills the whole earth.

- In Christian eschatology, Babylon's fall prefigures the final judgment when all worldly powers will be overthrown, and God's kingdom will be established. The head of gold is merely the first in a succession of kingdoms, all of which will be destroyed in favor of the divine kingdom that will last forever.

Babylon as the Head of Gold

The head of gold in Nebuchadnezzar's dream symbolizes the Babylonian Empire, a kingdom of immense wealth, power, and grandeur under Nebuchadnezzar II. Babylon, in all its glory, represents the pinnacle of human achievement, but it is also a symbol of pride, arrogance, and rebellion against God. The gold head highlights both the splendor and the ephemeral nature of human empires, which, despite their strength, are ultimately subject to divine judgment.

Babylon's role as the head of gold is significant not only historically but also prophetically. Its eventual fall to the Medo-Persians fulfills biblical prophecy and serves as a reminder that no human kingdom is eternal. In the broader eschatological framework, Babylon becomes a symbol for the worldly powers that oppose God's rule, destined to be destroyed at the Second Coming of Christ.

Ultimately, Babylon's place as the head of gold in Nebuchadnezzar's dream is a cautionary tale about the limitations of human power and the inevitable triumph of God's eternal kingdom.

Babylon's Significance in the Book of Revelation

In the Book of Revelation, Babylon is not merely a reference to the historical Babylonian Empire but a potent symbol for the worldly systems of power, corruption, and rebellion against God that are prevalent in human history. Throughout Revelation, Babylon represents idolatry, materialism, and the oppressive structures that stand in opposition to the Kingdom of God. The imagery of Babylon is used to depict the final climactic conflict between these forces and the ultimate victory of God's kingdom over all forms of evil.

This chapter will explore the significance of Babylon in Revelation, focusing on the following aspects: Babylon as a symbol of corruption and idolatry, the fall of Babylon as a prophetic judgment, and how these elements connect to the overarching theme of eschatological fulfillment in Revelation. It will also examine how the portrayal of Babylon in Revelation draws on Old Testament imagery, particularly from Daniel and Isaiah, and serves as a key to understanding the end times and the final judgment.

1. Babylon as a Symbol of Worldly Power, Idolatry, and Oppression

In Revelation, Babylon the Great is depicted as the ultimate expression of worldly power in opposition to God. The symbol of Babylon is not limited to a specific geographical location or historical empire; instead, it represents the broader system of corruption that influences the nations and peoples of the earth. This system is characterized by its economic exploitation, moral depravity, and spiritual rebellion against God.

A. Babylon as the "Mother of Prostitutes"

In Revelation 17:1-6, Babylon is described as a woman sitting on a scarlet beast, adorned with gold, precious stones, and pearls. She holds a golden cup filled with "abominations and the filth of her adulteries." This woman is called Babylon the Great, the Mother of Prostitutes and the abominations of the earth.

- Revelation 17:4-5: "The woman was dressed in purple and scarlet, and was glittering with gold, precious stones, and pearls. She held a golden cup in her hand, filled with abominable things and the filth of her adulteries. The name written on her forehead was a mystery: Babylon the

Great, the mother of prostitutes and of the abominations of the earth."

The description of Babylon as a prostitute reflects her moral and spiritual unfaithfulness. She symbolizes a world system that seduces people into idolatry, greed, and immorality. The imagery of prostitution is used throughout the Bible to describe spiritual infidelity, where human beings turn away from God to pursue false gods, wealth, and power.

- Wealth and Idolatry: Babylon's adornment with gold, precious stones, and pearls emphasizes her material wealth and luxurious lifestyle. However, this wealth is obtained through unrighteous means, representing the exploitation and oppression of the weak. Babylon becomes a symbol of materialism and economic oppression, as her wealth is built on the suffering of others.

- Spiritual Infidelity: The cup of abominations that Babylon holds symbolizes her role in spreading idolatry and moral corruption throughout the earth. In Revelation, Babylon's seduction leads nations to forsake God and engage in false worship. This reflects the broader theme in Revelation of spiritual warfare, where the forces of evil seek to draw humanity away from true worship of God.

B. Babylon as the Persecutor of God's People

Babylon in Revelation is also depicted as a persecutor of God's people, symbolizing the political and spiritual forces that oppose the followers of Christ.

- Revelation 17:6: "I saw that the woman was drunk with the blood of God's holy people, the blood of those who bore testimony to Jesus."

Babylon's oppression of God's people, described as being "drunk with the blood of the saints," highlights her role as the enemy of the Church. Throughout Revelation, Babylon symbolizes the worldly systems that persecute and oppress Christians, seeking to suppress the Gospel and extinguish the light of Christ.

The portrayal of Babylon as the enemy of the Church parallels the historical persecution of Christians by the Roman Empire, which many early Christians saw as the embodiment of Babylon. The Roman Empire's demand for emperor worship and its persecution of those who refused to comply (including early Christians) reflect the broader theme in Revelation of worldly power opposing God's kingdom.

2. The Fall of Babylon: A Prophetic Judgment

The fall of Babylon in Revelation is one of the central events in the book's prophetic narrative. Babylon's destruction is portrayed as the culmination of God's judgment against the forces of evil and corruption in the world. This event is a turning point in the eschatological timeline, marking the defeat of the world system that has opposed God and His people, and paving the way for the establishment of God's eternal kingdom.

A. Babylon's Sudden and Complete Destruction

In Revelation 18, the fall of Babylon is described in vivid, dramatic language. Her destruction is sudden and total, symbolizing the inevitable collapse of all worldly powers that oppose God.

- Revelation 18:2: "Fallen! Fallen is Babylon the Great! She has become a dwelling for demons and a haunt for every impure spirit, a haunt for every unclean bird, a haunt for every unclean and detestable animal."

The repeated proclamation of "Fallen! Fallen!" emphasizes the finality of Babylon's destruction. The once-great city, adorned with wealth and power, has now become a desolate ruin, inhabited by demons and unclean spirits. This imagery reflects the idea that the worldly systems represented by Babylon are destined to be utterly overthrown and left in ruin, stripped of their former power and glory.

B. Mourning Over Babylon's Fall

In Revelation 18:9-19, the kings, merchants, and sailors of the earth mourn Babylon's fall, lamenting the loss of their wealth and luxury. These figures represent the worldly elites who have benefited from Babylon's corrupt system, growing rich through exploitation and trade.

- Revelation 18:10-11: "Terrified at her torment, they will stand far off and cry: 'Woe! Woe to you, great city, you mighty city of Babylon! In one hour your doom has come!' The merchants of the earth will weep and mourn over her because no one buys their cargoes anymore."

The mourning of the kings and merchants reflects their dependence on Babylon's economic system. Babylon's fall not only marks the end of an empire but also the collapse of the economic and social structures built on greed, oppression, and materialism. The suddenness of her fall—"in one hour"—emphasizes the fragility of worldly power and wealth, no matter how secure it may seem.

C. Divine Judgment and Vindication

Babylon's fall is portrayed as an act of divine judgment, a vindication of God's justice and a response to the persecution of His people.

- Revelation 18:20: "Rejoice over her, you heavens! Rejoice, you people of God! Rejoice, apostles and prophets! For God has judged her with the judgment she imposed on you."

The destruction of Babylon is not just a punishment for her sins but a vindication for those she has oppressed and persecuted. The heavens, along with God's people, are called to rejoice over Babylon's fall, for her destruction is the fulfillment of God's righteous judgment.

This moment of divine judgment parallels the Old Testament prophecies of Babylon's fall, particularly in Isaiah 13 and Jeremiah 50-51, where Babylon is portrayed as a corrupt and oppressive power destined for destruction. In these prophecies, the fall of Babylon represents the downfall of human pride and the vindication of God's people, themes that are fully realized in Revelation.

3. The Eschatological Significance of Babylon's Fall

The fall of Babylon in Revelation is more than just the destruction of a corrupt city or empire; it symbolizes the defeat of evil and the end of the world system that has opposed God since the beginning. The fall of Babylon is a key event in the eschatological timeline, marking the transition from the current age of human rebellion to the age of divine rule. This event is followed by the establishment of God's eternal kingdom, where Christ reigns supreme over all creation.

A. The Defeat of Evil Powers

Babylon's fall is part of the broader defeat of the forces of evil described in Revelation. After Babylon is destroyed, Revelation 19 depicts the return of Christ as the victorious King, defeating the beast, the false prophet, and the kings of the earth who have aligned themselves with Babylon's corrupt system.

- Revelation 19:11-16: "I saw heaven standing open and there before me was a white horse, whose rider is called Faithful and True. With justice He judges and wages war... On His robe and on His thigh He has this name written: King of kings and Lord of lords."

Christ's return symbolizes the final overthrow of all earthly powers and the complete victory of God's kingdom. Babylon's fall is a key part of this victory, as it marks the destruction of the economic, political, and spiritual forces that have stood in opposition to God's rule.

B. The Establishment of God's Kingdom

With the fall of Babylon, the way is cleared for the establishment of God's eternal kingdom, symbolized by the new heaven and new earth in Revelation 21-22.

- Revelation 21:1-2: "Then I saw a new heaven and a new earth, for the first heaven and the first earth had passed away, and there was no longer any sea. I saw the Holy City, the new Jerusalem, coming down out of heaven from God, prepared as a bride beautifully dressed for her husband."

The fall of Babylon represents the end of the current world system, characterized by corruption, oppression, and rebellion. In its place, God establishes a new creation, where

His will is perfectly fulfilled, and His people dwell with Him in eternal peace and righteousness.

This new creation, symbolized by the New Jerusalem, stands in stark contrast to Babylon the Great. Where Babylon was a city of corruption and immorality, the New Jerusalem is a city of holiness, justice, and the presence of God. The establishment of the New Jerusalem marks the fulfillment of God's promises to His people and the consummation of His plan for creation.

4. Babylon in Revelation and the Broader Biblical Narrative

The portrayal of Babylon in Revelation draws heavily from the broader biblical narrative, particularly the Old Testament prophecies concerning Babylon's rise and fall. Babylon's significance in Revelation is not limited to its role as a symbol of corruption and evil; it also serves as a theological link between the past judgments of God against oppressive empires and the future final judgment of all human systems that oppose His rule.

A. Old Testament Roots of Babylon's Symbolism

In the Old Testament, Babylon is often portrayed as the archetype of human rebellion and pride, especially in its defiance of God's sovereignty. This portrayal begins in Genesis 11 with the story of the Tower of Babel, where humanity attempts to build a tower to reach the heavens, symbolizing their desire to usurp divine authority. God's judgment on Babel, resulting in the confusion of languages and the scattering of people, serves as an early example of how God opposes human arrogance.

- Isaiah 13-14 and Jeremiah 50-51 contain prophecies against the historical city of Babylon, predicting its destruction due to its pride and oppression of God's people. These prophecies serve as a backdrop for the portrayal of Babylon the Great in Revelation, where the themes of pride, idolatry, and oppression are expanded to represent the broader system of worldly powers that oppose God.

B. Theological Implications of Babylon's Fall

The fall of Babylon in Revelation has deep theological implications for understanding God's justice and sovereignty. Babylon's destruction demonstrates that no power, no matter how wealthy or powerful, can ultimately stand against God. The judgment of Babylon is a vindication of God's justice and a reminder that worldly systems built on greed, corruption, and rebellion are destined to fall.

- God's Sovereignty: The fall of Babylon underscores the biblical theme of God's sovereignty over history. Just as God judged Babylon in the past, He will judge the final world system that opposes His kingdom. Revelation presents God as the ultimate ruler who controls the destiny of nations and will bring all things to their rightful conclusion.

- The Hope of Restoration: The destruction of Babylon also points to the hope of restoration for God's people. Just as the fall of historical Babylon led to the return of the Jewish exiles and the rebuilding of Jerusalem, the fall of Babylon the Great in Revelation leads to the establishment of the New Jerusalem, where God will dwell with His people forever.

Babylon's Eschatological Significance in Revelation

In the Book of Revelation, Babylon represents the culmination of worldly power, idolatry, and moral corruption. It is a symbol of the systems that oppose God and lead humanity into rebellion and exploitation. Babylon's fall in Revelation signifies the overthrow of these systems, marking the end of the current age and the beginning of God's eternal reign.

The portrayal of Babylon in Revelation draws on the broader biblical narrative, where Babylon serves as a symbol of human pride and rebellion. The fall of Babylon is an expression of divine judgment, demonstrating that no kingdom, no matter how powerful, can stand against God. This judgment is also a vindication for God's people, who have suffered under Babylon's oppression.

Ultimately, Babylon's fall clears the way for the establishment of God's kingdom, symbolized by the New Jerusalem. The destruction of Babylon the Great marks the defeat of evil and the restoration of creation, where God's people will dwell with Him in peace and righteousness for eternity.

Babylon's Role as a World Empire and the Beginning of the Prophecy

In Nebuchadnezzar's dream as recorded in Daniel 2:31-45, Babylon is represented as the head of gold, symbolizing its dominance as a world empire. The Babylonian Empire under Nebuchadnezzar II not only achieved great power and wealth but also became a pivotal figure in the unfolding of biblical prophecy. As the first of the empires symbolized in the dream, Babylon marks the beginning of the sequence of world kingdoms that would rise and fall, leading ultimately to the establishment of God's eternal kingdom.

This chapter will explore Babylon's role as a world empire, emphasizing its historical importance, its position as the head of gold in Daniel's prophecy, and its significance in the broader biblical narrative. We will also delve into how the rise of Babylon sets the stage for the unfolding of divine prophecy and what it signifies in the eschatological timeline.

1. Babylon's Rise as a World Empire

A. Nebuchadnezzar II and the Glory of Babylon

The Babylonian Empire under Nebuchadnezzar II (reigned 605-562 BCE) represented the height of Babylon's political, military, and cultural power. Babylon was located in Mesopotamia (modern-day Iraq) and had a long history of dominance in the ancient Near East, but it was under Nebuchadnezzar's rule that the empire reached its zenith. The city of Babylon itself was a marvel of the ancient world, known for its impressive architecture, including the Hanging Gardens, one of the Seven Wonders of the Ancient World.

- Nebuchadnezzar's Achievements: Nebuchadnezzar expanded Babylon's territory significantly, creating a vast empire that stretched from Egypt to Persia. He is most famous for his conquests, including the destruction of Jerusalem in 586 BCE and the subsequent Babylonian Exile of the Jewish people, an event that had profound theological and historical significance.

- Cultural and Economic Power: Babylon was not only a military force but also a center of learning, culture, and commerce. The city boasted magnificent temples, palaces, and city walls, reflecting the wealth and technological advancement of the empire.

As the head of gold, Babylon represents the splendor and power of human kingdoms, embodying both their heights and their inherent flaws. The golden head is a fitting symbol for Babylon's wealth and grandeur, but it also foreshadows the empire's eventual decline.

B. Babylon's Impact on the Ancient Near East

Babylon's dominance reshaped the ancient Near East, influencing politics, culture, and religion. Nebuchadnezzar's empire brought about significant changes in the region, not only through military conquest but also through his policies of deportation and resettlement.

- The Babylonian Exile: The conquest of Judah and the destruction of the First Temple in Jerusalem in 586 BCE had a lasting impact on Jewish history and theology. The Babylonian Exile, during which many Jews were taken to Babylon, forced the Jewish people to rethink their relationship with God in the absence of the Temple. The exile led to the development of new religious practices, including the rise of the synagogue as a place of worship and the compilation of sacred texts, which laid the foundation for Rabbinic Judaism.

- Cultural Exchange: Babylon's position as a crossroads between different civilizations facilitated cultural exchange. The empire absorbed influences from its neighbors, including the Persians, Egyptians, and Greeks, contributing to a blending of artistic, scientific, and religious ideas that would shape the development of the region for centuries.

The Babylonian Empire's legacy is not only found in its political and military achievements but also in its influence on the cultural and religious life of the ancient world.

2. Babylon in Biblical Prophecy: The Head of Gold

In Nebuchadnezzar's dream, the statue's head of gold symbolizes the Babylonian Empire. Gold, as the most precious and valuable of metals, reflects the grandeur, wealth, and influence of Babylon. However, the prophecy in Daniel 2 reveals that despite its greatness, Babylon's reign is temporary and will be followed by other empires, each represented by different metals of lesser value and strength.

A. The Significance of Gold in the Prophecy

The symbolism of gold in the Bible often conveys notions of glory, power, and purity. Gold was used to adorn the Temple in Jerusalem, emphasizing its sacredness and beauty. In the context of Daniel's prophecy, gold represents the pinnacle of human achievement, but it is also malleable and perishable, symbolizing the fragility of even the most powerful human kingdoms.

- Babylon's Temporal Glory: While Babylon is depicted as the most glorious of the empires in Nebuchadnezzar's dream, the prophecy foretells that its dominance will not last forever. Gold, while beautiful and valuable, is still a human material and thus subject to decay.

This indicates that Babylon's power, though immense, is impermanent in the face of divine sovereignty.

- Babylon as the Beginning of the Prophetic Sequence: The Babylonian Empire represents the beginning of a divinely ordained timeline in which successive empires will rise and fall. This timeline is not random but is guided by God's providence, leading ultimately to the establishment of His eternal kingdom. As the head of the statue, Babylon's fall sets in motion the unfolding of this prophetic sequence.

B. Babylon as the Model for Human Empires

In biblical prophecy, Babylon is often seen as the archetype of human empires—a kingdom that rises to great heights but is brought low due to its pride and opposition to God. Babylon's greatness, though real, is tempered by its ultimate rejection of divine authority. This theme of human pride and rebellion is central to the biblical narrative, and Babylon's fall serves as a warning to all subsequent empires.

- Pride and Rebellion Against God: In Daniel 4, Nebuchadnezzar's pride is depicted as a key reason for his temporary fall from power. After boasting of his achievements—"Is not this the great Babylon I have built as the royal residence, by my mighty power and for the glory of my majesty?" (Daniel 4:30)—Nebuchadnezzar is humbled by God, losing his sanity and living like a beast until he acknowledges God's sovereignty. This episode highlights the danger of human arrogance and the belief that earthly kingdoms are independent of divine rule.

- Babylon's Role in God's Plan: Despite its rebellion, Babylon is used by God as an instrument of judgment against Judah and other nations. The Bible often portrays human empires as tools in God's hand, even when they act in opposition to His will. In Jeremiah 25:9, Babylon is referred to as God's "servant," used to punish the unfaithfulness of Israel. This paradox—that a rebellious empire can still serve God's purposes—reveals the complexity of Babylon's role in biblical prophecy.

3. The Fall of Babylon and the Transition to the Next Empire

Though Babylon is symbolized by the most valuable metal, the prophecy makes clear that its reign will come to an end. The chest and arms of silver, representing the Medo-Persian Empire, will replace Babylon, signifying a transfer of power as part of God's divine plan. Babylon's fall is an essential part of the prophetic sequence, marking the transition from one era of human rule to the next.

A. The Historical Fall of Babylon

Babylon fell in 539 BCE to the Persian Empire under Cyrus the Great. The fall of Babylon was relatively peaceful; according to historical accounts, Cyrus entered the city without significant resistance, taking control of the empire and bringing an end to Babylon's dominance in the ancient Near East.

- Cyrus and the Jewish Return: Cyrus's conquest of Babylon had profound implications for the Jewish exiles in Babylon. In fulfillment of biblical prophecy, Cyrus issued a decree allowing the exiles to return to Jerusalem and rebuild the Temple (Ezra 1:1-4). This event was seen by the Jewish people as a sign of God's continuing faithfulness and a fulfillment of His promises.

- Daniel's Prophecy Fulfilled: The fall of Babylon and the rise of the Medo-Persian Empire represented the fulfillment of Daniel's prophecy, which foretold the succession of empires that would lead to the eventual establishment of God's kingdom. Babylon, despite its greatness, was not immune to the forces of history and divine will.

B. The Transition to the Medo-Persian Empire

The prophecy of the statue in Daniel 2 transitions from the head of gold (Babylon) to the chest and arms of silver (the Medo-Persian Empire). The decreasing value of the metals reflects the diminishing grandeur of the successive empires, though each one remains powerful in its own right.

- The Dual Nature of the Medo-Persian Empire: The two arms of silver likely symbolize the dual nature of the Medo-Persian Empire, which was composed of the Medes and the Persians. Though the empire was vast and powerful, it lacked the cultural and architectural splendor of Babylon, represented by the less valuable metal of silver.

- The Continuation of God's Plan: The transition from Babylon to the Medo-Persian Empire demonstrates that human history is guided by divine providence. Each empire serves its purpose within God's overarching plan, but none of them, not even Babylon, is permanent. The fall of each empire brings the world closer to the establishment of God's eternal kingdom, symbolized by the stone in Nebuchadnezzar's dream.

4. Babylon's Role in the Broader Eschatological Timeline

Babylon's role as the head of gold in Nebuchadnezzar's dream is not only significant for understanding the rise and fall of human empires but also for interpreting the broader eschatological timeline. Babylon marks the beginning of the prophetic sequence that will eventually culminate in the Kingdom of God, symbolized by the stone cut without human hands. The rise and fall of

Babylon and the subsequent empires represent the transience of human power and the inevitability of God's kingdom.

A. Babylon as the Archetype of Human Empires

In the Bible, Babylon serves as the archetype of human empires that achieve great power and wealth but ultimately fall due to their pride and opposition to God. Babylon's rise to power is part of the natural progression of history, but its fall is inevitable because no human empire can withstand the judgment of God.

- Isaiah 13:19: "Babylon, the jewel of kingdoms, the glory of the Babylonians' pride, will be overthrown by God like Sodom and Gomorrah." This prophecy reflects the theme of Babylon as a symbol of human pride that will be brought low by divine judgment.

B. Babylon's Legacy in Apocalyptic Literature

In Revelation, Babylon's legacy is extended as a symbol of the final world system that opposes God. Babylon the Great in Revelation represents the culmination of human rebellion against God, characterized by materialism, idolatry, and moral corruption. The fall of Babylon the Great, like the fall of the historical Babylon, marks the beginning of the end times and the transition to the eternal kingdom of God.

- Revelation 18:2: "Fallen! Fallen is Babylon the Great! She has become a dwelling for demons and a haunt for every impure spirit." This passage, echoing the fall of the historical

Babylon, symbolizes the final judgment against the corrupt systems of the world and the establishment of God's rule.

Babylon as the Beginning of Prophecy

As the head of gold in Nebuchadnezzar's dream, Babylon represents the beginning of the prophetic sequence that foretells the rise and fall of successive empires, leading to the establishment of God's eternal kingdom. Babylon's wealth, power, and influence made it the most magnificent of the ancient empires, but it was also a symbol of human pride and rebellion against God, destined to fall under divine judgment.

The fall of Babylon to the Medo-Persians marked the fulfillment of Daniel's prophecy and set in motion the unfolding of God's plan for history. Babylon's role as both a historical empire and an archetype of human rebellion continues to resonate throughout the Bible, particularly in apocalyptic literature, where it symbolizes the final defeat of worldly powers before the return of Christ and the establishment of the Kingdom of God.

The Fall of Babylon to the Persians: Historical Details and Biblical Significance

The fall of Babylon to the Persian Empire under Cyrus the Great in 539 BCE marked one of the most significant events in the ancient Near East, bringing an end to

Babylonian dominance and establishing Persian control over a vast territory. This event was pivotal not only in the political history of the region but also in biblical prophecy, fulfilling predictions in the books of Isaiah, Jeremiah, and Daniel.

In this chapter, we will delve into the historical context and key events surrounding the fall of Babylon, explore the role of Cyrus the Great, and examine the biblical significance of this event, particularly its fulfillment of prophecy and its impact on the Jewish people.

1. The Rise of the Persian Empire Under Cyrus the Great

A. Cyrus the Great's Ascension to Power

Cyrus II, known as Cyrus the Great, was the founder of the Achaemenid Empire, which would go on to become one of the largest empires in the ancient world. Before his conquest of Babylon, Cyrus had already established himself as a powerful ruler, having united the Persians and the Medes into a single empire and expanded his territories through military campaigns.

- Cyrus' Early Conquests: Cyrus began his rise to power by defeating the Medes around 550 BCE, thereby establishing the Persian Empire. He then turned his attention to other regions, conquering Lydia in Asia Minor (modern-day Turkey) and extending his control into central Asia.

- Military Strategy and Diplomacy: Cyrus was known not only for his military prowess but also for his strategic diplomacy. He often allowed local rulers to maintain a degree of autonomy and was respectful of local religions and customs, which earned him a reputation as a liberator rather than a conqueror in many of the regions he subdued.

By the time Cyrus set his sights on Babylon, he had already established a formidable empire and was recognized as one of the most powerful rulers of the ancient world.

B. The Persian Empire's Expansion Toward Babylon

Babylon, under the rule of Nabonidus, was experiencing internal unrest and declining influence by the late 6th century BCE. Nabonidus, the last king of Babylon, was often absent from the capital, having left the city for extended periods to stay in Tayma, a city in Arabia, due to religious disputes and political tensions within Babylon.

- Internal Weakness in Babylon: The absence of Nabonidus from Babylon and his conflicts with the Babylonian priesthood (particularly over his devotion to the moon god Sin rather than the traditional Babylonian god Marduk) weakened his authority. These factors contributed to the Babylonian people's disillusionment with their king and the internal instability of the empire.

- Cyrus' Approach to Babylon: Sensing an opportunity, Cyrus prepared to invade Babylon. His conquest of the surrounding territories, including Elam (modern-day southwestern Iran), allowed him to gain control of key strategic areas before launching his campaign against Babylon.

Cyrus' approach was marked by careful planning, both militarily and diplomatically, as he sought to win the favor of the people of Babylon by presenting himself as a liberator rather than a conqueror.

2. The Fall of Babylon: The Conquest in 539 BCE

The actual fall of Babylon to Cyrus the Great is considered one of the most significant military and political events of the ancient world. Remarkably, it occurred with minimal bloodshed, a factor that contributed to Cyrus' reputation as a just and capable ruler. Babylon's fall is notable for both its military success and its symbolic importance in the broader context of history and prophecy.

A. The Battle of Opis

The first major confrontation between the Persian and Babylonian forces took place at the Battle of Opis in September 539 BCE, near the Tigris River, north of Babylon.

- Persian Victory: The Persian army, under Cyrus' command, defeated the Babylonians at Opis, effectively breaking the Babylonian defense and opening the way for Cyrus to march on Babylon itself. The Persian army's superior strategy and discipline, combined with the weakened state of the Babylonian military, contributed to the decisive victory.

- Babylon's Vulnerability: After the defeat at Opis, Babylon was left vulnerable to attack. The city was well-fortified, with massive walls and a network of defensive systems, but its internal instability, compounded by the absence of strong leadership from Nabonidus, left it susceptible to conquest.

B. The Entry into Babylon

Following the Battle of Opis, Cyrus advanced toward Babylon. According to historical accounts, including those of the Greek historian Herodotus and the Babylonian Chronicles, Cyrus employed a clever military strategy to capture the city.

- Diverting the Euphrates River: One of the key factors in the conquest of Babylon was the Persian army's ability to divert the course of the Euphrates River, which flowed through the center of the city. By diverting the river, Cyrus' forces were able to enter Babylon through the riverbed, bypassing the city's formidable defenses.

- Minimal Resistance: Remarkably, Cyrus faced little to no resistance when entering the city. Many historical sources suggest that the Babylonian population, disillusioned with Nabonidus and his policies, welcomed Cyrus as a liberator.

Additionally, Babylon's religious elite had grown increasingly frustrated with Nabonidus' neglect of their traditional religious practices, making them more open to Cyrus' rule.

C. The Capture of Babylon and the Fate of Nabonidus

On October 12, 539 BCE, Babylon officially fell to the Persian army, and Cyrus the Great entered the city. Nabonidus, who had returned to Babylon shortly before its fall, was captured. His fate after the conquest is somewhat unclear, though some accounts suggest that Cyrus allowed him to live in exile.

- Cyrus' Peaceful Takeover: Cyrus' peaceful entry into Babylon was notable for the absence of widespread destruction or looting. He positioned himself as a liberator of the Babylonian people, promising to restore their religious traditions and respect their customs.

- The Cylinder of Cyrus: The Cyrus Cylinder, an ancient clay artifact, provides further insight into Cyrus' approach to ruling Babylon. The inscription on the cylinder describes how Cyrus was chosen by Marduk, the chief god of Babylon, to bring peace and justice to the city. This propagandistic message helped solidify Cyrus' image as a benevolent ruler in the eyes of the Babylonian population.

3. The Role of Cyrus the Great in Biblical Prophecy

The fall of Babylon and the rise of Cyrus the Great hold immense significance in biblical prophecy, particularly in the books of Isaiah, Jeremiah, and Daniel. Cyrus is portrayed as a divinely chosen instrument, used by God to fulfill His plans for the Jewish people and the world. Cyrus' conquest of Babylon marks the fulfillment of prophecies that foretold the end of Babylonian rule and the beginning of a new era.

A. The Prophecies of Isaiah and Jeremiah

The fall of Babylon was foretold in the prophecies of Isaiah and Jeremiah, both of whom predicted that Babylon, despite its grandeur, would eventually fall under divine judgment.

- Isaiah 13:19-22: "Babylon, the jewel of kingdoms, the pride and glory of the Babylonians, will be overthrown by God like Sodom and Gomorrah." This prophecy foretells the destruction of Babylon, emphasizing its pride and eventual downfall.

- Jeremiah 25:12: "But when the seventy years are fulfilled, I will punish the king of Babylon and his nation, the land of the Babylonians, for their guilt, declares the Lord, and will make it desolate forever." Jeremiah's prophecy links the fall of Babylon with the return of the Jewish exiles after seventy years, a significant period that reflects God's judgment on the Babylonian Empire.

B. Cyrus as God's Chosen Instrument

In the book of Isaiah, Cyrus is specifically named as the chosen servant of God who would fulfill God's purpose by conquering Babylon and allowing the Jewish people to return to their homeland.

- Isaiah 44:28: "Who says of Cyrus, 'He is my shepherd and will accomplish all that I please; he will say of Jerusalem, 'Let it be rebuilt,' and of the temple, 'Let its foundations be laid.'"

- Isaiah 45:1-4: "This is what the Lord says to his anointed, to Cyrus, whose right hand I take hold of to subdue nations before him and to strip kings of their armor, to open doors before him so that gates will not be shut."

These passages present Cyrus as an instrument of God's will, chosen to fulfill the divine plan of restoring the Jewish people to Jerusalem and rebuilding the Temple. Cyrus is the only non-Jewish ruler in the Bible to be referred to as "God's anointed", highlighting his unique role in biblical history.

C. The Return of the Jewish Exiles

One of the most significant outcomes of Cyrus' conquest of Babylon was his decree allowing the Jewish exiles to return to Jerusalem and rebuild the Temple. This event is recorded in the book of Ezra.

- Ezra

1:1-4: "In the first year of Cyrus king of Persia, in order to fulfill the word of the Lord spoken by Jeremiah, the Lord moved the heart of Cyrus king of Persia to make a proclamation throughout his realm and also to put it in writing: 'This is what Cyrus king of Persia says: The Lord, the God of heaven, has given me all the kingdoms of the earth and He has appointed me to build a temple for Him at Jerusalem in Judah.'"

Cyrus' decree marked the end of the Babylonian Exile and the beginning of a new chapter in Jewish history. The return of the exiles and the rebuilding of the Temple were seen as the fulfillment of God's promises to His people, restoring their relationship with Him and reestablishing Jerusalem as the center of Jewish worship.

4. The Impact of Babylon's Fall on the Ancient World

The fall of Babylon had far-reaching consequences for the political, cultural, and religious landscape of the ancient Near East. The Persian Empire, under Cyrus the Great, would go on to become one of the largest and most influential empires in history, shaping the development of the region for centuries.

A. The Persian Empire's Influence

Under Cyrus and his successors, the Persian Empire expanded its territories, incorporating a vast array of peoples and cultures. The Persian policy of religious tolerance and respect for local customs helped maintain stability within the empire and allowed it to flourish for over two centuries.

- Cultural Integration: The Persian Empire is often credited with fostering a sense of unity and cooperation among its diverse subjects. By respecting the traditions and religions of the peoples they conquered, the Persians were able to govern a vast and culturally heterogeneous empire with relative peace.

- Administrative Innovations: The Persian Empire also introduced significant administrative reforms, including the use of satrapies (provinces) governed by local officials, which allowed for more efficient governance of its extensive territories.

B. The Decline of Babylonian Influence

Although the city of Babylon remained an important cultural and economic center under Persian rule, its influence as an independent empire came to an end. Babylon's fall marked the beginning of a new era in which Persia would dominate the ancient Near East, while the legacy of Babylon would be remembered primarily through its historical and symbolic significance in both secular and biblical traditions.

- The Shift in Power: With the rise of the Persian Empire, the political and military dominance of Babylon was supplanted by the Persians, who would go on to play a key role in shaping the history of the ancient world. Babylon's significance would increasingly be viewed through the lens of its role in biblical prophecy and its symbolic representation of worldly power in opposition to God.

The Fall of Babylon and the Fulfillment of Prophecy

The fall of Babylon to the Persians in 539 BCE was a momentous event in both world history and biblical prophecy. Under Cyrus the Great, the Persian Empire not only conquered Babylon but also fulfilled the prophecies of Isaiah, Jeremiah, and Daniel, bringing an end to Babylonian dominance and initiating the return of the Jewish exiles to their homeland.

Babylon's fall marked the end of a significant chapter in the history of the ancient Near East, as the city's grandeur and power gave way to Persian rule. However, the impact of Babylon's fall extended far beyond its political consequences. In biblical terms, it represented the fulfillment of divine judgment against a kingdom that, despite its wealth and influence, had opposed God's people and defied His sovereignty.

The role of Cyrus as a divinely appointed ruler highlights the theme of God's sovereignty over human history, using even foreign kings to accomplish His purposes. The fall of Babylon and the rise of Persia serve as reminders of the transience of human power and the ultimate authority of God's kingdom, a theme that continues to resonate in eschatological discussions of worldly powers and their eventual judgment.

The Prophecies of Isaiah and Jeremiah Regarding Babylon's Fall

The fall of Babylon was one of the most significant events prophesied in the Old Testament, and both Isaiah and Jeremiah dedicated substantial portions of their writings to predicting and explaining this monumental event. These prophecies portray Babylon as the epitome of human pride, oppression, and idolatry, destined to fall under the judgment of God. The fall of Babylon was not only a geopolitical event but also a profound theological statement about the sovereignty of God over human history and the fate of nations.

In this section, we will explore the detailed prophecies in Isaiah and Jeremiah concerning the fall of Babylon, highlighting their themes of divine judgment, the role of Babylon as God's instrument, and the eventual restoration of God's people after Babylon's downfall. These prophecies also carry deep eschatological significance, foreshadowing the ultimate judgment of all worldly powers that stand in opposition to God's kingdom.

1. Isaiah's Prophecies Against Babylon

The prophet Isaiah lived in the 8th century BCE, long before the rise of Babylon as a dominant world empire. Nevertheless, Isaiah's prophecies foresaw the eventual destruction of Babylon, which became a reality more than a century later. These prophecies focus on the arrogance and pride of Babylon, the judgment of God against it, and the restoration of God's people.

A. Isaiah 13: The Destruction of Babylon as Divine Judgment

Isaiah 13 is one of the most direct and vivid prophecies concerning the fall of Babylon. Although Babylon had not yet risen to prominence during Isaiah's time, this prophecy looks forward to its eventual downfall.

- Isaiah 13:1-3: "An oracle concerning Babylon that Isaiah son of Amoz saw: Raise a banner on a bare hilltop, shout to them; beckon to them to enter the gates of the nobles. I have commanded those I prepared for battle; I have summoned my warriors to carry out my wrath—those who rejoice in my triumph."

In this passage, God declares that He is summoning foreign nations, described as "His warriors," to carry out His judgment against Babylon. The language emphasizes that Babylon's fall is not a result of mere human ambition but is divinely orchestrated as part of God's plan.

- Isaiah 13:9: "See, the day of the Lord is coming—a cruel day, with wrath and fierce anger—to make the land desolate and destroy the sinners within it."

Here, Isaiah describes the fall of Babylon as part of the Day of the Lord, a theme that runs throughout biblical prophecy. The Day of the Lord represents a time of divine intervention in history, where God acts decisively to judge the wicked and bring about justice. Babylon's destruction is depicted as a central event in this apocalyptic vision, highlighting the empire's sins and pride as reasons for its downfall.

- Isaiah 13:19-20: "Babylon, the jewel of kingdoms, the glory of the Babylonians' pride, will be overthrown by God like Sodom and Gomorrah. She will never be inhabited or lived in through all generations; there no nomads will pitch their tents, there no shepherds will rest their flocks."

Isaiah compares the destruction of Babylon to the overthrow of Sodom and Gomorrah, emphasizing the totality and finality of Babylon's judgment. The prophecy predicts that Babylon will be left desolate, never to be inhabited again. This apocalyptic imagery symbolizes the irreversible nature of God's judgment and serves as a warning to future empires that similarly exalt themselves in opposition to God.

B. Isaiah 14: The Fall of the King of Babylon

Isaiah 14 continues the theme of Babylon's fall, but this chapter focuses more on the king of Babylon, who represents the empire's arrogance and opposition to God. The king's fall is portrayed as a dramatic reversal of fortune, from the heights of power to the depths of humiliation.

- Isaiah 14:4: "You will take up this taunt against the king of Babylon: How the oppressor has come to an end! How his fury has ended!"

Isaiah envisions the fall of Babylon's king as a moment of triumph for the oppressed. The king of Babylon, once a symbol of power and oppression, is now the subject of mockery and derision. This "taunt" emphasizes the transience of worldly power and the inevitability of divine justice.

- Isaiah 14:12-15: "How you have fallen from heaven, morning star, son of the dawn! You have been cast down to the earth, you who once laid low the nations! You said in your heart, 'I will ascend to the heavens; I will raise my throne above the stars of God... But you are brought down to the realm of the dead, to the depths of the pit.'"

This famous passage is often associated with the fall of Lucifer, but in its original context, it refers to the king of Babylon. The king's fall from heaven symbolizes his pride and ambition to exalt himself above God, which ultimately leads to his downfall. This imagery is a powerful reminder that no human ruler can defy God's sovereignty and escape judgment.

- Isaiah 14:22-23: "I will rise up against them, declares the Lord Almighty. I will wipe out Babylon's name and survivors, her offspring and descendants, declares the Lord. I will turn her into a place for owls and into swampland; I will sweep her with the broom of destruction, declares the Lord Almighty."

God's judgment against Babylon is described as absolute and final. The imagery of desolation and wasteland reinforces the idea that Babylon's fall is a demonstration of God's power over the greatest empires of the world. The prophecy reflects the fate of all human kingdoms that oppose God's will—they will be wiped out, and their memory will fade.

2. Jeremiah's Prophecies Against Babylon

The prophet Jeremiah lived during the final years of the Kingdom of Judah and witnessed the Babylonian conquest of Jerusalem and the destruction of the First Temple. While much of Jeremiah's message warned of impending judgment on Judah, he also delivered extensive prophecies concerning the eventual fall of Babylon. These prophecies focus on Babylon as both God's instrument of judgment and a nation destined for destruction due to its own sins.

A. Jeremiah 25: Babylon as God's Instrument of Judgment

n Jeremiah 25, the prophet explains that God is using Babylon as His instrument to bring judgment on the nations, including Judah. However, he also foretells that Babylon itself will be punished after completing its role in God's plan.

- Jeremiah 25:8-9: "Therefore the Lord Almighty says this: 'Because you have not listened to my words, I will summon all the peoples of the north and my servant Nebuchadnezzar king of Babylon, and I will bring them against this land and its inhabitants and against all the surrounding nations. I will completely destroy them and make them an object of horror and scorn, and an everlasting ruin.'"

In this passage, God calls Nebuchadnezzar "my servant," emphasizing that even though Babylon is a foreign and pagan empire, it is being used by God to accomplish His purposes. Nebuchadnezzar's conquest of Judah and other nations is part of God's judgment for their disobedience and rebellion.

However, Babylon's role as God's servant is temporary, and Jeremiah makes it clear that Babylon itself will not escape judgment.

- Jeremiah 25:12: "But when the seventy years are fulfilled, I will punish the king of Babylon and his nation, the land of the Babylonians, for their guilt, declares the Lord, and will make it desolate forever."

Here, Jeremiah introduces the concept of the seventy years, during which Babylon would dominate the region and Judah would be in exile. After this period, God promises to punish Babylon for its own sins, just as He punished Judah. The prophecy implies that Babylon's arrogance, cruelty, and idolatry will ultimately lead to its downfall.

B. Jeremiah 50-51: The Judgment of Babylon

Chapters 50 and 51 of Jeremiah contain some of the most detailed and dramatic prophecies concerning the fall of Babylon. These chapters describe Babylon's destruction as an act of divine retribution for its pride, violence, and idolatry.

Jeremiah 50:2-3: "Announce and proclaim among the nations, lift up a banner and proclaim it; keep nothing back, but say, 'Babylon will be captured; Bel will be put to shame, Marduk filled with terror. Her images will be put to shame and her idols filled with terror.' A nation from the north will attack her and lay waste her land."

This passage foretells the defeat of Babylon by a nation from the north, traditionally understood as the Medo-Persians. The prophecy also emphasizes the humiliation of Babylon's gods, including Marduk, the chief deity of Babylon. This reflects the broader biblical theme that false gods will be brought low and that only the God of Israel reigns supreme.

- Jeremiah 50:9-10: "For I will stir up and bring against Babylon an alliance of great nations from the north. They will take up their positions against her, and from the north she will be captured. Their arrows will be like skilled warriors who do not return empty-handed. So Babylon will be plundered; all who plunder her will have their fill, declares the Lord."

Jeremiah describes Babylon's defeat as the work of an alliance of nations, likely referring to the Medes and Persians who would eventually conquer the city. The prophecy vividly portrays the conquest of Babylon as an act of divine retribution, with Babylon's wealth being plundered by the victorious nations.

- Jeremiah 50:23-24: "How broken and shattered is the hammer of the whole earth! How desolate is Babylon among the nations! I set a trap for you, Babylon, and you were caught before you knew it; you were found and captured because you opposed the Lord."

Babylon, once the "hammer of the whole earth", is now broken and shattered. This dramatic reversal underscores the idea that no empire, no matter how powerful, can stand against the judgment of God. Babylon's pride and opposition to God have led to its downfall.

C. Jeremiah 51: The Complete Destruction of Babylon

Chapter 51 of Jeremiah continues the theme of Babylon's impending destruction, offering detailed prophecies about how the city will fall and the consequences for its people.

- Jeremiah 51:6: "Flee from Babylon! Run for your lives! Do not be destroyed because of her sins. It is time for the Lord's vengeance; He will repay her what she deserves."

Here, Jeremiah calls on the people to flee from Babylon, symbolizing the urgency of escaping the impending judgment. Babylon's destruction is described as divine vengeance, a repayment for the empire's sins and cruelty.

- Jeremiah 51:25-26: "'I am against you, you destroying mountain, you who destroy the whole earth,' declares the Lord. 'I will stretch out my hand against you, roll you off the cliffs, and make you a burned-out mountain. No rock will be taken from you for a cornerstone, nor any stone for a foundation, for you will be desolate forever,' declares the Lord."

Babylon is metaphorically described as a "destroying mountain", emphasizing its role as a force of destruction and conquest. However, God declares that He will destroy Babylon and leave it desolate. The prophecy also suggests that Babylon's fall will be so complete that it will never be rebuilt or used as a foundation for future empires.

- Jeremiah 51:62-64: "Then say, 'Lord, you have said you will destroy this place, so that neither people nor animals will live in it; it will be desolate forever.' When you finish reading this scroll, tie a stone to it and throw it into the Euphrates. Then say, 'So will Babylon sink to rise no more because of the disaster I will bring on her. And her people will fall.'"

The final symbolic act described in this prophecy is the casting of a scroll into the Euphrates River. This act signifies that Babylon will "sink" like the stone tied to the scroll, never to rise again. The irreversibility of Babylon's judgment is a key theme in Jeremiah's prophecies, reinforcing the idea that Babylon's fall is permanent and divinely ordained.

3. The Eschatological Significance of Babylon's Fall

The prophecies of Isaiah and Jeremiah concerning the fall of Babylon have far-reaching implications beyond the historical destruction of the Babylonian Empire. These prophecies contain strong eschatological themes, pointing to the ultimate defeat of worldly powers and the establishment of God's eternal kingdom.

A. Babylon as a Symbol of Worldly Power

Throughout biblical prophecy, Babylon serves as a symbol of the pride, oppression, and idolatry that characterize human kingdoms that reject God. The arrogance of the Babylonian king, the city's wealth, and its dominance over other nations make Babylon the archetype of human rebellion against God's sovereignty.

- In the Book of Revelation, Babylon reappears as "Babylon the Great," a symbol of the final world system that opposes God in the last days. The fall of Babylon the Great in Revelation 18 mirrors the destruction of the historical Babylon, representing the final defeat of all human powers that oppose God.

- Revelation 18:2: "Fallen! Fallen is Babylon the Great! She has become a dwelling for demons and a haunt for every impure spirit."

The fall of Babylon in Isaiah and Jeremiah thus serves as a foreshadowing of the ultimate judgment of all worldly empires that set themselves against God's kingdom.

B. The Restoration of God's People

The fall of Babylon is not only an act of judgment against a wicked empire but also a moment of restoration for God's people. Both Isaiah and Jeremiah connect the fall of Babylon with the return of the Jewish exiles and the rebuilding of Jerusalem.

- Isaiah 44:28: "Who says of Cyrus, 'He is my shepherd and will accomplish all that I please; he will say of Jerusalem,

'Let it be rebuilt,' and of the temple, 'Let its foundations be laid.'"

- Jeremiah 29:10: "This is what the Lord says: 'When seventy years are completed for Babylon, I will come to you and fulfill my good promise to bring you back to this place.'"

These promises of restoration point to a broader eschatological hope—the return of God's people from exile and the establishment of a new covenant. In the New Testament, this theme is extended to include the ultimate restoration of all creation when Christ returns to establish His eternal reign.

The Prophecies of Isaiah and Jeremiah on the Fall of Babylon

The prophecies of Isaiah and Jeremiah concerning the fall of Babylon reveal a complex and multifaceted view of divine judgment and human history. Babylon is depicted as both an instrument of God's judgment and a symbol of human pride and rebellion, destined to fall under God's wrath.

Isaiah's vivid descriptions of Babylon's destruction emphasize the complete and irreversible nature of its fall, while Jeremiah's prophecies highlight Babylon's role in God's plan and the ultimate restoration of God's people after the seventy years of exile. Together, these prophecies provide a powerful theological framework for understanding the transience of human power and the sovereignty of God over history.

The fall of Babylon also carries significant eschatological meaning, foreshadowing the final judgment of all human empires and the establishment of God's eternal kingdom. In the biblical narrative, Babylon's fall is not only a historical event but also a symbolic representation of the ultimate victory of God over the forces of evil and rebellion.

The Prophetic Role of Cyrus as a Liberator and Restorer of God's People

The role of Cyrus the Great, the Persian king who conquered Babylon in 539 BCE, holds profound prophetic significance in the Bible. Despite being a foreign king and non-Israelite, Cyrus is described in the Book of Isaiah as an instrument of God's will, specifically chosen to liberate the Jewish people from exile and to facilitate the rebuilding of Jerusalem and the Temple. His unique status as a Gentile Messiah figure in the prophetic narrative highlights themes of divine sovereignty, liberation, and restoration.

In this chapter, we will dive deeper into the prophetic role of Cyrus, exploring the biblical passages that describe him, the theological implications of his actions, and his significance in the broader biblical narrative. We will also examine how his role as a restorer of God's people not only fulfilled immediate historical needs but also foreshadowed larger eschatological themes in the Bible.

1. Cyrus in the Prophecy of Isaiah

Cyrus is one of the few non-Israelite figures in the Bible to be directly called by God to fulfill a divine mission. The prophecies concerning Cyrus, found primarily in Isaiah 44 and Isaiah 45, reveal that God specifically chose him to play a pivotal role in the restoration of Israel after the Babylonian exile. These passages emphasize that, despite his status as a foreign king, Cyrus was used by God as a "shepherd" and "anointed" to carry out His purposes.

A. Isaiah 44:28 – Cyrus, God's Shepherd

In Isaiah 44:28, God refers to Cyrus by name, describing him as a shepherd who will fulfill God's will by ordering the rebuilding of Jerusalem and the restoration of the Temple.

- Isaiah 44:28: "Who says of Cyrus, 'He is my shepherd and will accomplish all that I please; he will say of Jerusalem, 'Let it be rebuilt,' and of the temple, 'Let its foundations be laid.'"

Here, Cyrus is called "my shepherd," a title typically reserved for Israelite leaders like King David, and later applied to Jesus in the New Testament. The use of this term highlights Cyrus' role as someone who will guide and protect God's people. In this case, the protection comes in the form of political liberation from Babylon and the decree that allows the Jewish exiles to return to their homeland and rebuild the Temple in Jerusalem.

The fact that God specifically names Cyrus in Isaiah, long before Cyrus would rise to power, is a striking example of the biblical theme that God controls the course of history. Even foreign rulers, who do not know or worship Him, can be used by God to fulfill His purposes.

B. Isaiah 45:1-7 – Cyrus, God's Anointed

In Isaiah 45, Cyrus is referred to as God's "anointed" (Hebrew: mashiach, or "Messiah"), a term that is traditionally used for Israelite kings and priests. This is the only instance in the Bible where a foreign ruler is given this title, emphasizing the uniqueness of Cyrus' role in God's plan.

- Isaiah 45:1: "This is what the Lord says to his anointed, to Cyrus, whose right hand I take hold of to subdue nations before him and to strip kings of their armor, to open doors before him so that gates will not be shut."

By calling Cyrus His anointed, God designates him as a chosen instrument for carrying out divine purposes, specifically the conquest of Babylon and the subsequent liberation of the Jewish people. The imagery of God taking Cyrus' right hand implies divine support and empowerment, ensuring that Cyrus' military victories, including the fall of Babylon, are seen as acts of God's will.

- Isaiah 45:2-3: "I will go before you and will level the mountains; I will break down gates of bronze and cut through bars of iron. I will give you hidden treasures, riches stored in secret places, so that you may know that I am the Lord, the God of Israel, who summons you by name."

These verses emphasize God's direct intervention in Cyrus' success, ensuring that the conquest of Babylon and other nations would be swift and decisive. The treasures and riches referred to here could be a reference to the wealth of Babylon, which Cyrus would capture. However, the key theological point is that Cyrus' victories are portrayed as acts of God's sovereign power, not simply the result of his own strength or ambition.

- Isaiah 45:4-5: "For the sake of Jacob my servant, of Israel my chosen, I summon you by name and bestow on you a title of honor, though you do not acknowledge me. I am the Lord, and there is no other; apart from me there is no God. I will strengthen you, though you have not acknowledged me."

This passage underscores the fact that Cyrus did not know or worship the God of Israel, yet he was still chosen by God to carry out His will. This reflects the broader biblical theme that God is the sovereign ruler of all nations and can use anyone, regardless of their personal faith or nationality, to accomplish His purposes. The liberation of Israel from Babylon, orchestrated through Cyrus, is presented as a demonstration of God's unique power and control over the destiny of His people.

2. Cyrus as the Liberator of the Jewish Exiles

The fall of Babylon in 539 BCE and Cyrus' subsequent decree allowing the Jewish exiles to return to Jerusalem represent the fulfillment of prophetic promises. The Babylonian Exile, which began in 586 BCE with the destruction of Jerusalem and the Temple, was a time of deep theological crisis for the Jewish people. Many believed that God had abandoned them due to their unfaithfulness. However, the prophecies of Isaiah and Jeremiah promised that after a period of seventy years, God would raise up a liberator to restore them to their land.

A. The Decree of Cyrus and the Return to Jerusalem

One of the most significant acts of Cyrus' reign was his decree allowing the Jewish exiles to return to Jerusalem and rebuild the Temple. This decree is recorded in the opening verses of the book of Ezra and marks the official end of the Babylonian Exile.

- Ezra 1:1-4: "In the first year of Cyrus king of Persia, in order to fulfill the word of the Lord spoken by Jeremiah, the Lord moved the heart of Cyrus king of Persia to make a proclamation throughout his realm and also to put it in writing: "This is what Cyrus king of Persia says: The Lord, the God of heaven, has given me all the kingdoms of the earth and he has appointed me to build a temple for him at Jerusalem in Judah. Any of his people among you may go up to Jerusalem in Judah and build the temple of the Lord, the God of Israel, the God who is in Jerusalem, and may their God be with them.'"

Cyrus' decree reflects the fulfillment of prophecies in both Jeremiah and Isaiah. It was prophesied that after seventy years of exile, God would bring His people back to the land He promised to their ancestors. Cyrus' proclamation highlights the fact that even though he did not personally worship the God of Israel, he recognized that his victories were part of a divine plan.

The return of the Jewish people to their homeland marked a new era in their relationship with God. It was a sign of God's faithfulness to His covenant promises, despite the disobedience that had led to the exile. The decree also set the stage for the rebuilding of the Second Temple, which would become the spiritual center of Jewish life in the post-exilic period.

B. The Role of Jeremiah's Prophecy

The return from exile and the role of Cyrus in liberating the Jewish people were also part of Jeremiah's prophetic message. Jeremiah had warned of the coming destruction of Jerusalem, but he also offered hope that the exile would not be permanent.

- Jeremiah 25:11-12: "This whole country will become a desolate wasteland, and these nations will serve the king of Babylon seventy years. But when the seventy years are fulfilled, I will punish the king of Babylon and his nation, the land of the Babylonians, for their guilt, declares the Lord, and will make it desolate forever."

- Jeremiah 29:10: "This is what the Lord says: 'When seventy years are completed for Babylon, I will come to you and fulfill my good promise to bring you back to this place.'"

The return of the Jewish exiles under Cyrus' decree was seen as the fulfillment of Jeremiah's prophecy. The seventy years of exile were over, and now God was fulfilling His promise to restore His people. The fall of Babylon and the rise of Cyrus were not random historical events but were part of God's providential plan to bring about the redemption and restoration of Israel.

3. The Theological Significance of Cyrus as a Liberator

The role of Cyrus as a liberator and restorer of God's people holds deep theological significance, particularly in how it illustrates God's sovereignty over history and His ability to use even foreign rulers to accomplish His purposes. Cyrus' actions also provide important foreshadowing of the Messianic deliverance that is central to Christian theology.

A. God's Sovereignty Over History

One of the key theological lessons from the story of Cyrus is the demonstration of God's sovereignty over human history. The fact that God called and used a pagan king like Cyrus to liberate His people shows that God's plans are not limited by human politics or national boundaries. God can and does use anyone—whether they acknowledge Him or not—to fulfill His purposes.

- Isaiah 45:7: "I form the light and create darkness, I bring prosperity and create disaster; I, the Lord, do all these things."

In this verse, God declares His total control over the events of the world, both good and bad. Cyrus' rise to power and his subsequent decree allowing the Jewish people to return to their land were not coincidences—they were part of God's providential plan to fulfill His promises.

B. Cyrus as a Foreshadowing of the Messiah

The language used to describe Cyrus in the Book of Isaiah has Messianic overtones, particularly in how he is referred to as God's "anointed" (Hebrew: mashiach). This title is most often associated with the Davidic kings and ultimately with the Messiah, who is prophesied to come and bring about the final restoration of Israel and the world.

- Isaiah 45:1: "This is what the Lord says to his anointed, to Cyrus."

Cyrus, as God's anointed, is a type of Christ, in that he prefigures the role of the ultimate Messiah, who will bring about spiritual deliverance and restore God's people not just to a physical land but to a right relationship with God. Just as Cyrus liberated the Jewish people from their physical exile, Jesus, the ultimate Messiah, will liberate humanity from the spiritual exile of sin.

The restoration of Jerusalem and the rebuilding of the Temple under Cyrus also foreshadow the ultimate restoration of creation that will occur when Christ returns. The new Jerusalem described in the Book of Revelation represents the final fulfillment of God's plan, where His people will dwell with Him forever in a renewed and perfected creation.

- Revelation 21:2-3: "I saw the Holy City, the new Jerusalem, coming down out of heaven from God, prepared as a bride beautifully dressed for her husband. And I heard a loud voice from the throne saying, 'Look! God's dwelling place is now among the people, and he will dwell with them.'"

C. The Universal Scope of God's Plan

The fact that Cyrus was a Gentile highlights the universal scope of God's redemptive plan. God's choice of a non-Israelite to bring about the liberation of His people foreshadows the inclusion of the Gentiles in the plan of salvation. This is an important theme in both the Old and New Testaments, where the blessings of Abraham are ultimately extended to all nations.

- Isaiah 45:22-23: "Turn to me and be saved, all you ends of the earth; for I am God, and there is no other. By myself I have sworn, my mouth has uttered in all integrity a word that will not be revoked: Before me every knee will bow; by me every tongue will swear."

This passage, which comes just after the prophecy concerning Cyrus, emphasizes that God's plan for salvation is not limited to Israel but extends to "all the ends of the earth." Cyrus, though a Gentile, is used by God to accomplish a crucial part of this plan, illustrating that God's sovereignty and salvation are not bound by ethnic or national distinctions.

4. The Legacy of Cyrus in Biblical and Historical Tradition

Cyrus' legacy as a liberator and restorer continued to be celebrated in both biblical and historical tradition. His reputation for justice, tolerance, and respect for local customs made him a beloved figure not only among the Jews but also among many other peoples who lived under his rule.

A. The Cyrus Cylinder: A Historical Record

The Cyrus Cylinder, an ancient clay artifact discovered in Babylon in 1879, provides historical evidence of Cyrus' policies of religious tolerance and liberation. The cylinder contains a declaration by Cyrus in which he describes his conquest of Babylon and his decision to allow exiled peoples to return to their homelands and restore their religious practices.

While the Cyrus Cylinder does not specifically mention the Jews, its general description of Cyrus' policies aligns with the biblical account of his decree allowing the Jewish exiles to return to Jerusalem. The cylinder has been hailed as one of the earliest declarations of human rights, and it solidifies Cyrus' reputation as a just and enlightened ruler.

B. Cyrus in Jewish Tradition

Cyrus is remembered in Jewish tradition as a divinely appointed liberator and a symbol of God's faithfulness to His people. The return from exile under Cyrus marked a new chapter in the history of Israel, and the rebuilding of the Temple became a central focus of the post-exilic community.

In Second Temple Judaism, the return from exile was seen as a partial fulfillment of God's promises, but many Jews continued to look forward to the coming of the Messiah, who would bring about a final and complete restoration. Cyrus' role as a type of Messiah helped shape Jewish expectations of the ultimate deliverer who would come to establish God's kingdom.

C. Cyrus in Christian Theology

In Christian theology, Cyrus is often seen as a prefigurement of Christ, particularly in how he is described as God's "anointed" and how his actions led to the restoration of God's people. Just as Cyrus liberated the Jews from physical exile, Christ liberates humanity from spiritual exile through His death and resurrection.

The connection between Cyrus and Christ highlights the broader biblical theme that God works through history to bring about redemption and restoration. Cyrus' role in the return from exile is seen as a foreshadowing of the ultimate return from spiritual exile, which will be fulfilled in Christ's second coming and the establishment of the new Jerusalem.

Cyrus as a Liberator and Restorer

The prophetic role of Cyrus the Great as a liberator and restorer of God's people is one of the most remarkable examples of God's sovereignty over history. Despite being a pagan king who did not know or worship the God of Israel, Cyrus was chosen by God to fulfill a central role in the redemption of the Jewish people. His decree allowing the exiles to return to Jerusalem and rebuild the Temple marked the fulfillment of Isaiah's and Jeremiah's prophecies and demonstrated that God's plans are not confined by national or religious boundaries.

Cyrus' role in the biblical narrative serves as a powerful reminder that God uses unexpected people and circumstances to accomplish His will. His actions prefigure the Messianic deliverance that is central to the Christian faith, and his inclusion in the biblical story points to the universal scope of God's plan for salvation, which extends to all nations and peoples.

Ultimately, the story of Cyrus highlights the themes of liberation, restoration, and divine sovereignty, offering hope to those who await the fulfillment of God's promises and the establishment of His eternal kingdom.

Connection to Apocalyptic Literature and Prophecy in the Hebrew Bible

The fall of Babylon and the role of Cyrus as a liberator in the Hebrew Bible not only mark key historical and prophetic events but also serve as critical themes in the development of apocalyptic literature. Apocalyptic prophecy, with its visions of divine judgment, the ultimate defeat of evil, and the establishment of God's eternal kingdom, is deeply influenced by the imagery and themes related to Babylon, Cyrus, and the broader concept of God's sovereignty over nations.

In Section we will explore the connections between the prophecies concerning Babylon and Cyrus in the Hebrew Bible and the apocalyptic literature that emerges in later Jewish and Christian texts. Specifically, we will examine how Babylon's fall and Cyrus' role as God's chosen instrument foreshadow the larger apocalyptic vision of the end of human kingdoms and the triumph of God's eternal reign, as seen in books like Daniel and Revelation.

1. The Apocalyptic Elements in Prophecies Concerning Babylon

The prophetic oracles against Babylon in the books of Isaiah and Jeremiah contain several elements that foreshadow the development of apocalyptic literature. These elements include the theme of divine judgment on worldly powers, the idea of a cosmic battle between good and evil, and the promise of God's ultimate victory over the forces of oppression.

A. Divine Judgment as a Foretaste of Apocalyptic Themes

In the prophecies concerning the fall of Babylon, we see the early development of apocalyptic themes, particularly in the emphasis on divine judgment against human arrogance, idolatry, and injustice. Babylon, as the archetype of human pride and rebellion, becomes a symbol for all oppressive world systems that defy God's rule.

- Isaiah 13:9-11: "See, the day of the Lord is coming—a cruel day, with wrath and fierce anger—to make the land desolate and destroy the sinners within it. The stars of heaven and their constellations will not show their light. The rising sun will be darkened, and the moon will not give its light. I will punish the world for its evil, the wicked for their sins."

This passage contains clear apocalyptic imagery. The Day of the Lord is described as a time of cosmic upheaval, with celestial bodies darkened and the natural order disrupted. This imagery later becomes a hallmark of apocalyptic texts, where divine judgment is portrayed as an event that affects not only human kingdoms but also the entire cosmos. Babylon's fall is thus presented as part of a larger narrative of God's judgment against evil and the ultimate renewal of the world.

- Isaiah 13:19-20: "Babylon, the jewel of kingdoms, the glory of the Babylonians' pride, will be overthrown by God like Sodom and Gomorrah. She will never be inhabited or lived in through all generations."

The destruction of Babylon is likened to the catastrophic destruction of Sodom and Gomorrah, another event often associated with divine judgment in the Hebrew Bible. This connection further underscores the apocalyptic nature of Babylon's fall, presenting it as part of the ongoing struggle between human rebellion and divine justice.

B. The Cosmic Battle and the Defeat of Evil

The prophecies against Babylon also introduce the concept of a cosmic battle between the forces of good and evil. Babylon represents not just a historical empire but a broader symbol of the kingdoms of this world that stand in opposition to God's kingdom. The prophetic vision of Babylon's fall foreshadows the final defeat of evil that becomes central to later apocalyptic literature.

- Jeremiah 51:25: "I am against you, you destroying mountain, you who destroy the whole earth," declares the Lord. "I will stretch out my hand against you, roll you off the cliffs, and make you a burned-out mountain."

Babylon is described as a destroying mountain—a symbol of immense power that oppresses the nations. But God promises to bring it low, emphasizing His ultimate sovereignty over even the most powerful of human kingdoms. This image of Babylon as the embodiment of destructive power resonates with later apocalyptic texts, where worldly empires are depicted as agents of evil that will be defeated by God in the final judgment.

2. The Book of Daniel: Apocalyptic Visions and Babylon's Fall

The Book of Daniel stands as a pivotal text in the development of apocalyptic literature in the Hebrew Bible. Written during a time of intense persecution under foreign rule, likely during the reign of Antiochus IV Epiphanes (2nd century BCE), Daniel contains visions of divine judgment and the ultimate triumph of God's kingdom over the kingdoms of this world. The themes of Babylon, Cyrus, and God's sovereignty continue to play a major role in these visions.

A. The Four Kingdoms and the Final Kingdom of God

One of the most important visions in Daniel is the dream of Nebuchadnezzar, where the Babylonian king sees a great statue representing a series of four empires. Each part of the statue is made of different materials, symbolizing successive kingdoms, and the head of gold represents Babylon.

- Daniel 2:31-35: "Your Majesty looked, and there before you stood a large statue—an enormous, dazzling statue, awesome in appearance. The head of the statue was made of pure gold, its chest and arms of silver, its belly and thighs of bronze, its legs of iron, its feet partly of iron and partly of baked clay. While you were watching, a rock was cut out, but not by human hands. It struck the statue on its feet of iron and clay and smashed them."

In this vision, Babylon is the head of gold, the first of the great world empires. However, the prophecy foretells that all human empires—including Babylon—will eventually be destroyed by a kingdom represented by a stone "cut out, but not by human hands." This stone symbolizes the Kingdom of God, which will ultimately replace all earthly kingdoms and endure forever.

- Daniel 2:44: "In the time of those kings, the God of heaven will set up a kingdom that will never be destroyed, nor will it be left to another people. It will crush all those kingdoms and bring them to an end, but it will itself endure forever."

The destruction of the statue and the rise of the eternal kingdom reflect the apocalyptic belief that human history will culminate in the final defeat of evil and the establishment of God's reign. Babylon, as the head of gold, represents the beginning of the sequence of human empires that will eventually give way to the Kingdom of God.

B. The Role of Daniel as a Model for Apocalyptic Figures

In the Book of Daniel, the prophet Daniel himself is depicted as a figure who has access to divine wisdom and is able to interpret apocalyptic visions. Daniel's role as a visionary parallels that of later apocalyptic figures, such as

John in the Book of Revelation, who receive similar revelations about the end of the world and the coming of God's kingdom.

- Daniel 7:13-14: "In my vision at night I looked, and there before me was one like a son of man, coming with the clouds of heaven. He approached the Ancient of Days and was led into his presence. He was given authority, glory and sovereign power; all nations and peoples of every language worshiped him. His dominion is an everlasting dominion that will not pass away, and his kingdom is one that will never be destroyed."

This vision of the Son of Man is a key moment in the development of apocalyptic prophecy. The Son of Man is seen as a messianic figure who receives authority over all the nations from the Ancient of Days (God). The imagery of divine authority, the defeat of the beastly kingdoms, and the eternal dominion of the Son of Man provide a clear eschatological framework that would influence later Jewish and Christian apocalyptic thought.

3. Cyrus and the Apocalyptic Hope of Restoration

While Cyrus is not an explicitly apocalyptic figure in the Hebrew Bible, his role as a liberator and restorer of Israel has significant apocalyptic overtones. His decree allowing the exiles to return to Jerusalem and rebuild the Temple is seen as the fulfillment of prophecy and a foretaste of the ultimate restoration that would come with the Messiah.

A. Cyrus as a Prototype of the Messianic Deliverer

In Isaiah 45, Cyrus is called God's anointed (Hebrew: mashiach), a term usually reserved for the kings of Israel and later applied to the Messiah. This designation highlights the messianic role that Cyrus plays in the immediate context—bringing the Jewish people back from exile and facilitating the rebuilding of the Temple.

- Isaiah 45:1: "This is what the Lord says to his anointed, to Cyrus, whose right hand I take hold of to subdue nations before him."

Cyrus' role as a political and religious liberator prefigures the eschatological role of the Messiah, who would bring about the final and ultimate restoration of Israel and establish God's kingdom. Just

as Cyrus overthrew Babylon and restored the Jewish people to their land, the future Messiah would overthrow the kingdoms of this world and establish the new Jerusalem, where God's people would dwell in peace and righteousness.

B. The Rebuilding of the Temple and Apocalyptic Themes

Cyrus' decree allowing the rebuilding of the Second Temple was a pivotal event in the restoration of Israel after the Babylonian exile. The Temple symbolized God's presence among His people and was central to Jewish worship and identity. The rebuilding of the Temple under Cyrus thus served as a precursor to the larger apocalyptic vision of the new Jerusalem and the establishment of God's eternal dwelling with His people.

- Haggai 2:9: "The glory of this present house will be greater than the glory of the former house, says the Lord Almighty. And in this place I will grant peace, declares the Lord Almighty."

This prophecy, given during the rebuilding of the Second Temple, expresses the hope that the restored Temple will one day surpass even the splendor of Solomon's Temple. This hope is taken up in apocalyptic literature, where the new Jerusalem is envisioned as a city of unparalleled beauty and divine presence.

- Revelation 21:3: "And I heard a loud voice from the throne saying, 'Look! God's dwelling place is now among the people, and he will dwell with them. They will be his people, and God himself will be with them and be their God.'"

The new Jerusalem in Revelation represents the ultimate fulfillment of the restoration that Cyrus began. Just as Cyrus allowed the Jewish people to rebuild the Temple, the final Messiah will bring about the new creation, where God will dwell with His people forever in perfect peace and righteousness.

4. Babylon in Apocalyptic Literature: A Symbol of Ultimate Judgment

The image of Babylon as a symbol of oppressive world power continues to play a central role in later apocalyptic literature, particularly in the Book of Revelation. In this context, Babylon the Great becomes the ultimate embodiment of human rebellion against God, and its destruction signals the final defeat of evil and the establishment of God's kingdom.

A. Babylon the Great in the Book of Revelation

In Revelation 17-18, Babylon the Great is described as a wealthy, corrupt city that embodies the evils of idolatry, oppression, and materialism. The city is symbolized as a prostitute who seduces the kings of the earth and leads them into rebellion against God.

- Revelation 17:5: "The name written on her forehead was a mystery: Babylon the Great, the mother of prostitutes and of the abominations of the earth."

Babylon's fall in Revelation mirrors the prophecies in Isaiah and Jeremiah concerning the destruction of the historical Babylon. Just as the Babylonian Empire was overthrown by the Medo-Persians, so too will Babylon the

Great be overthrown in the apocalyptic vision of John. Its destruction represents the final judgment on all human systems that stand in opposition to God.

- Revelation 18:2: "Fallen! Fallen is Babylon the Great! She has become a dwelling for demons and a haunt for every impure spirit."

This dramatic announcement of Babylon's fall echoes the language of Isaiah 21:9, where the prophet similarly declares the fall of historical Babylon. The repetition of "Fallen! Fallen!" emphasizes the finality of Babylon's destruction in both historical and eschatological contexts.

B. The Eschatological Hope of God's Kingdom

The destruction of Babylon the Great in Revelation leads to the establishment of God's eternal kingdom, just as the fall of the historical Babylon under Cyrus led to the restoration of Israel. The apocalyptic vision culminates in the coming of the new Jerusalem, where God's people will dwell with Him forever.

- Revelation 21:1-2: "Then I saw a new heaven and a new earth, for the first heaven and the first earth had passed away, and there was no longer any sea. I saw the Holy City, the new Jerusalem, coming down out of heaven from God, prepared as a bride beautifully dressed for her husband."

This new Jerusalem represents the final fulfillment of the prophetic hope for restoration that began with Cyrus' decree to rebuild the Second Temple. In the apocalyptic vision, the new creation is not just a return from exile but the ultimate renewal of the entire cosmos, where God's kingdom will reign supreme and His people will experience eternal peace and joy.

The Connection to Apocalyptic Literature and Prophecy in the Hebrew Bible

The prophecies concerning Babylon and Cyrus in the Hebrew Bible are deeply connected to the development of apocalyptic literature. The fall of Babylon, prophesied by Isaiah and Jeremiah, serves as a precursor to the apocalyptic theme of divine judgment on human kingdoms that oppose God. The role of Cyrus as a liberator and restorer points to the broader hope for the ultimate restoration of God's people and the establishment of His eternal kingdom.

In the Book of Daniel, the fall of Babylon is incorporated into a larger apocalyptic vision of the end of human history, where God's kingdom will replace all earthly powers. The imagery of the statue and the stone cut from the mountain without human hands encapsulates the eschatological hope for the defeat of evil and the triumph of God's rule.

Finally, in the Book of Revelation, Babylon the Great serves as the ultimate symbol of worldly rebellion, whose fall marks the beginning of the new creation and the establishment of the new Jerusalem. The destruction of Babylon in both historical and apocalyptic contexts illustrates the sovereignty of God over human history and the inevitability of His judgment on all forces that oppose His will.

The Role of Babylon the Great in Christian Apocalyptic Literature

In Christian apocalyptic literature, particularly in the Book of Revelation, Babylon the Great serves as a powerful and symbolic representation of worldly systems that oppose God. Unlike the historical Babylon, which fell to the Persian Empire in 539 BCE, Babylon the Great in Revelation symbolizes not only the evils of a specific empire but also the broader forces of corruption, idolatry, and rebellion that characterize the kingdoms of this world. It embodies the ultimate symbol of evil in its opposition to God's kingdom, making its destruction a central theme in the apocalyptic vision of the end times.

This chapter will explore the role of Babylon the Great in Christian apocalyptic thought, examining its symbolic meaning, how it relates to historical and spiritual themes in the Bible, and its place within the broader eschatological narrative of Revelation. We will also delve into the significance of its destruction and the transition from Babylon the Great's fall to the establishment of the new Jerusalem and the eternal kingdom of God.

1. Babylon the Great: Symbolism and Meaning in Revelation

In Revelation 17-18, Babylon the Great is portrayed as a wealthy, corrupt, and seductive entity that embodies the evils of human power, idolatry, and oppression. While it draws on the historical imagery of ancient Babylon, the Babylon in Revelation transcends any specific historical empire, becoming a metaphor for the entirety of the world's rebellious systems that resist God's authority.

A. The Prostitute of Babylon: Idolatry and Worldly Seduction

One of the most striking images of Babylon the Great in Revelation is her portrayal as a prostitute who seduces the nations with her wealth and immorality. This depiction emphasizes the allure of worldly power and materialism, as well as the idolatrous nature of Babylon's influence over the rulers of the earth.

- Revelation 17:1-2: "One of the seven angels who had the seven bowls came and said to me, 'Come, I will show you the punishment of the great prostitute, who sits by many waters. With her the kings of the earth committed adultery, and the inhabitants of the earth were intoxicated with the wine of her adulteries.'"

The image of Babylon as a prostitute reflects her role in leading the nations into spiritual adultery—turning them away from worshiping the true God and drawing them into idolatry and moral corruption. The "many waters" symbolize her global influence, spreading her corrupting influence over the rulers and peoples of the world. The "wine of her adulteries" signifies the intoxication of wealth, power, and false worship that blinds people to God's truth.

- Revelation 17:4-5: "The woman was dressed in purple and scarlet, and was glittering with gold, precious stones, and pearls. She held a golden cup in her hand, filled with abominable things and the filth of her adulteries. The name written on her forehead was a mystery: Babylon the Great, the mother of prostitutes and of the abominations of the earth."

Babylon's lavish appearance—her clothing of purple and scarlet, her adornment with gold and jewels—represents the extravagance and wealth associated with her. This wealth, however, is ill-gotten and tied to the abominations of her false worship and exploitation. The phrase "mother of prostitutes" underscores Babylon's role as the originator and perpetuator of spiritual infidelity and abominations across the earth.

B. The Beast and Babylon: Political Power and Corruption

In addition to her role as a symbol of idolatry and immorality, Babylon the Great is also associated with political power. In Revelation 17, she is seen riding a scarlet beast, which represents the worldly empires and political systems that support her and are complicit in her corruption.

- Revelation 17:3: "Then the angel carried me away in the Spirit into a wilderness. There I saw a woman sitting on a scarlet beast that was covered with blasphemous names and had seven heads and ten horns."

The beast represents the political structures that are in opposition to God's kingdom. The "seven heads and ten horns" echo the descriptions of beastly kingdoms in Daniel 7, further drawing the connection between Babylon's spiritual corruption and the political empires of the world. Babylon is depicted as sitting on the beast, symbolizing her reliance on and association with worldly power.

- Revelation 17:12-13: "The ten horns you saw are ten kings who have not yet received a kingdom, but who for one hour will receive authority as kings along with the beast. They have one purpose and will give their power and authority to the beast."

The ten kings symbolize earthly rulers who, though they may rise and fall in power, are ultimately aligned with the beast and its rebellion against God. Babylon's influence over these rulers represents her ability to seduce and corrupt those in positions of authority, leading them to give their power to the beastly kingdom in defiance of God.

2. The Judgment and Destruction of Babylon the Great

The climax of Babylon the Great's role in Revelation is her judgment and destruction. As the embodiment of all that opposes God, Babylon must be overthrown to make way for the coming of God's kingdom. Her destruction is described in vivid and catastrophic terms, emphasizing the finality of her judgment and the inevitability of God's justice.

A. The Sudden Fall of Babylon

In Revelation 18, the fall of Babylon is proclaimed as a decisive moment in the apocalyptic narrative. The grandeur, wealth, and power that Babylon once possessed are destroyed in an instant, highlighting the fragility of human kingdoms and their ultimate submission to divine authority.

- Revelation 18:2: "Fallen! Fallen is Babylon the Great! She has become a dwelling for demons and a haunt for every impure spirit, a haunt for every unclean bird, a haunt for every unclean and detestable animal."

The repetition of "Fallen! Fallen!" emphasizes the finality of Babylon's destruction. The once-great city, the symbol of worldly power and wealth, is now reduced to desolation, inhabited only by demons and unclean spirits. This imagery echoes the destruction of ancient Babylon, which was prophesied by Isaiah and Jeremiah to become a desolate ruin, devoid of life.

- Revelation 18:8: "Therefore in one day her plagues will overtake her: death, mourning and famine. She will be consumed by fire, for mighty is the Lord God who judges her."

Babylon's fall is swift and catastrophic—"in one day" her destruction comes. This highlights the divine judgment that overtakes her, signaling that no amount of wealth, power, or human influence can protect her from the wrath of God. The reference to fire evokes the idea of total destruction, a judgment that leaves nothing of Babylon's former glory intact.

B. The Lament of the Kings and Merchants

Following the announcement of Babylon's fall, there is a lament from the kings and merchants of the earth, who mourn the loss of her wealth and the collapse of the economic system that sustained them. This lament underscores the materialism and greed that Babylon represents.

- Revelation 18:9-10: "When the kings of the earth who committed adultery with her and shared her luxury see the smoke of her burning, they will weep and mourn over her. Terrified at her torment, they will stand far off and cry: 'Woe! Woe to you, great city, you mighty city of Babylon! In one hour your doom has come!'"

The kings of the earth, who were once seduced by Babylon's luxury and power, now mourn her destruction from afar. Their lament reflects their self-interest, as Babylon's fall marks the end of the system that allowed them to flourish. The phrase "in one hour your doom has come" reinforces the suddenness and inevitability of Babylon's fall.

- Revelation 18:11-13: "The merchants of the earth will weep and mourn over her because no one buys their cargoes anymore—cargoes of gold, silver, precious stones and pearls; fine linen, purple, silk and scarlet cloth; every sort of citron wood, and articles of every kind made of ivory, costly wood, bronze, iron and marble."

The merchants mourn the collapse of Babylon's economic system, which was characterized by excessive materialism and the pursuit of luxury. The list of goods highlights the opulence of Babylon's trade, which was built on the exploitation of resources and people. The merchants' lament reveals the extent to which Babylon's economy was driven by greed and excess, reflecting the broader critique of materialism and worldly wealth in apocalyptic literature.

3. The Fall of Babylon and the Triumph of God's Kingdom

The destruction of Babylon the Great marks a turning point in the apocalyptic narrative of Revelation. With Babylon's fall, the forces of evil, corruption, and idolatry that have dominated the world are overthrown, paving the way for the establishment of God's eternal kingdom. This transition from Babylon's judgment to the coming of the new Jerusalem represents the ultimate fulfillment of apocalyptic prophecy.

A. The Hallelujah Chorus: Rejoicing at Babylon's Fall

In Revelation 19, following the destruction of Babylon, there is a celebration in heaven as the hosts of heaven and the saints rejoice over the victory of God's justice. The downfall of Babylon is seen as a cause for rejoicing, as it signals the end of oppression and the beginning of God's reign.

- Revelation 19:1-2: "After this I heard what sounded like the roar of a great multitude in heaven shouting: 'Hallelujah! Salvation and glory and power belong to our God, for true and just are his judgments. He has condemned the great prostitute who corrupted the earth by her adulteries. He has avenged on her the blood of his servants.'"

The hallelujah chorus reflects the righteousness of God's judgments and the vindication of those who suffered under Babylon's oppression. The destruction of the "great prostitute" represents the end of corruption, and the rejoicing in heaven is a foretaste of the final victory that will come with the establishment of God's kingdom.

B. The Establishment of the New Jerusalem

The fall of Babylon the Great is followed by the vision of the new Jerusalem, a city that represents the ultimate fulfillment of God's promise to dwell with His people. Unlike Babylon, the new Jerusalem is characterized by holiness, purity, and divine presence.

- Revelation 21:2-4: "I saw the Holy City, the new Jerusalem, coming down out of heaven from God, prepared as a bride beautifully dressed for her husband. And I heard a loud voice from the throne saying, 'Look! God's dwelling place is now among the people, and he will dwell with them. They will be his people, and God himself will be with them and be their God. He will wipe every tear from their eyes. There will be no more death or mourning or crying or pain, for the old order of things has passed away.'"

The new Jerusalem stands in direct contrast to Babylon the Great. Whereas Babylon was a city of idolatry, oppression, and immorality, the new Jerusalem is a place of righteousness, peace, and divine fellowship. It is the culmination of God's plan for salvation and restoration, where His people will dwell with Him forever, free from the evils of the fallen world.

C. Babylon as the Antithesis of God's Kingdom

In the overall narrative of Revelation, Babylon the Great represents the antithesis of the new Jerusalem and God's kingdom. Babylon embodies everything that is opposed to God's will—materialism, greed, corruption, idolatry, and oppression—while the new Jerusalem embodies the fulfillment of God's covenant and the establishment of His eternal reign.

The contrast between the destruction of Babylon and the creation of the new Jerusalem illustrates the central message of apocalyptic literature: the present world order, dominated by evil and rebellion, will be overthrown, and a new and perfect order will be established by God. The fall of Babylon signifies the end of the old order, while the new Jerusalem represents the dawning of the new creation, where God's people will live in harmony with Him.

4. Babylon the Great and the Eschatological Hope of Justice

The destruction of Babylon the Great is not only an act of divine judgment but also an expression of eschatological hope. In Christian apocalyptic thought,

Babylon represents the worldly systems that oppress and exploit, while its fall points to the ultimate victory of God's justice and the restoration of creation.

A. Vindication of the Martyrs

One of the key themes in the judgment of Babylon is the vindication of the martyrs—those who suffered persecution and death for their faithfulness to God. Throughout Revelation, Babylon is described as being "drunk with the blood of the saints", symbolizing its role in persecuting God's people.

- Revelation 17:6: "I saw that the woman was drunk with the blood of God's holy people, the blood of those who bore testimony to Jesus."

The destruction of Babylon is an act of divine retribution for the violence and injustice it perpetrated against the saints. In apocalyptic literature, the martyrs often serve as witnesses to God's justice, and their vindication is a sign of the coming judgment that will bring an end to all forms of oppression.

- Revelation 18:20: "Rejoice over her, you heavens! Rejoice, you people of God! Rejoice, apostles and prophets! For God has judged her with the judgment she imposed on you."

The call to rejoice reflects the eschatological hope that God's justice will ultimately prevail, even in the face of the world's injustice. The fall of Babylon is thus a sign that the sufferings of the righteous will not go unanswered, and that God will bring about ultimate justice in His timing.

B. The End of Oppression and the Renewal of Creation

Babylon's destruction also represents the end of oppression and the beginning of a new era of peace and justice. The worldly systems that Babylon represents—systems of exploitation, greed, and idolatry—are seen as inherently corrupt and unsustainable. Their fall is a necessary precondition for the renewal of creation.

- Revelation 21:5: "He who was seated on the throne said, 'I am making everything new!' Then he said, 'Write this down, for these words are trustworthy and true.'"

The new creation that follows Babylon's fall is marked by the restoration of all things, where evil and suffering are no more, and God's people experience eternal peace and communion with Him. This eschatological hope is at the heart of Christian apocalyptic literature, offering a vision of the future where God's justice prevails and creation is brought to its intended perfection.

The Role of Babylon the Great in Christian Apocalyptic Literature

In Christian apocalyptic literature, Babylon the Great serves as the ultimate symbol of worldly power, corruption, and rebellion against God. Drawing on the imagery of ancient Babylon, the city becomes a metaphor for the oppressive systems that dominate human history, leading nations and peoples into idolatry, materialism, and moral decay. Babylon's fall, as described in Revelation, marks the definitive end of these systems and the triumph of God's justice.

The destruction of Babylon the Great is a pivotal moment in the apocalyptic narrative, signaling the end of the old order and the beginning of the new creation. The contrast between Babylon and the new Jerusalem highlights the central message of Revelation: God's kingdom will ultimately prevail over the forces of evil, and His people will live in eternal fellowship with Him in the renewed creation.

Babylon's role in apocalyptic literature emphasizes the inevitability of divine judgment on human pride and rebellion, while also offering hope for those who have remained faithful to God. The fall of Babylon is not only a moment of destruction but also a moment of redemption, as it clears the way for the new Jerusalem and the full realization of God's eternal kingdom.

CHAPTER 04

THE SILVER CHEST AND ARMS – MEDO-PERSIA

In Nebuchadnezzar's dream as interpreted by the prophet Daniel (Daniel 2:31-45), the statue's chest and arms of silver represent the Medo-Persian Empire. This empire, which followed the Babylonian Empire, is often referred to as the second kingdom in the sequence of four empires symbolized by the statue in Nebuchadnezzar's vision. The Medo-Persian Empire is described as inferior to Babylon in terms of splendor (hence its representation by silver instead of gold), yet it achieved significant expansion and played a crucial role in the fulfillment of biblical prophecy.

This chapter explores the rise of the Medo-Persian Empire, its role in biblical prophecy as the silver kingdom, and how it served as the fulfillment of Daniel's vision. We will also examine how this empire's ascent set the stage for critical historical and theological developments, particularly the return of the Jewish exiles and the rebuilding of the Second Temple in Jerusalem.

1. The Rise of the Medo-Persian Empire

The Medo-Persian Empire, also known as the Achaemenid Empire, rose to prominence in the 6th century BCE, following the fall of the Neo-Babylonian Empire. It was a dual monarchy composed of the Medes and the Persians, with the Persians, under the leadership of Cyrus the Great, eventually assuming dominance.

A. The Medes and the Persians

The Medes were an ancient Indo-European people who lived in the region that is today known as Iran. Before the rise of the Persians, the Medes had established a powerful kingdom in the 7th century BCE, and they played a major role in the defeat of the Assyrian Empire. The Persians, originally a smaller tribe within the region, gradually gained power under the leadership of Cyrus II, also known as Cyrus the Great.

- Cyrus the Great (c. 600-530 BCE) united the Persians and the Medes around 550 BCE, effectively establishing the Achaemenid Empire. This empire quickly expanded, conquering vast territories, including the wealthy and powerful Lydian Empire in Asia Minor and, most notably, Babylon in 539 BCE.

B. The Conquest of Babylon

The conquest of Babylon by Cyrus the Great in 539 BCE marked the transition from the golden kingdom of Babylon to the silver kingdom of Medo-Persia as foretold in Nebuchadnezzar's dream. The fall of Babylon was significant not only for its political impact but also for its fulfillment of biblical prophecy.

- According to Daniel 5, the fall of Babylon occurred under Belshazzar, the last ruler of the Babylonian Empire, during a great feast where the famous "writing on the wall" appeared. Daniel interpreted the writing as a divine declaration that Babylon's days were numbered and that the kingdom would be divided and given to the Medes and Persians.

- Daniel 5:30-31: "That very night Belshazzar, king of the Babylonians, was slain, and Darius the Mede took over the kingdom, at the age of sixty-two."

The conquest of Babylon by Cyrus was not a violent takeover; according to historical records, it was relatively peaceful, with Cyrus being welcomed as a liberator. His entry into Babylon fulfilled not only the prophecies of Daniel but also those of Isaiah and Jeremiah, who had predicted Babylon's fall and the subsequent liberation of the Jewish exiles.

2. Medo-Persia as the Fulfillment of the Silver Kingdom

The chest and arms of silver in Nebuchadnezzar's dream symbolized the Medo-Persian Empire, which, though powerful and expansive, was considered inferior to Babylon in terms of splendor and wealth. Silver, while valuable, is less precious than gold, reflecting the relative decrease in cultural prestige and luxury of the Medo-Persian Empire compared to Babylon.

A. Duality of Medo-Persia

The statue's two arms of silver are often interpreted as representing the dual nature of the Medo-Persian Empire, composed of two distinct peoples: the Medes and the Persians. Although Cyrus the Great united these two groups, the Medes and Persians maintained separate identities, and the empire was marked by this duality.

- Darius the Mede (Daniel 5:31) is sometimes seen as a representative of the Median element of the empire, though historical details about Darius remain debated. It is possible that Darius was a title or a governor under the larger rule of Cyrus, or he could have been an official who administered Babylon after its fall.

- The Persians, under Cyrus, eventually became the dominant force within the empire, though they continued to honor the role of the Medes in the empire's governance and administration.

B. Expansion and Dominance of the Medo-Persian Empire

The Medo-Persian Empire was vast, stretching from the Indus Valley in the east to Greece and Egypt in the west, making it the largest empire the world had seen up to that point. Under Cyrus and his successors, the empire expanded significantly, absorbing many diverse cultures and regions into its fold.

- Cyrus' Successors: After Cyrus' death in 530 BCE, the empire continued to expand under his successors, particularly Cambyses II and Darius I. Darius I (reigned 522–486 BCE) consolidated and organized the empire, dividing it into satrapies (provinces) and instituting administrative reforms that allowed for efficient governance over vast territories.

The Medo-Persian Empire, though powerful, is considered inferior to Babylon in Daniel's prophecy because of its lack of the same cultural and architectural grandeur. However, it was far more successful in terms of military expansion and administrative organization. This reflects the transition from Babylon's wealth and luxury to Persia's focus on empire-building and governance.

3. The Role of Medo-Persia in Biblical Prophecy

The Medo-Persian Empire plays a significant role in the fulfillment of biblical prophecy, particularly in its connection to the return of the Jewish exiles and the rebuilding of the Second Temple in Jerusalem. The prophecies of Isaiah, Jeremiah, and Daniel all pointed to the fall of Babylon and the rise of a foreign ruler who would liberate God's people and allow them to return to their homeland.

A. The Prophecies of Isaiah and Jeremiah

Both Isaiah and Jeremiah predicted the fall of Babylon and the subsequent restoration of the Jewish people. Isaiah 44-45 specifically names Cyrus as God's chosen instrument to carry out His will, liberating the exiles and enabling the rebuilding of the Temple.

- Isaiah 44:28: "Who says of Cyrus, 'He is my shepherd and will accomplish all that I please; he will say of Jerusalem, 'Let it be rebuilt,' and of the temple, 'Let its foundations be laid.'"

- Isaiah 45:1: "This is what the Lord says to his anointed, to Cyrus, whose right hand I take hold of to subdue nations before him and to strip kings of their armor, to open doors before him so that gates will not be shut."

Cyrus is portrayed as an anointed one—a messianic figure chosen by God to bring about the return of His people.

The rise of the Medo-Persian Empire under Cyrus was thus seen as a fulfillment of these prophecies, highlighting God's control over history and His ability to use even non-Israelite rulers to accomplish His divine purposes.

B. The Decree of Cyrus and the Return of the Exiles

One of the most significant actions of Cyrus the Great was his decree allowing the Jewish exiles to return to Jerusalem and rebuild the Temple. This event is recorded in the opening chapters of the book of Ezra and is seen as the fulfillment of Jeremiah's prophecy that the exile would last seventy years.

- Ezra 1:1-3: "In the first year of Cyrus king of Persia, in order to fulfill the word of the Lord spoken by Jeremiah, the Lord moved the heart of Cyrus king of Persia to make a proclamation throughout his realm and also to put it in writing: 'This is what Cyrus king of Persia says: The Lord, the God of heaven, has given me all the kingdoms of the earth and he has appointed me to build a temple for him at Jerusalem in Judah. Any of his people among you may go up to Jerusalem and build the temple of the Lord, the God of Israel, the God who is in Jerusalem, and may their God be with them.'"

Cyrus' decree not only allowed the rebuilding of the Second Temple but also marked the beginning of a new chapter in Jewish history. The return from exile was a profound moment of restoration, symbolizing God's faithfulness to His covenant promises. It also set the stage for the Second Temple period, which would last until the Roman destruction of the Temple in 70 CE.

C. Medo-Persia in Daniel's Vision of the Beasts

The Medo-Persian Empire is also symbolized in Daniel 7, where it appears as the second of the four beasts in Daniel's vision. The second beast is described as a bear, representing the Medo-Persian Empire.

- Daniel 7:5: "And there before me was a second beast, which looked like a bear. It was raised up on one of its sides, and it had three ribs in its mouth between its teeth. It was told, 'Get up and eat your fill of flesh!'"

The image of the bear raised on one side is often interpreted as symbolizing the unequal partnership between the Medes and Persians, with the Persians being the dominant force. The three ribs in the bear's mouth may represent the three major conquests of the Medo-Persian Empire—Babylon, Lydia, and Egypt—which solidified its power and dominance.

4. The Legacy of the Medo-Persian Empire in Biblical and Historical Tradition

The legacy of the Medo-Persian Empire extends beyond its role in fulfilling biblical prophecy. Historically, the

Achaemenid Empire is remembered for its administrative innovations, cultural tolerance, and vast territorial expansion. In biblical tradition, it is remembered primarily for its role in liberating the Jewish exiles and allowing the rebuilding of the Temple in Jerusalem.

A. Cyrus as a Model of Just Rule

Cyrus the Great is often praised in both biblical and historical sources for his fairness and respect for local customs. Unlike many conquerors, Cyrus is remembered as a benevolent ruler who allowed subject peoples to retain their religious practices and local governance structures.

- The Cyrus Cylinder, an ancient artifact inscribed with a declaration by Cyrus, describes how he allowed exiled peoples to return to their homelands and restore their religious temples. Although the cylinder does not specifically mention the Jews, it aligns with the biblical account of Cyrus' decree in Ezra 1.

Cyrus' model of governance, which emphasized tolerance and justice, made him a highly respected figure in ancient history. This reputation is reflected in the Bible, where he is portrayed as God's chosen instrument for carrying out divine purposes, even though he was not an Israelite.

B. The Medo-Persian Empire and Biblical Eschatology

In the broader scope of biblical eschatology, the Medo-Persian Empire is seen as one stage in the unfolding of human history that will eventually culminate in the establishment of God's eternal kingdom. The Medo-Persian Empire, though powerful, is ultimately a temporary kingdom that will give way to the next empire in the prophetic sequence—Greece—and, ultimately, to the Kingdom of God.

- Daniel 2:44: "In the time of those kings, the God of heaven will set up a kingdom that will never be destroyed, nor will it be left to another people. It will crush all those kingdoms and bring them to an end, but it will itself endure forever."

The Medo-Persian Empire, like Babylon before it, serves as a reminder of the transience of human kingdoms and the ultimate sovereignty of God over history. Despite its power and influence, the Medo-Persian Empire would eventually fall to Alexander the Great and the Greek Empire, continuing the prophetic cycle that leads to the final establishment of God's kingdom.

The Silver Kingdom of Medo-Persia

The Medo-Persian Empire, represented by the chest and arms of silver in Nebuchadnezzar's dream, played a critical role in the unfolding of biblical prophecy and the course of human history. Though less splendid than Babylon, it was a vast and powerful empire that expanded across a wide territory, uniting diverse peoples under a relatively tolerant and just administration.

The rise of Cyrus the Great and his conquest of Babylon fulfilled the prophecies of Isaiah, Jeremiah, and Daniel, marking the beginning of the Jewish return from exile and the rebuilding of the Second Temple. As the silver kingdom, the Medo-Persian Empire stands as a symbol of transitional power, setting the stage for the next empire in the prophetic sequence while illustrating the broader biblical themes of God's sovereignty and the ultimate establishment of His kingdom.

The Bronze Kingdom – Greece

In Nebuchadnezzar's dream as recorded in Daniel 2:31-45, the bronze belly and thighs of the statue symbolize the third kingdom, widely understood to represent the rise of Greece. This bronze kingdom follows the Babylonian and Medo-Persian empires and represents the Greek Empire under the leadership of Alexander the Great. The Greek Empire was instrumental in shaping the ancient world through its conquests, its dissemination of Hellenistic culture, and its significant influence on both the East and West.

This chapter explores the rise of the Greek Empire under Alexander the Great, its prophetic significance as the bronze kingdom in Daniel's vision, and how its dominance fits into the larger narrative of biblical prophecy. Additionally, we will examine how the Hellenistic period following Alexander's death set the stage for later biblical events, especially the Maccabean Revolt and the Roman Empire, which would be the final empire in Daniel's prophetic sequence.

1. The Rise of the Greek Empire

The Greek Empire, led by Alexander the Great, emerged as a dominant force in the 4th century BCE. Alexander's conquests were unparalleled in their scope, as he established one of the largest empires in history, stretching from Greece to India. His rapid military success and the spread of Hellenistic culture marked a significant turning point in ancient history.

A. Alexander the Great and His Conquests

Alexander III of Macedon, known as Alexander the Great, was born in 356 BCE and ascended to the throne of Macedon in 336 BCE after the assassination of his father, King Philip II. At just 20 years old, Alexander embarked on a military campaign that would transform the ancient world.

- The Defeat of Persia: Alexander's most significant achievement was his conquest of the Persian Empire. In a series of decisive battles, including the Battle of Issus (333 BCE) and the Battle of Gaugamela (331 BCE), Alexander defeated Darius III, the last king of the Persian Achaemenid

Empire, effectively bringing an end to the silver kingdom and inaugurating the bronze kingdom of Greece.

- Expansion of the Greek Empire: Following his victory over Persia, Alexander continued his conquests, expanding his empire into Egypt, Mesopotamia, Central Asia, and parts of India. His empire stretched from Greece in the west to the borders of India in the east, making it one of the largest empires in the ancient world.

B. The Spread of Hellenistic Culture

One of the most enduring legacies of Alexander's conquests was the spread of Hellenistic culture across the vast territories he conquered. Hellenism—the blend of Greek language, art, architecture, philosophy, and religious practices—became the dominant cultural force throughout the ancient world.

- Hellenistic Influence: Greek culture, language, and ideas spread across the conquered regions, influencing not only the elites but also local populations. Greek became the lingua franca of the eastern Mediterranean and Near East, facilitating communication and cultural exchange across diverse regions.

- Cultural Synthesis: The Hellenistic period, which followed Alexander's death, saw the fusion of Greek culture with local traditions, particularly in Egypt, Mesopotamia, and

Persia. This cultural synthesis laid the groundwork for significant developments in philosophy, science, religion, and politics.

2. Greece as the Bronze Kingdom in Biblical Prophecy

The bronze belly and thighs of Nebuchadnezzar's statue in Daniel 2 are understood to represent the Greek Empire. While bronze is less valuable than gold (Babylon) or silver (Medo-Persia), it is a stronger metal, symbolizing Greece's military might and far-reaching influence.

A. The Prophetic Imagery of Bronze

In Daniel 2:39, Daniel explains that after the Medo-Persian Empire, there will arise "another kingdom, one of bronze, which will rule over the whole earth." This prophecy accurately describes the Greek Empire, which under Alexander, ruled vast territories and brought much of the known world under its control.

- Bronze as Strength: The choice of bronze as the metal representing Greece highlights the empire's strength in terms of military power. Greek armies, especially under Alexander, were known for their effectiveness in battle, using advanced tactics and weaponry such as the phalanx formation and the use of bronze armor.

- Global Rule: The prophecy states that this kingdom will "rule over the whole earth," a statement that reflects the global reach of Alexander's empire, which stretched from Europe to Asia. While not literally encompassing the entire earth, the extent of Greek rule was unprecedented in the ancient world and matched the scope of Daniel's vision.

B. Daniel 8: The Vision of the Ram and the Goat

In addition to Nebuchadnezzar's dream, the Book of Daniel contains another vision in Daniel 8 that further elaborates on the rise of Greece. In this vision, Daniel sees a ram (representing Medo-Persia) and a goat (representing Greece) engaged in battle.

- Daniel 8:5-7: "As I was thinking about this, suddenly a goat with a prominent horn between its eyes came from the west, crossing the whole earth without touching the ground. He came toward the two-horned ram I had seen standing beside the canal and charged at him in great rage. I saw him attack the ram furiously, striking the ram and shattering its two horns. The ram was powerless to stand against him; the goat knocked him to the ground and trampled on him, and none could rescue the ram from his power."

The goat with a prominent horn is understood to represent Alexander the Great, who came from the west (Greece) and decisively defeated the Medo-Persian Empire. The shattering of the ram's horns symbolizes the fall of Persia, and the dominance of the goat represents Greece's swift and uncontested rise to power.

- Daniel 8:8: "The goat became very great, but at the height of its power the large horn was broken off, and in its place four prominent horns grew up toward the four winds of heaven."

This verse alludes to the sudden death of Alexander the Great at the height of his power in 323 BCE. After Alexander's death, his empire was divided among his generals into four main kingdoms, represented by the four horns. This division led to the Hellenistic period, during which Greek influence persisted, but political unity was lost.

3. The Division of Alexander's Empire and the Hellenistic Period

Following the untimely death of Alexander the Great at the age of 32, his vast empire was divided among his generals, leading to the formation of the Hellenistic kingdoms. These successor states continued to spread Greek culture but also became embroiled in political and military conflict, particularly in the regions of Egypt, Syria, and Palestine.

A. The Division of the Empire

The diadochi (Alexander's generals) fought for control of the empire after his death, eventually dividing it into several major Hellenistic kingdoms. The most notable were the Ptolemaic Kingdom in Egypt and the Seleucid Kingdom in Syria and Mesopotamia.

- Ptolemaic Kingdom: Centered in Egypt and founded by Ptolemy I, this kingdom controlled Egypt and parts of the Levant, including Judea. It became a center of Greek culture and learning, with its capital in Alexandria becoming one of the greatest cities of the ancient world.

- Seleucid Kingdom: Founded by Seleucus I, this kingdom controlled Syria, Mesopotamia, and parts of Asia Minor. It became a dominant power in the eastern Mediterranean but was often in conflict with the Ptolemies over control of Judea and other territories.

B. The Impact on Judea

The division of Alexander's empire and the subsequent rivalry between the Ptolemies and Seleucids had a significant impact on Judea. Initially under the control of the Ptolemaic dynasty, Judea later came under Seleucid rule following the Battle of Panium in 198 BCE.

- Hellenization: Under both the Ptolemies and Seleucids, Judea experienced varying degrees of Hellenization, the process by which Greek culture, language, and practices were imposed on or adopted by local populations. While some Jews embraced elements of Greek culture, others resisted, leading to tensions within the Jewish community.

- Antiochus IV Epiphanes: One of the most significant figures during the Hellenistic period was Antiochus IV Epiphanes, the Seleucid king who sought to impose Hellenistic religion and practices on the Jewish people, including the desecration of the Temple in Jerusalem. His actions led to the Maccabe an Revolt (167-160 BCE), a pivotal event in Jewish history that resulted in the rededication of the Temple and the establishment of the Hasmonean dynasty.

4. The Prophetic Significance of the Greek Empire

The rise and fall of the Greek Empire are integral to the prophetic narrative in the Book of Daniel and play a significant role in the broader eschatological vision of the Bible. The bronze kingdom represents not only the strength and influence of Greece but also the transitory nature of human empires in contrast to the eternal kingdom of God.

A. The Temporary Nature of Human Kingdoms

The bronze kingdom of Greece, like the empires that preceded it (Babylon and Medo-Persia), was powerful but ultimately temporary. The vision of the statue in Daniel 2 emphasizes the fragility of human power and the inevitable fall of even the greatest empires.

- Daniel 2:39: "After you, another kingdom will arise, inferior to yours. Next, a third kingdom, one of bronze, will rule over the whole earth."

Although Greece ruled over much of the known world, it was not eternal. The division of Alexander's empire and the eventual conquest of the Hellenistic kingdoms by Rome illustrate the cyclical rise and fall of human kingdoms in contrast to the permanence of God's kingdom.

B. Foreshadowing the Kingdom of God

The sequence of empires in Nebuchadnezzar's dream serves to highlight the progression of history leading to the ultimate establishment of God's kingdom, symbolized by the stone cut without hands that will crush all earthly kingdoms.

- Daniel 2:44-45: "In the time of those kings, the God of heaven will set up a kingdom that will never be destroyed, nor will it be left to another people. It will crush all those kingdoms and bring them to an end, but it will itself endure forever."

The fall of the bronze kingdom of Greece and the subsequent rise of the iron kingdom (Rome) are seen as steps in the prophetic timeline leading to the coming of the Messiah and the establishment of God's eternal reign. The temporary nature of these empires contrasts sharply with the eternal nature of the Kingdom of God, which will never be overthrown.

C. The Greek Empire's Role in Shaping the World for the Coming of Christ

Although the Greek Empire was ultimately a temporary power, its influence played a significant role in preparing the world for the coming of Christ and the spread of the gospel.

- Hellenization facilitated the spread of the Greek language, which became the common language of the eastern Mediterranean and the Near East. This linguistic unity allowed for the rapid dissemination of the New Testament writings, which were originally written in Koine Greek.

- The spread of Greek philosophy and thought also laid the intellectual groundwork for early Christian theology, as ideas about ethics, metaphysics, and the nature of the divine were widely discussed in the Hellenistic world.

5. The Legacy of the Bronze Kingdom

The legacy of the Greek Empire endures in both biblical prophecy and historical tradition. As the bronze kingdom, Greece represents a pivotal moment in world history, where military might, cultural influence, and political dominance reshaped the ancient world.

A. The Hellenistic Influence on the Jewish World

The period of Hellenistic dominance had a profound impact on the Jewish world. The cultural tensions between Hellenism and Judaism during the reign of the Seleucids ultimately led to the Maccabean Revolt and the brief period of Jewish independence under the Hasmonean dynasty.

- The influence of Hellenistic culture also shaped the intellectual and religious environment of the Second Temple period, during which Greek ideas about the nature of God, the afterlife, and ethics interacted with Jewish beliefs.

B. The Greek Empire's Role in the Prophetic Narrative

In the prophetic narrative of Daniel, the bronze kingdom of Greece is an important stage in the succession of empires that leads to the coming of God's kingdom. Greece's rise and fall, though significant, are ultimately temporary events in the broader eschatological vision of the Bible.

- The bronze kingdom is a reminder that human power is fleeting and that all earthly kingdoms will eventually give way to the eternal kingdom of God. The fall of Greece and the subsequent rise of Rome continue the progression of history toward the final victory of God's kingdom.

The Bronze Kingdom and Its Prophetic Significance

The Greek Empire, represented by the bronze kingdom in Daniel's prophecy, played a crucial role in the unfolding of both world history and biblical prophecy. Under the leadership of Alexander the Great, Greece expanded its influence across vast territories, spreading Hellenistic culture and reshaping the ancient world. Yet, despite its strength and dominance, the Greek Empire, like the empires before it, was ultimately temporary, serving as one stage in the prophetic sequence leading to the establishment of God's eternal kingdom.

The legacy of Hellenistic culture continued to shape the world long after the fall of the Greek Empire, influencing Jewish history, early Christian theology, and the broader intellectual and cultural development of the ancient world. However, as prophesied in the Book of Daniel, the bronze kingdom would eventually give way to the iron kingdom of Rome, which in turn would set the stage for the coming of the Messiah and the establishment of God's kingdom.

The Iron Kingdom – Rome

In Nebuchadnezzar's dream as interpreted by Daniel (Daniel 2:31-45), the legs of iron symbolize the fourth kingdom, which is commonly understood to represent the Roman Empire. This empire, which followed the Greek Empire, was unmatched in its strength, durability, and brutality, characteristics fitting for the image of iron in the prophetic vision. The iron kingdom of Rome would dominate the Mediterranean world and beyond, establishing itself as one of the most powerful and enduring empires in human history. It also played a pivotal role in biblical prophecy, especially concerning the coming of the Messiah, the persecution of early Christians, and the eventual spread of the gospel.

This chapter explores the rise and dominance of the Roman Empire, its prophetic significance as the fourth kingdom in Daniel's vision, and how its rule fits into the larger biblical eschatological narrative. We will also examine the role of Rome in Jewish history, including the destruction of the Second Temple, and the empire's influence on the early Christian church.

1. The Rise and Dominance of the Roman Empire

The Roman Empire, symbolized by the legs of iron, emerged from a small city-state in central Italy to become a vast and powerful empire that would shape the course of Western history for centuries. Known for its military strength, political organization, and legal system, Rome established itself as the most powerful empire of the ancient world, with influence stretching across Europe, North Africa, and the Near East.

A. The Rise of Rome

Rome began as a small kingdom, eventually becoming a republic in the 6th century BCE, and then transitioning into an empire by the 1st century BCE under the rule of Julius Caesar and his successor, Augustus Caesar. The Roman Republic's expansion through warfare and diplomacy laid the groundwork for the empire's rise to power.

- The Punic Wars: Rome's early expansion involved a series of conflicts with the Carthaginian Empire during the Punic Wars (264–146 BCE), culminating in the destruction of Carthage and Rome's dominance over the western Mediterranean.

- Conquest of Greece and the East: Rome gradually extended its influence into the Hellenistic world, conquering Macedonia, Greece, and the remnants of Alexander's empire. By 30 BCE, following the defeat of Cleopatra and Mark Antony in Egypt, the entire Mediterranean basin had come under Roman control.

B. The Power and Structure of the Roman Empire

Rome's military prowess was central to its dominance. The Roman legions were highly disciplined and effective, ensuring the empire's control over vast territories. Additionally, Rome's political and administrative structures allowed it to maintain authority over diverse peoples and cultures.

- Political Structure: The Roman Empire was highly organized, with a complex system of governors, senators, and local administrators overseeing its vast territories. The empire was divided into provinces, each ruled by a governor appointed by the emperor.

- Infrastructure and Law: Rome's roads, aqueducts, and architecture were key to maintaining its control over the empire. Additionally, the development of Roman law had a lasting impact on the Western legal tradition, emphasizing the importance of citizenship, legal rights, and justice.

- Military Strength: Iron, the metal associated with Rome in Nebuchadnezzar's dream, symbolizes the strength and rigidity of the Roman Empire. Roman military power was unmatched in the ancient world, and the empire used its legions to secure its borders, suppress rebellions, and expand its territory.

2. Rome as the Iron Kingdom in Biblical Prophecy

The legs of iron in Nebuchadnezzar's dream represent the Roman Empire, characterized by its strength, durability, and power. Iron, unlike gold, silver, or bronze, is a hard, unyielding metal, symbolizing Rome's ability to conquer and subjugate other nations through military might. However, as strong as the Roman Empire was, it too would eventually give way to the Kingdom of God, which is symbolized by the stone cut without hands in Daniel's vision.

A. Iron: A Symbol of Strength and Harshness

The use of iron in the prophecy emphasizes the military and political dominance of Rome. Iron is stronger and more durable than gold, silver, or bronze, making it an appropriate symbol for an empire that ruled with iron discipline and brutality.

- Daniel 2:40: "Finally, there will be a fourth kingdom, strong as iron—for iron breaks and smashes everything—and as iron breaks things to pieces, so it will crush and break all the others."

This description accurately reflects the expansionist policies of Rome, which crushed other kingdoms under its rule. Rome's armies were often ruthless in their conquests, as seen in the destruction of Carthage, the suppression of Jewish revolts, and the sacking of Jerusalem in 70 CE.

- Rome's Crushing Power: The phrase "it will crush and break all the others" captures the reality of Rome's dominance over the ancient world. No other kingdom, whether Greek, Egyptian, or Jewish, could withstand the might of the Roman legions.

B. The Two Legs: The Division of the Roman Empire

Some interpretations of the two legs of iron suggest that they may symbolize the eventual division of the Roman Empire into Eastern and Western halves. This division, which occurred in the 4th century CE, marked a significant moment in Roman history.

- Western Roman Empire: The Western Roman Empire, centered in Rome, began to weaken by the 4th century due to internal corruption, invasions by Germanic tribes, and economic difficulties. It eventually fell in 476 CE when the last Roman emperor, Romulus Augustulus, was deposed by the Germanic king Odoacer.

- Eastern Roman Empire (Byzantine Empire): The Eastern Roman Empire, centered in Constantinople, survived for another thousand years as the Byzantine Empire. It remained a major power in the Eastern Mediterranean until its fall to the Ottoman Turks in 1453.

The two legs of iron can be seen as a representation of the East-West division, with each leg symbolizing one half of the empire, which continued to have influence long after the fall of the Western Roman Empire.

3. Rome's Role in Biblical History

The Roman Empire played a significant role in biblical history, particularly during the New Testament period. Roman rule had a profound impact on Jewish history, the life of Jesus, and the early Christian church. This section explores how Rome's political and military dominance interacted with key events in the Bible.

A. Rome's Influence in Jewish History

During the 1st century BCE, Judea became a client state of the Roman Empire. By 63 BCE, the Roman general Pompey had conquered Jerusalem, bringing the Jewish homeland under Roman control. This period of Roman dominance led to tensions between the Jewish people and their foreign rulers, culminating in several Jewish revolts.

- Herod the Great: Rome appointed Herod the Great as king of Judea in 37 BCE. Herod was a Roman client king who maintained power through his close ties to Rome. Although he oversaw the expansion of the Second Temple, he was deeply unpopular among many Jews due to his allegiance to Rome and his brutal policies.

- Jewish Revolts: The tensions between Rome and the Jewish population came to a head in the Jewish Revolt (66-70 CE), which ultimately led to the destruction of the Second Temple by the Roman general Titus in 70 CE. The loss of the Temple was a devastating event for the Jewish people, and it significantly shaped Jewish religious life in the following centuries.

B. The Life of Jesus and the Roman Empire

The Roman Empire serves as the political backdrop for many events in the New Testament, especially concerning the life and ministry of Jesus Christ. The Pax Romana ("Roman Peace"), the relative peace and stability provided by Roman rule, allowed for the spread of ideas, including the message of Jesus and the early Christian gospel.

- The Census and Birth of Jesus: According to Luke 2:1, it was a Roman decree by Caesar Augustus that led to Joseph and Mary traveling to Bethlehem, where Jesus was born. This Roman census fulfilled the prophecy that the Messiah would be born in Bethlehem (Micah 5:2).

- Pontius Pilate and the Crucifixion: The Roman governor Pontius Pilate played a central role in the trial and crucifixion of Jesus. While Jewish authorities condemned Jesus for blasphemy, it was ultimately the Roman administration that carried out the crucifixion, a method of execution reserved for criminals and political rebels under Roman law.

- The Cross as a Roman Symbol: The crucifixion of Jesus was not only a fulfillment of Old Testament prophecy but also a symbol of Rome's oppressive power. The cross, an instrument of Roman execution, became the central symbol of Christian salvation, representing the victory of God's kingdom over the forces of sin and death.

C. The Persecution of Early Christians

After the death and resurrection of Jesus, the early Christian movement spread throughout the Roman Empire. However, Christians often faced persecution under Roman authorities, who viewed their refusal to worship the emperor and the Roman gods as a threat to the social and political order.

- Nero's Persecution: One of the earliest and most infamous persecutions of Christians occurred under the

Roman Emperor Nero in 64 CE. After the Great Fire of Rome, Nero blamed the Christians for the disaster, leading to widespread persecution and the martyrdom of key figures like the apostles Peter and Paul.

- Domitian's Persecution: In the late 1st century, under the emperor Domitian, Christians faced renewed persecution. The Book of Revelation, written during this period, reflects the tension between the Christian community and Roman authority, with Rome symbolized as Babylon the Great, a corrupt and oppressive force in opposition to God's kingdom.

4. The Iron Kingdom's Prophetic Role in Eschatology

The Roman Empire, as the iron kingdom in Daniel's vision, plays a crucial role in biblical eschatology, serving as the backdrop for the coming of the Messiah and the spread of the gospel. Rome's dominance also sets the stage for the fulfillment of apocalyptic prophecies, particularly concerning the end times and the final establishment of God's kingdom.

A. The Fall of Rome and the Kingdom of God

While the Roman Empire was the strongest of the four kingdoms in Nebuchadnezzar's dream, it was not destined to last forever. According to the prophecy, the stone cut without human hands—representing the Kingdom of God—would strike the feet of the statue, symbolizing the end of all human kingdoms, including Rome.

- Daniel 2:44-45: "In the time of those kings, the God of heaven will set up a kingdom that will never be destroyed, nor will it be left to another people. It will crush all those kingdoms and bring them to an end, but it will itself endure forever."

The eventual fall of Rome, symbolized by the feet of iron and clay, points to the transitory nature of human empires. Despite its strength, Rome, like Babylon, Medo-Persia, and Greece, was subject to the sovereignty of God. The prophecy of the stone represents the coming of the Messiah, whose kingdom would be eternal and unshakable.

B. The Feet of Iron and Clay: The Fragility of Human Rule

The prophecy in Daniel 2 describes the feet of the statue as being made of iron mixed with clay, a combination that is inherently unstable. This imagery suggests that the later period of the Roman Empire, despite its military strength, would be marked by internal division and weakness.

- Daniel 2:41-43: "Just as you saw that the feet and toes were partly of baked clay and partly of iron, so this will be a divided kingdom; yet it will have some of the strength of iron in it... but the people will be a mixture and will not remain united, any more than iron mixes with clay."

This mixture of iron and clay is often interpreted as representing the internal fragmentation of the Roman Empire, particularly in its later stages. The Roman Empire struggled with political instability, economic problems, and invasions from various barbarian tribes, all of which contributed to its eventual decline.

C. Rome and the Final Eschatological Events

The Roman Empire also plays a key role in later apocalyptic literature, particularly in the Book of Revelation, where it is depicted as the great worldly power in opposition to God's kingdom. Rome, symbolized by Babylon the Great, is portrayed as a corrupt and oppressive force, whose downfall is prophesied as part of the final judgment.

- Revelation 18:2: "Fallen! Fallen is Babylon the Great! She has become a dwelling for demons and a haunt for every impure spirit."

The fall of Rome, as symbolized by the fall of Babylon in Revelation, marks the end of worldly power and the establishment of God's eternal kingdom. Just as the Babylonian Empire fell to the Persians, and the Roman Empire eventually collapsed, so too will all worldly systems that oppose God's rule.

The Iron Kingdom and Its Prophetic Significance

The Roman Empire, represented by the legs of iron in Nebuchadnezzar's dream, was the strongest and most enduring of the four kingdoms in Daniel's vision. Its rise to power marked a pivotal moment in world history, shaping the political, cultural, and religious landscape of the ancient world. Rome's military strength, political organization, and legal system allowed it to dominate the Mediterranean world and beyond for centuries.

However, as the fourth kingdom in Daniel's prophecy, Rome was ultimately a temporary empire, destined to be replaced by the Kingdom of God. The imagery of iron and clay in the feet of the statue symbolizes the fragility of human power and the inevitable collapse of all worldly kingdoms before the establishment of God's eternal reign. The fall of Rome, like the empires that preceded it, demonstrates that no earthly kingdom, no matter how powerful, can endure forever.

In the context of biblical eschatology, Rome plays a significant role in the events leading to the coming of the Messiah, the spread of Christianity, and the eventual fulfillment of God's prophetic plan. The iron kingdom of Rome, with all its strength and dominance, is ultimately superseded by the Kingdom of Heaven, which will last for eternity.

The Influence of Persia on Religious Thought – Zoroastrian Apocalypticism and Its Impact on Judaism and Christianity

The Persian Empire, particularly under the influence of Zoroastrianism, played a significant role in shaping religious thought during the period of its dominance, especially in relation to apocalyptic beliefs. Zoroastrianism, the religion of the ancient Persians, contained distinct apocalyptic themes, including the cosmic struggle between good and evil, the final judgment, and the ultimate triumph of good. These ideas profoundly influenced Jewish thought during the Second Temple period, especially after the Babylonian exile, and later contributed to Christian eschatology.

This chapter explores the religious influence of Persia, focusing on Zoroastrian apocalypticism, its core beliefs, and how these beliefs interacted with and shaped Jewish and Christian apocalyptic thought. By examining this intersection of ideas, we can understand how Persian religious beliefs contributed to the development of eschatological themes in the Bible and early Christian theology.

1. An Overview of Zoroastrianism and Its Apocalyptic Beliefs

Zoroastrianism is one of the world's oldest monotheistic religions, founded by the prophet Zoroaster (or

Zarathustra) in ancient Persia, likely sometime between the 10th and 6th centuries BCE. The religion centered on the worship of Ahura Mazda, the supreme deity, and promoted a cosmic dualism between good and evil.

A. The Cosmic Struggle Between Good and Evil

At the heart of Zoroastrianism is the belief in the ongoing struggle between good and evil, embodied by two opposing forces: Ahura Mazda (the god of truth and light) and Angra Mainyu (the spirit of lies, chaos, and darkness). This cosmic battle is central to Zoroastrian theology and shapes its eschatological vision.

- Ahura Mazda: The benevolent and omniscient god of light and goodness, who created the world and is destined to defeat evil. He represents order, justice, and truth (asha).

- Angra Mainyu: Also known as Ahriman, this malevolent spirit is the embodiment of chaos, deceit, and destruction. He opposes Ahura Mazda and seeks to corrupt creation, but his power is ultimately limited and will be overcome at the end of time.

B. Zoroastrian Eschatology: The End of the World and Final Judgment

Zoroastrianism presents a clear and detailed apocalyptic framework that includes the eventual defeat of evil, the resurrection of the dead, and a final judgment. These elements would later resonate with Jewish and Christian apocalyptic thought.

- The Saoshyant: Zoroastrianism teaches that a savior figure, known as the Saoshyant, will appear at the end of time to bring about the final defeat of Angra Mainyu and the forces of evil. The Saoshyant will lead humanity in the final cosmic battle and bring about the renewal of creation.

- Resurrection of the Dead: At the end of time, the dead will be resurrected, and there will be a final judgment. The righteous will be rewarded with eternal life, while the wicked will be purified or condemned.

- Frashokereti: This term refers to the ultimate restoration of the world. After the final victory of good over evil, the world will be purified, evil will be eradicated, and creation will be restored to its original perfect state. This apocalyptic vision emphasizes a renewed, incorruptible world, free from suffering, death, and evil.

2. Persian Influence on Jewish Apocalyptic Thought

The Persian period (539–332 BCE), during which the Jews returned from exile and rebuilt the Second Temple, was a critical time in the development of Jewish eschatology and apocalyptic thought. During this period, the Jewish people came into contact with Zoroastrian ideas, many of which influenced their own theological concepts, particularly in relation to the end times, the final judgment, and the resurrection of the dead.

A. Contact Between Jews and Zoroastrians

The Jewish exile in Babylon and the subsequent Persian conquest of Babylon under Cyrus the Great facilitated significant interaction between the Jewish community and Persian religious beliefs. Under Persian rule, the Jewish exiles were allowed to return to their homeland and rebuild the Temple in Jerusalem, but the influence of Persian thought remained pervasive.

- Cyrus and Zoroastrian Tolerance: Cyrus the Great, who was hailed as a liberator by the Jews, followed Zoroastrian principles of tolerance and respect for different religious traditions. This tolerance allowed for the free exchange of ideas, and it is likely that Jewish religious leaders encountered Zoroastrian eschatological beliefs during this period.

B. The Development of Jewish Apocalypticism

During the Second Temple period, Jewish texts began to reflect ideas that bear strong resemblance to Zoroastrian apocalypticism, particularly in relation to the final judgment, the cosmic struggle between good and evil, and the resurrection of the dead.

- Dualism in Jewish Apocalyptic Thought: The notion of a cosmic dualism—a struggle between the forces of light and darkness—became a prominent feature of Jewish apocalyptic literature, particularly in texts like the Book of Daniel and the Dead Sea Scrolls. This dualism mirrors Zoroastrian ideas about the battle between Ahura Mazda and Angra Mainyu.

- Daniel 12:1-2: "At that time Michael, the great prince who protects your people, will arise. There will be a time of distress such as has not happened from the beginning of nations until then. But at that time your people—everyone whose name is found written in the book—will be delivered. Multitudes who sleep in the dust of the earth will awake: some to everlasting life, others to shame and everlasting contempt."

This passage reflects a clear apocalyptic expectation of a future resurrection and final judgment, ideas that likely found resonance with Zoroastrian beliefs about the end of time.

- Resurrection and Final Judgment: The idea of a bodily resurrection of the dead, which became a core tenet of Jewish eschatology and later Christian theology, has parallels in Zoroastrianism's teaching of the resurrection at the end of the world. This concept is particularly emphasized in later Jewish apocalyptic texts, such as the Apocalypse of Baruch and the Book of Enoch.

C. Jewish Texts Reflecting Persian Influence

Several Jewish texts from the Second Temple period reflect Persian influence, particularly in their apocalyptic visions. These texts often emphasize the final triumph of good over evil, the coming of a messianic figure, and the establishment of an eternal kingdom.

- The Book of Daniel: Written during a time of persecution, the Book of Daniel includes vivid apocalyptic imagery, including visions of heavenly beings, the resurrection of the dead, and the final judgment. These themes parallel Zoroastrian ideas of the cosmic struggle and the end of the world.

- The Dead Sea Scrolls: The Qumran community, which produced the Dead Sea Scrolls, held strong apocalyptic beliefs, viewing themselves as the children of light engaged in a cosmic battle against the forces of darkness. Their texts contain references to angelic warfare, the coming of a messiah, and the ultimate victory of God—all themes that reflect an influence of Zoroastrian apocalypticism.

3. Persian Influence on Early Christian Eschatology

The apocalyptic themes that developed in Second Temple Judaism carried over into early Christian eschatology. Many of the central concepts in Christian teachings about the end times and the Kingdom of God—such as the final judgment, the resurrection of the dead, and the cosmic battle between good and evil—bear striking similarities to Zoroastrian beliefs.

A. The Concept of the Messiah and Final Judgment

Christianity inherited from Judaism the expectation of a messianic figure who would bring about the final victory of good and the establishment of God's kingdom. The notion of a savior figure, akin to the Zoroastrian Saoshyant, is central to Christian theology, with Jesus Christ fulfilling this role.

- Jesus as the Messiah: Christians believe that Jesus is the promised Messiah who fulfills the Old Testament prophecies and will return at the end of time to bring about the final judgment and the establishment of the Kingdom of God.

- Matthew 24:30-31: "Then will appear the sign of the Son of Man in heaven. And then all the peoples of the earth will mourn when they see the Son of Man coming on the clouds of heaven, with power and great glory. And he will send his angels with a loud trumpet call, and they will gather his elect from the four winds, from one end of the heavens to the other."

The Influence of Persia on Religious Thought – Zoroastrian Apocalypticism and Its Impact on Judaism and Christianity

The messianic expectations in both Judaism and Christianity bear strong similarities to the Zoroastrian belief in a future savior known as the Saoshyant. In Christianity, Jesus Christ is identified as the Messiah, who, like the Saoshyant in Zoroastrianism, is expected to bring about the final victory over evil, resurrect the dead, and initiate the final judgment.

- Jesus as the Savior and the Judge: In Christian eschatology, Jesus' second coming is portrayed as the moment when He will act as the judge of the living and the dead. This final judgment will determine the eternal fate of humanity, similar to the Zoroastrian idea of a final judgment presided over by Ahura Mazda at the end of the world.

- Matthew 25:31-32: "When the Son of Man comes in His glory, and all the angels with Him, He will sit on His glorious throne. All the nations will be gathered before Him, and He will separate the people one from another as a shepherd separates the sheep from the goats."

This apocalyptic imagery of Christ's return and judgment reflects the widespread Jewish and Christian belief in the Day of the Lord, a time when God will intervene in human history to defeat evil and establish divine justice. The concept of judgment, resurrection, and the ultimate triumph of righteousness are also seen in Zoroastrianism, where Ahura

Mazda and the Saoshyant will preside over the final eradication of Angra Mainyu (Ahriman), and the world will be renewed.

B. The Resurrection of the Dead

The resurrection of the dead is a key theme in both Zoroastrian eschatology and Christian theology, and it also became a prominent concept in Judaism during the Second Temple period. This belief in a future resurrection was likely influenced by Zoroastrian thought, which had a well-established doctrine of the dead being raised and judged at the end of time.

- Resurrection in Zoroastrianism: According to Zoroastrian belief, the dead will be resurrected at the time of the Frashokereti (the final renovation of the world), and they will be judged based on their deeds. The righteous will be rewarded with eternal life, while the wicked will undergo purification or be consigned to eternal punishment.

- Resurrection in Christianity: The belief in the resurrection of the dead is central to Christian eschatology. The Apostle Paul emphasizes this doctrine in his letters, particularly in 1 Corinthians 15, where he discusses the resurrection of Christ as a firstfruits of the general resurrection of believers at the end of the age.

- 1 Corinthians 15:52: "In a flash, in the twinkling of an eye, at the last trumpet. For the trumpet will sound, the dead will be raised imperishable, and we will be changed."

This passage, like others in the New Testament, reveals how Zoroastrian ideas of resurrection and final judgment found parallels in Christian teachings about the end times. The notion that the dead will rise, followed by a judgment where each individual's deeds are evaluated, reflects the apocalyptic vision shared across religious traditions influenced by Persian thought.

C. Cosmic Dualism and the Final Triumph of Good Over Evil

The theme of cosmic dualism, particularly the struggle between good and evil, is another area where Zoroastrianism left a lasting imprint on Jewish and Christian apocalyptic thought. Zoroastrianism's focus on the ongoing conflict between Ahura Mazda (representing good and order) and Angra Mainyu (representing evil and chaos) profoundly shaped later concepts of a final cosmic battle.

- Zoroastrian Cosmic Dualism: In Zoroastrianism, the battle between good and evil is not eternal; it will culminate in the eventual defeat of Angra Mainyu. This belief in a final victory of good over evil is crucial to Zoroastrian apocalypticism. At the end of time, the forces of evil will be destroyed, and the universe will be restored to its original perfection, free from corruption, death, and suffering.

- Jewish and Christian Apocalypticism: The apocalyptic visions in Jewish and Christian literature share this view of a final battle between good and evil. In the Book of Daniel, for example, the vision of the Son of Man and the Ancient of Days is a clear reference to a final judgment in which God will defeat the beastly kingdoms that oppose His rule.

- Daniel 7:13-14: "In my vision at night I looked, and there before me was one like a son of man, coming with the clouds of heaven. He approached the Ancient of Days and was led into his presence. He was given authority, glory and sovereign power; all nations and peoples of every language worshiped him. His dominion is an everlasting dominion that will not pass away, and his kingdom is one that will never be destroyed."

This passage reflects the eschatological hope for a divine intervention that will destroy the forces of evil and establish God's eternal kingdom. Similarly, in the Book of Revelation, the final chapters describe the defeat of Satan and the forces of evil in a cosmic struggle, followed by the establishment of a new heaven and new earth.

- Revelation 20:10: "And the devil, who deceived them, was thrown into the lake of burning sulfur, where the beast and the false prophet had been thrown. They will be tormented day and night for ever and ever."

In both Zoroastrianism and Christian eschatology, the ultimate victory of good over evil is not merely symbolic but is envisioned as a real event in which the powers of darkness will be defeated, and a new, perfect creation will emerge.

4. Zoroastrian Influence on Early Christian Apocalyptic Writings

The influence of Zoroastrian apocalypticism is evident not only in the themes of resurrection and cosmic dualism but also in specific literary elements found in early Christian apocalyptic writings, such as the Book of Revelation.

A. The Role of Angels and Spiritual Warfare

Zoroastrianism emphasizes the role of angelic beings in the cosmic struggle between good and evil, with Ahura Mazda and his divine servants waging war against Angra Mainyu and his demonic forces. This focus on spiritual warfare is mirrored in the apocalyptic literature of both Judaism and Christianity, where angels and demons play crucial roles in the unfolding of divine judgment.

- Angels in Zoroastrianism: In Zoroastrian belief, Amesha Spentas (Holy Immortals) serve Ahura Mazda, assisting him in maintaining order and fighting against the forces of evil. These beings are akin to angels in their role as protectors of creation and executors of divine justice.

- Angels in Revelation: In the Book of Revelation, angels are frequently depicted as messengers of God, carrying out His judgment and waging war against the forces of Satan. The archangel Michael, in particular, plays a leading role in the cosmic battle.

- Revelation 12:7-9: "Then war broke out in heaven. Michael and his angels fought against the dragon, and the dragon and his angels fought back. But he was not strong enough, and they lost their place in heaven. The great dragon was hurled down—that ancient serpent called the devil, or Satan, who leads the whole world astray. He was hurled to the earth, and his angels with him."

This imagery of spiritual warfare between the forces of good and evil, led by angelic beings, resonates with the Zoroastrian depiction of the battle between Ahura Mazda's angelic servants and the demonic forces of Angra Mainyu.

B. The New Heaven and New Earth

Both Zoroastrian eschatology and Christian apocalypticism envision the final triumph of good over evil as leading to a new creation, where the world is restored to a state of perfection. In Zoroastrianism, this process is called the Frashokereti, and it involves the purification of the cosmos and the renewal of the world. Similarly, Christian eschatology speaks of a new heaven and a new earth, where God will dwell with His people in eternal peace.

- Frashokereti: In Zoroastrian belief, after the final defeat of Angra Mainyu, the world will be purified by fire and renewed. The dead will be resurrected, and all souls will be judged. The righteous will live in a perfect, incorruptible world, free from evil and suffering.

The Influence of Persia on Religious Thought – Zoroastrian Apocalypticism and Its Impact on Judaism and Christianity

B. The New Heaven and New Earth in Revelation

The concept of a new heaven and new earth in Christian eschatology closely mirrors the Zoroastrian idea of the Frashokereti, which envisions the ultimate restoration of the world to a state of perfection. Both Zoroastrianism and Christianity share the belief that after the final defeat of evil, creation will be renewed, purified, and restored to a perfect state, where there will be no more suffering, corruption, or death. This apocalyptic hope for the renewal of the cosmos is central to the Book of Revelation and aligns with the Zoroastrian vision of the world's final transformation.

- Revelation 21:1-4: "Then I saw 'a new heaven and a new earth,' for the first heaven and the first earth had passed away, and there was no longer any sea. I saw the Holy City, the new Jerusalem, coming down out of heaven from God, prepared as a bride beautifully dressed for her husband. And I heard a loud voice from the throne saying, 'Look! God's dwelling place is now among the people, and he will dwell with them. They will be his people, and God himself will be with them and be their God. He will wipe every tear from their eyes. There will be no more death or mourning or crying or pain, for the old order of things has passed away.'"

This passage from Revelation describes the new creation that follows the defeat of evil, in which the new Jerusalem descends from heaven, symbolizing the eternal presence of God among His people. This vision of a transformed world, free from suffering and death, mirrors Zoroastrian eschatology, where the final triumph of Ahura Mazda leads to the purification of the universe and the establishment of a perfect, incorruptible world.

- Frashokereti in Zoroastrianism: In the Zoroastrian belief system, the Frashokereti represents the final renovation or making wonderful of the world. After the final battle between good and evil, the forces of evil and destruction will be vanquished, and the world will be made new. The elements of fire and molten metal will be used to purify the earth, and the righteous will live in a renewed world without suffering, disease, or death.

The parallelism between the Christian and Zoroastrian apocalyptic visions is striking: both depict the end of history as a time when the material world is transformed into a divine, everlasting state in which God (or Ahura Mazda) reigns supreme and all things are made right.

C. The Final Judgment and the Defeat of Evil

The final judgment is another key element shared between Zoroastrianism, Judaism, and Christianity, where the final victory of good over evil is solidified by divine judgment. This judgment not only determines the eternal fate of individuals but also serves as the culmination of history, bringing an end to the reign of evil forces in both the physical and spiritual realms.

- Zoroastrian Final Judgment: In Zoroastrian eschatology, at the end of time, the Saoshyant, the savior figure, will appear to lead humanity through the final battle against Angra Mainyu and his demonic forces. After the battle, the dead will be resurrected and judged according to their deeds. The righteous will be rewarded with eternal life in paradise, while the wicked will undergo purification before being granted a place in the renewed world.

- Christian Final Judgment: The Book of Revelation also describes a final judgment in which all the dead are raised and judged by God based on their deeds. This judgment culminates in the defeat of Satan and the casting of evil into the lake of fire, where it will remain for all eternity, unable to harm the new creation.

- Revelation 20:12-15: "And I saw the dead, great and small, standing before the throne, and books were opened. Another book was opened, which is the book of life. The dead were judged according to what they had done as recorded in the books. The sea gave up the dead that were in it, and death and Hades gave up the dead that were in them, and each person was judged according to what they had done. Then death and Hades were thrown into the lake of fire. The lake of fire is the second death. Anyone whose name was not found written in the book of life was thrown into the lake of fire."

The final judgment in Christianity is a key event in apocalyptic literature, reflecting the ultimate justice of God. Similar to Zoroastrianism, it involves both rewards for the righteous and punishment for the wicked, culminating in the restoration of the world and the eternal reign of God. In both traditions, this judgment serves as a cosmic turning point, leading to the defeat of evil and the establishment of a world governed by divine order and peace.

5. The Lasting Impact of Zoroastrian Apocalypticism on Judaism and Christianity

The Zoroastrian apocalyptic framework—with its concepts of a cosmic struggle, final judgment, resurrection of the dead, and renewal of the world—left a profound and lasting impact on the development of Jewish and Christian eschatology. The Persian period, during which the Jews were under Achaemenid rule, provided fertile ground for the exchange of religious ideas, and the apocalyptic themes found in Second Temple Judaism and early Christianity reflect a significant degree of interaction with Zoroastrian thought.

A. Jewish Apocalypticism and Zoroastrian Influence

During the Second Temple period, Jewish apocalyptic literature flourished, particularly in response to foreign oppression and the hope for divine intervention. Many of the key features of Jewish apocalyptic thought, such as the expectation of a Messiah, the resurrection of the dead, and the final judgment, bear the imprint of Persian influence.

- The Book of Daniel: Written during a time of Jewish persecution, the Book of Daniel is a prime example of Jewish apocalyptic literature that incorporates ideas of a cosmic battle between good and evil, angelic warfare, and the coming of a divine kingdom. The influence of Persian thought is evident in the dualistic structure of Daniel's visions, where the forces of light and darkness are locked in a struggle that will culminate in the triumph of God's kingdom.

- The Dead Sea Scrolls: The Qumran community also held to an apocalyptic worldview that emphasized the final battle between the sons of light and the sons of darkness, mirroring Zoroastrian cosmic dualism. This apocalyptic expectation of a Messianic deliverer and the eventual triumph of good over evil reflects the broader influence of Persian religious concepts on Jewish thought during this period.

B. Christian Eschatology and Zoroastrian Parallels

In early Christian eschatology, the influence of Zoroastrianism can be seen in the way Christian thinkers conceptualized the end times and the second coming of Christ. The themes of resurrection, judgment, and the final defeat of Satan all resonate with Zoroastrian apocalyptic beliefs.

- The Revelation of John: The Book of Revelation, with its vivid imagery of a final battle between the forces of good and evil, angelic participation in the cosmic conflict, and the establishment of a new heaven and new earth, bears clear similarities to Zoroastrian apocalypticism. The final victory of Christ and the establishment of God's eternal kingdom echoes the Zoroastrian vision of the Saoshyant's triumph and the Frashokereti.

- Paul's Letters: The apostle Paul frequently speaks of the resurrection of the dead and the return of Christ to bring about the final judgment and renewal of the world. His emphasis on the victory over death and sin reflects a Zoroastrian-like dualism, where good will ultimately overcome evil in a cosmic sense.

Persian Influence on Jewish and Christian Apocalypticism

The Persian period, and specifically the rise of Zoroastrianism, had a profound impact on the development of Jewish and Christian apocalyptic thought. Zoroastrian ideas about the cosmic struggle between good and evil, the resurrection of the dead, the final judgment, and the renewal of the world resonated deeply with Jewish and Christian thinkers, shaping the way they envisioned the end times and the ultimate triumph of God.

For both Jews and Christians, the apocalyptic hope for a future Messianic deliverer, the destruction of the forces of evil, and the establishment of a new, eternal kingdom where righteousness prevails became central to their religious worldviews. The influence of Zoroastrianism can be seen in many of the key features of Jewish and Christian apocalyptic literature, particularly in texts like Daniel and Revelation.

As history moved forward, the apocalyptic vision of a world renewed by God and the ultimate defeat of evil would continue to inspire Jewish messianic movements and

Christian eschatology, leaving a legacy of hope and divine justice that echoes through both traditions to this day.

The Prophetic Undertones of the Medo-Persian Empire

In Nebuchadnezzar's dream and Daniel's visions, the Medo-Persian Empire holds a unique prophetic significance. Represented by the chest and arms of silver in the great statue (Daniel 2:31-45) and by the ram with two horns in Daniel 8:3-4, the Medo-Persian Empire emerges as a kingdom that plays a pivotal role in the unfolding of God's plan for history. Although portrayed as a powerful and expansive empire, it is one that ultimately serves as a transitional kingdom in the biblical prophetic narrative, setting the stage for the later rise of Greece and, more importantly, the eventual establishment of God's eternal kingdom.

This chapter delves into the prophetic significance of the Medo-Persian Empire, exploring its role within the context of biblical prophecy and the broader eschatological narrative. The rise and eventual fall of the Medo-Persian Empire are presented not only as historical events but as part of God's sovereign plan, which foreshadows the ultimate establishment of His kingdom that will transcend all earthly powers.

1. The Silver Chest and Arms in Nebuchadnezzar's Dream

In Daniel 2, the Medo-Persian Empire is symbolized by the chest and arms of silver in Nebuchadnezzar's dream. As the second empire in the succession of world powers represented by the statue, Medo-Persia follows the Babylonian Empire and precedes the Greek Empire (symbolized by the belly and thighs of bronze).

A. Silver as a Symbol of Inferiority and Strength

The choice of silver to represent the Medo-Persian Empire carries significant symbolic meaning. While silver is a precious metal, it is less valuable than gold, which was used to symbolize Babylon (the head of gold). This difference in the value of the metals reflects the relative inferiority of Medo-Persia compared to Babylon in terms of splendor and wealth. However, the use of silver also emphasizes the strength and durability of the Medo-Persian Empire, particularly its ability to dominate vast territories and maintain order.

- Daniel 2:39: "After you, another kingdom will arise, inferior to yours. Next, a third kingdom, one of bronze, will rule over the whole earth."

This inferiority is not a matter of political power or military might, as the Medo-Persian Empire was vast and formidable. Rather, it refers to the glory and prestige associated with the empires. Babylon, with its grandeur and monumental architecture, is viewed as more majestic, whereas

Medo-Persia is seen as a strong but transitional empire, one that prepares the way for later developments in the biblical narrative.

B. The Duality of the Empire: Medes and Persians

The representation of the Medo-Persian Empire as having two arms of silver in Nebuchadnezzar's dream is significant because it reflects the dual nature of the empire—comprising two distinct but united powers, the Medes and the Persians. The Medes initially held political dominance, but the Persians, under Cyrus the Great, eventually became the more prominent force within the empire.

- Two Arms as Duality: The two arms of the statue symbolize the partnership between the Medes and Persians, though they were eventually unified under Persian leadership. This duality highlights the diverse origins of the empire but also its unified strength in conquest and governance.

2. The Ram with Two Horns in Daniel's Vision

In Daniel 8, the Medo-Persian Empire is depicted as a ram with two horns in a vision given to Daniel. This symbolic imagery provides further prophetic insights into the empire's power and its role in God's unfolding plan.

A. The Two Horns: The Medes and the Persians

The two horns of the ram, which represent the Medes and the Persians, are described as being of different sizes, with one horn larger than the other. This reflects the dominance of the Persian Empire over the Medes within the dual monarchy.

- Daniel 8:3: "I looked up, and there before me was a ram with two horns, standing beside the canal, and the horns were long. One of the horns was longer than the other but grew up later."

This imagery emphasizes the asymmetry between the Medes and Persians in terms of political power, with Persia eventually surpassing Media in prominence, especially under the leadership of Cyrus the Great.

B. The Ram's Power and Expansion

The ram in Daniel's vision is described as charging westward, northward, and southward, conquering all that stood in its way. This imagery corresponds to the military conquests of the Medo-Persian Empire, which expanded across a vast territory that included Babylon, Egypt, Lydia, and many other regions.

- Daniel 8:4: "I watched the ram as it charged toward the west and the north and the south. No animal could stand against it, and none could rescue from its power. It did as it pleased and became great."

This description highlights the unmatched power of the Medo-Persian Empire during its height, as no other kingdom was able to resist its advance. The empire's ability to dominate and subjugate neighboring territories is portrayed as part of God's sovereign plan for the rise and fall of nations.

However, the prophecy also indicates that the ram's dominance is temporary, as the next phase of history will see the rise of Greece (symbolized by the goat with a prominent horn), which will overthrow Medo-Persia.

3. Prophetic Fulfillment: The Fall of Babylon and Cyrus the Great

The prophetic significance of the Medo-Persian Empire is most clearly seen in its role in the fall of Babylon and the subsequent restoration of the Jewish people to their homeland. This pivotal event, prophesied by Isaiah, Jeremiah, and Daniel, highlights the sovereignty of God over the rise and fall of empires and His ability to use pagan rulers like Cyrus to accomplish His divine purposes.

A. The Fall of Babylon and Cyrus as God's Instrument

The fall of Babylon to the Medo-Persians in 539 BCE, under the leadership of Cyrus the Great, is one of the most significant fulfillments of biblical prophecy. Both Isaiah and Jeremiah had foretold Babylon's downfall as part of God's judgment on the empire for its arrogance and oppression.

- Isaiah 45:1: "This is what the Lord says to his anointed, to Cyrus, whose right hand I take hold of to subdue nations before him and to strip kings of their armor, to open doors before him so that gates will not be shut."

In this passage, Cyrus is referred to as God's anointed (Hebrew: mashiach), a term usually reserved for the kings of Israel. By using this term for a pagan ruler, the prophecy emphasizes God's sovereignty over all nations and His ability to use foreign powers to fulfill His purposes.

B. The Decree of Cyrus and the Restoration of the Jews

Cyrus' conquest of Babylon also fulfilled Jeremiah's prophecy that after seventy years of exile, the Jewish people would be allowed to return to their homeland and rebuild the Temple in Jerusalem.

- Ezra 1:1-2: "In the first year of Cyrus king of Persia, in order to fulfill the word of the Lord spoken by Jeremiah, the Lord moved the heart of Cyrus king of Persia to make a proclamation throughout his realm and also to put it in writing: 'This is what Cyrus king of Persia says: The Lord, the God of heaven, has given me all the kingdoms of the earth and he has appointed me to build a temple for him at Jerusalem in Judah.'"

Cyrus' decree allowed the Jewish exiles to return to Jerusalem and begin the process of rebuilding the Second Temple. This event marked a new chapter in Jewish history and signified the faithfulness of God in fulfilling His promises. The Medo-Persian Empire thus served as an instrument of divine restoration, allowing the Jewish people to reestablish their religious practices and identity in their homeland.

4. The Medo-Persian Empire's Role in the Larger Prophetic Narrative

Although the Medo-Persian Empire is significant in biblical prophecy, it is ultimately presented as a transitional kingdom—one that serves as part of the larger eschatological narrative leading to the coming of God's eternal kingdom. In Daniel's vision, the succession of empires (Babylon, Medo-Persia, Greece, and Rome) is meant to illustrate the temporary nature of human kingdoms, which will eventually be replaced by the kingdom of God.

A. Temporary but Significant

The Medo-Persian Empire, despite its power and accomplishments, is portrayed as temporary in the grand scheme of history. It is followed by the rise of Greece, symbolized by the goat with the prominent horn in Daniel 8, which ultimately defeats the ram and takes its place as the dominant world power.

- Daniel 8:7: "I saw him [the goat] attack the ram furiously, striking the ram and shattering its two horns. The ram was powerless to stand against him; the goat knocked him to the ground and trampled on him, and none could rescue the ram from his power."

This passage signifies the end of the Medo-Persian Empire and the beginning of the Hellenistic period under Alexander the Great. Despite its initial power and dominance, Medo-Persia is overthrown in accordance with God's plan, showing that no earthly empire, no matter how strong, can stand forever.

B. Foreshadowing the Eternal Kingdom of God

The prophetic narrative of the Medo-Persian Empire, along with the other kingdoms in Daniel's visions, ultimately points to the coming of God's eternal kingdom, which will supersede all human empires.

- Daniel 2:44: "In the time of those kings, the God of heaven will set up a kingdom that will never be destroyed, nor will it be left to another people. It will crush all those kingdoms and bring them to an end, but it will itself endure forever."

The rise and fall of the Medo-Persian Empire serve as a reminder that human kingdoms are temporary, and that the kingdom of God—symbolized by the stone cut without hands—is the only kingdom that will endure forever. In this sense, the Medo-Persian Empire, like the other kingdoms in Daniel's prophecy, foreshadows the ultimate establishment of God's reign over all the earth.

The Prophetic Role of the Medo-Persian Empire

The Medo-Persian Empire, represented by the silver chest and arms in Nebuchadnezzar's dream and the ram with two horns in Daniel's vision, plays a crucial role in the prophetic narrative of the Bible. Although powerful and expansive, it is ultimately a transitional empire that serves to fulfill God's purposes, particularly in relation to the fall of Babylon and the restoration of the Jewish people.

The Medo-Persian Empire's significance lies not only in its military and political achievements but also in its role as a divinely appointed instrument in the unfolding of salvation history. Through the conquest of Babylon and the decree of Cyrus the Great, the empire paved the way for the rebuilding of the Temple and the restoration of Israel, both of which are central to the biblical vision of God's faithfulness and His ultimate plan for the world.

However, like all human kingdoms, the Medo-Persian Empire is portrayed as temporary in the prophetic timeline. Its rise and fall, along with the other empires in Daniel's visions, serve as a reminder that only God's kingdom is eternal, and that all earthly powers will eventually give way to the divine reign of God.

THE BRONZE BELLY AND THIGHS – GREECE

In Nebuchadnezzar's dream, described in Daniel 2:31-45, the bronze belly and thighs of the statue symbolize the Greek Empire, which succeeded the Medo-Persian Empire. As the third kingdom in the succession of empires revealed in this prophetic vision, Greece, under the leadership of Alexander the Great, played a critical role in shaping the ancient world, both politically and culturally. The Greek Empire's influence extended far beyond military conquest, as the spread of Hellenism reshaped the Mediterranean and Near Eastern worlds, leaving a lasting legacy on language, philosophy, and religion.

This chapter explores the prophetic significance of the bronze kingdom and the role of Alexander the Great in establishing a vast empire that introduced Greek culture, language, and thought to a broad swath of the world. We will also examine how the spread of Hellenism had profound effects on Jewish thought and later on Christianity, laying the groundwork for the cultural and religious interactions that would shape both the Jewish and Christian apocalyptic visions.

1. Alexander the Great and the Rise of the Greek Empire

The Greek Empire, symbolized by the bronze belly and thighs in Nebuchadnezzar's dream, rose to prominence under the leadership of Alexander the Great in the 4th century BCE. Alexander's conquests were unparalleled in their speed and scope, as he established one of the largest empires in the ancient world, stretching from Greece in the west to India in the east.

A. Alexander's Conquests

Alexander III of Macedon, commonly known as Alexander the Great, was born in 356 BCE and ascended to the throne of Macedon in 336 BCE after the assassination of his father, King Philip II. Almost immediately, Alexander embarked on a series of military campaigns that would transform the political landscape of the ancient world.

- The Defeat of Persia: One of Alexander's primary goals was to conquer the Persian Empire, which had long been the dominant power in the Near East. In a series of decisive battles, including the Battle of Issus (333 BCE) and the Battle of Gaugamela (331 BCE), Alexander defeated Darius III, the last king of the Achaemenid Empire, bringing an end to the Medo-Persian Empire.

- Expansion into Egypt and Asia: After defeating Persia, Alexander continued his conquests, moving south into Egypt, where he was welcomed as a liberator and proclaimed pharaoh. He founded the city of Alexandria, which would become a major center of Hellenistic culture. From Egypt, Alexander moved east, conquering Babylonia, Persia, and eventually pushing into India, where his army halted after a series of hard-fought battles.

By the time of his death in 323 BCE at the age of 32, Alexander had created an empire that stretched from the Balkans to the Punjab, and he had brought the influence of Greek culture and philosophy to lands far beyond the Greek homeland.

B. The Spread of Hellenism

While Alexander's military conquests were impressive, his most lasting legacy was the spread of Hellenism—the dissemination of Greek language, culture, and ideas—across the territories he conquered. This process, known as Hellenization, had profound effects on the ancient world, particularly in the regions of the Near East, Egypt, and Judea.

- Hellenistic Culture: Hellenism combined elements of Greek culture with local traditions, creating a unique blend of art, philosophy, religion, and science that influenced the entire Mediterranean world. Greek became the lingua franca of the eastern Mediterranean, facilitating communication and the spread of ideas across diverse cultures.

- Philosophical Influence: Greek philosophy, particularly the teachings of Plato, Aristotle, and the Stoics, spread widely during this period. These philosophical schools explored questions of ethics, metaphysics, and the nature of the divine, laying the intellectual groundwork for later religious developments, including early Christian theology.

- Impact on Jewish Thought: In Judea, the influence of Greek culture created both opportunities for engagement with Hellenism and tensions between traditional Jewish religious practices and the new cultural influences. The Septuagint, the Greek translation of the Hebrew Scriptures, was produced during this period, making Jewish religious texts accessible to the broader Hellenistic world.

Hellenism thus left an indelible mark on the regions that Alexander conquered, shaping the religious and cultural environment in which both Judaism and Christianity would later develop.

2. The Prophetic Symbolism of Bronze

In Nebuchadnezzar's dream, the bronze belly and thighs of the statue symbolize the Greek Empire. The choice of bronze as the metal representing Greece is significant both in terms of its symbolic meaning and its historical context. Bronze, being stronger than gold or silver, represents a kingdom characterized by military strength and durability, qualities that were evident in the Greek Empire's rapid expansion and far-reaching influence.

A. Bronze as a Symbol of Strength and Warfare

In the ancient world, bronze was widely used in the production of weapons and armor, making it a fitting symbol for the Greek Empire, which was known for its military innovations and effectiveness in battle. Alexander's army was highly disciplined and made use of advanced tactics, including the phalanx formation, which allowed his forces to defeat much larger armies, such as those of the Persian Empire.

- Bronze Weapons: The Greek hoplites (heavily armed soldiers) were equipped with bronze shields and spears, which were critical to their success on the battlefield. The use of bronze for weapons and armor gave the Greek army a technological advantage, symbolizing the strength and resilience of the Greek Empire.

- Military Expansion: The bronze imagery also reflects the expansionist nature of the Greek Empire under Alexander, who sought to conquer and unite a vast territory under Greek control. His empire became known not only for its military conquests but also for the cultural and intellectual achievements that followed in the wake of his victories.

B. Bronze as a Transitional Kingdom

While bronze is stronger than gold or silver, it is less valuable, symbolizing the transitory nature of the Greek Empire in comparison to earlier empires. Greece, while powerful and influential, was ultimately a temporary kingdom in the succession of empires described in Daniel's vision. After Alexander's death, the Greek Empire quickly fractured into smaller Hellenistic kingdoms, which were eventually absorbed into the Roman Empire, symbolized by the legs of iron in Nebuchadnezzar's dream.

- Daniel 2:39: "Next, a third kingdom, one of bronze, will rule over the whole earth."

The bronze kingdom is presented as a global power, one that would extend its influence across the known world, but it would eventually give way to a stronger empire, symbolized by iron. This reflects the historical reality of the Greek Empire's fragmentation after Alexander's death and the eventual rise of Rome as the dominant power in the Mediterranean world.

3. The Hellenistic Kingdoms and Their Impact on the Jewish World

After Alexander's death in 323 BCE, his empire was divided among his generals, known as the Diadochi, who established a series of Hellenistic kingdoms that continued to spread Greek culture and influence throughout the ancient world. The most significant of these kingdoms were the Ptolemaic Kingdom in Egypt and the Seleucid Kingdom in Syria. These kingdoms played a crucial role in the history of Judea and had a profound impact on the development of Jewish thought during the Second Temple period.

A. The Ptolemies and the Seleucids

The division of Alexander's empire among the Diadochi led to a long period of rivalry between the Ptolemaic and Seleucid dynasties, both of which sought control over Judea. Initially, Judea fell under the control of the Ptolemies, but after the Battle of Panium in 200 BCE, it was annexed by the Seleucids.

- Ptolemaic Rule: Under the Ptolemies, Judea experienced a period of relative peace, with Greek culture gradually influencing Jewish society. The production of the Septuagint, the Greek translation of the Hebrew Scriptures, during this period, reflects the integration of Jewish religious life into the broader Hellenistic world.

- Seleucid Rule: The Seleucid rulers, particularly Antiochus IV Epiphanes, sought to impose Hellenistic religion and culture more forcefully on the Jewish population. Antiochus' attempts to Hellenize Judea, including the desecration of the Temple in Jerusalem and the prohibition of Jewish religious practices, sparked the Maccabean Revolt in 167 BCE.

B. The Maccabean

Revolt and Jewish Resistance to Hellenism

The Maccabean Revolt was a direct response to the oppressive policies of Antiochus IV Epiphanes and the forced Hellenization of the Jewish people. Led by Judas Maccabeus and his brothers, the revolt succeeded in expelling the Seleucid forces from Judea and rededicating the Temple in Jerusalem in 164 BCE, an event commemorated by the Jewish festival of Hanukkah.

- Resistance to Hellenism: While many Jews embraced elements of Greek culture, others, particularly the Hasidim (the pious ones), strongly resisted Hellenistic influences, viewing them as a threat to Jewish identity and religious practice. The conflict between Hellenizers and traditionalists played a central role in the Maccabean Revolt and the subsequent establishment of the Hasmonean dynasty.

- Religious Implications: The Maccabean Revolt had profound implications for Jewish religious thought, particularly in relation to apocalyptic expectations. The persecution suffered under Antiochus IV and the eventual victory of the Maccabees reinforced the belief in divine intervention and the coming of a Messianic age, themes that would later influence Christian eschatology.

4. The Prophetic Role of the Greek Empire in the Biblical Narrative

The rise and fall of the Greek Empire, as depicted in Daniel's prophetic vision, serves as a crucial stage in the unfolding of God's plan for human history. While Greece, symbolized by the bronze belly and thighs, was a powerful and influential kingdom, it was ultimately a transitory empire that gave way to the next phase in the prophetic timeline—the rise of Rome, symbolized by the legs of iron.

A. The Temporary Nature of Human Kingdoms

The Greek Empire's rise to power and its eventual fragmentation after Alexander's death highlight the temporary nature of human kingdoms. Despite its military strength and cultural achievements, Greece, like the empires that preceded it (Babylon and Medo-Persia), was destined to fall, emphasizing the transience of earthly power in contrast to the eternal kingdom of God.

- Daniel 2:44: "In the time of those kings, the God of heaven will set up a kingdom that will never be destroyed, nor will it be left to another people. It will crush all those kingdoms and bring them to an end, but it will itself endure forever."

The prophetic narrative of the succession of empires in Daniel ultimately points to the coming of God's eternal kingdom, which will replace all earthly powers. The bronze kingdom of Greece, despite its strength, is merely one phase in this larger eschatological vision.

B. The Role of Hellenism in Preparing the Way for the Gospel

While the Greek Empire was ultimately temporary, the spread of Hellenism played a crucial role in preparing the ancient world for the spread of the gospel. The widespread use of the Greek language and the dissemination of Greek ideas created a common cultural and intellectual framework that facilitated the communication of the Christian message in the New Testament period.

- Koine Greek: The New Testament was written in Koine Greek, the common language of the eastern Mediterranean world, allowing the message of Jesus Christ to be spread quickly and effectively across diverse regions.

- Philosophical Engagement: Early Christian thinkers engaged with Greek philosophy, particularly the ideas of Plato and Stoicism, as they developed Christian theology. The Hellenistic worldview, with its emphasis on the immortality of the soul and the nature of the divine, provided a conceptual framework for the articulation of Christian doctrines about resurrection and the kingdom of God.

The Bronze Kingdom and Its Prophetic Role

The Greek Empire, symbolized by the bronze belly and thighs in Nebuchadnezzar's dream, played a pivotal role in the unfolding of biblical prophecy. Under the leadership of Alexander the Great, the Greek Empire expanded rapidly, spreading Hellenistic culture and shaping the ancient world in profound ways. Yet, despite its strength and influence, the Greek Empire was ultimately a temporary kingdom that prepared the way for the rise of Rome and the eventual fulfillment of God's eschatological plan.

The prophetic symbolism of bronze reflects both the strength and transitory nature of the Greek Empire. While Greece ruled over much of the known world, it was destined to give way to the legs of iron—the Roman Empire—which would in turn be replaced by the eternal kingdom of God.

Greece's Significance in Nebuchadnezzar's Dream

In Nebuchadnezzar's dream (Daniel 2:31-45), the Greek Empire is symbolized by the bronze belly and thighs of the great statue. Greece's significance in this vision lies not only in its role as a powerful empire that succeeded the Medo-Persian Empire but also in its unique contribution to the broader biblical prophetic narrative. Greece represents the third of the four great world empires, followed by the Roman Empire (symbolized by the legs of iron) and ultimately succeeded by the eternal kingdom of God.

This chapter explores the symbolic meaning of Greece in Nebuchadnezzar's dream and its role in shaping the historical and spiritual landscape of the ancient world. Through Alexander the Great's conquests and the subsequent spread of Hellenistic culture, Greece played a critical part in preparing the world for the coming of Christ and the spread of the gospel. We will also examine how Greece fits into the overall prophetic narrative, pointing to the transient nature of human kingdoms and the ultimate triumph of God's eternal kingdom.

1. Greece as the Bronze Belly and Thighs in Nebuchadnezzar's Dream

The image of the bronze belly and thighs in Nebuchadnezzar's dream represents the Greek Empire—a powerful and expansive kingdom that followed the Medo-Persian Empire. In Daniel's interpretation of the dream, Greece is identified as the third kingdom in the sequence of four, which also includes Babylon (gold) and Medo-Persia (silver).

A. The Significance of Bronze

The choice of bronze to represent Greece is significant for several reasons. In the ancient world, bronze was associated with strength and military power, particularly in the production of weapons and armor. The use of bronze to symbolize Greece emphasizes the military might of the Greek Empire, which under Alexander the Great became one of the most formidable forces in the ancient world.

- Bronze as a Strong Metal: Bronze is stronger than gold or silver, symbolizing the military strength of Greece compared to its predecessors. The Greek armies, particularly under Alexander, were known for their advanced tactics, discipline, and effective use of bronze weapons, such as spears, shields, and armor.

- The Bronze Age Connection: The symbolism of bronze also connects Greece to the Bronze Age, a period in which bronze was widely used for tools and weapons. This historical connection reinforces the idea of Greece as a civilization that, through its military prowess, dominated large parts of the known world.

B. The Belly and Thighs: A Divided Empire

The belly and thighs of the statue represent the Greek Empire, but they also foreshadow the division of the empire following Alexander's death. After his untimely death in 323 BCE, the vast Greek Empire was divided among his generals, known as the Diadochi, leading to the formation of several Hellenistic kingdoms. The imagery of the statue, with the bronze belly giving way to the two thighs, reflects this fracturing of the empire.

- Division of the Greek Empire: The Greek Empire was divided into multiple regions, with the most prominent being the Ptolemaic Kingdom in Egypt and the Seleucid Kingdom in Syria. This division weakened the empire and set the stage for the rise of the Roman Empire.

This division is significant in the prophetic timeline, as it underscores the transitory nature of human kingdoms. Despite its strength and influence, the Greek Empire could not maintain its unity, and its fragmentation paved the way for the next great empire—Rome.

2. Alexander the Great's Conquests and the Spread of Hellenism

The Greek Empire's significance in Nebuchadnezzar's dream cannot be understood apart from the figure of Alexander the Great, whose military conquests transformed the political and cultural landscape of the ancient world. Under Alexander's leadership, the Greek Empire expanded rapidly, conquering Persia, Egypt, and large portions of Asia Minor and India.

A. The Military Expansion of the Greek Empire

Alexander's conquests were unparalleled in their scope and speed. In just over a decade, he established one of the largest empires the world had ever seen, stretching from Greece to the Indus Valley. His victories over the Persian Empire, particularly the decisive battles of Issus and Gaugamela, brought an end to Medo-Persian dominance and established Greece as the leading power in the ancient world.

- Conquest of Persia: Alexander's victory over the Achaemenid Empire not only fulfilled the prophetic vision of Greece's rise but also symbolized the transition from the silver kingdom (Medo-Persia) to the bronze kingdom (Greece) in the prophetic timeline. The fall of Persia to Greece was a pivotal moment in the history of the ancient Near East, marking the end of Persian control over Babylonia, Egypt, and Asia Minor.

- Cultural Expansion: In addition to his military conquests, Alexander sought to spread Greek culture (Hellenism) throughout the territories he conquered. He founded numerous cities, most notably Alexandria in Egypt, which became centers of Greek learning, art, and philosophy. This cultural expansion had a lasting impact on the ancient world and played a key role in the later development of Jewish and Christian thought.

B. The Spread of Hellenism

One of the most significant aspects of Alexander's legacy was the spread of Hellenism—the diffusion of Greek language, culture, and philosophy across the territories he conquered. This process, known as Hellenization, had profound effects on the political and cultural life of the ancient world.

- Greek Language: Greek became the lingua franca of the eastern Mediterranean, facilitating communication and the exchange of ideas across a wide geographic region. This linguistic unity played a crucial role in the spread of Christianity, as the New Testament was written in Koine Greek, making the message of the gospel accessible to a broad audience.

- Philosophical Influence: The spread of Greek philosophy, particularly the ideas of Plato and Aristotle, influenced both Jewish and Christian thought. Greek concepts of ethics, metaphysics, and the nature of the divine provided a philosophical framework that early Christian theologians would later engage with as they developed Christian doctrine.

- Impact on Judaism: The Hellenistic period also had a significant impact on Jewish life. The translation of the

Hebrew Scriptures into Greek (the Septuagint) made Jewish religious texts accessible to the broader Greek-speaking world. At the same time, the encounter with Greek culture created tensions between traditional Jewish practices and the Hellenizing influences of the surrounding culture, leading to movements such as the Maccabean Revolt.

3. The Greek Empire in the Broader Prophetic Narrative

In Nebuchadnezzar's dream, the bronze kingdom of Greece is presented as a transitory phase in the broader prophetic narrative. While Greece played a significant role in shaping the ancient world, it was ultimately a temporary kingdom that would be succeeded by the Roman Empire (symbolized by the legs of iron) and eventually by the eternal kingdom of God.

A. The Temporary Nature of the Greek Empire

The bronze belly and thighs of the statue represent the strength and dominance of the Greek Empire, but they also highlight the impermanence of human kingdoms. Despite its military power and cultural influence, Greece, like the empires that came before it, was destined to fall.

- Daniel 2:39: "Next, a third kingdom, one of bronze, will rule over the whole earth."

Although Greece was prophesied to rule over the known world, its rule was not eternal. After Alexander's death, the empire fractured into several Hellenistic kingdoms, which were eventually absorbed by the Roman Empire. This fragmentation underscores the transience of human power and sets the stage for the rise of Rome, symbolized by the legs of iron in the statue.

B. Greece's Role in Preparing for the Coming of Christ

Despite its temporary nature, the Greek Empire played a crucial role in preparing the ancient world for the coming of Christ and the spread of the gospel. The widespread use of Greek language, the philosophical discourse that emerged from Greek culture, and the political stability brought by Hellenistic kingdoms all contributed to creating a world that was ready for the message of salvation.

- Koine Greek and the New Testament: The use of Koine Greek as the common language of the eastern Mediterranean allowed the New Testament writings to reach a broad audience, facilitating the rapid spread of Christianity across the Roman Empire.

- Hellenistic Influence on Theology: Greek philosophical ideas about ethics, the nature of the soul, and the divine played a significant role in shaping early Christian thought.

The engagement with Greek philosophy allowed Christian theologians to articulate their faith in a way that was intellectually compelling to the Hellenistic world.

Greece's Prophetic Significance in Nebuchadnezzar's Dream

The Greek Empire, symbolized by the bronze belly and thighs in Nebuchadnezzar's dream, holds a unique place in the prophetic timeline. Under the leadership of Alexander the Great, Greece became a powerful empire that spread Hellenistic culture across vast territories. However, despite its strength and influence, the Greek Empire was ultimately a transitory kingdom, destined to be replaced by the Roman Empire and eventually by the eternal kingdom of God.

The symbolism of bronze reflects both the military strength of Greece and the temporary nature of its rule. As part of the broader prophetic narrative, the rise and fall of the Greek Empire underscore the transience of human kingdoms and point to the coming of God's eternal kingdom, which will endure forever.

Connection Between the Crusades and the Resurgence of Greek Ideas Through Byzantine Influences

The Crusades, a series of religiously motivated military campaigns that took place between the 11th and 13th centuries, were significant not only for their impact on the political and religious dynamics of the medieval world but also for their role in the resurgence of Greek ideas in the West. This revival of classical Greek thought was largely facilitated by the Byzantine Empire, which served as the custodian of Greek culture and philosophy after the fall of the Western Roman Empire. The interaction between the Latin West and the Byzantine East during the Crusades led to a renewed interest in Greek philosophy, science, and theology in Europe.

This chapter explores the connection between the Crusades and the resurgence of Greek ideas through the influence of the Byzantine Empire. We will examine how the intellectual heritage of ancient Greece, preserved by Byzantine scholars, was transmitted to the Latin West during the Crusades and how this intellectual exchange contributed to the Renaissance and the development of Christian theology in medieval Europe.

1. The Byzantine Empire as the Custodian of Greek Ideas

After the fall of the Western Roman Empire in the 5th century CE, the Byzantine Empire (Eastern Roman Empire) continued to thrive for another millennium, with its capital in Constantinople. The Byzantines preserved and transmitted the rich intellectual heritage of the Greeks, including the works of Plato, Aristotle, and other classical philosophers. Unlike the Latin West, which experienced a period of intellectual stagnation during the early Middle Ages, the Byzantine Empire maintained a flourishing tradition of scholarship and learning, particularly in the fields of philosophy, theology, science, and medicine.

A. Preservation of Classical Greek Texts

The Byzantines were instrumental in preserving classical Greek texts that had been largely lost or neglected in the West. These texts included the works of major Greek philosophers such as Plato, Aristotle, Hippocrates, and Galen, as well as important theological writings by the Church Fathers, many of whom were deeply influenced by Greek thought.

- Byzantine Libraries and Scholars: The libraries of Constantinople housed extensive collections of classical Greek manuscripts, which were copied, studied, and taught by Byzantine scholars. Intellectual centers such as the University of Constantinople were dedicated to the study of Greek philosophy, rhetoric, and law.

- Greek Thought in Christian Theology: Theologians in the Byzantine Empire, such as Gregory of Nazianzus, Basil the Great, and John of Damascus, integrated Greek philosophical concepts into Christian theology, particularly in the areas of metaphysics, ethics, and Christology. This synthesis of Greek philosophy with Christian thought was a hallmark of Byzantine intellectual life and would later influence Scholasticism in the Latin West.

B. The Decline of Learning in the West

In contrast to the Byzantine East, the Latin West experienced a significant decline in intellectual life after the fall of the Western Roman Empire. The loss of access to classical Greek texts, combined with the political instability of the early Middle Ages, resulted in the deterioration of classical learning in Europe. Latin scholars in the West had limited access to the works of Greek philosophers, and much of Greek science and philosophy was unknown or poorly understood.

- Monastic Preservation of Knowledge: While some classical knowledge was preserved in monastic communities in Western Europe, these communities primarily focused on preserving Latin texts rather than Greek ones. As a result, much of the intellectual heritage of the Greeks remained inaccessible to Latin scholars until the later Middle Ages.

2. The Crusades and Cultural Exchange

The Crusades brought the Latin West into direct contact with the Byzantine Empire and the Islamic world, both of which had preserved and built upon the intellectual traditions of ancient Greece. Although the primary motivation for the Crusades was religious—to reclaim the Holy Land from Muslim control—the Crusaders' encounters with the Byzantines and Muslims facilitated a broader cultural and intellectual exchange.

A. The First Crusade and Byzantine-Latin Relations

During the First Crusade (1096–1099), the Byzantine Empire played a key role in facilitating the Crusaders' journey to the Holy Land. Alexios I Komnenos, the Byzantine emperor, provided military and logistical support to the Crusaders, who had traveled from Western Europe to assist the Byzantines in their conflict with the Seljuk Turks. While the relationship between the Crusaders and the Byzantines was often marked by mutual suspicion and political tension, the Crusades opened up new avenues for cultural interaction between the Latin West and the Byzantine East.

- Exchange of Knowledge: As the Crusaders passed through Byzantine territory, they were exposed to Greek culture and learning. Many Latin scholars, soldiers, and clergy encountered the rich intellectual traditions of the Byzantine Empire for the first time, sparking a renewed interest in Greek philosophy and science.

- Tensions Between East and West: Despite the exchange of knowledge, tensions between the Eastern Orthodox Church and the Roman Catholic Church deepened during the Crusades, particularly after the sacking of Constantinople by the Fourth Crusade in 1204. Nevertheless, the Crusades facilitated a cultural bridge that allowed for the transmission of Greek ideas to the West.

B. The Role of Greek Manuscripts in the Crusader States

The establishment of Crusader states in the Holy Land (such as the Kingdom of Jerusalem) also contributed to the exchange of knowledge between the Latin West and the Byzantine East. Crusaders and Latin settlers in these regions had access to Byzantine scholars and manuscripts, many of which were brought to the West through these interactions.

- Greek Manuscripts and Latin Scholars: As Latin scholars gained access to Greek manuscripts, they began translating these works into Latin, making them accessible to a broader audience in Western Europe. This process of translation laid the foundation for the revival of Greek philosophy and science in the West during the later Middle Ages.

- Rediscovery of Aristotle: One of the most significant outcomes of this cultural exchange was the rediscovery of Aristotle's works. Aristotle's metaphysics, logic, and natural philosophy had a profound impact on the development of Scholasticism, the dominant intellectual movement in medieval Europe. The translations of Aristotle's works from

Greek (and sometimes from Arabic translations) into Latin provided the intellectual tools that later scholars such as Thomas Aquinas would use to develop a systematic Christian theology.

3. The Intellectual Revival in the West: The Influence of Greek Ideas

The Crusades played a pivotal role in facilitating the revival of Greek philosophy and science in the Latin West. The transmission of Greek texts through Byzantine and Islamic intermediaries helped to ignite a broader intellectual movement in medieval Europe that culminated in the Renaissance and the rise of Scholasticism.

A. The Rise of Scholasticism

One of the most important outcomes of the resurgence of Greek ideas in the West was the development of Scholasticism, an intellectual movement that sought to reconcile Christian theology with Greek philosophy, particularly the works of Aristotle. Scholasticism dominated the medieval universities and laid the foundations for the later development of modern science and philosophy.

- Thomas Aquinas and Aristotle: One of the most influential Scholastic thinkers was Thomas Aquinas (1225–1274), whose works integrated Aristotelian philosophy with Christian doctrine. Aquinas's use of Aristotle's metaphysics and logic to explain Christian theological concepts, such as the existence of God, the nature of the soul, and natural law, became foundational to Christian thought in the West.

- Theological Debates: The reintroduction of Greek philosophical ideas sparked significant debates within the medieval Church. Some theologians embraced the rationalism of Aristotle, while others viewed Greek philosophy as a potential threat to Christian doctrine. These debates eventually led to the formulation of new approaches to understanding faith and reason, a central theme in medieval and Renaissance philosophy.

B. The Renaissance and the Revival of Classical Learning

The Renaissance (14th–17th centuries), often described as a rebirth of classical learning, was deeply influenced by the resurgence of Greek ideas that had been transmitted through Byzantine and Islamic intermediaries. Greek philosophy, science, and art experienced a revival in the Italian city-states, where scholars sought to recover and study the works of the ancient Greeks.

- Humanism and Greek Philosophy: The Renaissance humanists looked to the works of Greek philosophers for inspiration in their efforts to create a new intellectual and artistic culture. Plato's philosophy, in particular, experienced a revival during the Renaissance, as scholars such as Marsilio

Ficino translated and commented on Plato's dialogues, blending Greek philosophical ideas with Christian thought.

- Byzantine

Refugees and the Fall of Constantinople: The fall of Constantinople to the Ottoman Turks in 1453 brought an influx of Byzantine scholars to the West, many of whom carried with them important Greek manuscripts. These scholars played a key role in the revival of Greek learning during the Renaissance, helping to reintroduce the works of Plato, Aristotle, and other classical Greek thinkers to the West.

4. The Theological Impact of Greek Ideas on the Crusades

The resurgence of Greek philosophy and science through Byzantine influences during the Crusades also had a profound impact on medieval Christian theology. As Latin scholars engaged with the Greek philosophical tradition, they began to integrate these ideas into their theological frameworks, leading to new approaches to Christian doctrine and the interpretation of biblical prophecy.

A. Greek Philosophy and Christian Theology

The rediscovery of Greek philosophical ideas, particularly the works of Aristotle and Plato, provided Christian theologians with new intellectual tools for understanding the nature of God, the soul, and the cosmos. These ideas were not without controversy, as some theologians feared that rational philosophy might undermine the mystical and spiritual dimensions of the Christian faith.

- Plato's Influence: Platonic ideas about the immortality of the soul, the nature of the divine, and the ideal forms resonated with many Christian theologians, who saw parallels between Platonic philosophy and Christian teachings on the spiritual world. The Neoplatonic tradition, which emphasized the unity of the divine and the ascent of the soul, was particularly influential in shaping Christian mysticism and eschatology.

- Aristotle and Natural Theology: Aristotle's philosophy had a profound impact on the development of natural theology—the idea that human reason and observation of the natural world could provide insights into the existence of God and the moral order of the universe. This approach, championed by thinkers like Thomas Aquinas, sought to harmonize faith and reason by demonstrating that philosophical inquiry could complement divine revelation.

B. Eschatological Themes and the Crusades

The resurgence of Greek ideas during the Crusades also influenced medieval Christian eschatology, particularly in relation to prophecies about the end times and the role of human action in bringing about the Kingdom of God. The

Crusades were often viewed as part of the apocalyptic narrative, with many Christians believing that the recovery of the Holy Land would pave the way for the second coming of Christ.

- Apocalyptic Expectations: Many medieval Christians believed that the Crusades were divinely ordained and that the success of the Crusades would lead to the fulfillment of biblical prophecies about the end of the world. Greek eschatological ideas, particularly those influenced by Plato's concept of the ideal state and Aristotle's teleological view of history, were integrated into Christian apocalyptic thought, shaping the medieval understanding of God's plan for history.

The Crusades and the Resurgence of Greek Ideas

The Crusades played a significant role in the resurgence of Greek ideas in the Latin West, largely through the Byzantine Empire's preservation of classical Greek texts and the cultural exchanges that took place during the Crusader period. The rediscovery of Greek philosophy and science had a profound impact on medieval Christian theology, contributing to the development of Scholasticism and laying the intellectual foundations for the Renaissance.

The transmission of Greek ideas during the Crusades also influenced Christian eschatology, with Greek philosophical concepts being integrated into the medieval understanding of biblical prophecy and the end times. This intellectual revival not only enriched medieval European thought but also helped to shape the religious, cultural, and scientific developments of the later Middle Ages and beyond.

Chapter 5: Aristotle's Works and the Development of Scholasticism, and Apocalyptic Expectations During the Crusades

The resurgence of Greek philosophy during the Crusades, particularly through the transmission of Aristotle's works, had a profound impact on the intellectual and theological development of medieval Europe. The recovery of Aristotle's writings through Byzantine and Islamic intermediaries provided medieval scholars with new tools for engaging with questions of philosophy, theology, and ethics, leading to the emergence of Scholasticism. At the same time, the Crusades ignited apocalyptic expectations in the medieval Christian world, with many viewing the Crusades as part of a broader divine plan leading to the fulfillment of biblical prophecy and the second coming of Christ.

This chapter explores the role of Aristotle's works in the development of Scholasticism, the dominant intellectual tradition of medieval Europe, and examines the apocalyptic expectations that arose in connection with the Crusades. These two themes—the revival of Aristotelian philosophy and the eschatological fervor of the Crusades—played significant roles in shaping the religious and intellectual life of medieval Christendom.

1. Aristotle's Works and the Development of Scholasticism

The recovery of Aristotle's works during the 12th century marked a turning point in medieval intellectual history. Aristotle's writings on logic, metaphysics, ethics, and natural philosophy provided medieval scholars with a comprehensive framework for understanding the natural world and the relationship between faith and reason. This revival of Aristotelian thought laid the foundation for the development of Scholasticism, a system of learning that sought to harmonize Christian theology with classical philosophy.

A. The Rediscovery of Aristotle in the West

Although much of Aristotle's philosophy had been lost to the Latin West after the fall of the Roman Empire, his works were preserved in the Byzantine Empire and later translated into Arabic by Islamic scholars. During the Crusades and through contacts with the Muslim world, Latin scholars regained access to Aristotle's works, particularly through translations made in Spain and Sicily, where Muslim, Jewish, and Christian scholars worked together to translate these texts from Arabic and Greek into Latin.

- Islamic Philosophers and Aristotle: Islamic philosophers such as Avicenna (Ibn Sina) and Averroes (Ibn Rushd) played a crucial role in preserving and commenting on Aristotle's works. Their interpretations of Aristotle, particularly in the fields of metaphysics and natural philosophy, were highly influential in shaping how Scholastic thinkers would engage with Aristotle's ideas.

- Translations into Latin: By the mid-12th century, Latin translations of Aristotle's works began to circulate in Europe, and by the 13th century, his entire corpus, including works on logic, ethics, natural science, and metaphysics, was available to Latin scholars. These translations had a profound impact on European intellectual life, leading to the creation of a new philosophical system that sought to reconcile Aristotle's thought with Christian doctrine.

B. Aristotle's Influence on Scholasticism

The Scholastic method, which emerged in the medieval universities, was characterized by the use of dialectical reasoning and the careful analysis of texts. Scholastic scholars employed Aristotle's logic and metaphysics as tools for understanding theology, particularly in addressing questions about the nature of God, creation, and the soul. Aristotle's emphasis on rational inquiry and empirical observation provided a framework for Scholastic thinkers to explore complex theological issues while remaining grounded in philosophical rigor.

- Aristotle's Logic: Aristotle's Organon, a collection of his works on logic, became the foundation for Scholastic reasoning. The syllogism, a form of deductive reasoning introduced by Aristotle, was adopted by Scholastic scholars as a tool for theological and philosophical argumentation. The Summa Theologica of Thomas Aquinas, one of the most famous Scholastic works, is structured around the use of logical arguments to address theological questions.

- Natural Philosophy and Theology: Aristotle's natural philosophy, particularly his views on the nature of the physical world and causality, influenced Scholastic interpretations of the creation and the relationship between God and the natural world. Thomas Aquinas and other Scholastic theologians drew on Aristotle's concept of the Prime Mover as a way of explaining God's role as the ultimate cause of all things in the universe.

- Metaphysics and Ethics: Aristotle's metaphysical ideas about substance, form, and essence provided Scholastic thinkers with a framework for exploring theological doctrines, such as the nature of Christ and the immortality of the soul. In ethics, Aristotle's concept of the golden mean influenced Scholastic discussions of virtue and the moral life, leading to the integration of Aristotelian ethics with Christian moral teachings.

C. Thomas Aquinas and the Integration of Aristotle's Philosophy

Among the Scholastic thinkers, Thomas Aquinas (1225–1274) stands out as the most influential figure in integrating Aristotle's philosophy with Christian theology. In his magnum opus, the Summa Theologica, Aquinas systematically employed Aristotle's logic, metaphysics, and ethics to address central questions of Christian doctrine. Aquinas viewed Aristotle as a valuable source of philosophical insight, but he also recognized the need to correct certain aspects of Aristotle's thought in light of Christian revelation.

- Aquinas on Faith and Reason: Aquinas argued that faith and reason were not in conflict but rather complemented each other. While reason could lead to certain truths about the natural world and human nature, faith was necessary to understand the mysteries of divine revelation, such as the Trinity and the Incarnation. By harmonizing Aristotle's rational philosophy with Christian theology, Aquinas created a comprehensive system of thought that influenced Christian doctrine for centuries.

- Aristotle's Legacy in Scholasticism: Through the work of Aquinas and other Scholastic thinkers, Aristotelian philosophy became a cornerstone of medieval Christian intellectual life. Scholasticism, with its emphasis on dialectical reasoning and the integration of faith and reason, laid the groundwork for later developments in Western philosophy and theology.

2. Apocalyptic Expectations During the Crusades

The Crusades were not only military campaigns but also deeply religious endeavors that ignited apocalyptic expectations among medieval Christians. Many saw the Crusades as part of a divine plan to reclaim the Holy Land and hasten the fulfillment of biblical prophecy, particularly in relation to the end times and the second coming of Christ. The intersection of eschatological fervor and military action during the Crusades created a powerful narrative in which the Crusaders were seen as agents of God's will, tasked with bringing about the Kingdom of God.

A. Apocalyptic Prophecies and the Recovery of Jerusalem

The recovery of Jerusalem from Muslim control was central to the apocalyptic expectations surrounding the Crusades. In Christian eschatology, Jerusalem held a special place as the city where Christ would return to establish his millennial reign. Many Christians believed that the conquest of Jerusalem by the Crusaders would pave the way for the fulfillment of prophecies related to the end times.

- Jerusalem as the Center of Apocalyptic Prophecy: According to medieval interpretations of biblical prophecy, the rebuilding of the Temple in Jerusalem and the restoration of Christian control over the city were seen as necessary steps before the second coming of Christ. The Book of Revelation and other apocalyptic texts describe Jerusalem as the focal point of eschatological events, including the final battle between the forces of good and evil.

- The First Crusade and the Capture of Jerusalem: When the Crusaders captured Jerusalem in 1099 during the First Crusade, it was widely seen as a fulfillment of God's will and a sign that the end times were near. The victory was interpreted by many as a divine confirmation that the Crusaders were playing a central role in God's plan for the last days. The Holy Sepulchre, the site of Christ's crucifixion and resurrection, was reclaimed by Christians, further fueling apocalyptic expectations.

B. The Crusades as a War Against the Forces of Evil

Medieval Christians often framed the Crusades as part of a cosmic battle between the forces of good (represented by the Christian Crusaders) and the forces of evil (represented by the Muslims). This dualistic worldview was deeply influenced by apocalyptic thought, particularly the belief that Satan and his followers would be defeated in a final confrontation before the establishment of the Kingdom of God.

The Antichrist and the Crusades: In some apocalyptic interpretations, the Muslim rulers of Jerusalem were seen as precursors to the Antichrist, who would appear before the end of the world. The Crusades were thus viewed as a holy war not only to reclaim Jerusalem but also to prevent the rise of the Antichrist and delay his reign of terror on earth.

- Final Judgment and the Crusaders: The Crusaders were often portrayed as warriors of Christ, fighting to ensure the ultimate triumph of the Kingdom of God. Many Crusaders believed that by participating in the holy war, they were earning divine favor and securing their place in the Kingdom of Heaven. The promise of indulgences (forgiveness of sins) for those who fought in the Crusades further reinforced the idea that the Crusades were part of God's apocalyptic plan.

C. The Role of Apocalyptic Preachers

Apocalyptic preachers played a significant role in promoting the eschatological significance of the Crusades. Figures such as Bernard of Clairvaux and Peter the Hermit called on Christians to join the Crusades by emphasizing the spiritual and apocalyptic importance of the campaign. They framed the Crusades as a divine mission to bring about the end times and the return of Christ.

- Bernard of Clairvaux: A leading figure in promoting the Second Crusade, Bernard of Clairvaux preached that the Crusade was divinely ordained and that the Crusaders were fulfilling God's will by reclaiming Jerusalem. His sermons were filled with apocalyptic imagery, and he urged Christians to see their participation in the Crusades as part of their spiritual duty to bring about the Kingdom of God.

- Peter the Hermit: One of the key figures in mobilizing popular support for the First Crusade, Peter the Hermit preached that the end of the world was imminent and that Christians needed to fight to reclaim the Holy Land from Muslim control. His apocalyptic message resonated with many medieval Christians, who believed that by joining the Crusades, they were hastening the return of Christ.

Aristotle's Influence on Scholasticism and Apocalyptic Expectations During the Crusades

The recovery of Aristotle's works during the Crusades played a critical role in shaping the intellectual landscape of medieval Europe, particularly through the development of Scholasticism, which sought to harmonize Christian theology with Greek philosophy. At the same time, the Crusades ignited apocalyptic expectations among medieval Christians, who viewed the Crusaders as agents of God's will tasked with reclaiming the Holy Land and preparing the world for the second coming of Christ.

The intersection of Aristotelian thought and Christian eschatology during this period reflects the broader cultural and intellectual exchange that took place between the Latin West, the Byzantine Empire, and the Islamic world. This exchange not only enriched medieval theology and philosophy but also deepened the apocalyptic fervor that accompanied the Crusades, contributing to the religious and political dynamics of the medieval world.

The Rediscovery of Aristotle and Its Influence on the Renaissance

The rediscovery of Aristotle's works during the late Middle Ages was one of the most important intellectual developments leading to the Renaissance. Aristotle's philosophy, particularly his writings on logic, metaphysics, natural science, and ethics, had a profound influence on the scholars and thinkers of the Renaissance, who sought to reconcile the classical wisdom of antiquity with the growing humanistic and scientific inquiries of their time. The integration of Aristotelian thought into Renaissance philosophy, education, and science set the stage for the intellectual flourishing that characterized this period.

This chapter delves into how the rediscovery of Aristotle shaped the Renaissance—an era of profound cultural, intellectual, and artistic transformation that emerged in the 14th and 15th centuries. We will explore how Aristotle's works influenced the development of Renaissance humanism, the natural sciences, and political theory, and how his ideas were adapted by Renaissance thinkers to address new philosophical and scientific challenges.

1. The Rediscovery of Aristotle in the Late Middle Ages

Although Aristotle's works had been known to scholars in the Byzantine Empire and the Islamic world, they were largely lost to the Latin West following the collapse of the Western Roman Empire. However, during the 12th and 13th centuries, as a result of contact with the Muslim world during the Crusades and the efforts of translators in Spain and Italy, Aristotle's writings were reintroduced to Western Europe.

A. The Role of Islamic Scholars in Preserving Aristotle

Islamic philosophers played a pivotal role in preserving, interpreting, and transmitting Aristotle's works to the West. Scholars such as Averroes (Ibn Rushd) and Avicenna (Ibn Sina) produced commentaries on Aristotle's works, particularly in the fields of logic, metaphysics, and natural philosophy, which were later translated into Latin.

- Averroes: Known as "The Commentator" in medieval Europe, Averroes' interpretations of Aristotle had a significant impact on both medieval Scholasticism and Renaissance thought. His works helped revive interest in Aristotelian philosophy and provided a foundation for later philosophical debates on the nature of the soul, reason, and God.

- Translations from Arabic and Greek: By the mid-12th century, scholars working in centers such as Toledo and Palermo translated Aristotle's works from both Arabic and Greek into Latin, making them accessible to Western intellectuals. These translations sparked a revival of interest in classical philosophy and laid the groundwork for the Renaissance.

B. The Influence of Aristotle on Medieval Scholasticism

The rediscovery of Aristotle during the High Middle Ages profoundly influenced the development of Scholasticism, the dominant intellectual tradition of the medieval period. Scholars such as Thomas Aquinas, Albertus Magnus, and John Duns Scotus integrated Aristotelian logic and metaphysics into Christian theology, seeking to reconcile faith and reason.

- Thomas Aquinas: The work of Thomas Aquinas in the 13th century is particularly significant in this regard. In his Summa Theologica, Aquinas used Aristotle's logic and metaphysical framework to systematically address theological questions, creating a synthesis of Christian doctrine and classical philosophy that would dominate Western thought for centuries.

Although Aristotle's influence was already well established in the medieval universities, it was during the Renaissance that his ideas were reexamined and adapted to fit new humanistic, scientific, and political contexts.

2. Aristotle and Renaissance Humanism

The Renaissance was marked by a renewed interest in classical antiquity, particularly the works of Greek and Roman philosophers. The humanists of the Renaissance were scholars and thinkers who sought to revive the classical ideals of wisdom, virtue, and eloquence, emphasizing the importance of human experience, reason, and moral development. Aristotle's philosophy played a central role in this revival, providing a philosophical foundation for Renaissance humanism.

A. The Humanist Educational Program

Aristotle's works became foundational to the humanist educational program that emerged during the Renaissance. Humanist scholars sought to educate individuals in the liberal arts, which included rhetoric, grammar, poetry, history, moral philosophy, and natural science—all areas in which Aristotle's writings were influential.

- The Role of Aristotle in Education: Aristotelian logic and ethics were central to the humanist curriculum, as scholars believed that studying Aristotle's writings would cultivate reason, virtue, and eloquence in their students. Humanist educators like Petrarch and Erasmus emphasized the importance of reading Aristotle alongside Plato, Cicero, and other classical authors to develop a well-rounded and morally upright individual.

- Aristotle's Ethics and Political Thought: Aristotle's Nicomachean Ethics and Politics were particularly important to Renaissance humanism. His emphasis on the virtues of prudence, justice, courage, and temperance aligned with the humanist goal of cultivating moral and civic virtues. Humanists believed that by studying Aristotle's ethical thought, individuals could develop the moral character necessary for participation in public life.

B. Aristotle's Impact on Renaissance Art and Science

Aristotle's influence extended beyond philosophy and education to other fields, particularly art and science. His writings on aesthetics, poetics, and natural philosophy shaped the artistic and scientific developments of the Renaissance.

- Aristotle's Aesthetics: In his Poetics, Aristotle provided a framework for understanding the structure and purpose of tragedy, which influenced Renaissance writers and dramatists. The Aristotelian concept of catharsis—the emotional cleansing experienced by the audience during a tragic play—was particularly influential on Renaissance playwrights such as Shakespeare and Marlowe.

- Natural Philosophy and Science: Aristotle's works on natural philosophy, particularly his writings on biology, physics, and cosmology, were studied by Renaissance scientists such as Leonardo da Vinci and Galileo Galilei. Although some of Aristotle's ideas were later challenged by the discoveries of the Scientific Revolution, his emphasis on empirical observation and the classification of the natural world provided a foundation for Renaissance scientific inquiry.

3. Aristotle and the Renaissance Scientific Revolution

The Renaissance was also a time of significant developments in natural science, and Aristotle's works played a key role in shaping the scientific thought of the period. Although some of Aristotle's scientific theories were eventually superseded by the discoveries of Copernicus, Galileo, and Kepler, his method of empirical observation and his emphasis on systematic inquiry into the natural world laid the groundwork for the Scientific Revolution.

A. Aristotle's Influence on Early Scientific Thought

Aristotle's writings on natural philosophy—including his works on physics, biology, and astronomy—were foundational to the scientific investigations of the Renaissance. His approach to scientific inquiry emphasized the importance of empirical observation and the classification of phenomena, which resonated with the Renaissance desire to explore and understand the natural world.

- Aristotle's Biology: Aristotle's studies in biology, particularly his efforts to classify animals and plants, influenced Renaissance naturalists such as Andreas Vesalius and William Harvey. Although Aristotle's ideas about the functioning of the body were later revised, his method of systematic observation remained influential in the development of anatomy and medicine during the Renaissance.

- The Aristotelian Cosmos: Aristotle's geocentric model of the universe, which placed the earth at the center of the cosmos, dominated scientific thought throughout the Middle Ages and into the Renaissance. However, this model was eventually challenged by Nicholas Copernicus, whose heliocentric theory proposed that the sun was at the center of the universe. While Copernicus' theory marked a departure from Aristotelian cosmology, the methodological rigor and logical structure of Aristotle's approach to science continued to influence Renaissance thinkers.

B. The Challenge to Aristotelian Science

As the Renaissance progressed, new discoveries in astronomy, physics, and anatomy began to challenge some of Aristotle's scientific theories. The works of Copernicus, Galileo, and Kepler overturned the Aristotelian model of the cosmos and laid the foundations for a new understanding of the natural world.

- Copernican Revolution: In 1543, Nicholas Copernicus published his groundbreaking work, On the Revolutions of the Heavenly Spheres, which proposed a heliocentric model of the universe. This theory directly challenged the Aristotelian geocentric model that had been accepted for centuries. Although Copernicus' work was controversial, it set the stage for further scientific exploration and the eventual development of modern astronomy.

- Galileo and the Laws of Motion: Galileo Galilei, often called the "father of modern science," built upon the work of Copernicus and further challenged Aristotle's ideas about motion and the structure of the cosmos. Galileo's observations of the moons of Jupiter through his telescope provided evidence against Aristotle's geocentric theory, while his experiments on the laws of motion laid the groundwork for Newtonian physics.

Despite these challenges to Aristotle's scientific theories, his methodological contributions—particularly his emphasis on empirical observation and the use of logical reasoning to understand the natural world—remained central to the scientific developments of the Renaissance.

4. Aristotle's Influence on Renaissance Political Theory

In addition to his impact on science and philosophy, Aristotle's ideas also shaped the development of political theory during the Renaissance. Renaissance thinkers, particularly those engaged in debates about the nature of government and human society, turned to Aristotle's Politics for insights into the functioning of the state, the role of virtue in governance, and the relationship between citizens and their rulers.

A. Aristotle's Political Philosophy

In his Politics, Aristotle argued that the polis (city-state) was the highest form of human community and that the purpose of government was to promote the common good and virtue among its citizens. He also emphasized the importance of moderation in government, advocating for a mixed constitution that combined elements of democracy, oligarchy, and monarchy.

- Aristotle's Influence on Renaissance Political Thought: Renaissance political theorists, such as Niccolò Machiavelli and Jean Bodin, drew on Aristotle's ideas about the nature of political authority and the role of virtue in governance. Aristotle's emphasis on the moral responsibilities of rulers and the need for a balanced constitution resonated with the humanist concerns of the Renaissance, particularly in the Italian city-states, where debates about republicanism and monarchical power were central to political life.

- Civic Virtue and the Common Good: Aristotle's idea that the common good should be the primary aim of government influenced Renaissance humanists' views on civic virtue and the responsibilities of citizens. Humanist scholars argued that by cultivating virtue through education and participation in public life, individuals could contribute to the moral and political well-being of their communities.

B. The Legacy of Aristotle in Renaissance Political Theory

Aristotle's political philosophy provided Renaissance thinkers with a framework for addressing questions about the nature of power, the relationship between ruler and ruled, and the role of virtue in governance. His ideas about the mixed constitution and the importance of civic participation continued to influence political thought well into the modern period, particularly during the development of republican theory in Renaissance Italy and later during the Enlightenment.

Aristotle's Enduring Influence on the Renaissance

The rediscovery of Aristotle's works during the late Middle Ages and their integration into the intellectual life of the Renaissance had a profound impact on the development of humanism, science, and political theory. Aristotle's philosophy provided Renaissance thinkers with the tools to explore new questions about the nature of human existence, the natural world, and the structure of society, while his emphasis on empirical observation, logical reasoning, and virtue ethics helped shape the cultural and intellectual achievements of the period.

Although many of Aristotle's scientific theories were eventually challenged by the discoveries of the Scientific Revolution, his methodological contributions continued to influence the ways in which Renaissance scholars approached the study of the natural world and human society. As a result, Aristotle's legacy remained central to the intellectual life of the Renaissance, shaping the art, science, philosophy, and political thought of the era.

CHAPTER 06

THE IRON LEGS – ROME

In Nebuchadnezzar's dream, described in Daniel 2:31-45, the legs of iron represent the Roman Empire, the fourth great kingdom in the succession of world empires. Rome's significance in the prophetic vision is tied to its unmatched military strength, political dominance, and ability to conquer and govern vast territories for centuries. Unlike the previous empires symbolized by gold, silver, and bronze, the use of iron emphasizes the sheer power and resilience of the Roman Empire, which became the largest and most influential empire in the ancient world.

This chapter explores how Rome, as the iron kingdom in Nebuchadnezzar's dream, fulfilled the prophecy through its military conquests, political administration, and enduring legacy. We will also examine how the Roman Empire's rise and eventual decline fit into the broader biblical prophetic narrative, culminating in the emergence of the eternal kingdom of God.

1. Rome as the Iron Kingdom: Military and Political Strength

The imagery of the legs of iron in Nebuchadnezzar's dream is an apt representation of the Roman Empire, which was known for its unparalleled military power and ability to conquer and control vast territories. Rome's military might, combined with its efficient political administration, allowed it to dominate the Mediterranean world and beyond for centuries.

A. The Strength of Iron: Military Dominance

Iron, as a symbol of strength and durability, reflects the military prowess of the Roman Empire. The Roman legions, highly disciplined and organized, were unmatched in their ability to defeat enemy forces and expand Roman control over diverse regions. The Romans' use of advanced military tactics, engineering, and weaponry, including iron weapons, enabled them to establish a vast empire stretching from Britain in the north to Egypt in the south, and from Spain in the west to Mesopotamia in the east.

- Roman Legions: The Roman legions were the backbone of Rome's military power. Highly trained and equipped with iron swords (gladius), shields, and armor, the legions were capable of executing complex battlefield maneuvers, such as the testudo (tortoise) formation, which made them nearly invincible in combat. The military effectiveness of the Roman legions allowed Rome to defeat powerful adversaries, including Carthage, Macedonia, and the Seleucid Empire.

- Expansion of the Roman Empire: Rome's military conquests led to the creation of an empire that encompassed the entire Mediterranean Basin, often referred to as "Mare Nostrum" (Our Sea). This empire included Gaul, Britain, Greece, Egypt, Judea, and much of the Near East, making Rome the dominant power of the ancient world.

- Pax Romana: Following the conquests, the Roman Empire entered a period of relative peace and stability known as the Pax Romana (Roman Peace), which lasted for approximately two centuries (27 BCE–180 CE). This period allowed for the consolidation of Roman rule and the establishment of an extensive network of roads, cities, and trade routes, which facilitated communication and commerce across the empire.

B. Political Strength: Rome's Administrative Genius

In addition to its military power, the Roman Empire was known for its political and administrative innovations, which allowed it to effectively govern a diverse and far-reaching empire. Rome's legal and political institutions provided a framework for maintaining order and stability across its provinces, ensuring the long-term survival of the empire.

- Roman Law: One of Rome's most enduring legacies was its system of law. The Roman legal code provided a uniform set of laws that applied to all citizens and subjects of the empire, regardless of their ethnic or cultural background. This system of law, which emphasized justice, equity, and due process, helped maintain stability across the empire and provided a model for later legal systems in Europe and the Western world.

- Governance of Provinces: Rome's ability to govern such a vast and diverse empire was largely due to its provincial administration. Roman governors, appointed by the emperor or the Senate, were responsible for maintaining order, collecting taxes, and overseeing local affairs in their respective provinces. The Roman system of governance allowed for a high degree of local autonomy while ensuring loyalty to the central government.

- Infrastructure and Trade: The Romans were master builders, and their infrastructure projects, such as the construction of roads, aqueducts, and fortifications, facilitated the movement of troops, goods, and people throughout the empire. The extensive network of Roman roads connected major cities and provinces, promoting trade and cultural exchange. Roman engineering achievements, such as the Aqueducts of Rome, demonstrated the empire's ability to harness technology to serve its administrative and military needs.

The combination of military might and political acumen made Rome an empire of unmatched power and longevity, qualities that are reflected in the iron legs of Nebuchadnezzar's statue.

2. Rome in Biblical Prophecy: The Fourth Kingdom in Daniel's Vision

In the Book of Daniel, the Roman Empire is depicted as the fourth kingdom in the succession of world empires. This kingdom, symbolized by the legs of iron, is described as being stronger and more fearsome than the previous empires, but it is also depicted as a kingdom that will eventually be divided and weakened, represented by the feet of iron and clay.

A. The Unmatched Power of the Iron Kingdom

The description of the iron kingdom in Daniel 2:40 emphasizes its strength and its ability to crush and break all other kingdoms. This prophecy corresponds to the Roman Empire's unparalleled military power and its ability to subjugate and absorb the earlier empires of Babylon, Medo-Persia, and Greece.

- Daniel 2:40: "Finally, there will be a fourth kingdom, strong as iron—for iron breaks and smashes everything—and as iron breaks things to pieces, so it will crush and break all the others."

This passage highlights the brutal efficiency of Roman military conquest and its ability to impose its will on the known world. The Roman Empire not only defeated rival powers but also incorporated their cultures and territories into its vast imperial system, making it the most dominant force in the ancient world.

B. The Division and Decline of the Roman Empire

While the Roman Empire was initially characterized by its strength, Daniel's prophecy also alludes to the eventual division and weakening of the empire. This is symbolized by the feet of iron and clay, a mixture that represents the internal fragility and instability of the later Roman Empire.

- Daniel 2:41-43: "Just as you saw that the feet and toes were partly of baked clay and partly of iron, so this will be a divided kingdom; yet it will have some of the strength of iron in it... but the people will be a mixture and will not remain united, any more than iron mixes with clay."

The division of the Roman Empire into the Western Roman Empire and the Eastern Roman Empire (Byzantine Empire) in the late 4th century CE reflects this prophecy. The Western Roman Empire, plagued by internal strife, economic problems, and barbarian invasions, eventually fell in 476 CE, while the Eastern Roman Empire continued to survive for another millennium.

The iron and clay mixture also symbolizes the inherent weakness in Rome's later period, when internal divisions, political instability, and the integration of diverse peoples and cultures made the empire more vulnerable to external threats. Despite its strength, Rome, like the empires before it, was ultimately subject to the sovereignty of God, and its fall was part of the larger biblical narrative of the rise and fall of human kingdoms.

3. Rome's Role in Biblical History and the Coming of Christ

The Roman Empire's significance in biblical prophecy is not limited to its role as a powerful political and military entity. Rome also played a critical role in the unfolding of salvation history, particularly through its involvement in the events surrounding the birth, ministry, and crucifixion of

Jesus Christ. In this sense, Rome is depicted as both an instrument of God's plan and as an example of the temporary nature of human power.

A. The Roman Empire and the Birth of Christ

The Roman Empire provided the political and cultural context in which Jesus was born, lived, and carried out his ministry. The reign of Caesar Augustus, the first Roman emperor, is particularly significant in the biblical narrative, as it was during his rule that Jesus was born in Bethlehem, fulfilling the prophecy of the Messiah's birth in Micah 5:2.

- Luke 2:1-7: The account of Jesus' birth is set against the backdrop of a Roman census ordered by Caesar Augustus, which required Joseph and Mary to travel to Bethlehem. This event not only fulfilled the prophecy of Jesus' birth but also underscored the influence of Roman political authority over the Jewish people at the time.

B. The Crucifixion of Jesus under Roman Authority

Rome's involvement in the crucifixion of Jesus is another key aspect of its role in biblical history. Jesus was tried and sentenced to death by Pontius Pilate, the Roman governor of Judea, at the urging of the Jewish religious authorities. The method of execution—crucifixion—was a distinctly Roman punishment reserved for non-citizens and criminals.

- John 19:16-18: "Finally, Pilate handed him over to them to be crucified. So the soldiers took charge of Jesus. Carrying his own cross, he went out to the place of the Skull (which in Aramaic is called Golgotha). There they crucified him, and with him two others—one on each side and Jesus in the middle."

Rome's role in Jesus' crucifixion reflects the empire's authority over Judea and its role in fulfilling the messianic prophecies concerning the suffering and death of the Savior. At the same time, the crucifixion highlights the temporal nature of Roman power, as the empire, despite its might, could not prevent the resurrection of Christ and the establishment of his eternal kingdom.

4. The Fall of Rome and the Transition to the Eternal Kingdom

The Roman Empire, despite its strength and longevity, was ultimately subject to the same fate as the empires that preceded it. In Daniel's vision, the iron kingdom is destined to be replaced by a kingdom not made by human hands—the eternal kingdom of God, symbolized by the stone that strikes the statue and destroys it.

A. The Fall of the Roman Empire

The fall of the Western Roman Empire in 476 CE, marked by the deposition of the last emperor, Romulus Augustulus, by the barbarian chieftain Odoacer, signaled the end of ancient Rome as a political entity. However, the Eastern Roman Empire (Byzantine Empire) continued to survive for another thousand years, maintaining Roman culture and governance in the East.

- The Eastern and Western Empires: The division of the Roman Empire into East and West contributed to its eventual decline, as the two halves became increasingly autonomous and isolated from each other. While the Eastern Empire remained strong under the leadership of emperors such as Justinian, the West was unable to resist the pressures of barbarian invasions and internal decay.

- A Sign of Things to Come: The fall of the Roman Empire, as prophesied in Daniel's vision, serves as a symbol of the transitory nature of all human kingdoms. Despite its immense power, the Roman Empire, like the kingdoms of Babylon, Persia, and Greece before it, was ultimately replaced by the eternal kingdom of God—a kingdom that is not built by human hands but by divine intervention.

B. The Eternal Kingdom of God

In Daniel's vision, the statue representing the succession of world empires is ultimately destroyed by a stone that is "cut out, but not by human hands" (Daniel 2:34). This stone represents the kingdom of God, which will replace all earthly kingdoms and endure forever.

- Daniel 2:44: "In the time of those kings, the God of heaven will set up a kingdom that will never be destroyed, nor will it be left to another people. It will crush all those kingdoms and bring them to an end, but it will itself endure forever."

The eternal kingdom of God is described as indestructible and not subject to the rise and fall of human powers. This kingdom, established through the life, death, and resurrection of Jesus Christ, will ultimately supersede all earthly empires, including Rome, and bring about the fulfillment of God's plan for human history.

Rome as the Iron Kingdom and the Fulfillment of Prophecy

The Roman Empire, symbolized by the legs of iron in Nebuchadnezzar's dream, fulfilled the biblical prophecy through its unparalleled military and political strength. As the dominant power of the ancient world, Rome conquered and controlled vast territories, established a system of governance and law that influenced the entire Mediterranean world, and played a critical role in the events of salvation history, particularly in relation to the birth, crucifixion, and resurrection of Jesus Christ.

However, despite its immense power, the Roman Empire, like the empires that preceded it, was ultimately transitory. Its division and decline, symbolized by the feet of iron and clay, paved the way for the rise of the eternal kingdom of God, which is destined to endure forever. In this sense, Rome's role in the biblical narrative serves as a reminder of the sovereignty of God over human history and the inevitability of the coming of God's kingdom, which will surpass all earthly powers.

The Feet of Iron and Clay – Division and Decline of the Roman Empire

In Nebuchadnezzar's dream, the legs of iron represent the Roman Empire, but the feet and toes, made of a mixture of iron and clay, signify the empire's eventual division and weakening. This part of the vision, described in Daniel 2:41-43, emphasizes that while the Roman Empire was initially strong, like iron, it would later become divided and fragile, as iron does not mix with clay. This imagery captures the internal instability and the external pressures that led to the eventual fall of Rome, particularly the Western Roman Empire.

In this chapter, we will explore the symbolic meaning of the feet of iron and clay, examining how the Roman Empire became increasingly vulnerable due to internal fractures and the pressures of barbarian invasions. We will also delve into how these divisions set the stage for the rise of new powers and paved the way for the emergence of Christendom in the post-Roman world. Additionally, we will analyze the lasting legacy of Rome in shaping the early Christian Church, which flourished within the structures and institutions of the Roman Empire.

1. The Feet of Iron and Clay: Symbol of Division and Weakness

In Nebuchadnezzar's dream, the statue's feet, made of a mixture of iron and clay, represent the later stages of the Roman Empire. This mixed composition signifies the inherent weaknesses that would develop within the empire, leading to its eventual decline and collapse.

A. The Symbolism of Iron and Clay

Iron, as previously discussed, symbolizes strength and durability, qualities that characterized the Roman Empire at its height. However, when mixed with clay, which is fragile and easily broken, the strength of iron is compromised. This mixture reflects the contradictory nature of the later Roman Empire, which, while still retaining elements of its former military and political power, became increasingly unstable and vulnerable.

- Daniel 2:41-43: "Just as you saw that the feet and toes were partly of baked clay and partly of iron, so this will be a divided kingdom; yet it will have some of the strength of iron in it, even as you saw iron mixed with clay. As the toes were partly iron and partly clay, so this kingdom will be partly strong and partly brittle."

The iron and clay symbolize the internal divisions within the Roman Empire, as well as the external pressures from various barbarian tribes that contributed to its fragmentation. These internal and external factors weakened the empire, making it less cohesive and more prone to collapse.

B. The Division of the Roman Empire

One of the most significant developments in the history of the Roman Empire was its division into the Western Roman Empire and the Eastern Roman Empire (later known as the Byzantine Empire) in the late 3rd and early 4th centuries CE. This division was formalized by Emperor Diocletian in 285 CE as a way to manage the vast and unwieldy empire more effectively. Diocletian appointed a Tetrarchy, or rule by four emperors, with two emperors in the East and two in the West.

- Western and Eastern Roman Empires: The Western Roman Empire, based in Rome and later in Ravenna, encompassed Italy, Gaul, Spain, Britain, and North Africa. The Eastern Roman Empire, with its capital in Constantinople, included Greece, Anatolia, Egypt, and the Levant. While both halves of the empire shared the same imperial structure and laws, they became increasingly independent in terms of administration, culture, and military strategy.

- Increasing Instability: The division between the East and West exacerbated the internal weaknesses of the Roman Empire. The Western Roman Empire faced greater challenges, including economic decline, political corruption, and constant invasions by Germanic tribes, such as the Visigoths, Ostrogoths, Vandals, and Huns. The Eastern Roman Empire (Byzantium) was more stable and prosperous, largely due to its strategic location and wealth.

2. The Fall of the Western Roman Empire

The feet of iron and clay in Nebuchadnezzar's dream point to the fall of the Western Roman Empire in 476 CE, a watershed moment in history that marked the end of ancient Rome's dominance and the beginning of the medieval period. While the Roman Empire in the West crumbled, the Eastern Roman Empire continued to thrive for another millennium as the Byzantine Empire.

A. The Role of Barbarian Invasions

One of the primary factors contributing to the fall of the Western Roman Empire was the series of barbarian invasions that swept across its territories during the 4th and 5th centuries. As the empire weakened internally due to economic decline and political instability, it became increasingly difficult to defend its borders against migratory tribes and invaders from the north and east.

- Sack of Rome: In 410 CE, the city of Rome was sacked by the Visigoths under their leader Alaric I, marking the first time in nearly 800 years that the city had fallen to a foreign power. This event shocked the Roman world and symbolized the vulnerability of the once-mighty empire.

- Deposition of Romulus Augustulus: The traditional date for the fall of the Western Roman Empire is 476 CE, when the last Roman emperor, Romulus Augustulus, was deposed by the Germanic chieftain Odoacer. This event is often seen as the definitive end of the Roman Empire in the West, although Roman cultural and legal traditions continued to influence the successor kingdoms.

B. The Continued Survival of the Eastern Roman Empire

While the Western Roman Empire collapsed under the weight of barbarian invasions and internal disunity, the Eastern Roman Empire (Byzantium) managed to survive and even thrive. Centered in Constantinople, the Eastern Empire became a beacon of Roman culture, Orthodox Christianity, and Byzantine art and architecture.

- Byzantine Resilience: The Byzantine Empire was able to fend off invasions and maintain a relatively stable political structure, thanks in part to its wealth, strategic location, and strong leadership under emperors such as Justinian I and Heraclius. Byzantine diplomacy, combined with the empire's formidable military defenses, allowed it to survive for nearly a thousand years after the fall of Rome in the West.

- The Byzantine Influence: The Byzantine Empire played a critical role in the preservation of classical Greek and Roman knowledge and served as a bridge between the ancient world and the Middle Ages. Byzantine scholars preserved and copied important texts from Plato, Aristotle, and other classical authors, which would later be transmitted to the West during the Renaissance.

3. The Legacy of Rome in the Early Christian Church

Despite the fall of the Western Roman Empire, the legacy of Rome lived on through the Christian Church, which had grown significantly during the late Roman period. The Roman Empire provided the social, political, and cultural framework in which Christianity spread and became institutionalized, eventually becoming the dominant religion of the Roman world.

A. The Roman Empire and the Spread of Christianity

The Roman Empire played a crucial role in the spread of Christianity during the early centuries of the faith. The Pax Romana (Roman Peace) and the extensive network of Roman roads allowed Christian missionaries, such as Paul of Tarsus, to travel freely across the empire, preaching the gospel and establishing Christian communities.

- Paul's Missionary Journeys: The Apostle Paul took advantage of the Roman infrastructure to spread Christianity throughout the eastern Mediterranean, traveling to cities such as Ephesus, Corinth, and Rome itself. His letters to these early Christian communities, which form a significant portion of the New Testament, reveal the deep connections between the Roman world and the nascent Christian faith.

- Persecution and Conversion: Early Christians often faced persecution by Roman authorities, particularly under emperors like Nero, Domitian, and Diocletian. However, with the conversion of Emperor Constantine in the early 4th century and the subsequent Edict of Milan in 313 CE, Christianity was granted legal status within the Roman Empire, paving the way for it to become the state religion by the end of the century.

B. The Role of the Church in Preserving Roman Traditions

After the fall of the Western Roman Empire, the Christian Church became one of the primary institutions responsible for preserving and transmitting Roman cultural and legal traditions. The Church's hierarchical structure, modeled in part on Roman political organization, helped it to maintain continuity and authority during the chaotic early medieval period.

- Papal Authority: The bishop of Rome (later known as the Pope) became the most powerful figure in the Western Christian Church. The Papacy drew on the prestige and authority of the city of Rome to claim primacy over other Christian bishops, establishing the foundations of the Roman Catholic Church.

- Latin as a Sacred Language: The use of Latin as the official language of the Roman Empire was preserved by the Christian Church, which used Latin in its liturgies, scriptures, and theological writings. This ensured the continuity of Roman cultural and intellectual traditions, even after the political collapse of the empire in the West.

C. The Influence of Roman Law and Governance on the Church

Roman law and governance had a profound impact on the early Christian Church, shaping its development in both the East and West. The structure of the Roman Empire, particularly its legal and administrative systems, influenced the way the Church organized itself and interacted with secular authorities.

- Canon Law: The development of canon law, the body of laws governing the Christian Church, was heavily influenced by Roman legal traditions. Canon law regulated issues such as ecclesiastical governance, marriage, property, and the sacraments, and it provided a legal framework for resolving disputes within the Church.

- The Ecumenical Councils: The Ecumenical Councils of the Church, such as the Council of Nicaea (325 CE) and the Council of Chalcedon (451 CE), were convened by Roman emperors and followed Roman legal procedures. These councils played a key role in defining Christian doctrine and addressing theological controversies, such as the nature of Christ and the relationship between God the Father and the Son.

4. The Transition from the Roman Empire to Christendom

As the Western Roman Empire declined, the Christian Church filled the void left by the collapse of Roman political authority. The Church not only preserved Roman traditions but also began to build a new political and spiritual order, known as Christendom, which would dominate Europe during the Middle Ages.

A. The Rise of the Papacy

With the fall of the Western Roman Empire, the Papacy emerged as the most powerful institution in the West. The Pope assumed both spiritual and temporal authority, becoming the leader of the Christian Church and a key political figure in Europe. The Papacy's claim to authority was rooted in the idea of the Apostolic See, which traced its origins back to the Apostle Peter, whom Jesus had appointed as the leader of his disciples.

- Papal Authority in the Middle Ages: The Pope wielded considerable influence over the rulers of medieval Europe, often mediating disputes between kings and emperors. The crowning of Charlemagne as Holy Roman Emperor by Pope Leo III in 800 CE symbolized the close relationship between the Papacy and secular rulers in the creation of a new Roman Empire based on Christian principles.

B. The Legacy of Roman Law and the Church's Role in the Middle Ages

The Roman legal tradition also left a lasting legacy in medieval Europe, as canon law and Roman civil law became foundational elements of the legal systems of Christendom. The Church's role in preserving Roman law helped ensure that Roman legal principles, such as due process, property rights, and the rule of law, continued to influence European society for centuries.

- Roman Civil Law in the Middle Ages: The Corpus Juris Civilis, or Body of Civil Law, compiled by the Emperor Justinian in the 6th century, became a key legal text in the

Byzantine Empire and was later rediscovered in Western Europe during the 12th century. This rediscovery contributed to the development of the legal profession and the study of Roman law in the emerging medieval universities.

The Feet of Iron and Clay and the Legacy of Rome

The feet of iron and clay in Nebuchadnezzar's dream symbolize the division and weakening of the Roman Empire, leading to the eventual fall of the Western Roman Empire in 476 CE. This prophetic image reflects the internal and external pressures that eroded Rome's strength, but it also highlights the empire's enduring influence on the development of the Christian Church and medieval Christendom.

Despite the political collapse of the Roman Empire, the legacy of Roman law, governance, and cultural traditions lived on through the Christian Church, which played a central role in shaping the post-Roman world. The transition from the Roman Empire to Christendom represents both the end of one era and the beginning of another, as the Church became the dominant institution in Europe, carrying forward the traditions of Rome and paving the way for the Middle Ages.

Roman Law and Order, and Its Influence on Later Christian Eschatology

The Roman Empire, symbolized by the legs of iron in Nebuchadnezzar's dream, was renowned not only for its military strength but also for its development of a sophisticated system of law and order. Roman law became one of the most enduring legacies of the empire, shaping the legal and political frameworks of later civilizations, particularly in Europe. This system of law, along with the Roman Empire's approach to governance and order, played a crucial role in the emergence of Christian eschatology, the branch of theology concerned with the end times and the final judgment.

This chapter explores how Roman law and order served as the foundation for the governance of the empire and how the legacy of Roman legal traditions influenced medieval and modern law. We will also examine how the Roman Empire became central to later Christian eschatological thought, with Rome often being identified in apocalyptic literature as a key player in the unfolding of end-time events.

1. Roman Law and Order: The Foundation of Governance

The Roman Empire's ability to govern such a vast and diverse territory was due in large part to its development of a comprehensive legal system and a highly organized structure of administration. Roman law, characterized by its emphasis on justice, equity, and order, provided a stable framework for maintaining peace and control throughout the empire.

A. The Development of Roman Law

Roman law evolved over several centuries, beginning in the early days of the Roman Republic and reaching its peak during the imperial period. The Romans developed a sophisticated legal system that encompassed everything from private law (dealing with individuals' rights and obligations) to public law (governing the relationship between the state and its citizens). One of the key features of Roman law was its flexibility and adaptability, allowing it to evolve to meet the changing needs of the empire.

- The Twelve Tables: One of the earliest codifications of Roman law was the Twelve Tables (450 BCE), which laid out the legal rights and duties of Roman citizens. This code was intended to provide transparency in legal matters and prevent abuses of power by the ruling class. It became the foundation for later developments in Roman law.

- The Praetorian Edicts: As Roman society became more complex, the legal system expanded through the praetorian edicts—decrees issued by the praetors, who were judicial officials. These edicts allowed for flexibility in the application of the law and provided a mechanism for addressing new legal issues that arose as the empire grew.

- The Corpus Juris Civilis: One of the most significant achievements of Roman law was the compilation of the Corpus Juris Civilis (Body of Civil Law) under the Emperor Justinian I in the 6th century CE. This monumental work, which included the Digest, Institutes, and Code, summarized and systematized centuries of Roman legal thought. It became the foundation for the legal systems of many European nations and had a profound influence on both canon law (the law of the Church) and civil law in the medieval period.

B. Roman Order and Administration

In addition to its legal system, the Roman Empire was characterized by a highly organized system of administration and governance that allowed it to maintain order across its vast territories. The Roman approach to governance was pragmatic, relying on a combination of centralized authority and local autonomy to ensure stability and loyalty.

- Provinces and Governors: The Roman Empire was divided into provinces, each governed by a Roman official (either a governor or procurator) who was responsible for maintaining order, collecting taxes, and administering justice. These officials reported directly to the emperor, ensuring a high degree of central control, while also allowing for local customs and laws to continue, as long as they did not conflict with Roman authority.

- The Rule of Law: One of the key principles of Roman governance was the rule of law—the idea that all citizens, regardless of their status, were subject to the same laws. This principle helped to maintain order and prevent abuses of power, as even the emperor was expected to uphold the law. Roman legal procedures were highly formalized, with a clear system of courts, judges, and legal advocates.

- Pax Romana: The stability provided by the Roman legal and administrative system contributed to the establishment of the Pax Romana (Roman Peace), a period of relative peace and stability that lasted for over two centuries. During this time, the Roman Empire was able to maintain control over its vast territories, foster trade and cultural exchange, and spread its influence across the Mediterranean world.

2. The Legacy of Roman Law in Later Christian Thought

The Roman legal system not only influenced the governance of the empire but also left a lasting legacy on the development of Christian theology and Church law. As Christianity became the dominant religion of the Roman Empire, particularly after the Edict of Milan in 313 CE, Roman legal principles were incorporated into the administration of the Church, shaping the development of canon law and influencing later theological concepts of justice, order, and authority.

A. The Influence of Roman Law on Canon Law

As the Christian Church grew in influence, it adopted many aspects of Roman law to govern its internal affairs. The development of canon law, which regulated the practices and discipline of the Church, was heavily influenced by the Roman legal tradition.

- Canon Law and Roman Jurisprudence: The early Church councils, such as the Council of Nicaea (325 CE), used Roman legal procedures to debate theological issues and establish Church doctrine. The decisions made at these councils, known as canons, became the foundation for the Church's legal system. Many of these canons were modeled on Roman legal concepts, such as the idea of due process and the role of judicial authority.

- The Papacy and Roman Law: The development of the Papacy was also influenced by Roman law. The Pope, as the bishop of Rome, was seen as the successor to the Apostle Peter, and his authority was modeled on the Roman system of governance. The Papal courts and the system of ecclesiastical courts that developed during the Middle Ages were based on Roman legal principles, particularly the idea that legal authority flowed from a central figure (the Pope) who acted as the final arbiter of disputes.

B. Roman Law and the Concept of Justice in Christian Thought

The Roman emphasis on justice, equity, and the rule of law had a profound influence on Christian theology, particularly in relation to the concepts of divine justice and the final judgment. Early Christian thinkers, such as Augustine of Hippo and Thomas Aquinas, drew on Roman legal principles to articulate their understanding of God's justice and the role of law and order in the divine plan for humanity.

- Augustine's City of God: In his monumental work, City of God, Augustine contrasted the earthly city (represented by Rome and other temporal powers) with the City of God (the eternal kingdom of God). While acknowledging the importance of Roman law in maintaining order in the earthly city, Augustine argued that true justice could only be found in the City of God, where divine law reigned supreme. His writings helped shape the Christian understanding of the relationship between human law and divine law.

- Aquinas and Natural Law: Thomas Aquinas, one of the most influential medieval theologians, developed a theory of natural law that was deeply influenced by Roman legal thought. Aquinas argued that natural law was a reflection of divine law, accessible to human reason, and that it provided a moral framework for governing human society. His ideas about justice, law, and authority were drawn from Roman legal concepts and helped to shape the development of Christian political thought in the Middle Ages.

3. The Role of Rome in Christian Eschatology

The Roman Empire played a central role in the development of Christian eschatology, the branch of theology that deals with the end times and the final judgment. In the New Testament, Rome is often depicted as both a powerful force for order and a symbol of the world's opposition to God's kingdom. This dual role reflects the complex relationship between the early Christians and the Roman Empire, which both facilitated the spread of Christianity and, at times, persecuted the followers of Christ.

A. Rome as the Fourth Kingdom in Daniel's Prophecy

In Daniel 2, the Roman Empire is symbolized by the legs of iron, representing its unmatched strength and dominance. However, Daniel's prophecy also foretells the eventual fall of the Roman Empire and its replacement by the eternal kingdom of God. This eschatological vision would later influence Christian interpretations of Rome's role in the end times.

- The Stone Cut Without Hands: In Daniel's vision, the statue representing the succession of world empires is destroyed by a stone cut without hands, symbolizing the arrival of God's kingdom, which will replace all earthly powers, including Rome. This imagery suggests that while Rome may have been powerful, its rule was ultimately temporary, and it would be superseded by the eternal reign of God.

B. Rome and the Beast in Revelation

In the Book of Revelation, the Roman Empire is symbolically identified with the Beast and the great harlot (often referred to as Babylon the Great) that opposes God and persecutes His people. This apocalyptic imagery reflects the early Christians' experience of persecution under Roman authorities and their hope for divine justice at the end of time.

- Revelation 17:5-6: "On her forehead was written a name, a mystery: 'Babylon the Great, the mother of prostitutes and of the abominations of the earth.' I saw that the woman was drunk with the blood of God's holy people, the blood of those who bore testimony to Jesus."

In Revelation, Babylon (a symbolic reference to Rome) is depicted as a corrupt and oppressive power that will be overthrown by God in the final judgment. This portrayal reflects the Christian belief that while Rome may wield great temporal power, it will ultimately be judged and destroyed when Christ returns to establish His kingdom.

C. The Fall of Rome and the Rise of Christendom

The fall of the Western Roman Empire in 476 CE was seen by some early Christians as the fulfillment of the eschatological prophecies concerning the end of Rome's power. However, rather than marking the end of the world, the fall of Rome paved the way for the rise of Christendom, the Christian civilization that would dominate Europe during the Middle Ages.

- The Rise of the Papacy: After the fall of the Western Roman Empire, the Papacy emerged as the most powerful institution in the West, assuming both spiritual and temporal authority. The Pope, as the bishop of Rome, became the central figure in Christendom, and the Church adopted many of the administrative structures and legal traditions of the Roman Empire.

- The Holy Roman Empire: In the 9th century, the Holy Roman Empire was established in Western Europe, symbolizing the continuation of Roman political and religious authority under Christian rule. This new empire, crowned by the Pope, sought to revive the legacy of Rome and establish a Christian order based on Roman law and governance.

The Influence of Roman Law and the Eschatological Legacy of Rome

The Roman Empire's legal system and commitment to order left a profound and enduring legacy on both Western civilization and the development of the Christian Church. Roman law provided a foundation for the governance of the empire and influenced the development of canon law and Christian theological concepts of justice and divine authority. Even after the fall of the Western Roman Empire, the legacy of Rome continued to shape the political and legal structures of Europe through the Church and the establishment of Christendom.

At the same time, Rome played a pivotal role in Christian eschatology, with the empire often being portrayed as both a symbol of earthly power and a force of opposition to God's kingdom. The fall of Rome, as foretold in biblical prophecy, was seen as part of God's plan to bring about the final judgment and the establishment of the eternal kingdom of God.

The Role of Rome in Shaping and Perpetuating Apocalyptic Prophecy

The Roman Empire played a pivotal role in the shaping and perpetuation of apocalyptic prophecy within early Christianity. As both the most powerful empire of the ancient world and a central figure in biblical prophecy, Rome was often portrayed in apocalyptic literature as a symbol of oppressive world power and a key player in the unfolding of end-time events. In this chapter, we will explore how the Roman Empire influenced the development of apocalyptic prophecy, becoming both a fulfillment of certain prophecies and a symbol of the world's opposition to God's kingdom.

This examination will focus on how Rome's military, political, and cultural dominance shaped early Christian interpretations of prophecy, and how the eventual decline of the empire was seen as a fulfillment of biblical eschatology. Additionally, we will delve into the ongoing legacy of Rome in medieval and modern apocalyptic thought, where it continues to be referenced as a symbol of the worldly powers that will be judged and overthrown in the end times.

1. Rome in Early Christian Apocalyptic Thought

The Roman Empire's dominance over the Mediterranean world during the first few centuries of the Christian era profoundly influenced the eschatological outlook of early Christians. Living under Roman rule, with its military power, imperial cult, and periods of persecution, Christians interpreted their experiences through the lens of apocalyptic prophecy, seeing Rome as both a symbol of worldly power and a force that would ultimately be overthrown by God.

A. The Role of Rome in the Book of Revelation

One of the most explicit references to Rome in Christian apocalyptic literature is found in the Book of Revelation, where Rome is symbolically portrayed as Babylon the Great, the great harlot who sits on many waters (Revelation 17). This imagery draws on the prophetic tradition of the Old Testament, where Babylon was seen as a symbol of oppression and rebellion against God.

- Babylon as a Symbol of Rome: In the Book of Revelation, Babylon is used as a metaphor for Rome—a powerful, corrupt, and oppressive empire that exerts dominion over the world. The Roman Empire's wealth, military might, and pagan worship practices, including the imperial cult (where the emperor was venerated as a god), were seen as antagonistic to Christian faith. John, the author of Revelation, equates Rome with Babylon to evoke the imagery of a powerful city that will be destroyed for its defiance against God.

- Revelation 17:5-6: "And on her forehead was written a name of mystery: Babylon the Great, mother of prostitutes and of earth's abominations. And I saw the woman, drunk with the blood of the saints, the blood of the martyrs of Jesus."

In this context, the Roman Empire is depicted as being drunk with the blood of the saints, referring to its persecution of Christians, most notably under emperors such as Nero and Domitian. This persecution fueled the early Christian expectation that Rome's fall would be part of the final judgment and the victory of God's kingdom over the forces of evil.

B. Rome as the Fourth Beast in Daniel's Vision

The Book of Daniel, written centuries before the Roman Empire's rise to prominence, also provides imagery that early Christians interpreted as referring to Rome. In Daniel's vision of the four great beasts (Daniel 7), which represent successive world empires, the fourth beast, which is terrifying, dreadful, and exceedingly strong, is often identified with the Roman Empire.

- Daniel 7:7: "After this I saw in the night visions, and behold, a fourth beast, terrifying and dreadful and exceedingly strong. It had great iron teeth; it devoured and broke in pieces and stamped what was left with its feet. It was different from all the beasts that were before it, and it had ten horns."

This fourth beast, with its iron teeth, is commonly understood to represent the Roman Empire, particularly its military might and capacity for conquest. The ten horns are interpreted as representing either ten kings or kingdoms that would arise from the Roman Empire, pointing to a period of division and fragmentation, consistent with the imagery of the feet of iron and clay in Nebuchadnezzar's dream.

- Rome's Role in Eschatology: Early Christian interpreters saw the Roman Empire as the culmination of the oppressive worldly kingdoms foretold in Daniel, but they also believed that Rome would be overthrown by the Kingdom of God, which is represented by the Son of Man who receives dominion over all nations (Daniel 7:13-14).

C. The Roman Persecutions and Christian Eschatology

The persecutions of Christians under Roman rule significantly shaped the development of Christian eschatology. The Emperor Nero (r. 54-68 CE) became a central figure in Christian apocalyptic thought due to his brutal persecution of Christians following the Great Fire of Rome in 64 CE. Later Christian writers, such as Lactantius and Tertullian, identified Nero as a precursor to the Antichrist, a figure who would appear in the end times to oppose Christ and the Church.

- Nero as a Prototype of the Antichrist: The legend of Nero persisted well into the early medieval period, with some Christians believing that Nero would return in the last days as the Antichrist, leading a final rebellion against God's people before being destroyed by Christ at his second coming. This belief was closely tied to the broader apocalyptic expectation that Rome, as the seat of power, would play a key role in the last battle between good and evil.

- The Martyrdom of Saints: Roman persecution, particularly under Diocletian (r. 284-305 CE), reinforced the Christian belief that the suffering of the faithful was a sign of the coming end of the world. Many early Christian martyrs were seen as witnesses to the ultimate victory of God over the powers of this world, with their blood becoming symbolic of the final conflict between Christ and the forces of Satan.

2. The Fall of Rome and the Fulfillment of Prophecy

For many early Christians, the fall of the Western Roman Empire in 476 CE was seen as a sign of the end times and the fulfillment of the apocalyptic prophecies found in the Book of Revelation and Daniel. The collapse of Roman power, after centuries of dominance, was interpreted as part of the divine plan to replace earthly kingdoms with the eternal Kingdom of God.

A. The Fall of Rome as an Eschatological Event

The sacking of Rome by the Visigoths in 410 CE and the eventual fall of the Western Roman Empire in 476 CE were seen by many Christians as events with apocalyptic significance. The idea that Rome—once the center of the known world—could fall, reinforced the belief that no earthly power could withstand the judgment of God.

- Augustine's City of God: One of the most influential responses to the fall of Rome came from Augustine of Hippo, who wrote his seminal work, City of God, in the aftermath of the sack of Rome. Augustine argued that the fall of Rome was not the end of the world but rather a reminder that all earthly cities and empires are temporary. In contrast, the City of God, which represents the eternal Kingdom of God, would endure forever. Augustine's work helped to shift the Christian understanding of eschatology from an immediate expectation of the end to a more spiritual and theological focus on the eternal victory of God.

B. The Division of the Roman Empire and the Feet of Iron and Clay

The division of the Roman Empire into the Western Roman Empire and the Eastern Roman Empire (Byzantium) in the 4th century CE, and the eventual fall of the West, was seen by many as a fulfillment of the prophecy of the feet of iron and clay in Daniel 2:41-43. The imagery of the statue's feet, made of a mixture of strong iron and brittle clay, symbolizes a kingdom that is partly strong and partly fragile— a fitting description of the Roman Empire in its later years.

- Division and Fragmentation: The feet of iron and clay represent the internal divisions and weaknesses that plagued the Roman Empire in its later centuries. The Eastern

Empire (Byzantium) retained much of the strength of the Roman state and continued to flourish, while the Western Empire became increasingly fragmented, eventually succumbing to barbarian invasions.

- A Sign of the End Times: For early Christian interpreters, the fall of the Roman Empire was not only a political event but a sign that the end times were drawing near. The feet of iron and clay were seen as the final stage of the prophetic sequence of empires, with the collapse of Rome marking the beginning of the end and the imminent arrival of the Kingdom of God.

3. Rome's Continued Role in Apocalyptic Thought

Even after the fall of the Western Roman Empire, the imagery of Rome as a symbol of worldly power and corruption persisted in Christian apocalyptic thought throughout the Middle Ages and into the modern era. Rome's association with both empire and apostasy continued to shape interpretations of the end times, particularly in the context of the Holy Roman Empire and the Reformation.

A. The Holy Roman Empire and the Legacy of Rome

The establishment of the Holy Roman Empire in 800 CE, when Charlemagne was crowned emperor by the Pope, was seen by many as the revival of Roman power under Christian leadership. The Holy Roman Empire presented itself as the successor to the Roman Empire, with a mission to uphold Christian values and protect the Church.

- Rome as the Center of Christendom: Throughout the Middle Ages, Rome continued to be seen as the spiritual and political center of Christendom, with the Papacy wielding significant influence over European rulers. However, the apocalyptic associations with Rome persisted, particularly in times of corruption and decline within the Church.

- The Papacy and the Antichrist: During the Reformation in the 16th century, some Protestant reformers, such as Martin Luther and John Calvin, identified the Papacy with the Antichrist, drawing on the imagery of Babylon and the great harlot from Revelation. They argued that the corruption of the Roman Catholic Church was evidence that the end times were near, and that Rome, as the seat of the Papacy, was the embodiment of worldly power in opposition to God's kingdom.

B. Rome in Modern Apocalyptic Movements

In modern times, the symbolism of Rome continues to play a role in apocalyptic thought, particularly in movements that emphasize the imminent return of Christ and the final judgment. Some contemporary Christian groups interpret the prophecies of Daniel and Revelation as referring to modern political systems that they associate with the spirit of Rome—seen as a symbol of global power and secular authority.

- Rome as a Symbol of Worldly Powers: In modern apocalyptic literature, Rome is often used as a symbol of the secular world system that opposes God's kingdom. This interpretation can be seen in movements that view global institutions, such as the United Nations or the European Union, as fulfilling the role of Babylon or the Beast in Revelation.

- The Legacy of Rome in Popular Culture: The imagery of Rome's role in the end times has also been perpetuated in popular culture, particularly in films, books, and television series that explore apocalyptic themes. Rome, or cities modeled on its imagery, often represents a fallen world that will be destroyed in the final judgment.

Rome's Role in Shaping and Perpetuating Apocalyptic Prophecy

The Roman Empire played a critical role in shaping early Christian apocalyptic prophecy, both as a historical reality and as a symbol of the worldly powers that would be overthrown in the end times. In the Book of Revelation and the prophecies of Daniel, Rome is portrayed as both a powerful force and a temporary kingdom that would ultimately be replaced by the eternal Kingdom of God.

Even after the fall of the Western Roman Empire, the symbolism of Rome persisted in Christian eschatology, influencing interpretations of the Antichrist, the final judgment, and the rise of new worldly powers. From the Holy Roman Empire to the Reformation and beyond, Rome's legacy has continued to shape the Christian understanding of the end of history.

CHAPTER 07

THE FEET OF IRON AND CLAY – DIVIDED KINGDOMS

The feet of iron and clay in Nebuchadnezzar's dream (Daniel 2:31-45) represent a critical phase in the unfolding of world history, particularly as it relates to the divided kingdoms that emerged after the fall of the Roman Empire. The imagery of iron mixed with clay symbolizes a period of political fragmentation and instability, where the remnants of the Roman Empire gave way to a collection of weaker kingdoms that lacked the unity and strength of their predecessor. This chapter will delve into the symbolism of iron mixed with clay, interpreting how this mixture represents the divided kingdoms of medieval Europe and their role in biblical prophecy.

We will explore the fall of the Roman Empire and the subsequent formation of European kingdoms, the political and cultural fragmentation of the continent, and how this period fits into the broader prophetic narrative. In addition, we will examine how medieval Europe's divided states struggled with unity and power, mirroring the fragile mixture of iron and clay, and how this symbolism has continued to resonate in apocalyptic interpretations of world history.

1. Iron and Clay: Symbolism of Strength and Fragility

In Nebuchadnezzar's dream, the feet and toes of the great statue are made of a mixture of iron and clay, a composition that signifies both strength (iron) and weakness or fragility (clay). This combination is crucial to understanding the divided kingdoms that followed the fall of the Roman Empire, as it suggests a period characterized by disunity, internal weakness, and external threats, even as some remnants of Roman strength persisted.

A. Iron as a Symbol of Strength

The iron in the feet represents the lingering elements of Roman strength, particularly in the form of military power, law, and governance, which survived the collapse of the Roman Empire. Although the Western Roman Empire fell in

476 CE, the Eastern Roman Empire (Byzantium) continued to thrive, and the political and legal traditions of Rome persisted in various forms throughout Europe.

- Roman Legacy: The Byzantine Empire, centered in Constantinople, continued to claim the legacy of Rome, while various Germanic kingdoms in Western Europe adopted elements of Roman law and governance. The Holy Roman Empire, established in the 9th century under Charlemagne, sought to revive the Roman imperial tradition, emphasizing the strength of Rome's political and legal order.

B. Clay as a Symbol of Fragility

The clay represents the inherent weaknesses and divisions that plagued the post-Roman kingdoms of Europe. While some aspects of Roman power persisted, the fragmented political landscape of medieval Europe was marked by internal instability, competing kingdoms, and shifting alliances. The feudal system, which dominated much of Europe, further decentralized power, creating a political environment where unity was difficult to maintain.

- Fragility of Kingdoms: The mixture of iron and clay symbolizes the inability of these post-Roman kingdoms to achieve the strength and unity of the Roman Empire. While some kingdoms, like the Holy Roman Empire or the Frankish Kingdom, sought to consolidate power, their efforts were often undermined by internal conflicts, rival factions, and external threats from Vikings, Saracens, and other invaders.

2. The Fall of the Roman Empire and the Formation of Divided Kingdoms

The fall of the Western Roman Empire in 476 CE marked the beginning of a period of political fragmentation in Europe, as the once-unified Roman territories were divided among various barbarian kingdoms. These new kingdoms, while often retaining elements of Roman culture and governance, were fundamentally weaker and more divided than their imperial predecessor.

A. The Barbarian Kingdoms of Europe

In the wake of Rome's collapse, several Germanic tribes established their own kingdoms on former Roman territory. These kingdoms, such as the Visigoths, Ostrogoths, Franks, and Vandals, were the primary heirs to the Roman legacy in the West, though they struggled to maintain the same level of unity and administrative cohesion.

- The Visigothic Kingdom: The Visigoths, who sacked Rome in 410 CE, went on to establish a kingdom in Spain and southern Gaul. While the Visigoths adopted many Roman legal and cultural practices, their kingdom was marked by periods of internal strife and external pressure from the Byzantines and later the Muslims.

- The Ostrogoths and the Lombards: The Ostrogoths under Theodoric the Great ruled much of Italy after the fall of the Western Roman Empire. They maintained a degree of Roman governance, but their kingdom eventually fell to the Byzantines during the Gothic War. Similarly, the Lombards established a kingdom in Italy, but their rule was marked by fragmentation and conflict with the Papacy and the Byzantines.

- The Franks: The Frankish Kingdom, particularly under Clovis I and later under the Carolingians, became one of the most powerful of the post-Roman kingdoms. However, even the Franks experienced internal divisions, with the partitioning of the empire after the death of Charlemagne leading to the creation of distinct kingdoms in France, Germany, and Italy.

B. The Rise of the Feudal System

One of the defining features of the post-Roman period was the rise of feudalism, a system of governance based on land ownership, loyalty, and vassalage. In the absence of strong centralized power, local lords held significant authority over their territories, and political power was highly decentralized.

- Decentralization of Power: The feudal system further fragmented Europe, as kings often had limited control over their vassals, and political authority was distributed among a myriad of local rulers. This decentralized structure contributed to the political instability of medieval Europe, with frequent wars between competing lords and kingdoms.

- Fragmented Loyalties: The mixture of iron and clay in Nebuchadnezzar's dream also symbolizes the fragmented loyalties that characterized feudal Europe. While some kingdoms retained elements of Roman strength (iron), their rulers often struggled to maintain loyalty among their vassals, leading to a fragile and divided political landscape (clay).

3. The Holy Roman Empire: Iron and Clay in Medieval Europe

The establishment of the Holy Roman Empire in 800 CE by Charlemagne, and its subsequent development during the Middle Ages, is a prime example of the iron and clay symbolism. The Holy Roman Empire sought to revive the glory and strength of the ancient Roman Empire, but it was marked by internal divisions and weaknesses that prevented it from achieving true unity.

A. The Legacy of Rome in the Holy Roman Empire

The Holy Roman Empire, which was centered in Germany and included parts of Italy and central Europe, saw itself as the continuation of the Roman imperial tradition. The emperor, crowned by the Pope, was seen as the protector of Christendom and the successor to the Caesars.

- Charlemagne's Empire: Under Charlemagne (r. 768-814), the empire experienced a period of relative stability and expansion, incorporating much of western and central Europe. Charlemagne sought to emulate the governance of ancient Rome by promoting education, law, and religious unity.

- The Fragmentation of the Empire: However, after Charlemagne's death, the empire was divided among his heirs, leading to a period of political fragmentation. The Treaty of Verdun (843 CE) split the empire into three distinct kingdoms—West Francia (which would become France), East Francia (which would become Germany), and Middle Francia—a division that reflected the fragility symbolized by the feet of iron and clay.

B. The Internal Weaknesses of the Holy Roman Empire

The Holy Roman Empire was marked by internal divisions throughout its history. Unlike the centralized Roman Empire, the Holy Roman Empire was a loose confederation of duchies, kingdoms, and principalities, each with its own local rulers who often had competing interests. This lack of unity made the empire vulnerable to both internal strife and external threats.

- Power Struggles with the Papacy: One of the key sources of tension within the Holy Roman Empire was the ongoing power struggle between the emperors and the Popes. The conflict over who held ultimate authority—temporal rulers or the Church—weakened the empire and prevented it from achieving the kind of unity and strength that had characterized the Roman Empire.

- Regional Fragmentation: The empire was also divided by regionalism, with local rulers in Germany, Italy, and other parts of the empire often pursuing their own interests. This regional fragmentation mirrored the symbolic mixture of iron and clay, as the empire retained some of the strength of Rome but was weakened by internal divisions and a lack of cohesion.

4. The Feet of Iron and Clay in Prophetic Interpretation

The symbolism of the feet of iron and clay has long been interpreted as a representation of the divided kingdoms of post-Roman Europe, but it also carries broader prophetic implications. Many Christian interpreters, particularly in medieval and modern apocalyptic thought, have seen this imagery as indicative of a world order that is inherently unstable, marked by division and conflict, and destined to be replaced by the Kingdom of God.

A. Medieval Christian Interpretation

During the Middle Ages, many Christian theologians interpreted the divided kingdoms of Europe as part of the fulfillment of biblical prophecy. The idea that the successor kingdoms to the Roman Empire were part of the prophetic sequence outlined in Daniel's vision reinforced the belief that Europe's fragmented political landscape was a sign of the end times.

- Augustine's City of God: Augustine of Hippo, writing in the early 5th century, interpreted the fall of Rome and the subsequent fragmentation of the empire as part of the larger struggle between the earthly city (representing temporal power) and the City of God (representing the eternal kingdom). Augustine's work suggested that the divisions of Europe were part of the inevitable decline of earthly powers before the establishment of God's eternal reign.

B. Modern Apocalyptic Movements

In modern apocalyptic thought, the feet of iron and clay have been interpreted as a symbol of modern Europe's political divisions, particularly in the context of the European Union and the rise of global powers. Some interpreters see the ongoing fragmentation and instability of European and global politics as a continuation of the prophetic vision outlined in Daniel, with the ultimate fulfillment being the overthrow of all earthly powers and the establishment of the Kingdom of God.

- Europe and the End Times: In some modern apocalyptic interpretations, the European Union is seen as a revival of the Roman Empire, with its mixture of strong and weak nations reflecting the symbolism of iron and clay. These interpretations suggest that the political struggles within Europe and the rise of globalization are signs that the end times are drawing near.

The Divided Kingdoms and the Feet of Iron and Clay

The feet of iron and clay in Nebuchadnezzar's dream provide a vivid symbol of the divided kingdoms that emerged in the wake of the Roman Empire's fall. The mixture of strength (iron) and fragility (clay) represents the political and cultural fragmentation that characterized medieval Europe, where remnants of Roman power persisted but were weakened by internal divisions, regional conflicts, and external threats.

This period of division, which saw the rise of barbarian kingdoms, the development of the feudal system, and the establishment of the Holy Roman Empire, fits into the broader prophetic narrative of world history as outlined in Daniel's vision. The divided kingdoms of post-Roman Europe were seen by many as part of the unfolding of biblical prophecy, pointing to the eventual downfall of all earthly kingdoms and the establishment of the eternal Kingdom of God.

The Rise of the Holy Roman Empire and Its Role in the Crusades

The Holy Roman Empire, which emerged in the early Middle Ages as an attempt to revive the legacy of the ancient Roman Empire, played a significant role in the shaping of medieval Europe and the Christian world. The empire, which claimed to embody both Roman political traditions and Christian authority, sought to protect and expand Christendom. This chapter explores the rise of the Holy Roman Empire, its historical and political context, and its crucial role in the Crusades, a series of military campaigns that aimed to reclaim the Holy Land from Muslim control.

The Crusades, which began in the late 11th century, were deeply connected to the aspirations of the Holy Roman Empire and the broader vision of Christian unity under imperial and papal leadership. We will examine how the Holy Roman Empire, particularly under its leading emperors, contributed to the Crusades, balancing its own political ambitions with the religious goals of reclaiming the sacred places of Christianity.

1. The Rise of the Holy Roman Empire

The Holy Roman Empire was established in 800 CE when Pope Leo III crowned the Frankish king Charlemagne as Emperor of the Romans. This act symbolized the revival of the Roman imperial tradition in the West, a continuation of the legacy of the Roman Empire that had fallen more than three centuries earlier in the West. The Holy Roman Empire aimed to unite the territories of Western Europe under a Christian monarch who would be both a temporal ruler and a protector of the Christian faith.

A. Charlemagne and the Formation of the Empire

Charlemagne, also known as Charles the Great (r. 768–814 CE), was the first ruler to hold the title of Holy Roman Emperor. Under his leadership, the Carolingian Empire expanded significantly, encompassing modern-day France, Germany, Italy, and other parts of Europe. Charlemagne's empire represented the fusion of Germanic kingship, Roman imperial authority, and Christian ideals, forming the foundation for the Holy Roman Empire.

- The Coronation of Charlemagne: On Christmas Day, 800 CE, Charlemagne was crowned by Pope Leo III in St. Peter's Basilica in Rome. This coronation marked the symbolic union of Church and state, with the Pope bestowing imperial legitimacy on Charlemagne. The event also underscored the belief that the Holy Roman Emperor was the secular counterpart to the Pope, tasked with defending Christendom and spreading the Christian faith.

- Charlemagne's Reforms: Charlemagne introduced significant reforms in governance, education, and religion. He promoted the Carolingian Renaissance, a revival of learning and culture based on classical Roman and Christian ideals. His reign established the idea that the Holy Roman Empire was not only a political entity but also a spiritual protector of the Church and its teachings.

B. The Fragmentation of the Empire

After Charlemagne's death in 814 CE, his empire was divided among his heirs, leading to a period of political fragmentation. The Treaty of Verdun in 843 CE divided the empire into three separate kingdoms—West Francia (modern France), East Francia (modern Germany), and Middle Francia (stretching from the Low Countries to northern Italy). While the title of Holy Roman Emperor persisted, the political unity that characterized Charlemagne's reign was lost, leading to centuries of power struggles.

- East Francia and the Holy Roman Empire: By the 10th century, the eastern Frankish kingdom (East Francia) emerged as the core of the Holy Roman Empire under the Ottonian dynasty. Otto I (r. 936–973 CE) was crowned Holy Roman Emperor in 962 CE, solidifying the empire's connection to Germany. The emperors of the Holy Roman Empire saw themselves as the successors to Charlemagne and the protectors of Christendom.

C. The Role of the Papacy in the Empire

The relationship between the Holy Roman Emperor and the Pope was complex and often marked by tension. While the Pope provided religious legitimacy to the emperor's rule, there were frequent disputes over the balance of power between the secular and spiritual authorities. These conflicts culminated in the Investiture Controversy of the 11th century, in which emperors and popes clashed over the right to appoint bishops and other church officials.

- The Emperor as Protector of the Church: Despite these conflicts, the Holy Roman Empire was seen as the protector of the Roman Catholic Church. The emperor's role was to defend the Church against heretics, non-Christians, and external threats. This responsibility became particularly important during the Crusades, when Christian Europe faced the challenge of reclaiming the Holy Land from Muslim rule.

2. The Holy Roman Empire and the Crusades

The Crusades (1095–1291 CE) were a series of religious wars launched by Christian Europe to reclaim the Holy Land from Muslim control, particularly Jerusalem and other sacred Christian sites. The Holy Roman Empire played a significant role in these campaigns, with several emperors leading or supporting Crusades, despite the political and territorial ambitions that sometimes conflicted with purely religious goals.

A. The First Crusade and the Call of Urban II

The First Crusade (1096–1099 CE) was launched in response to a call by Pope Urban II at the Council of Clermont in 1095 CE. Urban urged the Christian nobility of Europe to take up arms against the Muslim Seljuk Turks, who had seized control of Jerusalem and other Christian holy sites. The First Crusade was marked by a wave of religious enthusiasm, as thousands of knights and commoners set out to reclaim the Holy Land.

- The Role of the Holy Roman Empire: Although the Holy Roman Emperor at the time, Henry IV, was engaged in the Investiture Controversy with Pope Urban II and was thus unable to directly participate in the First Crusade, the empire still played a role in supporting the Crusader effort. Many German nobles, including Godfrey of Bouillon, took part in the Crusade, and their contributions were crucial to the success of the Christian forces in capturing Jerusalem in 1099.

- Godfrey of Bouillon: Godfrey of Bouillon, a nobleman from the Holy Roman Empire, became one of the most famous leaders of the First Crusade. After the successful conquest of Jerusalem, he was offered the title of King of Jerusalem but refused it, instead taking the title Defender of the Holy Sepulchre, a reflection of the Crusaders' religious motivations.

B. The Second and Third Crusades: Imperial Leadership

The Second Crusade (1147–1149 CE) and Third Crusade (1189–1192 CE) saw the involvement of the Holy Roman Emperors more directly. The emperors of this period were motivated by both religious devotion and the desire to strengthen their political power in Europe and the East.

- The Second Crusade: Initiated by Pope Eugene III after the fall of the County of Edessa to Muslim forces, the Second Crusade was led by Emperor Conrad III of the Holy Roman Empire and King Louis VII of France. Although the Crusade ended in failure, with the Christian forces unable to recapture Edessa or make significant gains in the Holy Land, it demonstrated the Holy Roman Empire's commitment to the Crusading movement.

- The Third Crusade: The Third Crusade was launched in response to the Muslim leader Saladin's capture of Jerusalem in 1187 CE. The Holy Roman Emperor Frederick I Barbarossa took a leading role in this Crusade, gathering a massive army and marching towards the Holy Land. However, Barbarossa's untimely death during the campaign—he drowned in a river in Anatolia—dealt a significant blow to the Crusading effort. Despite this setback, his participation demonstrated the Holy Roman Empire's continued leadership in defending Christendom.

C. The Fourth Crusade and the Sacking of Constantinople

The Fourth Crusade (1202–1204 CE) was one of the most controversial Crusades in history. Originally intended to reclaim Jerusalem from Muslim control, it ended with the sacking of Constantinople, the capital of the Byzantine Empire, by Western Crusaders. The Holy Roman Empire, while not directly responsible for this outcome, played an indirect role in the broader power dynamics between Western and Eastern Christendom.

- Tensions Between East and West: The sacking of Constantinople during the Fourth Crusade deepened the divide between the Roman Catholic Church in the West and the Eastern Orthodox Church in the East. Although the Holy Roman Empire had long sought to assert its authority over the Eastern Roman (Byzantine) Empire, the destruction of Constantinople further complicated relations between the two Christian powers and weakened the overall unity of Christendom.

3. The Holy Roman Empire's Role in Shaping the Crusading Ideal

The Holy Roman Empire was central to the Crusading ideal, not only through its direct involvement in the military campaigns but also through its role in shaping the broader concept of Christian kingship and imperial authority. The empire, which saw itself as the defender of the Catholic faith and the Pope's protector, was integral to the ideology that underpinned the Crusades.

A. The Holy Roman Emperor as Defender of Christendom

The Holy Roman emperors viewed themselves as the defenders of Christendom, responsible for protecting the Christian faith from external enemies, particularly the Muslim powers that controlled the Holy Land. This self-image was rooted in the legacy of Charlemagne and his successors, who had waged campaigns against pagan and Muslim forces in Europe.

- Frederick II and the Sixth Crusade: One of the most notable examples of the Holy Roman Emperor's involvement in the Crusades was Frederick II, who led the Sixth Crusade (1228–1229 CE). Unlike previous Crusades, which relied on military conquest, Frederick II successfully negotiated the peaceful return of Jerusalem to Christian control through diplomacy with the Muslim ruler Al-Kamil. Frederick's unique approach to the Crusades reflected the Holy Roman

Empire's political influence and its ability to act as a mediator between the Christian and Muslim worlds.

B. The Impact of the Crusades on the Holy Roman Empire

The Crusades had a profound impact on the Holy Roman Empire, both politically and spiritually. The Crusading movement enhanced the empire's reputation as a protector of the Christian faith, but it also strained the empire's resources and contributed to internal conflicts.

- Strengthening of Papal-Imperial Tensions: The involvement of the Holy Roman emperors in the Crusades often exacerbated tensions with the Papacy. While the Popes relied on the emperors to lead Crusading efforts, there were frequent disputes over the emperor's authority and the extent to which the Church should control the Crusading movement. These tensions would ultimately contribute to the growing power struggles between the Holy Roman Empire and the Papacy in the late medieval period.

- The Legacy of the Crusades: The Crusades helped solidify the Holy Roman Empire's role as a central power in medieval Europe, but they also highlighted the limitations of imperial authority. The failure of several Crusades, combined with the empire's internal divisions, weakened the Holy Roman Empire's influence in the later medieval period. However, the ideal of Crusading kingship persisted, and later emperors continued to invoke the legacy of the Crusades in their efforts to defend and expand Christendom.

The Holy Roman Empire's Role in the Crusades

The Holy Roman Empire played a vital role in the Crusading movement, both as a political and military force and as a symbol of Christian kingship and imperial authority. From the First Crusade, in which German nobles like Godfrey of Bouillon took leading roles, to the later Crusades, where emperors such as Frederick I Barbarossa and Frederick II led campaigns to reclaim the Holy Land, the Holy Roman Empire was central to the defense and expansion of Christendom.

However, the Crusades also highlighted the internal weaknesses and political divisions within the empire, as well as its complex relationship with the Papacy. The Holy Roman Empire's involvement in the Crusades ultimately shaped its identity as the protector of Christendom, but it also contributed to the growing tensions between secular and spiritual authorities that would define the later medieval period.

How Divided Kingdoms Reflect the Instability That Continues Into Modern Times

The image of divided kingdoms symbolized by the feet of iron and clay in Nebuchadnezzar's dream has long been interpreted as a representation of the fragmented political landscape that emerged after the fall of the Roman Empire. This mixture of iron (strength) and clay (fragility) embodies the inherent instability that characterized the medieval period and continues to resonate in modern times. The division and fragility of these post-Roman kingdoms reflect a recurring theme of political fragmentation, regionalism, and competing powers, which still shape global political systems today.

This chapter will explore how the divided kingdoms that arose in medieval Europe following the collapse of the Roman Empire serve as a metaphor for the ongoing political instability that has persisted through the centuries, influencing nationalism, imperialism, and the modern geopolitical order. By examining how these divisions mirror the fragile state of international relations, we can better understand how the legacy of division and instability continues to impact modern societies, particularly in Europe and across the world.

1. The Divided Kingdoms After the Fall of the Roman Empire

The fall of the Western Roman Empire in 476 CE marked the beginning of a period of political fragmentation in Europe, as the once-unified empire fractured into various barbarian kingdoms and feudal territories. This era, often referred to as the Dark Ages, was characterized by a lack of central authority, with power being distributed among competing local rulers, kings, and noblemen.

A. The Emergence of Divided Kingdoms

In the wake of Rome's collapse, several Germanic tribes and barbarian groups established their own kingdoms on former Roman territories. These kingdoms, while often adopting Roman administrative practices and legal codes, lacked the political and military cohesion of the Roman Empire. Key examples include the Visigoths in Spain, the Franks in Gaul, the Ostrogoths in Italy, and the Anglo-Saxons in Britain.

- Fragmented Political Authority: The political landscape of medieval Europe was characterized by regionalism and local autonomy, with kings and lords exerting power over small territories. This fragmentation led to frequent conflicts between rival kingdoms and the emergence of feudalism, a system in which local lords wielded significant control over their vassals and lands.

- Feudal Loyalties: The mixture of iron and clay in Nebuchadnezzar's dream can be seen as a metaphor for the complex web of feudal loyalties that defined medieval politics. While some kings wielded considerable power (iron), their authority was often weakened by the competing interests of powerful nobles and local rulers (clay), leading to a fragile and decentralized political system.

B. The Holy Roman Empire as a Divided Kingdom

The Holy Roman Empire, which sought to revive the glory of the Roman Empire in the medieval period, provides a prime example of the iron and clay symbolism. Although it claimed to be the successor to the Roman Empire, the Holy Roman Empire was a loose confederation of kingdoms, duchies, and principalities that were often at odds with one another.

- Internal Divisions: The Holy Roman Empire was marked by internal divisions between the emperor and the various local rulers who controlled different parts of the empire. The emperor's authority was often challenged by powerful princes, leading to political instability and fragmentation.

- Struggles with the Papacy: In addition to internal divisions, the Holy Roman Empire also faced external challenges, particularly in its ongoing power struggle with the Papacy. The conflict between emperors and popes over the right to appoint bishops and exercise authority over the Church weakened the empire and contributed to its inability to achieve political unity.

2. The Continuation of Political Instability Into the Modern Era

The instability and division that characterized the post-Roman kingdoms of medieval Europe did not end with the Middle Ages. Instead, these divisions laid the groundwork for the national conflicts, imperial rivalries, and regional tensions that would define European politics in the modern era. The mixture of iron and clay continued to serve as an apt metaphor for the fragmented and often fragile political landscape of modern Europe.

A. The Rise of Nation-States and Nationalism

The rise of nation-states in the early modern period marked a shift away from the decentralized feudal order of medieval Europe. However, the formation of nation-states such as France, England, Spain, and the German principalities was often accompanied by conflict and division.

- The Hundred Years' War: One of the most prominent examples of the instability of this period is the Hundred Years' War (1337–1453) between England and France. This conflict, rooted in dynastic claims and the struggle for territorial control, reflects the ongoing fragmentation of political power in Europe. Although France and England eventually emerged as centralized nation-states, the war's devastation highlighted the fragility of these early modern kingdoms.

- German Fragmentation: The Holy Roman Empire remained a fragmented and decentralized entity well into the modern period. The various German principalities and duchies that made up the empire retained a high degree of autonomy, making it difficult for the emperor to unify the German-speaking lands under a single central authority. This division persisted until the eventual unification of Germany in the late 19th century.

B. European Imperialism and the Competition for Power

The instability of divided kingdoms was not limited to the internal politics of Europe. It also extended to the global stage, as European powers engaged in imperial expansion and colonial competition throughout the early modern period. The desire for power and wealth drove European nations to conquer and colonize large parts of the Americas, Africa, and Asia, often leading to conflicts between rival empires.

- The Scramble for Africa: The Scramble for Africa in the late 19th century is a prime example of how the division of power among European empires led to geopolitical instability. The competition between Britain, France, Germany, and other European powers for control of African territories reflected the broader struggle for dominance on the global stage. This division of the world into competing colonial empires mirrored the fragmentation of medieval Europe.

- World War I and the Collapse of Empires: The First World War (1914–1918) marked the culmination of these imperial rivalries, leading to the collapse of several European empires, including the Austro-Hungarian, Ottoman, and Russian Empires. The war also exposed the fragility of the European state system, as alliances between nation-states and empires (iron) were often undermined by internal dissent and nationalist movements (clay).

3. Modern Political Instability: A Legacy of Divided Kingdoms

The divided kingdoms that emerged after the fall of the Roman Empire continue to influence modern political systems. The national rivalries, regional conflicts, and political instability that characterized Europe in the medieval and early modern periods have left a lasting legacy that shapes contemporary geopolitics.

A. The Fragmentation of Europe in the 20th Century

The instability of Europe's divided political landscape persisted into the 20th century, as evidenced by the World Wars, the rise of totalitarian regimes, and the eventual division of Europe during the Cold War. The fall of empires, the redrawing of national borders, and the rise of competing ideologies contributed to the fragmentation and instability that characterized much of the century.

- World War II and the Division of Europe: After World War II, Europe was divided between the Western Bloc, led by the United States and its NATO allies, and the Eastern Bloc, dominated by the Soviet Union. This division, often referred to as the Iron Curtain, reflected the ongoing tension between competing political systems—capitalism in the West and communism in the East. The Cold War division of Europe into two hostile camps can be seen as a continuation of the fragmented political landscape that emerged after the fall of the Roman Empire.

- The Balkans and the Collapse of Yugoslavia: The Balkan region has long been a source of political instability in Europe. The collapse of Yugoslavia in the 1990s, which led to a series of violent conflicts and the redrawing of national borders, is a stark reminder of the fragility of political unity in the face of ethnic and regional divisions. The fragmentation of Yugoslavia into multiple independent states mirrors the divisions of the post-Roman kingdoms in medieval Europe.

B. Modern Nationalism and Regionalism

In the 21st century, the instability symbolized by the iron and clay continues to manifest itself in the form of nationalism and regionalism, particularly in Europe. The rise of separatist movements, the breakdown of international alliances, and the challenges posed by globalization have all contributed to a renewed sense of fragmentation.

- Brexit and the European Union: The decision by the United Kingdom to leave the European Union (Brexit) in 2016 is a key example of how modern political divisions echo the instability of the past. The European Union, which sought to unite Europe under a common political and economic framework, has struggled to maintain cohesion in the face of growing nationalist and populist movements. The tension between the desire for unity (iron) and the reality of political divisions (clay) remains a central challenge for Europe.

- Regional Separatist Movements: In several European countries, regional separatist movements continue to challenge national unity. Movements for independence in Catalonia (Spain), Scotland (United Kingdom), and Flanders (Belgium) reflect the ongoing tension between centralized states and regional identities. These movements underscore the difficulty of achieving lasting political stability in the face of deep-seated cultural and regional differences.

4. The Feet of Iron and Clay as a Symbol of Modern Instability

The feet of iron and clay in Nebuchadnezzar's dream serve as a powerful symbol of the fragile political order that has persisted throughout history and continues into modern times. The tension between strength and weakness, unity and division, remains a defining feature of global politics.

A. The Inherent Fragility of Political Systems

The mixture of iron and clay represents the inherent fragility of political systems, where even the most powerful empires and nation-states are susceptible to internal divisions and external pressures. From the fall of the Roman Empire to the collapse of modern empires and the rise of nationalist movements, the inability of political entities to achieve lasting unity and stability remains a central theme in world history.

- Divided Alliances: The modern geopolitical landscape is characterized by shifting alliances and fragile partnerships. International organizations such as the United Nations, NATO, and the European Union are often seen as attempts to foster global unity (iron), but they are frequently undermined by national interests and political divisions (clay).

- Globalization and Fragmentation: The rise of globalization has brought nations closer together in terms of trade, communication, and technology, but it has also exposed deep economic and cultural divisions. As nations become more interconnected, the potential for political fragmentation increases, as seen in the rise of populist and anti-globalization movements in recent years.

B. Apocalyptic Themes in Modern Times

The continuing instability of the modern political world has led some to view the current era through the lens of apocalyptic prophecy, particularly in relation to the imagery of Nebuchadnezzar's dream. The mixture of iron and clay, symbolizing a world order that is both strong and fragile, resonates with those who see modern political systems as unsustainable and destined for collapse.

- End-Times Interpretations: In some modern apocalyptic interpretations, the division of the world into competing powers is seen as a fulfillment of biblical prophecy, with the eventual collapse of these systems paving the way for the Kingdom of God. The ongoing political instability, environmental crises, and social upheaval of the 21st century have led some to believe that the world is approaching a final reckoning.

The Legacy of Divided Kingdoms and Modern Instability

The divided kingdoms that emerged after the fall of the Roman Empire represent a historical pattern of political fragmentation and instability that continues to shape the modern world. From the regional rivalries of medieval Europe to the imperial conflicts of the modern era, the tension between unity and division has remained a defining feature of global politics. The symbolism of the feet of iron and clay in Nebuchadnezzar's dream serves as a powerful metaphor for the fragility of political systems and the ongoing challenges of achieving lasting stability.

As we look to the future, the legacy of divided kingdoms reminds us that political stability is often elusive, and the forces of division and fragmentation continue to shape the world in profound ways. Whether through nationalism, regionalism, or globalization, the challenges of maintaining unity in a divided world remain as relevant today as they were in the aftermath of Rome's fall.

Apocalyptic Interpretations of Modern Global Events

Throughout history, periods of political upheaval, social unrest, and natural disasters have often been interpreted through an apocalyptic lens, drawing on biblical prophecies such as those found in the Book of Revelation and the Book of Daniel. In modern times, the ongoing instability in the world—marked by wars, economic crises, environmental degradation, and global pandemics—has reignited interest in apocalyptic prophecy and the belief that we may be living in the end times.

This chapter delves deeper into how modern global events are interpreted by various religious, cultural, and political groups through the framework of apocalyptic prophecy. We will explore specific events, such as wars, natural disasters, and globalization, that are often seen as signs of the coming end of the world and the fulfillment of biblical prophecy. Additionally, we will examine the role of modern technology, political power, and global institutions in shaping these interpretations, and how they connect with ancient prophecies like those found in Nebuchadnezzar's dream and Revelation's vision of the Beast.

1. The Resurgence of Apocalyptic Thought in Modern Times

The imagery of apocalyptic prophecy has reemerged in recent decades, driven by the perception that modern global events are echoes of biblical warnings about the end times. This resurgence of apocalyptic thinking can be attributed to a combination of geopolitical tensions, environmental crises, and the rapid pace of technological change that many believe could lead to catastrophic outcomes.

A. Global Instability and Apocalyptic Expectations

The instability in global politics—marked by wars, terrorism, and the rise of authoritarian regimes—has contributed to a growing sense of apocalyptic anticipation. Many interpret these events as fulfilling key prophecies from the Book of Revelation and other biblical texts, particularly those that foretell the rise of global powers, wars and rumors of wars, and the persecution of the faithful.

- Wars and Conflicts: The frequent outbreaks of conflict, particularly in the Middle East, are often viewed as signs that we are living in the end times. The wars in Iraq, Syria, and Afghanistan, alongside the Israeli-Palestinian conflict, are seen by some as modern manifestations of the apocalyptic wars foretold in biblical prophecy, especially those related to Armageddon (Revelation 16:16).

- Armageddon: The concept of Armageddon—a final battle between the forces of good and evil, fought near Mount Megiddo in Israel—is one of the most prominent apocalyptic themes in Christian eschatology. Modern wars in the region are often interpreted as precursors to this ultimate conflict, particularly by evangelical Christian groups who view these wars as a fulfillment of end-times prophecy.

- Rise of Authoritarianism: The emergence of authoritarian leaders and totalitarian regimes in various parts of the world has also been linked to the Beast described in Revelation. Some modern interpretations identify certain global leaders as Antichrist figures, whose rise to power will precede a period of great tribulation and persecution.

B. Natural Disasters and Environmental Catastrophes

The increase in natural disasters—including hurricanes, earthquakes, wildfires, and pandemics—has been interpreted by many as another sign of the end times. These disasters are often seen as manifestations of the plagues and judgments described in Revelation, which will be unleashed upon the world as part of God's plan to bring about the final judgment.

- Pandemics: The outbreak of global pandemics, most notably the COVID-19 pandemic, has been interpreted by some as a fulfillment of biblical prophecies concerning pestilence and disease in the end times. The global spread of COVID-19, alongside the rapid changes it caused in daily life, economic structures, and political systems, has fueled apocalyptic narratives. The imagery of plagues and pestilence (Revelation 6:8) is often cited in this context.

- Climate Change and Environmental Destruction: The looming threat of climate change and environmental destruction has also been interpreted through an apocalyptic lens. Rising global temperatures, melting ice caps, wildfires, and extreme weather patterns are often seen as evidence that humanity is reaching the limits of its dominion over the Earth, as described in Revelation's vision of the destruction of the earth (Revelation 11:18). For some, this environmental crisis is not only a sign of the end times but also a warning of divine judgment for humanity's failure to care for God's creation.

C. Globalization and Technological Surveillance

Modern technology, particularly advances in surveillance, data collection, and artificial intelligence, has contributed to growing concerns about the rise of a global order that echoes the apocalyptic warnings about the Beast and its mark (Revelation 13:16-17). In an age of rapid technological progress, many fear the potential for abuse of power by global authorities who could use technology to control populations.

- The Mark of the Beast: The Book of Revelation warns about a mark that will be placed on people's foreheads or hands, without which they will not be able to buy or sell (Revelation 13:16-17). In modern apocalyptic interpretations, this mark is often linked to emerging technologies such as digital currencies, RFID chips, and biometric identification systems. The concern is that these technologies could be used to create a system of total control, fulfilling the prophecy of the Beast's reign.

- Surveillance and Control: The rise of global surveillance systems, including the use of facial recognition, AI-driven data analysis, and social credit systems (such as those being developed in China), has further fueled apocalyptic fears. These technologies are seen by some as tools that could be used by an authoritarian global regime to exert total control over individuals, echoing the warnings about the Beast's dominion.

2. The Role of Global Institutions in Apocalyptic Interpretations

Global institutions, such as the United Nations, the European Union, and other international bodies, have often been viewed with suspicion by apocalyptic thinkers, particularly those who see the rise of global governance as a precursor to the establishment of the Antichrist's reign. These interpretations draw heavily on the imagery of Nebuchadnezzar's dream (Daniel 2) and the Beast from Revelation, which are often seen as symbolic of a future world government that will oppose God's kingdom.

A. The European Union as the Revival of the Roman Empire

In some interpretations of biblical prophecy, the European Union is seen as a revival of the Roman Empire, represented by the feet of iron and clay in Nebuchadnezzar's dream. The mixture of iron (strength) and clay (weakness) is often seen as a metaphor for the EU's combination of economic power and political fragility.

- Iron and Clay as the European Union: The EU's frequent struggles with internal division, as seen in debates over Brexit, economic crises, and the rise of populist movements, reflect the symbolism of iron mixed with clay. Some apocalyptic thinkers view the EU as the final phase of the Roman Empire, destined to play a key role in the rise of a global government before the return of Christ.

   - Ten Kings: The ten toes of the statue in Nebuchadnezzar's dream (Daniel 2:41-42) are sometimes interpreted as ten leaders or nations that will emerge from a revived Roman Empire in the last days. Apocalyptic interpretations often speculate that these ten leaders will work together to establish a global empire, which will ultimately be overthrown by the coming Kingdom of God.

B. The United Nations and Global Government

The United Nations and other international organizations are frequently viewed with suspicion by apocalyptic thinkers, who see these institutions as harbingers of a one-world government that could be controlled by the Antichrist. The UN's emphasis on global cooperation, peace, and human rights is sometimes reinterpreted as a veiled attempt to establish a secular global order that will ultimately persecute Christians and impose totalitarian control.

   - The Antichrist and World Government: The idea of a single global government, led by the Antichrist, is a key theme in many apocalyptic interpretations of modern events. The consolidation of power in global institutions is seen as a sign that the world is moving closer to the fulfillment of the prophecies in Revelation, where a global ruler will emerge to oppress the faithful and enforce the mark of the Beast.

- Globalism as a Sign of the End Times: For many apocalyptic interpreters, the rise of globalism and multilateralism in the 20th and 21st centuries is evidence that the world is moving toward the final phase of history. The establishment of global institutions, trade agreements, and international legal frameworks is often seen as a precursor to the end-times scenario in which the Antichrist will rule over a unified global system.

3. The Role of Israel in Modern Apocalyptic Prophecy

The modern state of Israel holds a central place in many apocalyptic interpretations of global events. The establishment of Israel in 1948, followed by the Six-Day War in 1967, which resulted in Israel gaining control of Jerusalem, are seen as key events in the fulfillment of biblical prophecy. For many, the return of the Jewish people to the Holy Land is a sign that the end times are near.

A. The Rebirth of Israel as a Fulfillment of Prophecy

The reestablishment of Israel as a nation in the 20th century is often interpreted as the fulfillment of Old Testament prophecies regarding the return of the Jewish people to their ancestral homeland. Prophecies such as those in Ezekiel 37 (the Valley of Dry Bones) and Isaiah 11:11-12 are seen as foretelling the modern return of the Jewish people to Israel, a key event that precedes the Second Coming of Christ.

- Jerusalem in Prophecy: The city of Jerusalem, which is central to both Jewish and Christian eschatology, plays a critical role in modern apocalyptic interpretations. The control of East Jerusalem and the Temple Mount is seen as particularly significant, with many believing that the rebuilding of the Third Temple will mark the final phase of human history before the return of the Messiah.

B. The Battle of Armageddon and Israel's Role

In apocalyptic prophecy, the nation of Israel is often seen as the setting for the final battle between the forces of good and evil. The Battle of Armageddon, described in Revelation 16:16, is believed to take place in Israel, near the site of Megiddo. This final battle, which will involve the nations of the world gathering against Israel, is interpreted as a key event that will precede the return of Christ.

- Support forIsrael in Apocalyptic Thought: Many Christian apocalyptic movements, particularly those in the United States, are staunch supporters of Israel, believing that the protection of Israel is crucial to the fulfillment of biblical prophecy. The geopolitical conflicts surrounding Israel, particularly its relationships with neighboring Muslim-majority nations, are seen as precursors to the prophesied end-times wars.

Apocalyptic Interpretations in the Modern Age

The apocalyptic lens through which many view modern global events continues to shape interpretations of political, environmental, and technological developments. Whether through wars and conflicts, natural disasters, or the rise of global governance, these events are often seen as signs that the world is approaching the end of history as foretold in biblical prophecy. The symbolism of Nebuchadnezzar's dream, with its feet of iron and clay, and the imagery of Revelation's Beast, resonate with those who believe that the instability and fragility of the modern world are harbingers of the final judgment.

As apocalyptic interpretations of global events persist, they continue to influence political, religious, and social movements, shaping how people understand the trajectory of history and their place within it. While these interpretations offer a sense of hope for those who anticipate the coming Kingdom of God, they also serve as a reminder of the challenges that humanity faces in navigating an uncertain and often unstable world.

The Role of Israel in Modern Apocalyptic Interpretations

The modern state of Israel occupies a central and unique position in apocalyptic prophecy, particularly in the eschatological frameworks of Christian Zionism, Evangelical Christianity, and certain branches of Judaism. The reestablishment of Israel in 1948 and subsequent geopolitical developments in the Middle East are frequently seen as key signs of the end times, fulfilling biblical prophecies regarding the return of the Jewish people to the Promised Land and the final stages of God's divine plan for humanity.

This chapter delves deeper into the role of Israel in modern apocalyptic interpretations, examining the theological, historical, and political contexts that link the nation's existence with eschatological expectations. We will explore how the creation of the state of Israel, the control of Jerusalem, and the potential rebuilding of the Third Temple are perceived as pivotal events in the fulfillment of biblical prophecy. Additionally, we will discuss the impact of these beliefs on modern geopolitics, particularly in the relationship between Israel and its international supporters, notably among Evangelical Christians in the United States.

1. The Reestablishment of Israel as a Fulfillment of Biblical Prophecy

One of the most significant modern developments in the context of apocalyptic prophecy is the reestablishment of the state of Israel in 1948. For many Christians and Jews, the rebirth of Israel is seen as the direct fulfillment of Old Testament prophecies concerning the return of the Jewish people to their ancestral homeland after centuries of exile.

A. Biblical Foundations of the Return to the Promised Land

Numerous prophecies in the Old Testament refer to the return of the Jewish people to their homeland after periods of exile. These prophecies, found in books like Isaiah, Jeremiah, Ezekiel, and Zechariah, are interpreted by many as foretelling the modern creation of Israel.

- Isaiah 11:11-12: "In that day the Lord will reach out his hand a second time to reclaim the surviving remnant of his people... He will raise a banner for the nations and gather the exiles of Israel; he will assemble the scattered people of Judah from the four quarters of the earth."

- Ezekiel 37:21-22: "This is what the Sovereign Lord says: I will take the Israelites out of the nations where they have gone. I will gather them from all around and bring them back into their own land."

These passages are interpreted as direct references to the modern return of Jews to Israel, a movement that began in the late 19th century with Zionism and culminated in the establishment of the state of Israel after World War II.

B. The State of Israel and Apocalyptic Expectations

For many Christians, particularly Evangelicals, the founding of Israel in 1948 is seen as a crucial event in the timeline of the end times. The return of the Jewish people to the land of Israel is understood as a necessary precursor to the Second Coming of Christ and the fulfillment of other end-time prophecies.

- Dispensationalism: A key theological framework that connects the establishment of Israel with the end times is dispensationalism. According to this interpretation, history is divided into distinct periods or "dispensations," and the current period—known as the "Church Age"—will culminate with the restoration of Israel and the return of Christ. Dispensationalists believe that Israel's rebirth as a nation is a clear sign that the final dispensation is unfolding, leading to the rapture, the tribulation, and the millennial reign of Christ.

- Significance of 1948: The year 1948 is seen by many apocalyptic interpreters as a turning point in history. The United Nations' recognition of Israel is viewed as a fulfillment of divine prophecy, marking the beginning of the final countdown toward the establishment of God's eternal kingdom. This interpretation is particularly strong among

Christian Zionists, who see the support of Israel as a biblical mandate.

2. Jerusalem in Prophecy: The City of Destiny

Jerusalem plays a central role in apocalyptic prophecy, as it is considered the city where the final events of human history will unfold. For both Jews and Christians, Jerusalem is seen as the spiritual center of the world, the place where God's presence dwelled in the Temple and where He will ultimately establish His eternal kingdom.

A. Jerusalem as the City of God

In biblical prophecy, Jerusalem is often referred to as Zion, the City of David, and the Holy City. It is depicted as the place where God will dwell with His people and where salvation and judgment will be enacted in the end times.

- Isaiah 2:2-3: "In the last days, the mountain of the Lord's temple will be established as the highest of the mountains... and all nations will stream to it. Many peoples will come and say, 'Come, let us go up to the mountain of the Lord, to the temple of the God of Jacob. He will teach us his ways, so that we may walk in his paths.' The law will go out from Zion, the word of the Lord from Jerusalem."

- Zechariah 12:2-3: "I am going to make Jerusalem a cup that sends all the surrounding peoples reeling... On that day, when all the nations of the earth are gathered against her, I will make Jerusalem an immovable rock for all the nations."

These passages are interpreted as describing the central role Jerusalem will play in the last days, where it will become the focal point of both divine judgment and salvation.

B. The Six-Day War and the Capture of Jerusalem

The Six-Day War in 1967 is another event that apocalyptic interpreters see as having profound prophetic significance. During this conflict, Israel captured East Jerusalem, including the Old City and the Temple Mount, areas that had been under Jordanian control since 1948.

- Jerusalem Reunited: The reunification of Jerusalem under Israeli control was seen by many as a further fulfillment of prophecy, especially the expectation that Jerusalem would once again be under Jewish sovereignty in preparation for the Messianic age. This event heightened expectations among Evangelical Christians and Orthodox Jews that the Third Temple could soon be rebuilt, which is seen as a key event in end-times prophecy.

- Jerusalem as the Capital: In recent years, the international recognition of Jerusalem as Israel's capital, notably through the United States' decision to move its embassy to the city in 2018, has further fueled apocalyptic speculation. Many Evangelicals view this political decision as aligning with biblical prophecy, reinforcing their belief that

Jerusalem's significance in God's plan is being fulfilled in their lifetime.

3. The Rebuilding of the Third Temple: A Key Apocalyptic Event

One of the most significant aspects of apocalyptic prophecy concerning Israel is the potential rebuilding of the Third Temple in Jerusalem. According to certain interpretations of biblical prophecy, the reconstruction of the Temple on the Temple Mount, where the First and Second Temples stood, is a critical event that must take place before the Messianic age can fully arrive.

A. The Prophecies of the Third Temple

Several passages in the Bible point to the rebuilding of the Temple as a pivotal moment in the end times. In particular, the prophecies of Ezekiel describe in great detail a future Temple that will be built as part of the restoration of Israel and the establishment of God's kingdom on earth.

- Ezekiel 40-48: In this extended vision, Ezekiel describes the dimensions and layout of a future Temple that will be built in Jerusalem. This vision is often interpreted as referring to the Third Temple, which will be the center of worship during the Millennial Kingdom—the thousand-year reign of Christ described in Revelation.

- Daniel's Prophecy: In Daniel 9:27, the prophet speaks of a covenant that will be broken by an abomination that causes desolation, which many interpreters believe refers to the defilement of a future Temple by the Antichrist. This prophecy is seen as further evidence that a Third Temple must be rebuilt before the tribulation period and the Second Coming of Christ.

B. The Temple Mount and Religious Tensions

The Temple Mount in Jerusalem is one of the most contentious and sacred places in the world. Currently, it is the site of the Dome of the Rock and the Al-Aqsa Mosque, two of the holiest sites in Islam. The possibility of rebuilding the Third Temple on this site is a source of great tension between Jews, Muslims, and Christians.

- The Role of the Temple Institute: Some Jewish groups, such as the Temple Institute in Jerusalem, are actively preparing for the reconstruction of the Temple. They have created ritual objects and garments that would be used in the Temple's worship, and they are training priests from the line of Levi in preparation for the day when the Temple can be rebuilt. For many Jews and Christians, the rebuilding of the Third Temple is a crucial step in fulfilling the prophecies of the Messianic age.

- The Antichrist and the Temple: Many Evangelical Christians believe that the rebuilding of the Temple is linked to the rise of the Antichrist, who will establish a covenant with Israel, allowing the Temple to be rebuilt, only to later defile it and proclaim himself as God (2 Thessalonians 2:3-4). This event is often seen as the start of the Great Tribulation, a period of intense persecution and suffering before the return of Christ.

4. Israel's Role in the Final Battle: Armageddon

The final battle between the forces of good and evil—Armageddon—is a central theme in apocalyptic prophecy, and Israel is often seen as the epicenter of this final conflict. According to the Book of Revelation, the nations of the world will gather against Israel in a climactic battle near the site of Megiddo (Revelation 16:16).

A. The Gathering of Nations Against Israel

The prophecies of Armageddon describe a time when the nations of the world will rise up against Israel, seeking to destroy the Jewish people. This final confrontation is often interpreted as the culmination of Satan's rebellion against God, with Israel at the heart of the conflict.

- Zechariah 14:2-3: "I will gather all the nations to Jerusalem to fight against it... Then the Lord will go out and fight against those nations, as He fights on a day of battle."

This passage, along with the Revelation 16:16 prophecy of Armageddon, is seen as describing the final attempt by Satan and his forces to defeat God's chosen people before Christ returns to establish His kingdom.

B. The Return of Christ and the Defeat of the Nations

In the apocalyptic scenario, the gathering of nations against Israel will be met by the Second Coming of Christ, who will defeat the forces of evil and establish His millennial reign on earth. The Battle of Armageddon is thus seen as the ultimate fulfillment of God's judgment on the nations and the vindication of Israel.

- Revelation 19:11-16: "I saw heaven standing open, and there before me was a white horse, whose rider is called Faithful and True... The armies of heaven were following Him... Out of His mouth comes a sharp sword with which to strike down the nations. He will rule them with an iron scepter."

This vivid imagery of Christ returning as a warrior-king to defeat the enemies of Israel and establish His reign is central to Christian eschatology and is often interpreted in the context of modern geopolitical events involving Israel and its enemies.

Israel's Central Role in Apocalyptic Interpretations

The modern state of Israel holds a place of profound significance in the apocalyptic imagination of many Christians and Jews. From the reestablishment of Israel in 1948, to the capture of Jerusalem in 1967, to the potential rebuilding of the Third Temple, these events are seen as direct fulfillments of biblical prophecy and as key markers on the road to the end times.

For many, Israel is not only a political entity but also a spiritual signpost pointing toward the Second Coming of Christ and the final judgment. The expectation that Israel will play a central role in the Battle of Armageddon and the eventual triumph of good over evil continues to shape modern apocalyptic interpretations and geopolitical discourse.

CHAPTER 08

THE ROCK NOT CUT BY HUMAN HANDS – GOD'S KINGDOM

In Nebuchadnezzar's dream (Daniel 2:31-45), the final and most pivotal image is that of a rock or stone, "not cut by human hands," which descends and destroys the statue representing the succession of world empires. This stone represents the Kingdom of God, a kingdom that will supersede all earthly powers and endure forever. The image of the rock shattering the statue symbolizes the ultimate sovereignty of God, the end of human history as it is currently understood, and the establishment of a divine kingdom that will never be destroyed.

This chapter explores the prophetic meaning of the rock, its symbolic role in biblical prophecy, and its interpretation as the Kingdom of God. We will delve into how this image represents the supremacy of God's eternal rule over all human kingdoms and what it signifies for the end times and eschatological fulfillment. Additionally, we will examine how this prophecy has been understood throughout Christian theology, particularly its connections to the Messiah and the Second Coming of Christ.

1. The Image of the Rock in Nebuchadnezzar's Dream

Nebuchadnezzar's dream, as interpreted by Daniel, describes a great statue composed of different materials—gold, silver, bronze, iron, and iron mixed with clay—each representing a succession of world empires. The statue is finally struck by a rock, which is described as being "not cut by human hands." This rock destroys the statue completely, reducing it to dust that is blown away by the wind. Afterward, the rock grows into a great mountain that fills the whole earth.

A. The Rock as a Symbol of God's Sovereignty

The rock in this dream represents a kingdom established not by human effort or power, but by divine intervention. Unlike the human kingdoms that preceded it—each symbolized by the materials of the statue—the rock is supernatural in origin, signifying that its authority and power come directly from God.

- Daniel 2:34-35: "While you were watching, a rock was cut out, but not by human hands. It struck the statue on its feet of iron and clay and smashed them. Then the iron, the clay, the bronze, the silver and the gold were all broken to pieces and became like chaff on a threshing floor in the summer. The wind swept them away without leaving a trace. But the rock that struck the statue became a huge mountain and filled the whole earth."

- Daniel 2:44: "In the time of those kings, the God of heaven will set up a kingdom that will never be destroyed, nor will it be left to another people. It will crush all those kingdoms and bring them to an end, but it will itself endure forever."

These passages underscore the divine origin of the rock, which stands in stark contrast to the man-made empires represented by the statue. The destruction of the statue symbolizes the temporary nature of human power and the inevitable triumph of God's eternal kingdom.

B. The Kingdom of God: A Supernatural Reality

The rock not cut by human hands is a clear metaphor for the Kingdom of God, which will be established through divine means rather than through human conquest or governance. This kingdom is described as one that will never be destroyed and will endure forever, outlasting all earthly powers.

The fact that the rock destroys the feet of iron and clay first—the final stage of human empire in the prophecy—signifies that God's kingdom will arrive during a time when human governments are divided, weak, and internally unstable, much like the feet of iron mixed with clay.

- Divine Kingdom: The rock is a symbol of the permanence and power of God's kingdom. It is not subject to the same rise and fall that characterize the earthly kingdoms. Unlike the fragile and fragmented human empires, God's kingdom is immutable, unshakable, and rooted in His sovereignty over all creation.

2. The Rock in the Broader Biblical Context

The imagery of the rock has deep symbolic significance throughout the Bible, often used to describe God's strength, refuge, and unchanging nature. The idea of a stone or rock representing divine power and authority is a common theme, appearing in both the Old Testament and the New Testament, and is frequently associated with the Messiah.

A. The Rock as a Messianic Symbol

In Christian theology, the rock in Nebuchadnezzar's dream is often seen as a messianic prophecy pointing to the arrival of Jesus Christ and the establishment of His kingdom. Several passages in the New Testament refer to Christ as a stone or rock, reinforcing the idea that He is the foundation of the eternal kingdom prophesied in Daniel.

- Isaiah 28:16: "So this is what the Sovereign Lord says: 'See, I lay a stone in Zion, a tested stone, a precious cornerstone for a sure foundation; the one who relies on it will never be stricken with panic.'"

This prophecy in Isaiah refers to the Messiah as a stone or cornerstone, which is often interpreted as a reference to Jesus Christ. In the New Testament, Christ is repeatedly referred to as the cornerstone of God's kingdom.

- 1 Peter 2:6-7: "For in Scripture it says: 'See, I lay a stone in Zion, a chosen and precious cornerstone, and the one who trusts in him will never be put to shame.' Now to you who believe, this stone is precious. But to those who do not believe, 'The stone the builders rejected has become the cornerstone.'"

Here, Peter identifies Jesus as the stone that the builders rejected—another reference to the Messianic fulfillment of the prophecy in Daniel, where the rock represents God's chosen one who will establish His eternal kingdom.

B. The Rock as a Foundation of Faith

Throughout the Bible, rock imagery is used to convey the stability and security of God's kingdom and His people's relationship with Him. In the Psalms and prophetic books,

God is frequently described as a rock—a refuge and source of strength for those who trust in Him.

- Psalm 18:2: "The Lord is my rock, my fortress and my deliverer; my God is my rock, in whom I take refuge, my shield and the horn of my salvation, my stronghold."

This imagery conveys the unchanging and reliable nature of God, who serves as a foundation for His people's faith. The symbolism of the rock in Nebuchadnezzar's dream builds on this theme, portraying God's kingdom as the ultimate refuge and foundation of all creation.

3. The Rock and the End Times: Christ's Kingdom and Final Judgment

In Christian eschatology, the rock that destroys the statue is often interpreted as the Second Coming of Christ, when He will return to establish His eternal kingdom and bring an end to the earthly powers that oppose God. The destruction of the statue symbolizes the overthrow of all human governments and the final judgment of the world.

A. Christ's Return and the Establishment of the Millennial Kingdom

According to many interpretations of Revelation and Daniel, the rock not cut by human hands represents the arrival of the Messiah's kingdom, which will be fully realized during the Millennial Reign of Christ. This period, often called the

Millennium, refers to the thousand-year reign of Christ on earth after His Second Coming, as described in Revelation 20:1-6.

- Revelation 11:15: "The seventh angel sounded his trumpet, and there were loud voices in heaven, which said: 'The kingdom of the world has become the kingdom of our Lord and of His Messiah, and He will reign for ever and ever.'"

This passage reflects the fulfillment of the prophecy in Daniel, where the earthly kingdoms, represented by the statue, are destroyed and replaced by the eternal Kingdom of God. The arrival of this kingdom marks the end of human history as it has been known, with Christ reigning as King of Kings.

B. The Final Judgment and the Destruction of Earthly Powers

The destruction of the statue in Nebuchadnezzar's dream is also a symbol of the final judgment that will come upon the world. The statue's fragmentation and the subsequent disappearance of the earthly empires represent the total eradication of human authority and power in the face of God's ultimate sovereignty.

- Revelation 19:19-21: In this passage, the final battle between the forces of evil and Christ's army is described, with the Beast and the kings of the earth being defeated and thrown into the lake of fire. This victory reflects the destruction of the statue, as all earthly rulers and powers are brought under God's judgment.

- Hebrews 12:28: "Therefore, since we are receiving a kingdom that cannot be shaken, let us be thankful, and so worship God acceptably with reverence and awe."

This unshakable kingdom, represented by the rock in Daniel, is the eternal Kingdom of God, which will outlast and overcome all human systems of governance.

4. The Growing Mountain: God's Kingdom Expands to All Nations

After the rock strikes the statue and destroys it, the rock grows into a great mountain that fills the whole earth. This image conveys the idea that the Kingdom of God will expand to encompass all of creation, bringing peace and righteousness to the entire world.

A. The Expansion of God's Kingdom

The growth of the rock into a mountain symbolizes the universal nature of God's kingdom. It will not be limited to one region or nation, but will cover the whole earth, bringing an end to the divided and fragile human empires.

- Isaiah 9:7: "Of the greatness of His government and peace there will be no end. He will reign on David's throne and over His kingdom, establishing and upholding it with justice and righteousness from that time on and forever."

- Isaiah 2:2: "In the last days, the mountain of the Lord's temple will be established as the highest of the mountains; it will be exalted above the hills, and all nations will stream to it."

These passages emphasize that the Kingdom of God will be global and eternal, surpassing all human boundaries and divisions.

B. The Ultimate Reign of Peace and Justice

The establishment of the Kingdom of God is also seen as the fulfillment of the Messianic age, a time when peace, justice, and righteousness will prevail over the entire earth. The growing mountain represents the universal reign of God, under which the world will be renewed and restored to its intended state.

- Micah 4:1-3: "In the last days, the mountain of the Lord's temple will be established as the highest of the mountains... They will beat their swords into plowshares and their spears into pruning hooks. Nation will not take up sword against nation, nor will they train for war anymore."

The mountain imagery signifies the permanence and universality of God's kingdom, which will bring about lasting peace and restoration to all of creation.

The Rock as the Fulfillment of God's Divine Plan

The rock not cut by human hands in Nebuchadnezzar's dream is a powerful symbol of the Kingdom of God, which will be established through divine power rather than human effort. This kingdom, represented by the rock that destroys the statue, will supersede all earthly powers and endure forever, marking the end of human history and the final victory of God's sovereignty.

The prophecy of the rock points to the Messiah, Jesus Christ, who will return to judge the nations and establish His eternal kingdom. The destruction of the statue signifies the end of earthly kingdoms, while the growth of the rock into a mountain represents the expansion of God's kingdom to encompass the whole world.

Would you like to explore how this interpretation fits into broader Christian eschatology, or delve deeper into the Millennial Kingdom and its significance in prophecy?

Chapter 8: Christ's Kingdom, Eschatological Fulfillment, and Its Role in Apocalyptic Prophecy

The Kingdom of Christ is the culmination of biblical prophecy, the final stage in the grand narrative of God's redemptive plan for humanity. This kingdom, often referred to as the Millennial Kingdom or the eternal Kingdom of God, is central to Christian eschatology. Its establishment marks the end of human history as it is known and the beginning of

God's eternal reign over all creation. This chapter will explore the eschatological fulfillment of Christ's kingdom, its connection to apocalyptic prophecy, and its role in Christian theology.

We will examine how the prophecies in Daniel, Revelation, and other biblical texts point to the establishment of Christ's kingdom on earth, how this kingdom is viewed in the context of end-time events, and what its establishment means for humanity and creation. We will also explore the various interpretations of Christ's reign, focusing on how different theological traditions view the Millennial Kingdom, the Second Coming, and the final judgment.

1. The Establishment of Christ's Kingdom: Prophecy and Fulfillment

The Bible contains numerous prophecies about the coming of a kingdom ruled by the Messiah, a kingdom that will last forever and bring peace, righteousness, and justice to the world. This kingdom is a central theme in both the Old Testament and the New Testament, where it is associated with the coming of Jesus Christ and His ultimate victory over the forces of sin and death.

A. Old Testament Prophecies of the Kingdom

The Old Testament prophets frequently spoke of a future kingdom that would be ruled by a descendant of David, the great king of Israel. This kingdom would bring salvation to God's people and justice to the nations.

- Isaiah 9:6-7: "For to us a child is born, to us a son is given, and the government will be on His shoulders. And He will be called Wonderful Counselor, Mighty God, Everlasting Father, Prince of Peace. Of the greatness of His government and peace there will be no end. He will reign on David's throne and over His kingdom, establishing and upholding it with justice and righteousness from that time on and forever."

This prophecy from Isaiah highlights the messianic hope of a kingdom established by a ruler from the line of David. This kingdom will bring endless peace, justice, and righteousness, themes that are later expanded upon in the New Testament as applying to Christ's reign.

- Daniel 7:13-14: "In my vision at night I looked, and there before me was one like a son of man, coming with the clouds of heaven. He approached the Ancient of Days and was led into His presence. He was given authority, glory and sovereign power; all nations and peoples of every language worshiped Him. His dominion is an everlasting dominion that will not pass away, and His kingdom is one that will never be destroyed."

In this passage, Daniel speaks of the Son of Man receiving an eternal kingdom from the Ancient of Days

(God). This vision is widely interpreted as a prophecy of Christ's kingdom, which will replace all earthly kingdoms and reign forever.

B. New Testament Fulfillment in Christ

The New Testament presents the life, death, and resurrection of Jesus Christ as the fulfillment of these Old Testament prophecies. Jesus Himself frequently spoke of the Kingdom of God, describing it as both a present reality and a future hope.

- Mark 1:15: "The time has come," He said. "The kingdom of God has come near. Repent and believe the good news!"

Jesus' announcement of the Kingdom of God signaled the beginning of its arrival through His ministry, yet its full realization is to occur in the future, at His Second Coming. The kingdom is both now and not yet—present in Christ's reign in the hearts of believers but awaiting its ultimate manifestation at the end of the age.

- Matthew 25:31-34: "When the Son of Man comes in His glory, and all the angels with Him, He will sit on His glorious throne. All the nations will be gathered before Him, and He will separate the people one from another as a shepherd separates the sheep from the goats... Then the King will say to those on His right, 'Come, you who are blessed by my Father; take your inheritance, the kingdom prepared for you since the creation of the world.'"

In this passage, Jesus refers to the final judgment, when He will return in glory to establish His kingdom fully. This future kingdom will be marked by the vindication of the righteous and the defeat of the wicked, as Christ takes His rightful place as the King of Kings.

2. Christ's Kingdom and the Eschatological Timeline

In Christian eschatology, the establishment of Christ's kingdom is the key event that brings an end to the current age and ushers in eternity. The timeline of events leading up to the full manifestation of Christ's kingdom varies across different theological traditions, but it generally revolves around key events such as the Second Coming, the Millennial Reign, and the final judgment.

A. The Second Coming of Christ

The Second Coming of Christ is central to Christian eschatological thought and is described as the moment when Christ will return to judge the world, defeat the forces of evil, and establish His eternal kingdom. This event is portrayed in vivid apocalyptic imagery in the Book of Revelation.

- Revelation 19:11-16: "I saw heaven standing open and there before me was a white horse, whose rider is called

Faithful and True... On His robe and on His thigh He has this name written: King of Kings and Lord of Lords."

In this vision, Christ returns as a conquering king, defeating the Beast and the nations that oppose Him. This triumphant return is seen as the decisive moment when the kingdom of God will replace the kingdoms of this world.

B. The Millennial Kingdom

One of the most debated aspects of Christian eschatology is the Millennial Kingdom—a thousand-year reign of Christ on earth, described in Revelation 20:1-6. The exact nature and timing of this kingdom have led to various interpretations within premillennial, amillennial, and postmillennial theological frameworks.

- Premillennialism: This view holds that Christ will return before the millennium and will establish a literal, thousand-year reign on earth. During this time, Christ will rule over the nations, and Satan will be bound. After the millennium, there will be a final rebellion, followed by the last judgment and the creation of a new heaven and new earth.

- Amillennialism: In this interpretation, the millennium is symbolic and represents the current Church Age, during which Christ reigns spiritually through the Church. The Second Coming will occur at the end of this age, followed immediately by the final judgment and the establishment of the eternal kingdom.

- Postmillennialism: Postmillennialists believe that Christ will return after the millennium, which they interpret as a golden age of Christian influence and gospel success on earth. The world will progressively become more aligned with Christian values, culminating in Christ's return and the final judgment.

C. The Final Judgment and New Creation

The final judgment is the culmination of Christ's kingdom, where all people—both the righteous and the wicked—will stand before Christ to be judged. This judgment is followed by the creation of a new heaven and a new earth, where God's eternal kingdom will be fully realized.

- Revelation 20:11-12: "Then I saw a great white throne and Him who was seated on it... And I saw the dead, great and small, standing before the throne, and books were opened... The dead were judged according to what they had done as recorded in the books."

After this final judgment, the current creation, which has been marred by sin, will be transformed into a new creation, where Christ will reign forever with His people.

- Revelation 21:1-4: "Then I saw a new heaven and a new earth, for the first heaven and the first earth had passed away... 'Look! God's dwelling place is now among the people, and He will dwell with them. They will be His people, and

God Himself will be with them and be their God. He will wipe every tear from their eyes.'"

This new creation is the ultimate fulfillment of God's plan for redemption, where there will be no more sin, death, or suffering. The Kingdom of Christ will be eternal, and God will dwell with His people in perfect harmony.

3. The Role of Christ's Kingdom in Apocalyptic Prophecy

The Kingdom of Christ is central to apocalyptic prophecy, particularly in the Book of Revelation, where it represents the final outcome of history. The prophecies of the end times are focused on the triumph of Christ over the forces of evil, the establishment of His rule, and the restoration of creation.

A. The Defeat of Evil: The Beast, the Dragon, and Babylon

In the apocalyptic prophecies of Revelation, Christ's return and the establishment of His kingdom are depicted as the final victory over the forces of evil, represented by the Beast, the Dragon (Satan), and Babylon (symbolizing the corrupt world system).

- Revelation 19:19-21: "Then I saw the Beast and the kings of the earth and their armies gathered to wage war against the rider on the horse and His army. But the Beast was captured, and with it the false prophet... The two of them were thrown alive into the fiery lake of burning sulfur."

This imagery of the final battle, often referred to as the Battle of Armageddon, represents the ultimate defeat of the Antichrist and his followers. Christ's kingdom will triumph, and the kingdoms of this world will be judged and destroyed.

B. Christ as the Eternal King

Throughout Revelation, Christ is presented as the eternal king, whose reign will have no end. His kingdom is described as one of peace, justice, and righteousness, in stark contrast to the oppressive and corrupt kingdoms of the world.

- Revelation 11:15: "The seventh angel sounded his trumpet, and there were loud voices in heaven, which said: 'The kingdom of the world has become the kingdom of our Lord and of His Messiah, and He will reign for ever and ever.'"

This passage underscores the final transfer of power from the earthly rulers to Christ, who will rule forever. The eschatological fulfillment of Christ's kingdom is not just a spiritual reality, but a cosmic event that will reshape all of creation.

4. The Eternal Kingdom: A New Heaven and a New Earth

The culmination of Christ's kingdom is the creation of a new heaven and a new earth, as described in Revelation 21. In this eternal state, the brokenness of the current world will be replaced by the perfect harmony of God's eternal kingdom.

A. The Restoration of All Things

The vision of the new creation is one of total restoration—a return to the ideal state that God intended at the beginning of creation. The curse of sin will be removed, and all of creation will be renewed and redeemed.

- Revelation 21:5: "He who was seated on the throne said, 'I am making everything new!'"

This declaration from God signifies the completion of His redemptive work and the full realization of His kingdom. The world will be restored to its original goodness, and humanity will dwell with God in perfect peace.

B. The Role of Believers in Christ's Kingdom

In the new heaven and new earth, believers will share in Christ's reign and will experience eternal life in His presence. The blessings of the kingdom—such as fellowship with God, eternal joy, and freedom from suffering—will be fully realized.

- Revelation 22:3-5: "No longer will there be any curse. The throne of God and of the Lamb will be in the city, and His servants will serve Him. They will see His face, and His name will be on their foreheads... And they will reign for ever and ever."

This promise of eternal life in God's kingdom is the ultimate hope of Christian eschatology, where believers will live in perfect communion with God and with one another.

Christ's Kingdom as the Fulfillment of Apocalyptic Prophecy

The establishment of Christ's Kingdom is the climax of biblical prophecy and the ultimate fulfillment of God's plan for the world. It represents the defeat of evil, the restoration of creation, and the eternal reign of Christ over all things. In the apocalyptic vision of Revelation, Christ's kingdom is not just the end of human history, but the beginning of eternity, where God's will is perfectly realized and His people live in His presence forever.

This eschatological fulfillment is central to Christian faith, offering hope for the future and a vision of a world where righteousness, peace, and justice prevail. Christ's return and the establishment of His kingdom are the ultimate answers to the brokenness of the world, as heaven and earth are united under His eternal rule.

Delving Deeper into the Symbols and Imagery Used in Revelation

The Book of Revelation is one of the most symbolically rich and mysterious texts in the Bible, filled with apocalyptic imagery that has fascinated readers for centuries. Written by the Apostle John while in exile on the island of Patmos, Revelation presents a prophetic vision of the end of the world, the final judgment, and the ultimate triumph of God over the forces of evil. The book's powerful symbols and metaphors offer profound insight into the eschatological fulfillment of God's plan but also present significant challenges for interpretation.

In this chapter, we will explore the key symbols and imagery used in Revelation, examining their theological meanings and prophetic significance. By analyzing recurring motifs such as the Lamb, the Beast, the Dragon, the seven seals, and the New Jerusalem, we will delve deeper into how these images reveal the cosmic battle between good and evil and the establishment of Christ's eternal kingdom.

1. The Lamb: Christ as the Sacrificial Savior and Conquering King

One of the most important and recurring symbols in Revelation is the Lamb, which represents Jesus Christ. Unlike traditional portrayals of kings and warriors as lions or other powerful animals, the Lamb in Revelation is both a symbol of sacrifice and of victory.

A. The Lamb Who Was Slain

In Revelation 5:6, Christ is introduced as the Lamb who was slain, standing at the center of the heavenly throne surrounded by angels and the four living creatures. The Lamb bears the marks of His sacrificial death, yet He is also described as being alive and worthy to open the scroll sealed with seven seals.

- Revelation 5:6-7: "Then I saw a Lamb, looking as if it had been slain, standing at the center of the throne, encircled by the four living creatures and the elders. The Lamb had seven horns and seven eyes, which are the seven spirits of God sent out into all the earth."

This imagery emphasizes the paradox of Christ's role as both the sacrificial victim and the victorious king. The Lamb's seven horns represent complete power, and the seven eyes signify divine wisdom and omniscience. Though slain, the Lamb's position at the throne shows His authority to rule and bring God's final plan to fruition.

B. The Lamb as the Conqueror

Throughout Revelation, the Lamb is also depicted as a conquering king who will defeat the forces of evil. In Revelation 19:11-16, Christ returns as a warrior riding a white horse, leading the armies of heaven to victory against the Beast and the nations aligned with Satan. Yet even in this moment of triumph, He is identified as the Lamb, signifying that His victory comes through His sacrificial death and resurrection.

- Revelation 17:14: "They will wage war against the Lamb, but the Lamb will triumph over them because He is Lord of lords and King of kings—and with Him will be His called, chosen and faithful followers."

The victory of the Lamb is central to the message of Revelation: the ultimate power in the universe does not lie in violence, domination, or oppression, but in self-giving love and sacrifice.

2. The Beast and the Dragon: Symbols of Evil and Oppression

Revelation vividly portrays the forces of evil through the figures of the Beast and the Dragon, representing the Antichrist, Satan, and the oppressive world systems that oppose God's kingdom.

A. The Beast from the Sea: Political Power and the Antichrist

The Beast is one of the most terrifying symbols in Revelation, described as rising out of the sea with seven heads and ten horns (Revelation 13:1). This image is a direct reference to the four beasts in the book of Daniel, which represent world empires. However, the Beast in Revelation combines elements of all four of Daniel's creatures, signifying that it is a culmination of all oppressive political powers throughout history.

- Revelation 13:1-2: "The Beast I saw resembled a leopard, but had feet like those of a bear and a mouth like that of a lion. The dragon gave the beast his power and his throne and great authority."

The Beast is often interpreted as representing a final, satanically empowered world empire, or more specifically, the Antichrist—a figure who will rise to power in the end times, deceive the nations, and demand worship. The seven heads and ten horns likely symbolize different rulers or kingdoms aligned with this figure, while the mortal wound the Beast receives (but recovers from) is thought to mimic Christ's death and resurrection, as part of the Beast's deception.

B. The Dragon: Satan as the Ancient Enemy

The Dragon in Revelation is explicitly identified as Satan, the enemy of God and His people. In Revelation 12, the Dragon is portrayed as pursuing the woman (representing Israel or the Church) and waging war against her offspring (believers). The Dragon's fall from heaven represents Satan's defeat in the spiritual realm, but his earthly influence continues through the Beast and the false prophet.

- Revelation 12:9: "The great dragon was hurled down—that ancient serpent called the devil, or Satan, who leads the whole world astray. He was hurled to the earth, and his angels with him."

This imagery of the Dragon connects back to the serpent in the Garden of Eden, emphasizing that the conflict in Revelation is not just political or historical but part of a cosmic battle that spans all of human history. Satan's ultimate defeat is assured, but not before a period of great suffering and deception.

3. The Seven Seals, Trumpets, and Bowls: Symbols of God's Judgment

The seven seals, seven trumpets, and seven bowls represent the progressive judgment of God upon the world, as He prepares to bring about the end of the age and the establishment of His kingdom.

A. The Seven Seals: The Unfolding of God's Plan

In Revelation 6, the Lamb begins to open the seven seals on the scroll, each one revealing a new aspect of God's judgment. These seals introduce the Four Horsemen of the Apocalypse—symbols of war, conquest, famine, and death—as well as martyrdom and natural disasters. The seventh seal initiates the trumpet judgments.

- Revelation 6:2-8: "I looked, and there before me was a white horse! Its rider held a bow, and he was given a crown, and he rode out as a conqueror bent on conquest... Another horse came out, a fiery red one... Its rider was given power to take peace from the earth... I looked, and there before me was a pale horse! Its rider was named Death, and Hades was following close behind him."

The Four Horsemen symbolize the chaos and destruction that will characterize the end times, as human systems collapse under the weight of God's judgment.

B. The Seven Trumpets: Cosmic Judgment

The seven trumpets represent escalating cosmic disturbances, affecting not only humanity but the very fabric of the natural world. The trumpets signal plagues, fiery destruction, and catastrophic events reminiscent of the plagues of Egypt in the book of Exodus, further intensifying God's judgment on the earth.

- Revelation 8:6-7: "Then the seven angels who had the seven trumpets prepared to sound them. The first angel sounded his trumpet, and there came hail and fire mixed with blood, and it was hurled down on the earth."

Each trumpet brings devastation upon the earth, culminating in the final trumpet, which heralds the coming of God's kingdom.

C. The Seven Bowls: The Wrath of God

The seven bowls of wrath, poured out in Revelation 16, represent the final and most severe judgments of God. These plagues are similar to those unleashed by the trumpets but more intense and destructive, culminating in the complete overthrow of the Beast and his kingdom.

- Revelation 16:1: "Then I heard a loud voice from the temple saying to the seven angels, 'Go, pour out the seven bowls of God's wrath on the earth.'"

These bowls of wrath represent the totality of God's judgment against sin, rebellion, and evil, leading to the final destruction of the forces that oppose His kingdom.

4. The New Jerusalem: The Glorious Fulfillment of God's Kingdom

The climax of Revelation's imagery is the vision of the New Jerusalem, a city that descends from heaven and symbolizes the new creation and the eternal dwelling place of God with His people.

A. The New Heaven and New Earth

In Revelation 21, after the final defeat of evil and the judgment of all humanity, John sees a new heaven and a new earth. The old world, corrupted by sin and death, has passed away, and in its place, God brings forth a new reality, free from suffering and pain.

- Revelation 21:1-4: "Then I saw a new heaven and a new earth, for the first heaven and the first earth had passed away... 'Look! God's dwelling place is now among the people, and He will dwell with them. They will be His people, and

God Himself will be with them and be their God. He will wipe every tear from their eyes.'"

This vision of the new creation is the ultimate fulfillment of God's plan: a world where death and sin no longer exist, and where God's presence is fully experienced by His people.

B. The City of the New Jerusalem

The New Jerusalem is depicted as a perfect city, filled with the glory of God and radiant with light. Its dimensions and features—such as streets of gold and gates made of pearls—symbolize its purity, beauty, and divine origin.

- Revelation 21:10-11: "And he carried me away in the Spirit to a mountain great and high, and showed me the Holy City, Jerusalem, coming down out of heaven from God. It shone with the glory of God, and its brilliance was like that of a very precious jewel."

The New Jerusalem is the eternal dwelling place of God and His people, where the divisions and suffering of the old world have been replaced by perfect peace and fellowship with God.

The Power of Symbols in Revelation's Apocalyptic Vision

The symbols and imagery of Revelation convey profound theological truths about the nature of God, the reality of evil, and the ultimate victory of Christ. Through images like the Lamb, the Beast, the Dragon, and the New Jerusalem, Revelation reveals the cosmic struggle between good and evil, culminating in the final judgment and the establishment of God's eternal kingdom.

These symbols not only speak to the eschatological hope of believers but also challenge readers to live in the light of the coming kingdom, where Christ will reign forever as the King of Kings and Lord of Lords.

How Nebuchadnezzar's Dream Connects to Christian Interpretations of the End of History

The dream of Nebuchadnezzar, as described in Daniel 2, has been foundational in shaping Christian eschatology—the study of the end times and the ultimate fulfillment of history. The image of the great statue and its eventual destruction by a rock not cut by human hands has been interpreted by Christians as a prophetic vision of the rise and fall of world empires, culminating in the establishment of God's eternal kingdom. In Christian theology, this prophecy is intimately connected to the Second Coming of Christ, the final judgment, and the end of human history as we know it.

This chapter will delve into how the elements of Nebuchadnezzar's dream—particularly the statue and the rock—are integrated into Christian interpretations of the end of history, exploring how these symbols align with the

Millennial Kingdom, the return of Christ, and the new creation. We will also examine how this dream has shaped theological perspectives on the nature of human empires, their inherent fragility, and their ultimate replacement by the Kingdom of God.

1. The Statue in Nebuchadnezzar's Dream: A Timeline of Human History

In Daniel 2:31-45, the dream of Nebuchadnezzar features a statue made of various metals, each representing a different kingdom or empire that would dominate the world. Christian interpreters have long viewed this statue as a timeline of human history, with each section of the statue corresponding to a particular world empire. This interpretation extends into Christian eschatology, where the dream is seen as a key prophecy leading up to the end times.

A. The Four Kingdoms: Human Empires in the Eschatological Timeline

The four metals that make up the statue—gold, silver, bronze, and iron—are generally interpreted as representing the Babylonian, Medo-Persian, Greek, and Roman empires, respectively. Each empire rises to power but is eventually replaced by the next, symbolizing the transience and fragility of human rule.

- Head of Gold – Babylon: Babylon represents the golden head of the statue, with Nebuchadnezzar's reign being the first in the series of empires. This empire, while powerful, is temporary.

- Chest and Arms of Silver – Medo-Persia: The silver chest and arms symbolize the Medo-Persian Empire, which followed Babylon and conquered much of the ancient Near East.

- Belly and Thighs of Bronze – Greece: The bronze section is interpreted as Alexander the Great's Greek Empire, known for its vast expansion and cultural influence.

- Legs of Iron – Rome: The iron legs represent the Roman Empire, often seen as the strongest and most enduring of these empires due to its unmatched military and political might.

- Feet of Iron and Clay – Divided Kingdoms: The feet made of iron mixed with clay represent the fragmented kingdoms that followed the fall of Rome. These are often interpreted as the divided nations of Europe, which were powerful yet weakened by internal divisions, represented by the brittle mixture of iron and clay.

This progression of empires is viewed by Christian theologians as the historical backdrop leading to the end times, where the final phase of human history is characterized by fragile, divided political powers, which set the stage for the coming of Christ's kingdom.

B. The Statue as a Symbol of Human Frailty

The statue, despite its grandeur, represents the frailty of human attempts to build lasting kingdoms. No matter how mighty or enduring each empire appears to be, all are ultimately destined for destruction. This theme resonates deeply with Christian theology, which teaches that all human systems of power are temporary and flawed, subject to sin and corruption. Only the Kingdom of God is eternal and unshakable.

- Hebrews 12:28: "Therefore, since we are receiving a kingdom that cannot be shaken, let us be thankful, and so worship God acceptably with reverence and awe."

This passage from Hebrews echoes the message of Nebuchadnezzar's dream, reinforcing the idea that human history is moving toward an inevitable conclusion, where God's unshakable kingdom will replace the fading kingdoms of the world.

2. The Rock Not Cut by Human Hands: Christ and the Kingdom of God

The most significant element of Nebuchadnezzar's dream is the rock that is not cut by human hands, which strikes the statue, destroying it completely. This rock, which grows into a great mountain, symbolizes the Kingdom of God, which will be established at the end of history, replacing all human rule. In Christian eschatology, this rock is often interpreted as representing Jesus Christ, whose return will mark the defeat of evil and the establishment of God's eternal reign.

A. The Rock as Christ: The Foundation of God's Kingdom

The rock in Nebuchadnezzar's dream is widely understood by Christians as a metaphor for Christ and His messianic kingdom. Unlike the empires represented by the statue, which are built by human hands and destined to crumble, the kingdom represented by the rock is established by divine power and will never be destroyed.

- Matthew 21:42-44: Jesus said to them, "Have you never read in the Scriptures: 'The stone the builders rejected has become the cornerstone; the Lord has done this, and it is marvelous in our eyes'... Anyone who falls on this stone will be broken to pieces; anyone on whom it falls will be crushed."

This passage aligns with the imagery of the rock destroying the statue. Jesus identifies Himself as the cornerstone of God's kingdom, and His arrival will result in the destruction of all worldly powers that oppose God.

B. The Rock's Growth into a Mountain: The Global and Eternal Kingdom of God

After the rock strikes and destroys the statue, it grows into a great mountain that fills the whole earth (Daniel 2:35). This mountain is a symbol of the universal scope of God's kingdom, which will expand and encompass all of creation, bringing an end to the divided and temporary nature of human kingdoms.

- Isaiah 2:2: "In the last days the mountain of the Lord's temple will be established as the highest of the mountains; it will be exalted above the hills, and all nations will stream to it."

This vision of a mountain reflects the global reign of Christ during the Millennial Kingdom and beyond. It represents a new world order where Christ rules over all nations, and His peace and justice prevail over the violence and instability that characterize human rule.

3. The Connection to the End of History in Christian Theology

The rock striking the statue and growing into a mountain is central to Christian interpretations of the end of history, as it symbolizes the final triumph of God's kingdom over the kingdoms of the world. This event is often understood to occur during the Second Coming of Christ, at which point all earthly powers will be judged and destroyed, making way for the eternal reign of Christ.

A. The Second Coming of Christ and the Destruction of World Powers

In Revelation 19:11-16, the return of Christ is portrayed as a decisive moment in history, where He defeats the forces of evil and establishes His rule over the nations. The imagery of Christ as a warrior who strikes down His enemies resonates with the rock that strikes and destroys the statue in Nebuchadnezzar's dream.

- Revelation 19:15: "Coming out of His mouth is a sharp sword with which to strike down the nations. 'He will rule them with an iron scepter.'"

This final battle, often referred to as Armageddon, represents the culmination of human history as worldly powers—represented by the statue in Daniel—are defeated and replaced by Christ's eternal kingdom. The destruction of the statue is thus viewed as a symbolic representation of this final victory over all human systems that oppose God's rule.

B. The Millennial Kingdom: Christ's Rule on Earth

Following Christ's return, Christian eschatology teaches that He will establish a Millennial Kingdom, a thousand-year reign where He will govern the earth with peace, justice, and righteousness. This period is seen as a fulfillment of the prophecy in Daniel 2, where the rock becomes a mountain and fills the earth, symbolizing Christ's global reign.

- Revelation 20:4: "They came to life and reigned with Christ a thousand years."

The Millennial Kingdom represents a period where evil is temporarily subdued, and Christ's rule is fully established. It is the initial stage of the eternal kingdom, where Satan is bound, and the saints reign with Christ over a renewed earth. This kingdom is often seen as the fulfillment of the rock's expansion in Nebuchadnezzar's dream.

C. The Eternal Kingdom: A New Heaven and a New Earth

After the Millennial Kingdom, Christian theology teaches that there will be a final judgment (Revelation 20:11-15), followed by the creation of a new heaven and a new earth (Revelation 21:1). This marks the ultimate fulfillment of God's kingdom, where all things are made new, and God's presence dwells fully with His people.

- Revelation 21:3: "And I heard a loud voice from the throne saying, 'Look! God's dwelling place is now among the people, and He will dwell with them. They will be His people, and God Himself will be with them and be their God.'"

In this new creation, the division and corruption that characterized the kingdoms of this world—symbolized by the feet of iron and clay—will be forever abolished. The eternal

Kingdom of God, symbolized by the great mountain, will fill the earth, and God's rule will be universal and eternal.

4. Christian Interpretations of the End of History: A Theological Perspective

The Christian interpretation of Nebuchadnezzar's dream sees history as a progression of worldly empires that ultimately give way to the Kingdom of God. This view emphasizes that human history is not circular or endless but has a definitive endpoint, marked by the return of Christ and the establishment of His kingdom.

A. Human Kingdoms Are Temporary

The image of the statue teaches that all human kingdoms, no matter how powerful, are ultimately temporary and will be replaced by God's eternal reign. This aligns with the Christian understanding that history is linear and moving toward a final conclusion.

- 1 Corinthians 15:24: "Then the end will come, when He hands over the kingdom to God the Father after He has destroyed all dominion, authority and power."

This passage reflects the theological belief that all worldly power is temporary, and history is moving toward a moment when Christ's kingdom will be fully established.

B. The Kingdom of God Is Eternal

The rock that becomes a mountain represents the eternity of God's kingdom, which will outlast and overshadow all human efforts to build lasting empires. This eternal kingdom is the culmination of history and the fulfillment of God's purpose for the world.

- Daniel 2:44: "In the time of those kings, the God of heaven will set up a kingdom that will never be destroyed, nor will it be left to another people."

This prophecy points to the final reality of God's kingdom, which will not be followed by any further human rule or division. Once established, God's kingdom will endure forever.

Nebuchadnezzar's Dream and the Christian Vision of the End of History

The dream of Nebuchadnezzar, as interpreted by Daniel, serves as a powerful prophetic vision that connects to the Christian understanding of the end of history. The statue symbolizes the rise and fall of human empires, while the rock not cut by human hands represents the coming of Christ's eternal kingdom, which will replace all worldly powers and bring about the consummation of history.

For Christians, this dream is a reminder that human history is moving toward a divinely appointed conclusion, where Christ's return will mark the end of the age and the beginning of God's eternal reign.

The Crusades in Apocalyptic Thought

The Crusades were a series of military campaigns undertaken by Christian Europe between the 11th and 13th centuries, aimed at reclaiming the Holy Land from Muslim control. While the Crusades are often understood through the lens of political, social, and economic factors, they were also deeply rooted in apocalyptic thought and theological motivations. For many of the Crusaders and their supporters, these campaigns were not simply about territorial conquest but were perceived as part of a divine mandate, framed within an apocalyptic vision of history.

This chapter explores the theological motivations behind the Crusades, particularly focusing on how apocalyptic prophecy influenced the call to arms and the belief that the end times were near. We will examine how Christian leaders invoked eschatological themes to inspire participation in the Crusades, how the events of the Crusades were interpreted within the framework of apocalyptic warfare, and the lasting impact of these beliefs on both Christian theology and European culture.

1. The Theological Context of the Crusades

The theological motivations for the Crusades were deeply influenced by the belief that the Christian world was engaged in a cosmic battle against the forces of evil, represented by Islam. The Pope, the clergy, and many Christian leaders framed the Crusades as a fulfillment of divine prophecy and as a necessary step in preparing for the Second Coming of Christ. The idea of holy war was not new, but in the context of the Crusades, it took on a distinctly apocalyptic tone.

A. The Holy Land and Christian Eschatology

For medieval Christians, the Holy Land held profound spiritual significance, as it was the land where Jesus Christ lived, died, and was resurrected. It was also where many believed the final events of human history—the Second Coming, the final judgment, and the establishment of God's kingdom—would take place.

- Jerusalem as the Center of Apocalyptic Expectations: Jerusalem was seen as the spiritual center of the world and the location where Christ would return to establish His millennial reign. Many believed that the city must be in Christian hands for these eschatological events to occur, making the recapture of Jerusalem a central goal of the Crusades. In this sense, the Crusades were not merely about reclaiming territory but were viewed as a critical step in the unfolding of God's plan for the world.

- Pope Urban II's Call for the First Crusade: In 1095, Pope Urban II called for the First Crusade at the Council of Clermont, framing it as a holy war to reclaim the Holy Land from Muslim control. He appealed to Christian unity and the need to defend fellow Christians in the East, but he also invoked apocalyptic themes, urging Christians to purify themselves through holy war and prepare for the final battle between good and evil.

- Urban II promised that those who participated in the Crusades would receive spiritual rewards, including indulgences (forgiveness of sins), and that their actions were directly connected to Christ's will. For many, this was interpreted as part of the cosmic struggle leading to the end times.

B. Eschatological Themes in Medieval Christianity

During the medieval period, there was a widespread belief that history was moving toward a climactic end, with many interpreting contemporary events in light of biblical prophecy. The idea of apocalyptic warfare, where Christians would battle the forces of evil, was a common theme in sermons, writings, and popular belief.

- Apocalyptic Sermons and Crusading Zeal: Clerics often preached that the Crusades were part of the battle between Christendom and Islam, with Islam being portrayed as a demonic force that had usurped the holy sites of Christianity. These sermons emphasized that participating in the Crusades would bring Christians closer to fulfilling God's ultimate plan for history.

- The Influence of Augustine: The theological writings of St. Augustine played a role in shaping how Christians viewed the Crusades. In his seminal work, "The City of God," Augustine argued that the earthly city (symbolizing human governments) was temporary and would eventually be replaced by the city of God (symbolizing God's eternal kingdom). This idea supported the belief that the Crusades were part of the divine mission to prepare for the coming of God's kingdom on earth.

2. The Crusades as Apocalyptic Warfare

The Crusades were seen by many as part of the cosmic battle between the forces of good and evil. This interpretation was fueled by a blend of biblical prophecy, eschatological expectation, and the desire to secure Christian control over the Holy Land before the Second Coming of Christ.

A. Jerusalem and the Eschatological Significance of the First Crusade

The capture of Jerusalem by the Crusaders in 1099 was seen as a fulfillment of prophecy and a key event in the apocalyptic timeline. For many Christians, the recapture of the Holy City was not merely a military victory but a divine sign that history was progressing toward its final consummation.

- Revelation and the New Jerusalem: The Book of Revelation describes a new Jerusalem descending from heaven as part of the establishment of the Kingdom of God (Revelation 21:2). Many Crusaders believed that their efforts to reclaim the earthly Jerusalem were part of this larger eschatological vision, preparing the way for Christ's return and the coming of the new heaven and new earth.

- The Massacre of Jerusalem: The massacre of Jerusalem by the Crusaders in 1099, during which many Muslim and Jewish inhabitants were killed, was framed as a purification of the city. Some Crusaders saw this act as part of the cleansing necessary for the return of Christ, echoing the Old Testament themes of Israel purifying the land before God's presence could dwell there.

B. The Second Crusade and Apocalyptic Interpretations of Failure

Not all of the Crusades were successful, and the failure of the Second Crusade (1147–1149) was a moment of theological crisis for many Christians. The Crusade, led by Louis VII of France and Conrad III of Germany, ended in defeat, raising questions about whether the Christian effort was still part of God's plan.

- Divine Judgment and Eschatological Reflection: The failure of the Second Crusade was often interpreted as a sign of divine judgment. Many theologians and preachers suggested that the failure occurred because of the sins of the Crusaders themselves, implying that God's favor would return only when Christians had sufficiently repented and reformed their behavior. This interpretation reinforced the idea that the Crusades were part of a larger apocalyptic struggle, and that moral purity was essential for victory.

- Bernard of Clairvaux's Response: One of the most prominent voices during this time was Bernard of Clairvaux, a key figure in promoting the Second Crusade. After its failure, he argued that the defeat was not the end of the mission but a test of faith, and he continued to call for further Crusades, maintaining the apocalyptic urgency of the fight for the Holy Land.

C. The Later Crusades and the Shift in Apocalyptic Thought

As the Crusades continued, with later campaigns such as the Third Crusade (1189–1192) and the Fourth Crusade (1202–1204), the eschatological zeal of the early Crusades began to shift. While the focus remained on the Holy Land, there was also an increasing emphasis on the political and material goals of the Crusades, diluting the original apocalyptic fervor.

- The Fourth Crusade and the Sack of Constantinople: The Fourth Crusade, which resulted in the sack of

Constantinople in 1204, is often viewed as a moment when the Crusades lost much of their original religious and apocalyptic motivation. Instead of reclaiming the Holy Land, the Crusaders turned their attention to plundering the Christian city of Constantinople, leading many to question the spiritual legitimacy of the Crusading movement.

- The Decline of Apocalyptic Zeal: As the Crusades became more entangled with European politics and economic interests, the original apocalyptic vision that had driven the First Crusade began to wane. However, the idea of holy war as part of a divine plan continued to influence Christian thought, particularly in the Reconquista (the Christian reconquest of Spain) and later European conflicts with the Ottoman Empire.

3. The Impact of Crusading Apocalyptic Thought on Later Christian Theology

The apocalyptic motivations of the Crusades left a lasting impact on Christian theology, shaping how later generations understood the relationship between war, religion, and the end times. The idea of divinely sanctioned warfare to reclaim holy territory continued to influence European thought well into the early modern period and beyond.

A. The Reconquista and Apocalyptic Warfare in Spain

The Reconquista, the centuries-long struggle to reclaim the Iberian Peninsula from Muslim rule, was often framed as a continuation of the Crusading movement. The theological justification for the Reconquista echoed the apocalyptic themes of the Crusades, with the eventual fall of Granada in 1492 viewed by many as a fulfillment of God's will.

- Ferdinand and Isabella: The victory of Ferdinand and Isabella in 1492 marked the end of Muslim rule in Spain and was celebrated as a divinely sanctioned event that brought Christian unity to the peninsula. For many, this victory was seen as a sign that God's kingdom was advancing, preparing the way for the final confrontation between Christendom and the forces of evil.

B. Apocalyptic Themes in Later European Conflicts

The theological framework developed during the Crusades also shaped the way Europeans interpreted later conflicts with the Ottoman Empire, particularly during the sieges of Vienna in 1529 and 1683. These battles, fought between Christian Europe and the Muslim Ottomans, were often framed as apocalyptic struggles similar to the Crusades, with Christian leaders invoking themes of holy war and divine mandate.

- The Ottoman Threat and Apocalyptic Fears: The growing power of the Ottoman Empire, which had captured Constantinople in 1453 and expanded into Europe, was often viewed as part of the final battle between Christianity and Islam. The Ottoman siege of Vienna in 1683 was interpreted by many as an apocalyptic moment, where the survival of Christian Europe seemed to hang in the balance. The eventual Christian victory at Vienna was celebrated as a divinely ordained victory that prevented the forces of darkness from overrunning Europe.

C. Modern Apocalyptic Movements and the Legacy of the Crusades

In the modern era, the legacy of Crusading apocalyptic thought continues to influence certain Christian movements, particularly those that focus on the Middle East and the state of Israel. Some modern apocalyptic thinkers view the ongoing conflicts in the Middle East, particularly between Israel and its neighbors, as a continuation of the apocalyptic struggles that began with the Crusades.

- Christian Zionism: In the 20th and 21st centuries, the rise of Christian Zionism—which supports the restoration of the Jewish people to the Holy Land as part of biblical prophecy—has drawn on many of the same apocalyptic themes that motivated the Crusades. For Christian Zionists, the conflict over the Holy Land is viewed as part of the final events of history, leading up to the Second Coming of Christ.

- Apocalyptic Warfare in Modern Conflicts: Some Christian movements have interpreted modern conflicts in the Middle East, particularly the wars involving Israel, as part of the ongoing apocalyptic struggle. The idea of holy war continues to resonate in certain theological circles, where these conflicts are seen as fulfilling biblical prophecies about the end times.

The Crusades and the Continuing Influence of Apocalyptic Thought

The Crusades were not merely military campaigns but were deeply rooted in apocalyptic theology, reflecting a belief that history was moving toward a divinely ordained climax. The idea of holy war as part of the cosmic battle between good and evil became a defining feature of the Crusades, shaping how Christian Europe viewed its relationship with the Muslim world and its role in God's plan for history.

While the original apocalyptic fervor of the Crusades waned over time, the theological legacy of these campaigns has continued to influence Christian thought, particularly in the context of later conflicts with the Ottoman Empire and modern-day interpretations of Middle Eastern conflicts. The vision of a final, apocalyptic confrontation over the Holy

Land remains a potent theme in certain theological movements, reflecting the enduring power of the Crusading ideal.

CHAPTER 09

THE APOCALYPTIC NARRATIVE DURING THE CRUSADES AND THE IDEA OF HOLY WAS AS THE FINAL BATTLE

The Crusades were not only military campaigns aimed at reclaiming the Holy Land but also deeply connected to apocalyptic narratives within medieval Christian thought. For many Christians in Europe, the Crusades were seen as part of the divine plan for history, heralding the final battle between good and evil that would culminate in the Second Coming of Christ. The concept of Holy War, or war sanctioned by God, was intertwined with apocalyptic expectations, especially as Christian Europe struggled against the rise of Islamic powers and the control of Jerusalem.

Let us explores the apocalyptic narratives that fueled the Crusades and how the idea of Holy War was interpreted as part of the final battle between the forces of Christendom and Islam. By examining theological writings, sermons, and the political climate of the time, we will uncover how these ideas shaped both the motivation for the Crusades and their broader eschatological significance in the minds of medieval Christians.

1. Apocalyptic Expectations in Medieval Christianity

During the medieval period, apocalypticism was a pervasive element in Christian thought, heavily influenced by interpretations of the Book of Revelation and other biblical prophecies. The end times were viewed as a historical inevitability, and many Christians believed that they were living in the final age before the return of Christ. This apocalyptic expectation became intertwined with the call for Holy War, as many saw the Crusades as the necessary preparation for Christ's Second Coming.

A. The Role of Jerusalem in Apocalyptic Thought

Jerusalem was central to Christian apocalyptic expectations, as it was seen as the place where the final events of human history would unfold. The city had immense symbolic significance, representing both the earthly Jerusalem—the site of Christ's ministry and crucifixion—and the New Jerusalem described in the Book of Revelation as the city that would descend from heaven at the end of the age.

- Revelation 21:2: "I saw the Holy City, the new Jerusalem, coming down out of heaven from God, prepared as a bride beautifully dressed for her husband."

This passage was often interpreted to mean that Jerusalem needed to be under Christian control in order for the apocalyptic vision of the New Jerusalem to be fulfilled. For this reason, reclaiming Jerusalem from Muslim control became a key goal of the Crusades, as it was seen as part of the divine plan to usher in the end of history.

B. Apocalyptic Sermons and the Call to Arms

The apocalyptic tone of the Crusades was evident in the sermons that called Christians to take up the cross and join the campaign. Preachers such as Pope Urban II and Bernard of Clairvaux framed the Crusades not simply as a political or territorial war but as part of a holy mission to prepare the world for the return of Christ.

- Pope Urban II at the Council of Clermont (1095): Urban II's speech, which launched the First Crusade, was filled with apocalyptic rhetoric. He described the Muslims as an evil force that had desecrated holy sites, and he called upon Christians to purify themselves by engaging in holy war. Urban promised remission of sins for those who joined the

Crusade, emphasizing that their participation would secure them a place in heaven, a message that resonated with those who believed they were living in the end times.

- Bernard of Clairvaux and the Second Crusade (1147-1149): Bernard, a powerful preacher and theologian, promoted the Second Crusade with a similar apocalyptic fervor. He called the Crusaders "soldiers of Christ", portraying their mission as part of a cosmic battle between good and evil. Bernard emphasized that the Crusade was God's will and that victory would bring about the fulfillment of divine prophecy.

2. Holy War and the Idea of a Final Battle

The concept of Holy War was central to the Crusades, with many viewing these campaigns as the final battle between Christendom and Islam. For medieval Christians, Islam was often portrayed as a demonic force and the greatest threat to the fulfillment of God's kingdom on earth. The Crusades were seen not just as military expeditions but as spiritual warfare—a battle between good and evil that was part of the unfolding apocalyptic timeline.

A. The Demonization of Islam in Crusading Rhetoric

In order to frame the Crusades as part of an apocalyptic struggle, Christian leaders often demonized Islam. Muslims were portrayed as agents of Satan, and their control of Jerusalem and other Christian holy sites was seen as part of a larger satanic plan to prevent the coming of God's kingdom.

- Islam as the Antichrist: In many medieval Christian texts, Islam and its leaders were associated with the figure of the Antichrist, a character from Christian eschatology who would appear before the end of the world to deceive the nations and lead a final rebellion against God. The belief that Islamic forces were fulfilling this apocalyptic role further fueled the Crusading zeal, as many believed that defeating the Muslims was a necessary step in the final battle before Christ's return.

- Muslims as "Infidels" and Enemies of God: The term "infidel" (from the Latin infidelis, meaning unfaithful) was used by Crusaders to describe Muslims, reinforcing the idea that they were not only political enemies but also spiritual enemies of Christendom. This language was intended to motivate Crusaders by framing their mission as God's will and their enemies as agents of darkness.

B. The Concept of the Final Battle and the Siege of Jerusalem

For many Crusaders, the battles they fought were seen as precursors to the final battle described in the Book of Revelation, where Christ would return to defeat the forces of evil and establish His eternal kingdom. The Crusaders believed that by participating in these battles, they were playing a direct role in bringing about the Second Coming and the fulfillment of God's plan for the world.

- Revelation 19:11-16: This passage describes Christ returning on a white horse, leading the armies of heaven to defeat the Beast and the forces of evil. For many medieval Christians, the Crusades were seen as a prelude to this final confrontation, with the Muslims cast in the role of the Beast's army. By capturing Jerusalem, the Crusaders believed they were helping to prepare the way for Christ's return.

- The Siege of Jerusalem (1099): The capture of Jerusalem during the First Crusade was seen as a momentous event with profound apocalyptic significance. The city, which had been under Muslim control, was now restored to Christian hands. The massacre that followed the city's capture was justified by many Crusaders as part of the purification of the Holy Land, a necessary step in preparing Jerusalem for the Second Coming. Many saw this victory as a sign that they were on the verge of the final battle between good and evil.

3. Theological Writings and Apocalyptic Thought During the Crusades

The idea of the Crusades as part of an apocalyptic Holy War was reinforced by the theological writings of the time, which often interpreted the Crusades within the framework of biblical prophecy. Many theologians believed that the Crusades were a fulfillment of prophecies from the Old Testament, as well as from Revelation, and that they were a sign that history was reaching its culmination.

A. The Influence of Augustine's "City of God"

St. Augustine's writings, particularly his seminal work "The City of God", played a significant role in shaping how medieval Christians viewed the concept of Holy War and the Crusades. Augustine's distinction between the earthly city (symbolizing human empires and sin) and the heavenly city (symbolizing the Kingdom of God) provided a theological framework for understanding the Crusades as part of the battle between the temporal world and God's eternal kingdom.

- Just War Doctrine and Holy War: Augustine's Just War Doctrine influenced the way Christians justified holy war during the Crusades. He argued that war could be considered just if it was waged for the purpose of defending the innocent or restoring peace. The Crusades, framed as a defense of Christian holy sites and a mission to restore Jerusalem, were seen as a righteous war sanctioned by God.

B. Joachim of Fiore and Apocalyptic Theology

Another significant figure in medieval apocalyptic thought was the 12th-century theologian Joachim of Fiore. Joachim developed a three-stage theory of history, in which the world was divided into three ages: the age of the Father (the Old Testament), the age of the Son (the New Testament and the Church), and the coming age of the Holy Spirit, which would be characterized by peace, unity, and the direct rule of God.

- Joachim's Influence on the Crusades: Joachim believed that the Crusades were part of the transition between the second and third ages of history. He interpreted the struggle between Christendom and Islam as part of the final conflict that would usher in the millennial kingdom. For Joachim and his followers, the Crusades were seen as necessary for bringing about the end times and the establishment of the Age of the Spirit.

C. The Apocalyptic Nature of Crusader Propaganda

Crusader propaganda often invoked apocalyptic themes to inspire recruits and maintain enthusiasm for the war effort. These messages emphasized that the Crusades were part of a divine plan and that the Crusaders were fulfilling their role as warriors of Christ in the final battle before the establishment of God's kingdom.

- Sermons and Papal Bulls: The Papal Bulls that called for the Crusades frequently used apocalyptic language, describing the Crusaders as instruments of God's will and urging them to cleanse the Holy Land of Muslim rule. These documents often promised spiritual rewards, such as the remission of sins, for those who took part in the Holy War, further reinforcing the sense that the Crusades were part of the ultimate battle between good and evil.

4. The Decline of Apocalyptic Fervor in Later Crusades

As the Crusades continued, especially after the failure of the Second and Third Crusades to achieve lasting success, the apocalyptic fervor that had characterized the early campaigns began to decline. The Crusading movement became more entangled with political and economic goals, leading to disillusionment among many participants.

A. The Fourth Crusade and the Sack of Constantinople

The Fourth Crusade (1202-1204) marked a turning point in the Crusading movement. Instead of marching to Jerusalem, the Crusaders diverted their campaign to the Christian city of Constantinople, which they sacked and plundered. This event was a profound shock to Christendom and was seen by many as a betrayal of the original apocalyptic vision of the Crusades.

- Disillusionment with the Crusading Ideal: The sack of Constantinople undermined the idea of the Crusades as a holy mission and called into question the spiritual legitimacy of the later campaigns. The Crusading movement increasingly became focused on political gain and economic interests, rather than the apocalyptic vision of reclaiming the Holy Land for Christ.

B. The Enduring Legacy of Apocalyptic Holy War

Despite the decline of apocalyptic fervor in the later Crusades, the idea of holy war as part of the final battle between good and evil continued to influence Christian thought. This legacy can be seen in the Reconquista in Spain, the ongoing conflicts between Christian Europe and the Ottoman Empire, and the development of Christian eschatological movements that continue to view the struggle over the Holy Land as part of the end times.

The Crusades as Apocalyptic Warfare

The Crusades were deeply rooted in the apocalyptic narratives of medieval Christianity, where the idea of Holy War was closely tied to the expectation of a final battle between Christendom and Islam. The capture of Jerusalem was seen as a necessary step in the unfolding of God's plan for the end of history, and the Crusaders believed they were participating in the cosmic struggle described in the Book of Revelation.

While the original apocalyptic fervor diminished in the later Crusades, the idea of holy war as part of the final conflict continued to shape Christian theology and influence subsequent wars and conflicts in Europe. The Crusades remain a powerful example of how apocalyptic thought can be used to motivate and justify warfare, and their legacy continues to resonate in modern eschatological movements that focus on the Holy Land and the Second Coming of Christ.

Modern Christian Interpretations of the Crusades within an Apocalyptic Framework

The legacy of the Crusades continues to influence certain strands of modern Christian thought, particularly in movements that focus on apocalyptic prophecy and the end times. Many of these modern Christian movements view the Crusades as not just a historical series of religious wars, but as part of a broader cosmic battle between Christianity and Islam—a struggle that some believe will continue until the final return of Christ. The idea of holy war, once so central to medieval Christian theology, has been reinterpreted by some modern movements to fit into an apocalyptic narrative that sees the Middle East, Israel, and the Holy Land as central to the end times scenario.

This chapter will delve further into how various modern Christian movements—including Christian Zionism, premillennial dispensationalism, and some branches of evangelical Christianity—interpret the Crusades within an apocalyptic framework. We will explore the theological perspectives that have developed around the Holy Land, the conflicts in the Middle East, and the anticipation of a final eschatological battle between the forces of good and evil.

1. The Influence of the Crusades on Modern Christian Eschatology

The Crusades occupy a complex place in modern Christian eschatology, particularly in movements that see apocalyptic prophecy as an unfolding process involving contemporary global events. In these interpretations, the Crusades are often viewed as a precursor to the final battle between Christendom and Islam, with the ongoing struggle over the Holy Land representing the next stage in this historical conflict.

A. Christian Zionism and the Restoration of Israel

Christian Zionism is one of the most prominent modern movements that interprets the Crusades within an apocalyptic framework. For Christian Zionists, the restoration of the Jewish people to the land of Israel is seen as a fulfillment of biblical prophecy and a necessary precursor to the Second Coming of Christ. In this context, the Crusades are often viewed as an early attempt by Christians to secure control of the Holy Land, setting the stage for the final end-times scenario.

- Jerusalem and the Crusades: For many Christian Zionists, the control of Jerusalem—both in the past during the Crusades and in the present—is crucial to fulfilling apocalyptic prophecy. They believe that the return of the Jews to Israel, and particularly to Jerusalem, is part of the divine plan outlined in biblical prophecy, and that this will lead to the return of Christ to reign on earth.

- The Holy Land as the Center of Apocalyptic Conflict: Christian Zionism sees the Holy Land as the focal point of the end times, much like the Crusaders did. The struggle over control of the Temple Mount and the status of Jerusalem are interpreted as part of the cosmic battle that will culminate in the final defeat of evil and the establishment of God's kingdom.

B. Premillennial Dispensationalism and the Final Battle

Premillennial dispensationalism, a theological framework that became popular in the 19th century, also interprets the Crusades within the context of apocalyptic prophecy. This view holds that history is divided into distinct dispensations or epochs, with the current era being the Church Age. According to premillennial dispensationalism, the world is rapidly moving toward the tribulation period, during which a final battle between good and evil will take place in the Middle East.

- The Crusades as a Precursor to the End Times: In this theological view, the Crusades are seen as part of the historical conflict between the forces of Christianity and Islam, which will ultimately culminate in the Great Tribulation. The battle for control of Jerusalem, which the Crusaders viewed as central to their mission, is interpreted as foreshadowing the Battle of Armageddon—the final confrontation between the Antichrist and the forces of Christ as described in the Book of Revelation.

- The Antichrist and the Middle East: Some premillennial dispensationalists believe that the Antichrist will emerge from the Middle East or Europe and lead the world into a final period of apostasy and persecution. In this view, the Crusades are seen as part of the long history of conflict that will culminate in the Second Coming of Christ, when Jesus will return to defeat the Antichrist and establish His millennial reign.

2. The Crusades as a Symbol of the Christian-Islamic Conflict

For many modern apocalyptic movements, the Crusades represent the historical beginning of the Christian-Islamic conflict that will play a central role in the end times. This perspective is especially prevalent among certain evangelical Christian groups that view Islam as a major force in the final battle between good and evil.

A. Apocalyptic Interpretations of Modern Middle Eastern Conflicts

Many modern Christian movements see the ongoing conflicts in the Middle East, particularly those involving Israel and its Arab neighbors, as a continuation of the apocalyptic struggle between Christianity and Islam that began during the Crusades. These movements often interpret events such as the Israeli-Palestinian conflict, the wars in Iraq and Syria, and the rise of Islamic extremism as signs that the world is moving closer to the end times.

- The Role of Islamic Powers in the End Times: In some interpretations, modern Islamic powers are seen as the continuation of the demonic forces that the Crusaders fought against. For instance, movements like ISIS and Al-Qaeda are viewed by some as part of the Antichrist's army, which will rise in opposition to God's kingdom in the final days. This perspective is a continuation of the medieval view that Islam represents a spiritual enemy in the apocalyptic conflict.

- The Battle of Armageddon: According to Revelation 16:16, the Battle of Armageddon will take place in the Middle East, near Mount Megiddo. Many modern interpreters connect this prophecy to the Crusader battles over Jerusalem and the broader Christian-Islamic conflict, viewing current events in the Middle East as setting the stage for this final apocalyptic battle.

B. The Influence of the Crusades on Christian Militancy and Apocalyptic Movements

The legacy of the Crusades has also influenced some modern Christian militant movements that see themselves as warriors in the final apocalyptic battle. These groups often invoke the imagery of the Crusades in their rhetoric, framing their mission as part of the larger cosmic struggle between Christianity and Islam that will culminate in the Second Coming of Christ.

- Crusader Imagery in Modern Christian Nationalism: In some forms of modern Christian nationalism, particularly in the United States and parts of Europe, the imagery of the Crusades is used to promote a militant defense of Christian values against perceived threats from Islam and secularism. These movements sometimes frame their efforts to defend Western civilization as part of the final battle between Christendom and the forces of evil. While these movements do not engage in actual warfare, their rhetoric draws heavily on the Crusader ideal of holy war.

- Militant Christian Groups: Some fringe groups, such as Christian militias that operate in conflict zones like the Middle East and Africa, have adopted the language of the Crusades to justify their actions. These groups often see themselves as part of an ongoing apocalyptic struggle, defending Christians from Muslim persecution and preparing for the final confrontation between Christ and the forces of evil.

3. The Crusades and the Restoration of the Temple in Apocalyptic Thought

Another key aspect of modern Christian apocalyptic thought that draws on the legacy of the Crusades is the belief in the eventual rebuilding of the Third Temple in Jerusalem. The Crusaders sought to reclaim Jerusalem, and modern movements see the restoration of Jewish control over the city as a critical step in preparing for the Second Coming.

A. The Crusader Goal of Securing Jerusalem for Christ

The Crusades were primarily focused on securing Jerusalem for Christendom, a goal driven by the belief that control of the Holy City was necessary for the fulfillment of biblical prophecy. For modern apocalyptic movements, this goal remains significant, with the control of Jerusalem seen as essential to the return of Christ.

- The Temple Mount and Apocalyptic Prophecy: In modern apocalyptic theology, the Temple Mount in Jerusalem is seen as the site where the Third Temple must be rebuilt in order for the end times to fully unfold. This belief is often connected to the Crusades, as the Crusaders' efforts to control Jerusalem are viewed as an early attempt to reclaim the holy city and prepare it for Christ's return.

- The Rebuilding of the Third Temple: Some modern evangelical and Christian Zionist movements are focused on the rebuilding of the Third Temple, believing that this event will trigger the final events of the Great Tribulation and the return of Christ. The Crusaders' desire to secure Jerusalem is often invoked as part of this narrative, with modern movements seeing themselves as continuing the Crusader mission of preparing the Holy Land for the Messiah.

B. Jerusalem's Role in the Final Eschatological Battle

In many modern interpretations, the city of Jerusalem is not only the location where Christ will return, but also the site of the final eschatological battle between the forces of good and evil. This belief is closely tied to the Book of Revelation, where Jerusalem is described as the focal point of the final conflict.

- Revelation 16:16: The gathering of the armies for the Battle of Armageddon is often connected to Jerusalem, as many interpret the final confrontation to be centered around the city and its surrounding regions. In this view, the Crusader struggle for Jerusalem was an early attempt to secure the city for God's kingdom, with modern events in Israel continuing this apocalyptic narrative.

4. Criticisms of Modern Apocalyptic Interpretations of the Crusades

While some modern Christian movements embrace the apocalyptic framework of the Crusades, others criticize this approach, arguing that it distorts both historical reality and theological understanding. These critics contend that viewing the Crusades as part of an ongoing cosmic battle ignores the political and economic factors that played a major role in the Crusades, while also fueling religious extremism in the modern world.

A. Historical Criticism of the Crusades as an Apocalyptic Event

Historians and theologians who adopt a more critical approach to the Crusades argue that they were largely driven by political and territorial motivations, rather than purely apocalyptic concerns. While apocalyptic rhetoric was certainly used to inspire Crusaders, these critics emphasize the complex socio-political dynamics that influenced the Crusades.

- Economic and Political Motivations: Many historians point out that the Crusades were motivated by a combination of economic interests, the desire for territorial expansion, and the ambition of European monarchs. The use of apocalyptic language was often a tool for rallying support, but the primary drivers of the Crusades were not always spiritual in nature.

- Religious Violence and Extremism: Some critics argue that modern movements that glorify the Crusades as part of a holy mission or apocalyptic battle risk promoting a dangerous form of religious extremism. By framing modern conflicts in the Middle East as part of the final battle between Christianity and Islam, these movements can contribute to the escalation of violence and religious intolerance.

B. Theological Criticism of Holy War in Modern Apocalyptic Thought

The concept of Holy War as part of the final battle has also faced significant theological criticism from within the Christian tradition. Many theologians argue that the New Testament calls for peace, forgiveness, and the rejection of violence, and that the use of military force in the name of Christ is incompatible with His teachings.

- Christ's Kingdom of Peace: The teachings of Jesus emphasize the establishment of a kingdom of peace rather than one built on warfare. Many Christian theologians reject the idea that the Crusades or modern conflicts can be justified as part of a holy war, arguing that Christ's return will bring about peace and the renewal of creation, rather than a militaristic victory over enemies.

- The Role of Nonviolence in Christian Eschatology: The emphasis on nonviolence in Christian eschatology suggests that the final battle will not be fought with earthly weapons but through the spiritual victory of Christ over the forces of sin and death. In this view, the use of the Crusades as a model for modern apocalyptic warfare is theologically misguided.

The Legacy of the Crusades in Modern Apocalyptic Thought

The Crusades continue to resonate in modern Christian apocalyptic thought, particularly in movements such as Christian Zionism, premillennial dispensationalism, and certain strands of evangelical Christianity. For these groups, the Crusades are viewed as part of a broader cosmic battle between Christianity and Islam, with the conflict over the Holy Land representing a key element in the unfolding of end-times prophecy.

However, this interpretation is not without controversy. Critics argue that viewing the Crusades through an apocalyptic lens can distort historical reality, contribute to religious extremism, and promote a theology of violence that is incompatible with the teachings of Christ. As modern Christian movements continue to grapple with the legacy of the Crusades, the question of how to interpret these events within the framework of biblical prophecy remains a point of both theological interest and debate.

CHAPTER 10

NEBUCHADNEZZAR'S DREAM AND THE END OF HISTORY

The dream of Nebuchadnezzar, as recorded in Daniel 2, has been one of the most analyzed and debated prophetic visions in both Christian theology and world history. The image of the great statue with its various sections made of different metals, symbolizing the succession of world empires, has been interpreted by theologians, historians, and philosophers for centuries as a prophetic roadmap for the end of history. These interpretations have evolved, particularly as new historical events unfolded, ranging from the fall of the Roman Empire to the World Wars and the emergence of global powers in the 20th and 21st centuries.

This chapter explores how later theologians and historians have interpreted Nebuchadnezzar's dream in light of modern history. It will examine how post-Reformation, Enlightenment, and modern thinkers have viewed the progression of empires, the role of the Church, and the idea of God's kingdom replacing the world's kingdoms. Additionally, it will delve into how the dream is interpreted within contemporary discussions about globalization, the decline of the West, and the future of civilization.

1. The Traditional Interpretation: Four Empires and the Rise of God's Kingdom

Throughout much of Christian history, the dream of Nebuchadnezzar has been understood as a prophetic vision outlining the rise and fall of four major empires, culminating in the establishment of God's eternal kingdom. This traditional interpretation sees the four metals of the statue as representing specific empires in world history.

A. The Four Empires in Traditional Theology

The traditional interpretation, accepted by early Christian theologians like Augustine and Jerome, identified the four empires as:

1. Head of Gold – Babylonian Empire: Representing Nebuchadnezzar's own kingdom, the Babylonian Empire is seen as the first in the succession of human governments that would eventually be replaced by God's kingdom.

2. Chest and Arms of Silver – Medo-Persian Empire: The silver portion of the statue represents the Medo-Persian

Empire, which succeeded Babylon after its conquest by Cyrus the Great.

3. Belly and Thighs of Bronze – Greek Empire: The bronze section represents the Greek Empire, established under Alexander the Great, known for its vast territorial expansion and cultural influence.

4. Legs of Iron – Roman Empire: The legs of iron symbolize the Roman Empire, whose military and political strength made it the most dominant empire of the ancient world.

5. Feet of Iron and Clay – Divided Kingdoms: The feet made of iron mixed with clay are interpreted as the fragmentation of the Roman Empire into weaker, divided kingdoms. This part of the vision is seen as the final stage of human history, where kingdoms are strong but fragile, setting the stage for God's eternal kingdom.

- Daniel 2:44: "In the days of those kings the God of heaven will set up a kingdom that will never be destroyed, nor will it be left to another people. It will crush all those kingdoms and bring them to an end, but it will itself endure forever."

This passage forms the basis of the eschatological hope in Christian theology: that Christ's return will bring an end to all earthly powers and inaugurate God's eternal reign.

B. The Rock Not Cut by Human Hands: Christ and the Kingdom of God

The rock that destroys the statue is traditionally understood as representing Jesus Christ and His eternal kingdom. According to this interpretation, Christ's first coming laid the groundwork for this kingdom, but its full realization will occur at His Second Coming, when all human governments will be overthrown, and the Kingdom of God will be established forever.

For centuries, this vision was viewed as literal prophecy guiding historical interpretation. The fall of Rome, the rise of feudal Europe, and even the Crusades were often seen through the lens of this prophecy, with theologians believing they were living in the final stages of human history.

2. Post-Reformation Interpretations: The End of the Church Age

The Reformation in the 16th century brought about significant changes in how Nebuchadnezzar's dream was interpreted, particularly among Protestant theologians. Figures like Martin Luther and John Calvin viewed the Roman Catholic Church as part of the apostasy prophesied in the Bible and linked their contemporary struggles with the idea of end-times events.

A. The Protestant View of the Roman Empire and the Papacy

For many Reformers, the Roman Empire, represented by the legs of iron, was seen not only as a historical empire but as a symbol of both political and religious oppression. In their eyes, the Roman Catholic Church had inherited the power of the Roman Empire and had become corrupted.

- Antichrist and the Papacy: Some Protestant theologians, such as Luther, viewed the Papacy as the Antichrist, the religious and political power that would be overthrown at the end of time. They saw the Reformation as part of the process of preparing the world for the return of Christ and the establishment of God's kingdom.

- Divided Kingdoms: The Protestant interpretation often emphasized the divided kingdoms of Europe, which emerged after the fall of the Roman Empire. These fractured political states, marked by religious conflict and war, were seen as the feet of iron and clay—strong yet divided, symbolizing the inherent weakness of human governments.

B. Apocalyptic Expectation and the Reformation

The Reformation period was marked by intense apocalyptic expectation, with many believing that they were living in the last days. Nebuchadnezzar's dream was frequently referenced in sermons and writings to justify the overthrow of corrupt powers and the purification of the Church in preparation for Christ's return.

The Thirty Years' War (1618–1648), which devastated Europe, was seen by some theologians as part of the final judgment prophesied in the Book of Daniel. The religious wars between Catholics and Protestants were interpreted as a spiritual battle preceding the destruction of the earthly kingdoms and the establishment of God's rule.

3. Enlightenment and Modern Historical Interpretations

The Enlightenment of the 18th century brought about a shift in how many historians and theologians viewed prophecy and history. As rationalism and secularism took hold, traditional interpretations of Nebuchadnezzar's dream were often re-evaluated through a more historical-critical lens. However, this period also saw new interpretations emerge, particularly as nationalism and revolution reshaped Europe.

A. The Rise of Secularism and Nationalism

During the Enlightenment, thinkers like Edward Gibbon began to view the fall of the Roman Empire and the subsequent rise of modern nations in a more secular context. Gibbon's famous work, "The Decline and Fall of the Roman Empire," interpreted the empire's collapse as a result of internal weakness and external pressures, rather than divine intervention.

- Decline of Prophetic History: While some theologians continued to interpret history through the lens of biblical prophecy, many Enlightenment thinkers rejected the notion that world events were dictated by divine prophecy. Instead, they focused on the political, economic, and social factors that contributed to the rise and fall of empires.

- Revolutions and the Fall of Monarchies: The French Revolution (1789) and subsequent Napoleonic Wars were seen by some as part of the final phase of divided kingdoms. The fall of European monarchies and the rise of republicanism and nationalism were interpreted as a further fragmentation of the old order, in line with the prophecy of the feet of iron and clay.

B. Modern Interpretations of Global Powers and Empires

In the 19th and 20th centuries, the dream of Nebuchadnezzar continued to be interpreted in light of global powers and world conflicts. The rise of the British Empire, the United States, and the Soviet Union was seen by some theologians as part of the final stage of the prophecy, where powerful but divided nations dominated the world.

- World Wars and the End of Empire: The two World Wars of the 20th century, particularly World War II, were interpreted by some as part of the apocalyptic timeline outlined in Daniel. The collapse of European empires after the wars, particularly the fall of the British Empire and the decolonization of Africa and Asia, was seen as part of the ongoing fragmentation of human power structures, symbolized by the feet of iron and clay.

- Cold War: The Cold War between the United States and the Soviet Union was often interpreted as a struggle between two divided yet powerful empires, echoing the fragile and divided nature of the final stage of the statue. The nuclear arms race and the threat of global destruction were seen as evidence that the world was on the brink of the final judgment, with many Christian thinkers anticipating Christ's return.

4. Contemporary Interpretations: Globalization, the Decline of the West, and the End of History

In the 21st century, the dream of Nebuchadnezzar continues to be a source of reflection for theologians, historians, and political thinkers. As the world becomes more interconnected through globalization, and as debates over the decline of Western power and the rise of China and other Eastern powers dominate geopolitics, many have revisited Nebuchadnezzar's dream as a prophetic guide to understanding the future.

A. Globalization and the Division of Nations

The idea of globalization—where national borders and distinctions are increasingly blurred through economic, political, and cultural integration—has been interpreted by some as a continuation of the divided kingdoms represented by the feet of iron and clay.

- Global Fragility: Some modern interpreters see globalization as creating a fragile world order, where nations are interdependent yet often in conflict. This mixture of strength and weakness, much like the iron and clay in the statue, is seen as a precursor to the collapse of human systems and the establishment of God's kingdom.

- Multinational Corporations and Global Governance: The rise of multinational corporations and the increasing influence of global governance organizations, such as the United Nations and the World Trade Organization, are sometimes viewed as part of the final phase of human history, where divided powers struggle for dominance but ultimately fall apart in the face of Christ's return.

B. The Decline of the West and the Rise of Eastern Powers

The perceived decline of Western powers, particularly the United States and Europe, in global influence has also been viewed in the context of Nebuchadnezzar's dream. As Eastern powers like China and India rise, some theologians and historians see this as a shifting of the global balance of power, which could lead to the fulfillment of the final stage of divided kingdoms.

- United States as the Last Great Empire: Some Christian interpreters view the United States as the final empire in the sequence of world powers symbolized by the statue. With its global military dominance and economic power, the U.S. has been likened to the legs of iron (Rome), yet many also see its internal divisions and growing political instability as evidence that it is the feet of iron and clay, a fragile empire destined to be replaced by God's kingdom.

- China and the New World Order: The rise of China as a global superpower is often discussed in terms of its potential to challenge Western dominance, leading some to speculate that this could be part of the final geopolitical shift before the Second Coming of Christ. In this view, the weakness of human governments is once again highlighted, as powerful empires face internal strife and division, setting the stage for the Kingdom of God.

C. The End of History and the Eternal Kingdom

In the post-Cold War era, the idea of the "end of history" gained traction through the work of political theorist Francis Fukuyama, who argued that the spread of liberal democracy and capitalism would mark the final stage of human government. While Fukuyama's thesis is secular, some Christian theologians have engaged with this idea, suggesting that the true end of history will come not through political systems but through the intervention of God.

- The Rock as the Final Reality: For modern Christian eschatology, the rock not cut by human hands remains the ultimate symbol of God's kingdom, which will come to crush all human governments and establish Christ's eternal reign. As modern powers rise and fall, many theologians assert that the end of history will only come when Christ returns, fulfilling the prophecy of Nebuchadnezzar's dream.

Nebuchadnezzar's Dream and the Modern World

From the Roman Empire to globalization, the dream of Nebuchadnezzar has been a profound tool for interpreting the rise and fall of human empires and their place in God's plan for history. While the details of interpretation have evolved, the core message remains: human power is temporary and fragile, and only the Kingdom of God will last forever. Modern theologians and historians continue to find relevance in this ancient vision, seeing in it the hand of God guiding the course of history toward its final fulfillment.

Comparisons to Contemporary Apocalyptic Movements

The vision of Nebuchadnezzar's dream in Daniel 2 has long been a cornerstone of Christian apocalyptic thought, providing a symbolic roadmap for the rise and fall of empires leading to the ultimate end of history. However, the influence of apocalyptic themes has extended beyond religious interpretations, inspiring both contemporary religious movements and secular thought on the end of history. Today, these themes resonate in the rhetoric of modern apocalyptic movements, whether religious or secular, reflecting humanity's ongoing fascination with eschatology—the study of the end times—and the collapse of civilization as we know it.

This chapter explores the comparisons between Nebuchadnezzar's dream and contemporary apocalyptic movements, examining how modern religious and secular ideologies interpret the end of history. We will discuss how different movements—ranging from Christian Zionism, premillennial dispensationalism, and Islamic apocalypticism to secular theories like Francis Fukuyama's "End of History" thesis and environmental doomsday predictions—draw on similar themes of global collapse, the rise of new orders, and the ultimate transcendence of human civilization.

1. Christian Apocalyptic Movements and Nebuchadnezzar's Dream

In contemporary Christian apocalyptic thought, Nebuchadnezzar's dream continues to be a central text, influencing movements that predict the imminent return of Christ and the establishment of God's kingdom. These movements often interpret global events—such as the rise of new powers, the Middle East conflict, and natural disasters—through the lens of biblical prophecy.

A. Christian Zionism and the Restoration of Israel

Christian Zionism is one of the most influential movements that sees the restoration of Israel and the control of Jerusalem as central to the end times narrative. For Christian Zionists, Nebuchadnezzar's vision of the statue represents the succession of earthly kingdoms, with Israel's return as a critical part of the fulfillment of prophecy before the Second Coming of Christ.

- Nebuchadnezzar's Dream and Israel: Christian Zionists often interpret the divided kingdoms represented by the feet of iron and clay as a symbol of the modern geopolitical landscape, particularly the fragility of current global powers and their inability to create lasting peace. For them, the restoration of Jewish sovereignty over Jerusalem is seen as a sign that the final age of history has begun.

- Apocalyptic Expectations: The movement's focus on the Temple Mount in Jerusalem and the rebuilding of the Third Temple echoes the millennial expectations set forth in Revelation and Daniel. Many believe that these events will trigger the final battle between Christendom and the forces of evil, including Islam, leading to the Second Coming of Christ as the rock that crushes the world's kingdoms.

B. Premillennial Dispensationalism and the Final Kingdom

Premillennial dispensationalism is another major strand of Christian apocalypticism that draws heavily on the symbolism of Nebuchadnezzar's dream. According to this theology, world history is divided into dispensations, with the current era being the Church Age, soon to be followed by a period of tribulation and the establishment of Christ's millennial kingdom.

- Interpretation of the Statue: For premillennial dispensationalists, the statue's feet of iron and clay represent the fragmented nature of modern political powers, especially the rise of global alliances and multinational entities like the European Union and the United Nations. These entities, though powerful, are seen as unstable and destined to fall when Christ returns to establish His millennial reign.

- Apocalyptic Chronology: The view holds that the world will soon experience a Great Tribulation, during which the Antichrist will rise and global conflict will ensue. The rock not cut by human hands, representing Christ, will destroy the world's kingdoms, bringing an end to human rule and ushering in the millennial kingdom.

C. Islamic Apocalypticism and Global Struggle

In Islamic apocalyptic thought, there are parallels to Christian interpretations of Nebuchadnezzar's dream. Islamic eschatology also emphasizes the rise and fall of empires, the ultimate battle between good and evil, and the establishment of a final, righteous caliphate under Mahdi, the Islamic redeemer.

- Conflict with Christian Prophecy: Some Islamic apocalyptic movements see current geopolitical tensions as part of the final struggle between Islam and Western powers (often symbolized as Christian empires). For these movements, the crumbling of Western nations, represented by the fragile feet of iron and clay, signals the imminent victory of Islam and the arrival of Mahdi to establish God's rule on earth.

- Parallel Expectations: Similar to Christian expectations of Christ's return, Islamic apocalyptic thought includes the belief in the return of Isa (Jesus), who will come alongside Mahdi to defeat al-Dajjal (the Antichrist). This final victory is seen as ushering in a new era of justice, replacing the corrupt and divided kingdoms of the world.

2. Secular Interpretations of the End of History

In the modern secular world, the idea of an end of history continues to influence philosophical and political discourse. While these interpretations do not typically reference biblical prophecy, they reflect similar concerns about the decline of civilizations, the rise of new global orders, and the eventual transcendence of current human institutions. These secular interpretations often focus on geopolitical shifts, technological advancements, and environmental crises.

A. Francis Fukuyama's "End of History" Thesis

One of the most famous secular interpretations of the end of history comes from political theorist Francis Fukuyama, who argued in his 1992 book "The End of History and the Last Man" that the collapse of the Soviet Union and the triumph of liberal democracy marked the final stage of human political evolution. In this view, Western liberal democracy would be the final form of government, representing the culmination of history's ideological battles.

- Liberal Democracy as the Final Empire: Fukuyama's thesis can be compared to Nebuchadnezzar's dream in the sense that he saw liberal democracy as the final, stable political system, replacing all previous forms of governance. However, unlike the prophecy in Daniel, Fukuyama's vision did not foresee a divine intervention but rather a secular triumph of human reason and governance.

- Criticisms and Post-Cold War Reality: Fukuyama's thesis has been widely critiqued, especially in the wake of events like the 9/11 attacks, the rise of authoritarian governments, and the global economic crises of the early 21st century. These developments challenged the idea that history had reached its final form, suggesting instead that the divisions between nations and the fragility of political systems (reminiscent of the feet of iron and clay) remain a central feature of the world order.

B. Environmental Apocalypse and Climate Change

Another prominent secular apocalyptic narrative centers around the impending environmental collapse due to climate change. For many environmentalists, the global failure to address issues like carbon emissions, deforestation, and species extinction signals the end of history—at least in terms of human civilization as it is currently structured.

- Environmental Doomsday: This narrative often portrays the human race as being on the brink of a self-inflicted apocalypse, where the Earth's ecosystems collapse under the weight of unchecked industrialization and consumption. The fragile nature of global efforts to mitigate climate change can be likened to the feet of iron and clay in Nebuchadnezzar's dream, symbolizing a world order that is powerful yet inherently unstable.

- Globalization and Environmental Instability: Just as Nebuchadnezzar's dream depicts human empires as ultimately flawed and destined for destruction, the environmental crisis reveals the inherent weaknesses in global governance, cooperation, and human foresight. Environmental movements often call for a radical transformation of human society, akin to the rock not cut by human hands destroying the old order and creating a new, sustainable future.

C. Technological Singularity and Post-Humanism

In the world of technological futurism, the concept of the technological singularity—a point at which artificial intelligence surpasses human intelligence—represents a different kind of end of history. For some theorists, the singularity will mark the transcendence of humanity, where human civilization will be fundamentally transformed or even replaced by post-human entities.

- Singularity as the New Order: In this view, the progression of empires in Nebuchadnezzar's dream might be likened to the stages of human development, with the final transformation representing a leap beyond human control. The rock could be seen as technology itself, reshaping the very foundations of civilization in ways that are beyond human comprehension.

- Transcendence or Collapse: Proponents of the singularity often frame it as a new dawn for humanity, while critics warn of a potential technological apocalypse, where AI and automation could lead to mass unemployment, the breakdown of social systems, or even existential threats to human existence.

3. The End of History as a Recurring Theme in Human Thought

Both religious and secular apocalyptic movements share a common thread: the belief that human history is progressing toward a definitive conclusion—whether it be a divine intervention, ecological collapse, or the rise of a post-human order. This reflects humanity's enduring fascination with the end of history and the desire to understand our place within a larger cosmic narrative.

A. The Human Need for Closure

Apocalyptic narratives, whether rooted in religion or secularism, often reflect a deep psychological need for closure and understanding in the face of an unpredictable and chaotic world. The vision of Nebuchadnezzar's statue, with its clear progression of empires and its ultimate destruction, provides a sense of order and purpose to history, reassuring believers that there is a divine plan that will bring about a just and eternal kingdom.

- Religious Apocalypses: For religious believers, particularly within Christianity and Islam, the end of history represents the triumph of God and the fulfillment of divine prophecy. It promises a new heaven and new earth, where suffering, injustice, and division are replaced by God's reign of peace and righteousness.

- Secular Apocalypses: For secular movements, the end of history often represents a warning or call to action—whether to avert environmental disaster, adapt to technological change, or preserve democratic values in the face of rising authoritarianism. These narratives focus on the fragility of human achievements and the need for collective transformation.

B. The Role of Prophecy in Shaping Human History

Nebuchadnezzar's dream is part of a broader tradition of prophetic literature that has been used throughout history to inspire action, justify conflict, or explain historical events. In both religious and secular contexts, prophecy serves as a tool for making sense of global trends, offering hope to those who believe in a better future or warning to those who fear impending collapse.

- Prophetic Movements and Social Change: Throughout history, apocalyptic movements have often led to periods of intense social upheaval and transformation. Whether through revolution, religious reform, or political activism, these movements have shaped the course of history, influencing the rise and fall of nations and the redirection of human effort toward new visions of the future.

Nebuchadnezzar's Dream and Modern Apocalyptic Thought

Nebuchadnezzar's dream continues to resonate in both religious and secular interpretations of the end of history, providing a framework for understanding the rise and fall of empires, the fragility of human systems, and the ultimate establishment of a new world order—whether divine or man-made. From Christian eschatology to secular predictions about the environment, technology, and political systems, the idea of a final apocalyptic conclusion remains a powerful narrative that shapes how we perceive the world and its future.

Prophetic Interpretations of Modern Historical Events

Throughout history, many major historical events have been viewed through the lens of biblical prophecy, with scholars and theologians looking to Nebuchadnezzar's dream in Daniel 2 as a guide to understanding the rise and fall of empires and the ultimate end of history. In recent decades, events such as the fall of the Soviet Union, financial crises, and the changing global order have been interpreted by various religious and apocalyptic movements as part of this prophetic narrative.

This chapter explores how specific modern historical events, including the collapse of the Soviet Union, the global financial crises, and the broader shifts in global politics, have been interpreted in light of Nebuchadnezzar's dream. We will examine how these events are seen as part of the final stage of world history, represented by the feet of iron and clay, and how contemporary apocalyptic movements view these developments as leading to the imminent return of Christ or the end of the current world system.

1. The Fall of the Soviet Union and the End of the Iron Curtain

The collapse of the Soviet Union in 1991 was one of the most significant geopolitical events of the 20th century, signaling the end of the Cold War and the dismantling of the communist bloc in Eastern Europe. For many Christian eschatological movements, the fall of the Soviet Union was interpreted as a fulfillment of prophetic signs outlined in Daniel 2 and Revelation, marking a critical shift in the balance of global power.

A. The Soviet Union as the Final Empire?

Prior to its collapse, some Christian theologians and prophetic interpreters viewed the Soviet Union as a possible representation of the final world empire in Nebuchadnezzar's dream. The Soviet Union's military might and atheistic ideology led some to associate it with the iron in the statue's legs, representing a strong but ultimately flawed power.

- Soviet Union as Iron: The legs of iron in Nebuchadnezzar's dream traditionally symbolize the Roman

Empire, known for its strength and ability to conquer. However, in modern times, some interpreters extended this symbolism to the Soviet Union, seeing it as a similarly strong and authoritarian power with a capacity for military domination. The Soviet atheism and suppression of religion were also seen as signs of spiritual opposition to God's kingdom.

- Collapse as Prophetic Fulfillment: The sudden and relatively peaceful collapse of the Soviet Union, along with the fall of communist regimes in Eastern Europe, was seen by many as a sign that the iron legs of human empires were starting to crumble, fulfilling the prophecy that no earthly kingdom could last. For some interpreters, this collapse symbolized the beginning of the final phase of human history, setting the stage for the feet of iron and clay—representing the unstable and divided nature of the post-Soviet world.

B. The Rise of Divided Kingdoms

With the disintegration of the Soviet Union, the global order transitioned from a bipolar world dominated by the United States and the USSR to a more multipolar and divided global system. For many prophetic interpreters, this shift mirrored the prophecy in Daniel 2, where the feet of iron and clay represent a world order that is both strong and weak, with nations and empires increasingly divided.

- Fragmentation of Power: After the Soviet Union's collapse, the Eastern bloc fragmented into various independent states, some of which experienced ethnic conflict, economic instability, and political upheaval. This fragmentation was seen by some as emblematic of the weakness of the clay in the statue's feet, suggesting that the new world order was inherently unstable and ripe for divine intervention.

- Russia's Role in Prophecy: Despite the Soviet collapse, Russia remained a significant global power. Some interpreters believed that Russia could still play a key role in end-times prophecy, particularly in connection with Gog and Magog, names mentioned in Ezekiel and Revelation as nations involved in a final apocalyptic war against Israel. Russia's involvement in the Middle East and its return to global prominence under Vladimir Putin has revived this interpretation for some.

2. Financial Crises and Economic Instability

The global financial crises of the late 20th and early 21st centuries, particularly the 2008 financial crisis, have also been interpreted through the lens of biblical prophecy. These crises, which caused widespread economic hardship and political instability, are seen by some as evidence of the fragility of human systems and the moral decay of modern economies, symbolized by the feet of iron and clay in Nebuchadnezzar's dream.

A. The 2008 Financial Crisis: A Sign of Collapse

The 2008 financial crisis, which led to the collapse of major financial institutions, massive government bailouts, and global economic downturns, was viewed by many apocalyptic interpreters as a fulfillment of biblical warnings about the end of the age. The financial crisis exposed the underlying instability of the global economic system, which some saw as a reflection of the prophecy in Daniel 2.

- Economic Fragility as Clay: The feet of iron and clay are often interpreted as representing modern global powers that are economically powerful yet fundamentally unstable. The 2008 financial crisis, driven by debt, corruption, and greed, was seen as evidence of this instability, with the clay symbolizing the weakness of human economic systems that are ultimately destined to collapse.

- Globalization and the Division of Wealth: The global financial system, which became increasingly interconnected through globalization, was also seen as part of this prophetic vision. While some nations appeared strong and prosperous, the crisis revealed deep divisions and inequalities in the global economy, with many countries struggling to recover from the shock. For some interpreters, this division reflects the iron and clay mixture, symbolizing the fragile state of the global order before Christ's return.

B. Moral and Spiritual Decay in Economic Systems

Beyond the financial instability, many prophetic interpreters saw the 2008 crisis as evidence of the moral decay of modern economies, where greed, corruption, and deception played central roles in the collapse. These economic failures were often seen as part of the final judgment on human systems that prioritize material wealth over spiritual values.

- Judgment on Materialism: In this view, the global financial system is part of the Babylonian system described in Revelation 18, which represents the materialistic and morally corrupt kingdoms of the world. The fall of Babylon is interpreted as the collapse of global economies driven by greed and idolatry. The 2008 financial crisis, along with other economic collapses, was seen as a precursor to the final judgment of the world's economic powers.

- Warnings of Future Collapse: Many apocalyptic movements view the 2008 crisis as a warning of greater financial disasters to come, predicting that future collapses will bring about the end of the current world order and the rise of God's kingdom. In this context, economic instability is not just a political or financial problem but a spiritual sign of the end times.

3. The Rise of China and the Shifting Global Power Structure

As the global balance of power shifts in the 21st century, with the rise of China and the perceived decline of Western powers, many apocalyptic interpreters see these developments as part of the prophetic framework of Daniel 2. The growing influence of China, particularly its economic and military strength, is often viewed as part of the final stage of divided kingdoms, where global powers are both strong and weak, leading to the eventual destruction of human empires and the establishment of God's eternal kingdom.

A. China as a New Global Superpower

China's rapid economic growth and increasing global influence have led some to speculate that it represents a new world empire in the prophetic timeline. For some, China's rise is seen as part of the feet of iron and clay, where its economic and political strength is contrasted with internal challenges, such as authoritarian governance, social unrest, and economic inequality.

- Economic and Political Strength as Iron: China's dominant role in the global economy and its growing military presence are often interpreted as the iron in the feet of Nebuchadnezzar's statue. Its ability to project power, influence global trade, and challenge the United States for supremacy in various regions of the world is seen as a sign of its significant, though ultimately temporary, strength.

- Internal Instability as Clay: However, despite its economic and military might, China also faces significant internal challenges, including human rights abuses, government control, and environmental crises. For some interpreters, these challenges represent the clay, symbolizing the fragility of China's internal structure. Despite its outward appearance of strength, these weaknesses are seen as indicators that China, like other human empires before it, is subject to the same inevitable collapse predicted in Nebuchadnezzar's dream.

B. China's Role in End-Times Prophecy

In addition to its geopolitical significance, some Christian apocalyptic movements have speculated about China's role in the final events leading up to the Second Coming of Christ. Certain interpretations of the Book of Revelation point to Eastern powers playing a critical role in the end times, often citing Revelation 16:12, which refers to the "kings from the East" in the context of the Battle of Armageddon.

- Kings from the East and Armageddon: Some interpreters view China's rise as part of this prophecy, suggesting that China could be among the nations that will march toward the Middle East in the final battle against God's kingdom. The growth of China's military capabilities and its increasing involvement in global affairs, especially in regions like the Middle East and Africa, is seen as potentially significant in this apocalyptic context.

- China and Globalization: Others see China's role in the globalized economy—through projects like the Belt and Road Initiative—as part of the fragile and interconnected system represented by the feet of iron and clay. As China continues to expand its influence through infrastructure and trade agreements, some apocalyptic thinkers interpret this as a part of the final stage of global empire-building, which will ultimately be shattered by the divine intervention of the rock not cut by human hands.

4.   European   Union,   Globalism,   and   the Fragmentation of the West

The creation and expansion of the European Union (EU), as well as the rise of globalist ideologies, have also been interpreted by some prophetic movements as the fulfillment of Nebuchadnezzar's dream. The EU, in particular, is often seen as a contemporary embodiment of the divided kingdoms symbolized by the feet of iron and clay, representing an attempt to create a unified power out of disparate and often competing nations.

A. The European Union as the Rebirth of the Roman Empire

Some Christian interpreters view the European Union as a revival of the Roman Empire, a key stage in the prophetic timeline. The Roman Empire, represented by the legs of iron, was historically seen as the last great earthly empire before the establishment of God's kingdom. As the EU seeks to unite many of the countries that were once part of the Roman Empire, some see this as a modern attempt to resurrect the old imperial structure.

- Iron and Clay Symbolism: The EU's structure—strong in some areas (economic and military cooperation) but weak and divided in others (sovereignty disputes, internal political conflicts)—mirrors the symbolism of the feet of iron and clay. The Brexit vote in 2016, where the United Kingdom chose to leave the EU, was viewed by many as evidence of this inherent instability, further reinforcing the interpretation that human attempts at global unity are destined to fail.

- Antichrist and Global Governance: Some apocalyptic interpreters connect the EU with prophecies about the Antichrist, suggesting that a future world leader could arise from the EU or a similar global institution. This figure would, according to prophecy, attempt to create a one-world government, only to be defeated by the return of Christ. The European Union's bureaucratic governance and its secular political orientation are seen as potentially laying the groundwork for this end-times ruler.

B. Globalization as a Precursor to the End

In addition to the EU, broader trends toward globalization are seen by some as part of the prophetic narrative of Nebuchadnezzar's dream. The increasing integration of economies, the rise of multinational corporations, and the creation of global governance bodies like the United Nations are interpreted as signs that the world is moving toward a final, fragile state of interconnectedness that will soon be shattered.

- Globalism and Iron and Clay: Just as the feet of iron and clay in the statue represent a mixture of strength and weakness, globalism is viewed as creating a world order that is powerful but inherently unstable. The dependence on global supply chains, international trade, and diplomatic alliances makes the world vulnerable to crises—whether economic, environmental, or political—that could trigger a collapse of the current system.

- Environmental and Political Instability: Many interpreters see the fragility of the current global order as manifesting in environmental crises, such as climate change, and political instability, such as the rise of nationalism and authoritarianism. These events are viewed as part of the final stage of human history, where the divisions and weaknesses in the global system will ultimately lead to its destruction, paving the way for the establishment of God's eternal kingdom.

5. Prophetic Warnings in Light of Modern Financial and Political Crises

Modern financial and political crises, from the global debt crisis to political instability in major world powers, have been interpreted by many apocalyptic thinkers as signs of the imminent fulfillment of Nebuchadnezzar's dream. These crises are seen as judgments on the materialism, corruption, and moral decay of modern nations, which have turned away from God's laws.

A. The Global Debt Crisis and Economic Collapse

The increasing levels of national debt in many countries, particularly in the United States and Europe, are viewed as a sign that the global economic system is approaching a breaking point. For many prophetic interpreters, the debt-fueled growth of modern economies is unsustainable, and the coming collapse will trigger a global financial crisis that will lead to the fall of the current world order.

- Debt as a Symbol of Clay: In this interpretation, national and global debt symbolizes the clay in Nebuchadnezzar's vision, representing the weakness and vulnerability of modern economies. While nations appear strong on the surface, their dependence on debt financing reveals their underlying fragility. When this debt-based system collapses, it is seen as the fulfillment of the prophecy of the feet of iron and clay being destroyed by the rock of God's kingdom.

B. Political Instability and the Rise of Nationalism

The rise of nationalism and populist movements in countries like the United States, the United Kingdom, and across Europe is also seen as part of the prophetic fulfillment of Daniel's vision. These movements, which often reject globalization and emphasize national sovereignty, are viewed as contributing to the division and instability of the modern world.

- Nationalism as Division: For many apocalyptic interpreters, the resurgence of nationalism is seen as evidence of the inherent divisions within the feet of iron and clay. While the world has sought to unite through institutions like the United Nations and global trade agreements, the rise of nationalism shows that these efforts are weakening, preparing the way for the final collapse and the end of human rule.

Modern Historical Events and Prophetic Fulfillment

The interpretation of modern historical events through the lens of Nebuchadnezzar's dream continues to shape how many Christian apocalyptic movements view the current state of the world. Events such as the fall of the Soviet Union, financial crises, the rise of China, and the fragmentation of global powers are all seen as signs that the final stage of world history is unfolding, with the world's current systems—represented by the feet of iron and clay—nearing their collapse.

For these interpreters, the fulfillment of prophecy is not just a future event but is unfolding in real time, as the world's powers weaken and fragment in preparation for the return of Christ and the establishment of God's eternal kingdom. As geopolitical tensions, economic crises, and environmental challenges continue to escalate, many believe that the world is approaching the moment when the rock not cut by human hands will destroy all human kingdoms and usher in the end of history.

The Connection Between the Crusades, Modern Middle Eastern Conflict, and Eschatological Thinking

Throughout Christian history, the Crusades have been seen not just as a series of military campaigns but as a deeply eschatological struggle—a conflict between good and evil with significant apocalyptic undertones. For many medieval Christians, the Crusades were viewed as part of a divine plan to reclaim the Holy Land, particularly Jerusalem, in preparation for the Second Coming of Christ. These apocalyptic themes continue to resonate in modern eschatological thinking, especially regarding ongoing Middle Eastern conflicts involving Israel, Palestine, and broader global powers.

Let us explore the connection between the Crusades, the modern Middle Eastern conflict, and eschatological thinking, and examine how the religious motivations behind the Crusades have shaped contemporary Christian views on the Middle East, how apocalyptic expectations influence modern Christian Zionism, and how Islamic eschatology intersects with both historical and contemporary events in the region.

1. The Crusades as an Eschatological Struggle

The Crusades (1096–1291) were framed by their leaders and many participants as part of an apocalyptic battle for the Holy Land, particularly Jerusalem, which was seen as central to end-times prophecy. From a theological perspective, the Crusades were often interpreted as a holy war that would lead to the purification of the land in preparation for Christ's return.

A. Theological Motivation for the Crusades

For many medieval Christians, the Holy Land was not only a place of spiritual significance but also the site where key events in apocalyptic prophecy would take place. The

Book of Revelation describes Jerusalem as central to the final battle between good and evil, making the recapture of the city from Muslim control a key part of the Crusades' eschatological mission.

- Jerusalem and the End Times: Many Crusaders believed that the return of Christian control over Jerusalem was necessary for the fulfillment of prophecies related to the Second Coming of Christ. The belief that Christ's millennial reign would occur in Jerusalem added urgency to the Crusades, as it was seen as part of a larger divine plan leading up to the end of history.

- Apocalyptic Rhetoric: Leaders such as Pope Urban II, who launched the First Crusade in 1095, used apocalyptic language to inspire participants. Urban described the conflict as a battle between Christendom and the forces of darkness, portraying the Muslim control of Jerusalem as an affront to God's will. For many Christians, the Crusades were part of a holy mission to bring about the ultimate victory of Christ's kingdom.

B. Jerusalem as the Fulcrum of Apocalyptic Expectation

The capture of Jerusalem in 1099 during the First Crusade was seen by many as a divine sign of God's favor and a step closer to the fulfillment of prophecy. The city's symbolic importance in Christian apocalyptic thought cannot be overstated; it was the place where Christ was crucified, where the resurrection occurred, and where the Second Coming was expected to take place.

- Purification of the Holy Land: The brutal massacre of the city's Muslim and Jewish inhabitants was justified by some Crusaders as a necessary purification of the Holy Land, clearing the way for Christ's reign. This violent conquest was framed within an apocalyptic narrative that saw the Crusaders as agents of God, preparing the world for the final battle between good and evil.

2. Modern Middle Eastern Conflict and Eschatological Thought

The Crusades continue to influence modern Christian eschatological thinking, particularly in relation to the ongoing Middle Eastern conflict. For many contemporary evangelical Christians and Christian Zionists, the return of Jewish sovereignty over Jerusalem and the establishment of the state of Israel in 1948 are seen as fulfillments of biblical prophecy, directly linked to the end times.

A. Christian Zionism and the State of Israel

Christian Zionism, which emerged in the late 19th and early 20th centuries, is a theological movement that views the return of the Jewish people to the Holy Land as a fulfillment of biblical prophecy and a necessary precursor to the Second

Coming of Christ. This movement is deeply connected to eschatological interpretations of the Crusades and the ongoing conflict in the Middle East.

- Israel's Creation as Prophetic Fulfillment: For many Christian Zionists, the establishment of the state of Israel in 1948 was a key moment in the unfolding of prophecy, signaling the beginning of the end times. Just as the Crusades sought to reclaim the Holy Land for Christendom, Christian Zionists see the modern state of Israel as reclaiming the land for God's chosen people, preparing for the eventual return of Christ.

- Jerusalem and the Temple Mount: The status of Jerusalem, especially the Temple Mount, remains a central focus of Christian Zionist eschatology. Many believe that the rebuilding of the Third Temple in Jerusalem is a critical event that will trigger the final battle between good and evil, leading to the Second Coming of Christ. This view echoes the medieval Crusader belief that control of Jerusalem was essential to bringing about the millennial kingdom.

B. The Arab-Israeli Conflict and Apocalyptic Interpretations

The ongoing Arab-Israeli conflict, particularly over Jerusalem and the West Bank, has also been viewed through an apocalyptic lens by many Christian movements. These conflicts are often interpreted as part of the final confrontation between the forces of God and the Antichrist, with Israel playing a central role in the end-times scenario.

- Battle of Armageddon: Many evangelical Christians see the escalating conflicts in the Middle East, especially between Israel and its Muslim neighbors, as leading toward the Battle of Armageddon—the final apocalyptic war described in Revelation 16:16. The Crusades are often referenced as an earlier manifestation of this cosmic struggle, with modern events viewed as the continuation of the battle for the Holy Land.

- Islam as a Modern Antichrist: Some apocalyptic interpreters view Islam as a modern manifestation of the Antichrist or as a spiritual force opposed to the establishment of God's kingdom. This view draws on the Crusader narrative, which cast Islam as the enemy of Christendom. In this eschatological framework, the ongoing conflict between Israel and Muslim-majority nations is seen as part of a larger spiritual war that will culminate in the Second Coming.

3. Islamic Eschatology and the Modern Conflict

Just as Christian eschatology has been shaped by the Crusades and the modern Middle Eastern conflict, so too has Islamic eschatology. In Islam, the end times will be marked by a series of cosmic battles between good and evil, with the return of Jesus (Isa) and the coming of the Mahdi, a messianic figure who will establish justice and defeat al-Dajjal, the Islamic equivalent of the Antichrist.

A. The Mahdi and the Battle for Jerusalem

In Islamic eschatology, Jerusalem holds significant importance, much like in Christian and Jewish traditions. The belief that Jerusalem will play a central role in the end times is shared across the Abrahamic faiths. Many Muslims believe that the Mahdi will come to lead the final battle against evil forces, including the Antichrist (al-Dajjal), and will establish peace and justice on earth.

- Jerusalem in Islamic Prophecy: The significance of Jerusalem in Islamic eschatology reflects a similar narrative to that of the Crusades and modern Christian Zionism. Just as medieval Muslims saw the Crusades as a direct threat to Islam, modern Muslims view the Israeli-Palestinian conflict and the presence of non-Muslim forces in Jerusalem as part of an apocalyptic struggle over the city's control.

- Modern Jihad and Apocalyptic Thinking: Some contemporary Islamic movements frame the ongoing conflict with Israel and Western powers as part of the final battle before the coming of the Mahdi. Much like the Christian interpretation of the Battle of Armageddon, these movements see the conflict in the Middle East as leading toward the ultimate victory of Islam in the end times.

B. Apocalyptic Parallels Between the Crusades and Modern Jihad

For many modern jihadist movements, the Crusades are not merely a historical episode but part of an ongoing spiritual battle between

Islam and Christianity. The rhetoric of modern jihad often invokes the Crusades as a symbol of Western aggression against the Muslim world, framing contemporary conflicts as a continuation of this historical struggle.

- Crusades as a Symbol in Modern Jihadist Ideology: Groups like Al-Qaeda and ISIS have frequently referred to Western military interventions in the Middle East as the actions of "Crusaders," drawing a direct link between medieval Christian invasions and modern Western imperialism. This language reinforces the idea that the conflict is apocalyptic in nature, with modern Muslim warriors taking on the role of defenders of Islam in the final struggle before the end of days.

- Eschatological Justifications for Modern Conflict: Much like the Christian Crusaders who believed they were fulfilling prophecy, modern jihadists see their struggle as part of an eschatological narrative, believing that their efforts will hasten the arrival of the Mahdi and the establishment of an

Islamic caliphate. This apocalyptic framework continues to fuel radical ideologies and violent conflicts in the region.

4. Contemporary Eschatological Movements and the Middle East

In both Christian and Islamic apocalyptic thinking, the Middle East, and particularly Jerusalem, remains the focal point of the end times. This has led to an intersection of religious ideologies, geopolitical strategies, and eschatological expectations, all centered on the modern Middle Eastern conflict.

A. Christian Apocalyptic Movements and Middle Eastern Geopolitics

For many modern Christian apocalyptic movements, the ongoing conflicts in the Middle East are seen as clear signs that the world is entering the final stage of history. Events such as the Israeli-Palestinian conflict, wars in Syria and Iraq, and the rise of terrorist organizations are viewed as direct fulfillments of biblical prophecy.

- Middle Eastern Wars as Apocalyptic Events: Christian apocalyptic thinkers frequently interpret wars and political unrest in the Middle East as part of the birth pains leading up to the Second Coming of Christ. Just as the Crusaders believed they were fighting in the final battles of history, modern eschatological movements view these conflicts as signs that the end is near.

- The Role of the United States: Many evangelical Christians in the United States see their country's support for Israel as part of the divine plan for the end times. U.S. foreign policy in the Middle East, particularly regarding the protection of Israel and Jerusalem, is often framed within an eschatological context, where American involvement is seen as part of the final stage before Christ's return.

B. The Role of Israel and Jerusalem in Modern Prophecy

For both Christian and Jewish apocalyptic movements, the state of Israel and the city of Jerusalem are central to the final fulfillment of prophecy. The restoration of the Jewish people to their ancestral homeland and the potential rebuilding of the Third Temple are seen as crucial steps in the apocalyptic timeline.

- Rebuilding the Temple: Many Christian Zionists believe that the rebuilding of the Third Temple on the Temple Mount in Jerusalem will be the trigger for the final events of the end times. The Crusader mentality, which sought to reclaim Jerusalem for Christendom, is echoed in the modern belief that Jerusalem must be fully under Jewish control for the Second Coming to occur.

- Jerusalem as the Spiritual Epicenter: Jerusalem remains the spiritual epicenter of end-times prophecy for

Christians, Jews, and Muslims. The ongoing struggle for control of the city is seen as part of a larger apocalyptic narrative, where the forces of good and evil will ultimately clash in the Holy Land, leading to the establishment of God's kingdom.

The Crusades, Modern Middle Eastern Conflict, and Apocalyptic Thinking

The Crusades have left a lasting legacy in both Christian and Islamic eschatological thought, influencing how modern believers interpret ongoing Middle Eastern conflicts. For many, the battles fought over Jerusalem and the Holy Land during the Crusades are seen as part of a larger spiritual war that continues today, with modern conflicts framed as the final struggle before the end of history.

In both Christian Zionism and Islamic apocalypticism, the Middle East, and especially Jerusalem, plays a central role in end-times prophecy. The Crusader legacy of reclaiming the Holy Land for God's kingdom echoes in contemporary eschatological movements, with believers on all sides expecting the imminent return of Christ or the arrival of the Mahdi to bring about the final battle and the establishment of a new world order.

Eschatological Texts from Christian and Islamic Traditions and Their Influence on Modern Middle Eastern Conflict

The ongoing Middle Eastern conflict, especially the tensions surrounding Jerusalem, has long been interpreted through an eschatological lens by both Christian and Islamic traditions. These interpretations are deeply rooted in key scriptural texts, which have shaped the way many believers understand current geopolitical events as part of a larger end-times narrative.

This chapter explores how specific eschatological texts from Christian and Islamic scripture have influenced modern perspectives on the Middle Eastern conflict. We will examine passages from the Bible and Quran, as well as key works of apocalyptic literature, to understand how they frame Jerusalem, Israel, and broader regional dynamics as part of the final stage of history.

1. Christian Eschatological Texts and the Middle Eastern Conflict

Christian apocalyptic thought, particularly as it relates to the Middle East, draws heavily on key texts from the Old and New Testaments. For many Christians, these scriptures prophesy the return of Jesus Christ, the battle of Armageddon, and the ultimate establishment of God's kingdom in the Holy Land. This theological framework shapes modern interpretations of events in Israel, Palestine, and the broader region as part of an unfolding end-times scenario.

A. The Book of Revelation

The Book of Revelation is the most influential eschatological text in Christian scripture. Written by John of Patmos, this final book of the New Testament provides a symbolic and visionary account of the end of the world. Several key passages from Revelation have shaped Christian interpretations of the Middle Eastern conflict, particularly regarding the final battle, the role of Jerusalem, and the return of Christ.

- Revelation 16:12-16 – The Battle of Armageddon: This passage describes the gathering of the kings of the earth at a place called Armageddon for the final battle. While Armageddon is typically associated with Megiddo in northern Israel, this prophecy is widely interpreted as signifying a climactic conflict centered on the Holy Land. For many Christians, the ongoing conflicts in the Middle East, particularly involving Jerusalem, are seen as precursors to this final battle.

- Revelation 11:1-2 – The Temple and Jerusalem: In this passage, John is instructed to measure the Temple of God, but he is told to leave out the outer court, as it has been given to the Gentiles, who will trample the holy city for 42 months. Many Christians interpret this as a prophecy of

Jerusalem being under non-Jewish control until the end times, when the Temple will be rebuilt, signaling the imminent return of Christ. The status of the Temple Mount remains a critical issue in Christian Zionism, with some seeing it as essential for fulfilling this prophecy.

B. Daniel 9:24-27 – The Seventy Weeks Prophecy

The Book of Daniel contains several key apocalyptic prophecies, but none is more influential than the Seventy Weeks prophecy found in Daniel 9:24-27. This passage is often interpreted as a timeline for the Messiah's return and the final judgment of the world.

- The Seventy Weeks: According to this prophecy, seventy weeks (understood by many as 490 years) are decreed for the people of Israel and for the holy city (Jerusalem). The prophecy speaks of the restoration of Jerusalem, the coming of an Anointed One, and a final period of desolation. Many Christian interpreters see this timeline as leading to the end times, with the final seven-year tribulation occurring after the re-establishment of Israel as a nation in 1948.

- Modern Interpretations: Many modern evangelical and premillennial dispensationalist interpretations of the Middle Eastern conflict focus on this prophecy, particularly regarding the status of Jerusalem and the possible rebuilding of the Third Temple. The Six-Day War in 1967, which resulted in Israel gaining control of East Jerusalem, is often seen as a major fulfillment of Daniel's prophecy, signaling the countdown to Christ's return.

C. Ezekiel 38-39 – The War of Gog and Magog

The War of Gog and Magog, described in Ezekiel 38-39, has become a central eschatological text for many Christian interpreters, particularly in relation to the Middle East. The prophecy describes an invasion of Israel by Gog, a leader from the land of Magog, and a coalition of nations.

- Ezekiel's Vision: In this prophecy, the armies of Gog and Magog invade the land of Israel, but they are ultimately defeated by divine intervention. Many Christian interpreters associate this war with the final battle of Armageddon and see it as part of the end-times conflict over Israel.

- Modern Middle Eastern Conflict: For some Christian theologians, modern political and military conflicts involving Israel, particularly those with nations like Iran (often identified with Persia in Ezekiel), are viewed as the beginning of the fulfillment of this prophecy. The alliance of Muslim-majority nations opposing Israel is sometimes seen as a coalition resembling Gog's army, preparing for a final showdown in the end times.

2. Islamic Eschatological Texts and the Middle Eastern Conflict

In Islam, the eschatological texts within the Quran and Hadith (sayings of the Prophet Muhammad) play a significant role in shaping how many Muslims interpret modern events, particularly in relation to Jerusalem, Palestine, and the broader Middle Eastern conflict. Islamic eschatology, much like Christian apocalypticism, sees Jerusalem as a central battleground in the final struggle between good and evil.

A. Surah Al-Isra (17:1) – The Night Journey

The Quran mentions the significance of Jerusalem in Surah Al-Isra (also known as the Night Journey), where the Prophet Muhammad is said to have traveled from Mecca to the Al-Aqsa Mosque in Jerusalem, ascending to the heavens from this site. This verse establishes Jerusalem as one of the holiest places in Islam.

- Jerusalem as a Holy City: The status of Al-Aqsa and Jerusalem is central to Islamic eschatology. Many Muslims believe that the final events of history, including the appearance of the Mahdi (the Islamic messianic figure) and the return of Isa (Jesus), will unfold in Jerusalem.

- Al-Aqsa and Modern Conflict: The conflict over the Temple Mount, known to Muslims as Haram al-Sharif, continues to be a focal point in the Israeli-Palestinian conflict. Islamic eschatological texts often reference this site as the place where the final battle will occur, and any perceived threat to Al-Aqsa is seen as a trigger for apocalyptic events.

B. Hadith on the Mahdi and Isa (Jesus)

The Hadith literature contains several eschatological sayings that describe the events leading to the end times in Islamic belief. Two key figures in these prophecies are the Mahdi and Isa (Jesus), who will both play roles in the final judgment and the defeat of the Dajjal (the Islamic Antichrist).

- The Mahdi and the Final Battle: According to Islamic eschatology, the Mahdi will emerge in the end times to restore justice and lead the Muslim community. The Mahdi's appearance is often associated with a final conflict centered on Jerusalem, where Muslim forces will clash with those of the Dajjal.

- Isa's Return: In Islamic belief, Isa (Jesus) will return to assist the Mahdi in defeating the Dajjal and bringing about God's kingdom on earth. Jerusalem is expected to be the focal point of this final battle. This belief mirrors Christian expectations of Christ's return, but with Isa acting as a prophet of Islam rather than as the Messiah in the Christian sense.

C. Islamic Eschatology and the Modern Middle Eastern Conflict

Many Muslim scholars and theologians view the modern conflict over Palestine and Jerusalem as part of the unfolding end-times scenario described in the Quran and Hadith. The continued presence of Israeli and Western military forces in the Middle East is often seen as a sign of the approaching final battle between good and evil.

- Western Influence and the Dajjal: Some Islamic interpretations view Western powers, particularly the United States and Israel, as forces aligned with the Dajjal, working to undermine the Muslim world. In this apocalyptic framework, the ongoing conflict in Palestine, the wars in Syria and Iraq, and the broader geopolitical struggles in the Middle East are seen as signs that the Mahdi will soon appear.

- Jerusalem as the Epicenter: For many Muslims, Jerusalem remains central to the eschatological narrative, with the belief that the final events of history will unfold in this city. The Al-Aqsa Mosque is seen as a critical site where the last battle will occur, and any conflict involving Jerusalem is interpreted as having cosmic significance.

3. Eschatological Texts and the Israeli-Palestinian Conflict

Both Christian and Islamic eschatological texts directly influence modern interpretations of the Israeli-Palestinian conflict, particularly in terms of the status of Jerusalem and the broader struggle for control of the Holy Land.

A. Christian Views on the Israeli-Palestinian Conflict

For many evangelical Christians, particularly those aligned with Christian Zionism, the state of Israel represents the fulfillment of biblical prophecy. The establishment of Israel in 1948, and its subsequent victories in wars against its neighbors, are seen as part of God's plan to restore the Jewish people to their ancestral homeland.

- Israel and Prophecy: Many Christians interpret the restoration of Israel as the beginning of the final stage of history, with Jerusalem's status as the capital of Israel seen as fulfilling key prophecies from Isaiah, Daniel, and Ezekiel. Any attempts to divide Jerusalem or compromise Israel's sovereignty are viewed as opposing God's will.

- The Peace Process as a Prophetic Sign: Some Christian interpreters view efforts to create a two-state solution between Israel and Palestine as part of the end-times timeline, seeing such efforts as attempts to divide God's chosen land, which, according to prophecy, will lead to divine intervention.

B. Islamic Perspectives on the Israeli-Palestinian Conflict

In Islamic eschatology, the Israeli occupation of Palestinian territories is often interpreted as a sign of the Dajjal's influence. The struggle for Jerusalem is seen as part of the final confrontation between good and evil, with the belief that the Mahdi will ultimately liberate the city and establish justice.

- Al-Aqsa and Liberation: For many Muslims, the liberation of Al-Aqsa Mosque from Israeli control is seen as a sacred duty and a prelude to the arrival of the Mahdi. Islamic eschatology teaches that Muslim forces will ultimately prevail in this battle, and Jerusalem will be restored as a center of Islamic worship and governance.

Eschatological Texts and the Shaping of Modern Conflict

The ongoing Middle Eastern conflict is deeply influenced by eschatological texts from both Christianity and Islam, with both traditions seeing the region—and particularly Jerusalem—as the focal point of end-times prophecy. These interpretations have shaped not only theology but also political views and foreign policy, especially among movements like Christian Zionism and Islamic eschatological revivalism.

The tension over Jerusalem and the Temple Mount, as well as broader regional conflicts involving Israel, Palestine, and neighboring nations, continues to be viewed as part of the cosmic battle foretold in both scripture and apocalyptic literature. As these interpretations continue to shape religious and political narratives, the Middle Eastern conflict remains entangled with deep-rooted beliefs about the end of history and the ultimate victory of God's kingdom.

CHAPTER 11

CONCLUSION

Nebuchadnezzar's dream, as recorded in Daniel 2, has been a powerful symbolic and theological tool for interpreting the course of human history and understanding its divine progression toward the end of time. The dream's depiction of a great statue composed of different metals, each representing successive world empires, offers a prophetic framework that has been applied to the rise and fall of nations, from the Babylonian Empire to the modern geopolitical landscape. For centuries, both Christian and Islamic theologians have used this vision to interpret history, particularly in light of apocalyptic prophecy and the final establishment of God's kingdom.

In this concluding chapter, we will summarize how Nebuchadnezzar's dream reflects key aspects of human history and theological progression, from ancient times to the modern era, and how it continues to shape eschatological thinking today.

1. Nebuchadnezzar's Dream as a Prophetic Timeline of Empires

At its core, Nebuchadnezzar's dream provides a prophetic timeline that traces the rise and fall of great empires, symbolized by the statue's head of gold, chest of silver, belly of bronze, legs of iron, and feet of iron and clay. The traditional interpretation of these symbols has connected them to major historical powers: Babylon, Medo-Persia, Greece, and Rome, followed by the divided kingdoms that characterize the fragmented political landscape after Rome's fall.

A. Historical Fulfillment

Each section of the statue corresponds to an empire that played a significant role in the history of Israel and the ancient world. The progression from the golden head of Babylon to the iron legs of Rome reflects not only the succession of powerful empires but also the increasing strength and brutality of human rule, culminating in the Roman Empire's unparalleled military might.

- Babylon (Head of Gold): As the first empire in the sequence, Babylon represented the height of pagan power and world dominance under Nebuchadnezzar II. This empire's fall, foretold in Isaiah and Jeremiah, symbolized the beginning of God's judgment on human kingdoms.

- Medo-Persia (Chest of Silver): The next empire, represented by silver, was Medo-Persia, known for its vast bureaucracy and strong legal systems. The empire's rise fulfilled the prophecy of Babylon's destruction and the liberation of the Jewish exiles under Cyrus the Great.

- Greece (Belly of Bronze): Greece, under Alexander the Great, spread Hellenistic culture across the known world. This expansion of Greek thought and philosophy had a lasting influence on Jewish and Christian theology, shaping the intellectual framework of the early Church.

- Rome (Legs of Iron): The Roman Empire, known for its strength and authoritarian rule, symbolized the pinnacle of human political power. Rome's influence on the early Christian Church was profound, as it not only persecuted the followers of Christ but also later adopted Christianity as the state religion under Constantine.

- Divided Kingdoms (Feet of Iron and Clay): The feet of iron mixed with clay represent the post-Roman world, characterized by the fragmentation of power and the emergence of divided kingdoms. The instability of this mixture reflects the ongoing tensions in modern history, where nations are powerful yet often fragile and divided, setting the stage for the ultimate divine intervention.

B. A Theological Progression Toward God's Kingdom

The statue's destruction by a rock not cut by human hands symbolizes the final divine judgment on all earthly kingdoms and the establishment of God's eternal kingdom. This part of the dream represents the culmination of history and the ultimate triumph of God's sovereignty over human empires.

In this vision, the progression from gold to iron and clay is not just a commentary on the political power of these empires but also a reflection of the moral decline and spiritual inadequacy of human rule. The feet of iron and clay, symbolizing the divided kingdoms of the modern world, indicate that human systems will eventually prove incapable of sustaining peace and justice. Only the Kingdom of God, symbolized by the rock, can bring about true and lasting righteousness.

2. Eschatological Implications: The Rock and the Eternal Kingdom

The final act in Nebuchadnezzar's dream—the rock that destroys the statue—has been a powerful symbol of

Christ's return and the establishment of the Kingdom of God. For many Christian eschatologists, this part of the dream reflects the Second Coming of Christ, who will overthrow the kingdoms of the world and establish an eternal kingdom that will never be destroyed.

A. Christ as the Rock

In Christian theology, the rock that smashes the statue is often interpreted as Jesus Christ, who is described in the New Testament as the cornerstone (Ephesians 2:20) and the stone that the builders rejected (Psalm 118:22). His kingdom, unlike the human empires of history, is described as one that will last forever.

- The Second Coming: The rock represents not only Christ's initial coming to establish His Church but also His Second Coming, when He will return in glory to defeat the Antichrist, judge the nations, and establish the millennial reign of peace.

B. The Destruction of Human Kingdoms

In Nebuchadnezzar's dream, the rock not cut by human hands strikes the feet of iron and clay, causing the entire statue to collapse and disintegrate. This dramatic image symbolizes the total destruction of all human governments and kingdoms that have risen and fallen throughout history. It signifies that the earthly powers, no matter how strong they appear, will ultimately be swept away by the arrival of God's kingdom.

- Human Empires as Temporary: The dream's progression, from the grandeur of Babylon's golden head to the fragmented feet of iron and clay, illustrates the ephemeral nature of human power. Each empire, though mighty in its time, eventually crumbles, suggesting that no human system or government is eternal. The rock's destruction of the statue emphasizes that God alone holds the ultimate authority over history.

- Judgment and Renewal: In Christian eschatology, this destruction is often associated with the final judgment at the end of time, when all human systems of power, corruption, and injustice will be judged and replaced by God's righteous kingdom. The Book of Revelation speaks of the final battle at Armageddon, where the forces of evil will be defeated, similar to how the rock obliterates the statue. In this sense, the destruction is both a judgment on human sinfulness and the beginning of a new creation, free from the flaws of human rule.

C. The Eternal Kingdom of God

The second half of the vision, in which the rock grows to become a mountain that fills the whole earth, represents the establishment of God's eternal kingdom, which will replace all human kingdoms. This kingdom is described as unshakable, everlasting, and ruled by justice and righteousness. In Christian thought, this is often seen as the Millennial Kingdom, followed by the creation of a new heaven and a new earth as described in Revelation 21.

- Christ's Reign: The Kingdom of God, symbolized by the rock that becomes a mountain, is often understood as the reign of Christ following His Second Coming. During this period, Christ will rule over the earth, bringing about a time of peace, harmony, and divine justice, which is in stark contrast to the divided and corrupt kingdoms of human history. This kingdom is described as a place where suffering and death will be no more, and where God's will is fully realized on earth as it is in heaven.

- New Creation: The imagery of the rock expanding into a mountain that fills the whole earth echoes the biblical vision of a new creation, where God's kingdom encompasses all things. As prophesied in the Book of Isaiah and Revelation, this new world is one where God will dwell with humanity, bringing an end to sin, suffering, and the curse of death. This final, eternal state is the fulfillment of the apocalyptic hope expressed in Nebuchadnezzar's dream and throughout Scripture.

3. Theological Progression and Influence on Eschatological Thought

Nebuchadnezzar's dream has profoundly shaped theological thought concerning the end of history and divine sovereignty. Both Christian and Jewish interpretations of the dream highlight its prophetic message regarding the futility of human rule and the certainty of God's ultimate plan.

A. Shaping Christian Eschatology

From the early Church Fathers to modern-day Christian eschatologists, Nebuchadnezzar's dream has played a pivotal role in shaping Christian views of apocalyptic prophecy. This vision aligns with the New Testament emphasis on Christ as the Messiah who will overthrow the corrupt kingdoms of the world and establish His eternal reign.

- Premillennial Dispensationalism: In particular, movements like premillennial dispensationalism have drawn heavily on the symbolism of Nebuchadnezzar's dream to understand current global events and predict the timeline of Christ's return. According to this view, we are living in the final stage of history, represented by the feet of iron and clay, and the imminent return of Christ, symbolized by the rock, will soon bring an end to the present world order.

- Christian Zionism: The dream has also influenced Christian Zionism, which sees the modern state of Israel as part of the prophetic timeline. The establishment of Israel and the restoration of Jerusalem are viewed as steps toward the Second Coming of Christ, echoing the expectation that God's kingdom will replace the divided and fragile kingdoms of the world.

B. Jewish Interpretations

For Jewish scholars, Nebuchadnezzar's dream is often seen as a prophecy about the Messianic Age, when the Messiah will come to restore Israel and establish a world of peace under God's direct rule. The emphasis on the eternal kingdom resonates with the Jewish expectation of a future where Israel is fully restored and the nations of the world acknowledge the one true God.

- Messianic Expectation: Jewish interpretations often focus on the messianic implications of the dream, seeing the rock as a symbol of the Messiah's kingdom, which will bring an end to foreign oppression and establish justice for Israel and all nations. This expectation is central to the apocalyptic hope within Jewish thought, where the kingdom of God is envisioned as the ultimate fulfillment of God's covenant with His people.

4. The Dream's Ongoing Relevance in Modern Eschatological Movements

Nebuchadnezzar's dream continues to influence modern apocalyptic movements and interpretations of current events. The themes of rising and falling empires, the instability of modern powers, and the imminent establishment of God's kingdom resonate with believers who see the present time as the final stage before the fulfillment of prophecy.

A. Middle Eastern Conflict and the Prophetic Timeline

The ongoing Middle Eastern conflicts, particularly involving Israel and Jerusalem, are often viewed through the lens of Nebuchadnezzar's dream. Many Christians and Jews see the modern State of Israel as part of the end-times scenario, with the restoration of Israel fulfilling ancient prophecies and preparing the way for the arrival of the Messianic kingdom.

- The Role of Jerusalem: Jerusalem, as the focal point of both Jewish and Christian eschatology, is often seen as the epicenter of the final cosmic conflict that will lead to the establishment of God's kingdom. The status of Jerusalem— its political, religious, and symbolic significance—remains critical to how many interpret current global tensions and their connection to biblical prophecy.

B. Political Instability and Economic Crises as Signs of the End

The fragility of modern governments, symbolized by the feet of iron and clay, is often cited in apocalyptic thought as evidence that the world is nearing the end of the age. Economic crises, political unrest, and the rise of authoritarian regimes are interpreted as signs that the current world order is collapsing, making way for the return of Christ and the final establishment of the Kingdom of God.

- Global Instability: In modern Christian eschatology, global instability—whether through financial collapse, environmental disaster, or geopolitical conflicts—serves as a reminder of the inherent weakness of human institutions and the necessity of divine intervention to bring about lasting peace and justice.

Nebuchadnezzar's Dream and the End of History

Nebuchadnezzar's dream offers a profound prophetic vision of the rise and fall of human empires, culminating in the establishment of God's eternal kingdom. It serves as a theological map of history, illustrating the temporary nature of human power and the sovereign rule of God over all creation. The symbolism of the statue and the rock has resonated throughout the ages, influencing Christian, Jewish, and even Islamic eschatology.

From the fall of Babylon to the modern-day conflicts in the Middle East, the dream provides a lens through which believers understand the progression of history and the ultimate fulfillment of God's plan. As modern political and social systems show increasing signs of instability, many believers look to Nebuchadnezzar's dream as evidence that the world is moving toward the end of history, when the

Kingdom of God will be fully realized, and human empires will give way to divine rule.

The Role of Prophecy in Shaping Perceptions of Past, Present, and Future World Events

Throughout history, prophecy has played a profound role in shaping how individuals, communities, and even entire civilizations interpret the past, make sense of the present, and anticipate the future. Prophetic visions, particularly in religious traditions, have provided a framework for understanding world events, offering explanations for the rise and fall of empires, the unfolding of human history, and the ultimate destiny of the world.

Prophecy has often functioned as both a guide and a lens, influencing everything from political decisions and military campaigns to personal beliefs about salvation and the end of time. In this chapter, we explore how prophetic texts—whether in biblical, Quranic, or other sacred traditions—have shaped perceptions of historical events, influenced contemporary worldviews, and continue to affect expectations for the future.

1. Prophecy and the Interpretation of Past Events

In many religious traditions, prophecy is not only a foretelling of future events but also a retrospective lens for understanding the past. Events that have already occurred, especially significant historical milestones like the rise of empires or natural disasters, are often interpreted as the fulfillment of earlier prophecies, reinforcing the validity of sacred texts and the divine plan in human history.

A. The Bible and the Rise and Fall of Empires

In Judeo-Christian thought, particularly within the Bible, prophecy is central to interpreting historical events. The prophets of the Old Testament, such as Isaiah, Jeremiah, and Daniel, frequently warned of the destruction of kingdoms and empires as a result of disobedience to God. These prophecies were later connected to major events, like the fall of Jerusalem in 586 BCE or the destruction of the Babylonian Empire.

- The Destruction of Jerusalem: The Babylonian exile is a key event that Jewish and Christian theologians often see as the fulfillment of prophetic warnings. Prophets like Jeremiah foretold the destruction of Jerusalem as a consequence of the people's unfaithfulness. When this event occurred, it was understood as proof of God's hand guiding history, offering a way for future generations to learn from the past.

- Empires in Daniel's Prophecies: The visions of Daniel, especially Nebuchadnezzar's dream of the statue in Daniel 2, have been used to interpret the successive empires of Babylon, Medo-Persia, Greece, and Rome. The fall of these empires has been viewed as the inevitable fulfillment of God's plan, reinforcing the idea that divine prophecy governs the fate of nations and empires.

B. Islamic Views on the Fall of Ancient Empires

In Islamic eschatology, prophecy is also used to retrospectively interpret the fall of great empires and the rise of Islamic civilization. The Quran and Hadith (sayings of the Prophet Muhammad) provide insights into how Muslims have understood the rise and fall of ancient empires as part of God's unfolding plan.

- The Fall of Persia and Rome: The Quran foretells the defeat of the Persians by the Romans in Surah Ar-Rum (Chapter 30), and this prophecy was fulfilled within a few years after it was revealed. For Muslims, this event confirmed the truth of revelation, showing that God controls the destinies of nations. The later collapse of both the Roman and Persian empires was viewed through the lens of prophecy, emphasizing that no power on earth can stand against divine will.

2. Prophecy and the Shaping of Present Worldviews

Prophecy also plays a critical role in shaping how people understand current events. Whether it is through the lens of apocalyptic prophecy in Christianity, messianic expectations in Judaism, or Mahdist beliefs in Islam, prophetic interpretations provide a framework for understanding the chaos, conflicts, and political developments of the present world.

A. Christian Prophecy and Contemporary Geopolitics

For many Christians, particularly those influenced by premillennial dispensationalism and Christian Zionism, current geopolitical events—especially in the Middle East—are seen as fulfillments of biblical prophecy. This worldview profoundly affects perceptions of international relations, wars, and diplomatic efforts.

- Israel and Christian Zionism: For Christian Zionists, the establishment of the State of Israel in 1948 is interpreted as the fulfillment of prophecies regarding the return of the Jewish people to their homeland. Many see the ongoing conflict over Jerusalem and the status of the Temple Mount as signs that the world is moving closer to the Second Coming of Christ. Prophetic passages from the Books of Ezekiel, Daniel, and Revelation are frequently cited to explain present tensions in the region.

- Wars and Natural Disasters: For some evangelical Christians, wars, natural disasters, and global political instability are viewed as signs of the end times. Events such as the Iraq War, the rise of terrorism, and global economic crises are often seen as precursors to the Battle of

Armageddon and the eventual establishment of God's kingdom.

B. Islamic Prophecy and Modern Conflict

In the Muslim world, eschatological prophecies, especially those relating to the Mahdi and the return of Isa (Jesus), shape perceptions of modern political and social upheavals. Events in the Middle East, particularly the Israeli-Palestinian conflict, are often viewed through the lens of Islamic prophecy, with many believing that these events are leading toward the fulfillment of the final battle between good and evil.

- The Mahdi and Modern Movements: In Shia Islam, the belief in the coming of the Mahdi—the prophesied redeemer who will appear before the Day of Judgment—remains central to interpretations of current events. Conflicts involving Western powers, particularly in countries like Iraq, Syria, and Iran, are seen as part of a larger eschatological narrative in which the Mahdi will emerge to restore justice and lead the Muslim community to victory over its enemies.

- Western Powers as Dajjal: Some Islamic scholars and movements view Western influence in the Middle East as part of the apocalyptic prophecy concerning Dajjal—the false messianic figure in Islamic eschatology. This view frames Western military interventions, especially in predominantly

Muslim countries, as part of the final conflict before the Mahdi's arrival.

C. Jewish Messianism and Contemporary Expectations

In Judaism, the expectation of the Messiah remains a central component of religious thought, particularly regarding the future of Israel. Many Jewish religious communities, especially in Israel, see the current political and social landscape as preparation for the eventual coming of the Messiah and the restoration of a divinely guided kingdom.

- Messianic Hopes and the Third Temple: Some Jewish religious movements advocate for the rebuilding of the Third Temple on the Temple Mount, which they believe is a necessary precursor to the Messiah's arrival. The political and religious tensions surrounding the Temple Mount, particularly its current status as a Muslim holy site, are often interpreted as part of the messianic process.

3. Prophecy and Future Expectations: Shaping the End of History

Perhaps the most significant role of prophecy is in shaping expectations for the future. Eschatological texts from different religious traditions provide a roadmap for how the world will unfold in its final stages, influencing everything from personal spiritual preparation to global political actions.

The belief in an ultimate destiny, as foretold in sacred texts, drives much of the world's eschatological thinking.

A. Christian Eschatology and the Second Coming

For many Christians, the future is seen through the lens of apocalyptic prophecy, particularly the expectation of the Second Coming of Christ. This expectation shapes how individuals and communities prepare for the end times and influences their perceptions of future world events.

- The Rapture and the Tribulation: Many Christians believe in a pre-tribulation rapture, where the faithful will be taken to heaven before a period of great tribulation on earth, culminating in the Battle of Armageddon. The return of Christ to establish His millennial kingdom is the ultimate fulfillment of Christian prophecy, and many believe that global conflicts and disasters are signs that this event is drawing near.

- New Heaven and New Earth: The final chapters of Revelation describe the creation of a new heaven and a new earth, where God will dwell with humanity in peace and justice. This prophetic vision provides hope for the future, promising an end to suffering, war, and death—and shaping how Christians understand the ultimate resolution of history.

B. Islamic Eschatology and the Final Battle

In Islam, the future is also seen through an apocalyptic lens, with the expectation of the Mahdi's return and the final battle against Dajjal shaping

Muslim eschatological thought. The events leading up to the Day of Judgment are believed to involve widespread conflict, but also the restoration of Islamic justice.

- The Mahdi and Isa: The return of Isa (Jesus) to assist the Mahdi in defeating Dajjal is a central aspect of Islamic prophecy. For many Muslims, the conflicts and turmoil in the modern world are seen as precursors to these eschatological events, and the belief in the ultimate victory of Islam provides a framework for interpreting future challenges and political developments.

- Final Judgment: Islamic eschatology also emphasizes the Day of Judgment, when all souls will be judged for their deeds. The righteous will be rewarded, and the wicked will face punishment, with the ultimate goal being eternal life in Paradise.

The Enduring Power of Prophecy

The role of prophecy in shaping perceptions of the past, present, and future is a testament to the enduring power of sacred texts to influence human thought and behavior. Whether providing explanations for historical events, guiding interpretations of current geopolitical conflicts, or shaping expectations for the end of history, prophecy remains a key element in how religious communities understand the divine plan for the world.

As believers continue to look to prophetic texts for guidance, the interpretation of prophecy will undoubtedly shape global affairs, influencing both personal spirituality and international politics. Whether through the lens of Christian, Islamic, or Jewish eschatology, the expectation of a divinely orchestrated future offers a framework for understanding the complexities of human history and the ultimate fulfillment of God's purposes in the world.

The Relevance of Prophetic Symbols Today in Understanding Both Historical and Future Events

Prophetic symbols, especially those drawn from religious traditions like Christianity, Islam, and Judaism, continue to hold great significance in how many people understand both the course of history and the unfolding of future events. These symbols are powerful, providing layers of meaning that go beyond literal interpretation and connect believers to a divine narrative that stretches across time. By linking past and future, prophetic symbols give believers a framework for interpreting historical events as part of a larger cosmic design, while also shaping their expectations for what is yet to come.

The statue in Nebuchadnezzar's dream, with its sequence of metals symbolizing the rise and fall of empires, remains one of the most compelling prophetic symbols in understanding the trajectory of human history. Similarly, symbols from the Book of Revelation, such as the four horsemen, the Beast, or the New Jerusalem, have been used throughout Christian history to interpret political upheavals, wars, and changes in global power dynamics.

In this section, we will explore how these prophetic symbols remain relevant today, offering insight into both historical events and contemporary developments in world affairs. We will also consider how these symbols shape people's understanding of the future, particularly in the context of global instability, political changes, and ongoing religious tensions.

1. Prophetic Symbols and Their Role in Understanding Historical Events

One of the primary ways prophetic symbols continue to influence modern thinking is through their application to historical events. Many religious communities interpret significant world events, particularly those involving war, the rise and fall of nations, and natural disasters, as the fulfillment of long-standing biblical or Quranic prophecies. This retrospective interpretation gives meaning to the past and provides reassurance that the course of history is part of a divine plan.

A. The Statue of Nebuchadnezzar: A Symbol of Historical Empires

Nebuchadnezzar's dream, as recorded in Daniel 2, provides a perfect example of how prophetic symbols have been used to make sense of historical empires. The progression from the head of gold (Babylon) to the feet of iron and clay (divided kingdoms) has been applied to the rise and fall of Babylon, Persia, Greece, Rome, and beyond. This sequence is not just a historical recounting but also a prophetic warning about the temporary nature of human empires.

- Application to Modern Empires: The symbolic statue has continued to be relevant, with modern interpreters applying its meanings to the fall of more recent powers, such as the Ottoman Empire, the British Empire, and the Soviet Union. The division and fragility symbolized by the feet of iron and clay resonate with today's geopolitical landscape, where nations may appear strong yet are riddled with internal divisions and contradictions, much like the clay mixed with iron.

- The Cyclical Nature of History: For many, the statue in Nebuchadnezzar's dream underscores the cyclical nature of history—the inevitable rise and fall of great powers—and the ultimate futility of relying on human governance for lasting peace. This symbol continues to speak to modern observers of history, offering both a diagnosis of human ambition and a reminder that true sovereignty belongs to God.

B. The Four Horsemen of the Apocalypse: Interpreting War and Conflict

Another powerful prophetic symbol comes from Revelation 6, where the four horsemen of the apocalypse—representing conquest, war, famine, and death—have been used throughout history to interpret periods of extreme conflict and suffering. These symbols have resurfaced in times of war, plague, and famine, offering a way to understand the devastation seen in human history.

- Modern War and Global Conflict: The imagery of the four horsemen has been applied to both world wars, the Cold War, and even contemporary conflicts in the Middle East, particularly with the rise of terrorism and the war on terror. Each horseman represents a different aspect of the human condition during times of crisis: conquest through imperialism, war through global conflicts, famine through economic collapse and environmental destruction, and death through widespread violence and disease. These symbols help believers contextualize modern warfare as part of a broader cosmic struggle between good and evil.

- Ongoing Relevance: In the 21st century, the four horsemen continue to be used as symbols of global instability, as seen in the Syria conflict, the Yemen war, and fears over nuclear escalation. The rise of pandemics, climate change, and economic inequality further enhances their relevance, making these ancient symbols an important lens through which many interpret the chaotic nature of the modern world.

2. Prophetic Symbols and Their Role in Understanding Future Events

The enduring power of prophetic symbols is perhaps most evident in how they shape expectations for the future. Many believers turn to symbols from the Bible, Quran, and other sacred texts to help anticipate the end times, the return of the Messiah or Mahdi, and the eventual establishment of God's kingdom on earth. These symbols often guide not just religious belief but also influence political behavior, social movements, and global policy.

A. The Rock in Nebuchadnezzar's Dream: A Symbol of Divine Intervention

One of the central symbols in Nebuchadnezzar's dream is the rock not cut by human hands, which strikes the statue and destroys all the human kingdoms, ultimately becoming a mountain that fills the earth. This rock represents the Kingdom of God, which will be established in the end times and replace all earthly powers.

- Messianic Expectations: For Christians, the rock symbolizes the return of Jesus Christ, who will overthrow the corrupted human systems and establish a kingdom of peace and justice. This interpretation has shaped Christian expectations for future world events, especially in relation to the Middle East, where conflicts over Jerusalem and the Temple Mount are seen as signs that the end times are drawing near.

- Political Implications: The symbol of the rock also influences political theology. Many Christian Zionists view the establishment of Israel and the ongoing conflict over its territory as key signs of the approaching fulfillment of this prophecy. The belief that Christ's kingdom will emerge from the destruction of current global systems motivates political engagement, particularly regarding support for Israel and opposition to global governance that might interfere with God's plan.

B. The Beast and the Mark in Revelation: Fears of Global Control

The Beast and the Mark of the Beast described in Revelation 13 have long been used to symbolize future oppressive governments and totalitarian regimes that seek to control the world's population, often seen as a warning about global control and the rise of evil in the end times.

- Modern Technology and Surveillance: In modern interpretations, the Mark of the Beast has been associated with fears surrounding technological advancements, including concerns over surveillance, microchipping, and global digital currencies. These fears are often heightened by anxieties about globalization and the potential for a one-world government that imposes restrictions on religious freedom and personal autonomy.

- Economic and Political Oppression: The Beast is also seen as a symbol of future oppressive political systems, and some interpret it as a metaphor for modern authoritarian regimes. Fears of economic and political oppression through systems of global control, often discussed in the context of multinational corporations and international organizations like the United Nations, are framed within this eschatological imagery.

C. The New Jerusalem: The Future of Hope

In contrast to the fearsome symbols of war, oppression, and destruction, the prophetic image of the New Jerusalem in Revelation 21 offers a hopeful vision of the future—a time when the world will be restored to peace and divine rule.

- A Vision of Restoration: For many Christians, the New Jerusalem is a symbol of the perfected world that will be established after the final judgment, where God's people will live in a renewed creation, free from suffering, death, and sin. This symbol provides a future hope that shapes Christian engagement in the world, offering believers comfort and encouragement to endure present trials in anticipation of the coming kingdom.

- Social and Ethical Implications: The vision of the New Jerusalem also has social implications, with some Christian movements using it as a call to work toward justice, environmental care, and peacebuilding in the present. The belief that God's kingdom will ultimately triumph encourages believers to participate in acts of mercy and righteousness, seeing their efforts as aligned with God's future plan.

3. Prophetic Symbols in a Contemporary Global Context

In today's global context, prophetic symbols continue to resonate, providing meaning and structure to how many people view geopolitical events, environmental crises, and technological advancements. Whether through fears of global government, hopes for a coming Messiah, or warnings about the end of human empires, prophetic symbols shape the narratives through which many interpret both the present and the future.

A. Global Instability and Apocalyptic Expectations

In times of political instability, economic crises, and environmental degradation, many believers look to prophetic symbols to make sense of what is happening. Events like the global pandemic, climate change, and rising international tensions are seen by some as signs of the end times, leading to an increase in apocalyptic expectations across various religious traditions.

- COVID-19 and Apocalyptic Thought: The COVID-19 pandemic prompted a resurgence in apocalyptic interpretations, with some seeing it as a sign of the plagues foretold in Revelation or as a precursor to the final tribulation period. The widespread disruption of daily life, along with the global economic downturn, has contributed to a sense of urgency in some eschatological circles.

B. Religious Tensions in the Middle East

The Middle East remains central to Christian, Jewish, and Islamic eschatology, with prophetic symbols from each tradition shaping how many perceive the ongoing conflicts over Jerusalem, Israel, and the Temple Mount. These tensions are often interpreted as part of the larger apocalyptic drama that will lead to the final fulfillment of prophecy.

- Jerusalem as a Prophetic Fulcrum: For Christians, the rebuilding of the Third Temple in Jerusalem is seen as a key event that must occur before the return of Christ. For Muslims, the Al-Aqsa Mosque on the Temple Mount holds deep eschatological significance, with many believing that the final battles of history will center around this holy site.

Prophetic Symbols as Timeless Guides

Prophetic symbols, like those found in Nebuchadnezzar's dream or the Book of Revelation, continue to shape perceptions of history and future events in profound ways. For many, these symbols are not just ancient relics but timeless guides that provide insight into the nature of human existence, the course of empires, and the ultimate destiny of the world.

As people face global uncertainties, these symbols offer both warnings and hope, reminding believers that the kingdoms of this world are temporary, while God's kingdom is eternal. Whether through interpreting past empires, understanding present conflicts, or anticipating the future, prophetic symbols remain powerful tools for making sense of history and the unfolding of God's plan.

The Role of Prophetic Symbols in Guiding Religious Practice and Activism Today

Prophetic symbols from sacred texts hold deep significance for many religious communities, not only as guides to understanding the past and future but also as catalysts for religious practice and activism in the present. These symbols, found in key passages of the Bible, Quran, and other religious texts, shape how believers engage with the world, offering a sense of divine purpose that influences everything from political movements and social justice initiatives to personal spiritual devotion.

In today's global context, prophetic symbols are particularly influential in shaping eschatological movements, political activism, and religious practices aimed at preparing for or hastening the fulfillment of prophecy. This chapter will explore how these symbols inspire modern religious communities to engage with contemporary issues, focusing on key movements such as Christian Zionism, Islamic eschatological movements, and broader social justice efforts rooted in apocalyptic or messianic expectations.

1. Prophetic Symbols and Christian Religious Practice

In Christianity, prophetic symbols drawn from Revelation, Daniel, and other eschatological texts deeply influence how certain movements engage with both religious practice and global issues. Whether through Christian Zionism, premillennial dispensationalism, or broader movements concerned with social justice, these symbols provide a framework for activism that is often linked to the anticipation of Christ's return and the establishment of God's kingdom on earth.

A. Christian Zionism and the Restoration of Israel

One of the most influential modern movements driven by prophetic symbols is Christian Zionism. Christian Zionists, particularly within evangelical Christianity, see the re-establishment of Israel in 1948 and its ongoing political conflicts as the fulfillment of biblical prophecies, particularly those found in Ezekiel, Isaiah, and Daniel. Central to this belief is the role of Jerusalem and the Temple Mount in the end times.

- Prophetic Focus on Israel: The return of the Jewish people to their homeland is seen by Christian Zionists as a critical part of God's plan for the end times, where Israel plays a central role in the unfolding of prophecy. Symbols such as the fig tree in Matthew 24:32-34, often interpreted as representing the modern state of Israel, are used to justify both political support for Israel and spiritual efforts to prepare for the Second Coming of Christ.

- Activism and Political Support: Prophetic symbols motivate Christian Zionists to engage in political activism aimed at supporting Israel. This often involves lobbying for pro-Israel policies in countries like the United States, advocating for Israel's security and sovereignty over Jerusalem, and opposing any political moves that might divide the city or compromise Jewish control over the Temple Mount. These efforts are viewed not just as political acts but as fulfilling a divine mandate to support the unfolding of biblical prophecy.

- Religious Pilgrimage and Practice: Beyond political activism, Christian Zionists often engage in pilgrimages to Israel, particularly to sites in Jerusalem associated with the end times. These pilgrimages serve as acts of devotion, reinforcing the belief that Christians are witnessing the fulfillment of prophecy and preparing for the Second Coming. Many Christian Zionist churches also incorporate prayer for Israel into their regular worship, often citing prophetic passages related to the restoration of Zion.

B. Premillennial Dispensationalism and Preparation for the Rapture

Premillennial dispensationalism, another influential movement within evangelical Christianity, places great emphasis on prophetic symbols from the Book of Revelation, Daniel, and Thessalonians as guides to understanding current events and preparing for the future. Central to this movement is the belief in the rapture, the tribulation, and the millennial reign of Christ.

- Rapture Preparation: For dispensationalists, prophetic symbols such as the seven seals and the four horsemen from Revelation are seen as precursors to the Great Tribulation, during which Christ will return to rapture His followers. This belief shapes a range of religious practices aimed at spiritual preparedness, including Bible study, prayer, and a focus on evangelism, all intended to ensure that believers are ready for the imminent return of Christ.

- Apocalyptic Activism: In addition to personal spiritual preparation, many within this movement engage in apocalyptic activism, which includes supporting Israel politically (similar to Christian Zionists) and advocating for moral reforms in society. Prophetic symbols of the Beast and the Antichrist often shape their opposition to perceived threats to Christian values, such as secularism, globalization, and modern technology (which is sometimes linked to the Mark of the Beast).

- Moral and Social Justice Efforts: While some premillennial groups focus on spiritual readiness, others emphasize the importance of moral purity and social justice as preparations for Christ's return. Movements focused on pro-life advocacy, opposition to same-sex marriage, and religious freedom are often framed within an apocalyptic context, with believers seeing their activism as part of a broader effort to combat the forces of evil in the end times.

2. Islamic Eschatology and Activism: The Mahdi and the Final Battle

In Islam, prophetic symbols from the Quran and Hadith related to the end times play a significant role in shaping both religious practice and political activism. These symbols, particularly those concerning the Mahdi and the return of Isa (Jesus), guide how many Muslims interpret current global events and inspire activism aimed at preparing for or hastening the fulfillment of Islamic eschatology.

A. The Mahdi and Islamic Messianic Movements

The belief in the coming of the Mahdi—the prophesied redeemer who will establish justice on earth before the Day of Judgment—is central to Shia Islam but also holds significance in Sunni traditions. Prophetic symbols surrounding the Mahdi's arrival influence not only personal piety but also broader political movements that seek to create conditions for the Mahdi's emergence.

- Messianic Activism: In Shia Islam, particularly in Iran, the government and religious authorities often frame political actions within the context of preparing for the Mahdi's return. This includes social justice initiatives, resistance against Western powers, and the promotion of Islamic governance as steps toward the end times. Symbols such as the black banners prophesied in the Hadith, which are said to appear from the east in connection with the Mahdi's army, inspire both religious devotion and political militancy.

- Religious Practices Focused on Eschatology: In anticipation of the Mahdi, many Shia communities engage in specific religious practices, including prayers and commemorations of Imam Hussein's martyrdom (which is seen as a precursor to the final cosmic battle between good and evil). These practices not only deepen spiritual commitment but also serve to align believers with the righteous cause that the Mahdi will champion.

B. The Dajjal and Global Conflict in Sunni Eschatology

In Sunni eschatology, the figure of Dajjal, the Islamic equivalent of the Antichrist, plays a central role in shaping how Muslims understand current global conflicts, particularly those involving Western nations and Israel. The prophetic symbols associated with Dajjal's rise and the final battle guide both spiritual practices and political responses to modern global events.

- Prophetic Symbols and Modern Politics: Many Sunni movements interpret modern conflicts in the Middle East—such as the wars in Syria, Iraq, and the ongoing Israeli-Palestinian conflict—as part of the final battle between good and evil foretold in Islamic prophecy. Some groups see the actions of Western governments and Israel as aligned with the Dajjal's forces, motivating both militant resistance and religious devotion aimed at preparing for the arrival of Isa (Jesus) and the Mahdi.

- Eschatological Activism: Activism in response to these prophecies includes a wide range of efforts, from humanitarian aid and social justice work to more militant actions aimed at defending Muslim lands from perceived aggression. Religious symbols of the final battle and the establishment of God's justice are invoked in sermons, political speeches, and grassroots movements, motivating believers to act in alignment with prophetic expectations.

3. Social Justice Movements Rooted in Prophetic Symbols

In addition to overtly eschatological movements, many social justice initiatives within religious communities are inspired by prophetic symbols of justice, mercy, and the coming kingdom of God. These movements see their work as part of the larger divine narrative of restoring justice and righteousness on earth, aligning with the prophetic visions of a future where God reigns supreme.

A. Prophetic Justice in Christian Activism

Many Christian social justice movements, particularly within progressive Christianity, draw on prophetic symbols of the New Jerusalem and the Kingdom of God to guide their efforts to combat injustice, promote peace, and care for the environment.

- Environmental Activism: The biblical vision of the new heaven and new earth in Revelation 21 inspires many

Christian activists to engage in environmental conservation and climate justice efforts. This work is often framed within a theological vision of stewardship over God's creation, with activists seeing themselves as participating in the restoration of the earth in preparation for the coming kingdom of God.

- Social Justice and Racial Equality: Prophetic symbols of justice, such as those found in the Book of Amos—"Let justice roll down like waters, and righteousness like an ever-flowing stream" (Amos 5:24)—are used to motivate Christian involvement in racial equality, poverty alleviation, and prison reform movements. These initiatives are often seen as anticipatory acts of God's justice, reflecting the belief that the kingdom of God will be a place of perfect justice and equality.

B. Islamic Social Justice Inspired by Prophecy

In Islam, prophetic symbols related to the Day of Judgment and the establishment of divine justice also motivate social justice efforts. The Quran's emphasis on justice, charity, and care for the poor is often interpreted in light of the final judgment, where individuals will be judged on how they treated the vulnerable and oppressed.

- Charitable Giving (Zakat): The concept of zakat (charitable giving) in Islam is deeply tied to the belief that acts of mercy and justice will be rewarded on the Day of Judgment. Many Islamic social justice organizations focus on providing humanitarian aid, particularly in regions affected by war and poverty, seeing their work as fulfilling the prophetic mandate to establish justice on earth.

Prophetic Symbols as Catalysts for Activism

Prophetic symbols continue to inspire and guide religious practice and activism in the modern world. For Christians, Muslims, and Jews, these symbols are not just abstract theological concepts but serve as blueprints for how believers should engage with the world, both in terms of personal piety and broader efforts to shape political and social landscapes in alignment with divine prophecy.

From Christian Zionists lobbying for Israel to Islamic movements advocating for justice in preparation for the Mahdi's return, prophetic symbols motivate believers to act in ways that they believe will hasten the fulfillment of prophecy and align their lives with the will of God. In a time of global uncertainty, these symbols offer both comfort and a sense of purpose, driving engagement in everything from political activism to social justice work, all aimed at preparing for a future divinely foretold in sacred texts.

NEBUCHANEZZAR'S DREAM: PROPHECY, EMPIRES, AND THE END OF HISTORY

Appendix A: The Full Text of Nebuchadnezzar's Dream (Daniel 2:31-45)

Daniel 2:31-45 (NIV) – Nebuchadnezzar's Dream and Its Interpretation:

31 "Your Majesty looked, and there before you stood a large statue—an enormous, dazzling statue, awesome in appearance.

32 The head of the statue was made of pure gold, its chest and arms of silver, its belly and thighs of bronze,

33 its legs of iron, its feet partly of iron and partly of baked clay.

34 While you were watching, a rock was cut out, but not by human hands. It struck the statue on its feet of iron and clay and smashed them.

35 Then the iron, the clay, the bronze, the silver and the gold were all broken to pieces and became like chaff on a threshing floor in the summer. The wind swept them away without leaving a trace. But the rock that struck the statue became a huge mountain and filled the whole earth.

36 "This was the dream, and now we will interpret it to the king.

37 Your Majesty, you are the king of kings. The God of heaven has given you dominion and power and might and glory;

38 in your hands, he has placed all mankind and the beasts of the field and the birds in the sky. Wherever they live, he has made you ruler over them all. You are that head of gold.

39 "After you, another kingdom will arise, inferior to yours. Next, a third kingdom, one of bronze, will rule over the whole earth.

40 Finally, there will be a fourth kingdom, strong as iron—for iron breaks and smashes everything—and as iron breaks things to pieces, so it will crush and break all the others.

41 Just as you saw that the feet and toes were partly of baked clay and partly of iron, so this will be a divided kingdom; yet it will have some of the strength of iron in it, even as you saw iron mixed with clay.

42 As the toes were partly iron and partly clay, so this kingdom will be partly strong and partly brittle.

43 And just as you saw the iron mixed with baked clay, so the people will be a mixture and will not remain united, any more than iron mixes with clay.

44 "In the time of those kings, the God of heaven will set up a kingdom that will never be destroyed, nor will it be left to another people. It will crush all those kingdoms and bring them to an end, but it will itself endure forever.

45 This is the meaning of the vision of the rock cut out of a mountain, but not by human hands—a rock that broke the iron, the bronze, the clay, the silver, and the gold to pieces.

"The great God has shown the king what will take place in the future. The dream is true, and its interpretation is trustworthy."

Appendix B: Prophetic Symbols and Their Interpretations

Symbol	Prophetic Meaning	Historical/Modern Interpretation
Head of Gold	Represents the **Babylonian Empire**, led by King Nebuchadnezzar.	Historically tied to Babylon (605–539 BCE). Seen as the **height of power**, symbolizing the splendor of human kingdoms, later destroyed by Persia.
Chest and Arms of Silver	Represents the **Medo-Persian Empire**, which followed Babylon.	Identified with **Cyrus the Great** (539–331 BCE). A less wealthy but larger and more enduring kingdom, known for its legal and administrative systems.
Belly and Thighs of Bronze	Represents the **Greek Empire**, specifically under Alexander the Great.	Associated with the **Hellenistic period** (331–146 BCE). The spread of **Hellenistic culture** influenced the world but later fell to Rome.
Legs of Iron	Represents the **Roman Empire**, known for its strength, military power, and dominance.	Rome (27 BCE–476 CE) was the longest-lasting of the empires, known for its legal and political influence, symbolized by its **iron strength**.
Feet of Iron and Clay	Represents a **divided kingdom**, strong in some	Often interpreted as the **post-Roman world**, or modern global powers,

	parts but weak in others, unstable and brittle.	symbolizing the fractured nature of nations and alliances today.
Rock Cut Without Hands	Represents the **Kingdom of God**, which will destroy all earthly kingdoms and establish a lasting, eternal kingdom.	Interpreted as the **Messianic reign of Christ** or the **divine kingdom** in both Christian and Jewish thought, symbolizing the end of history.

Appendix C: Timeline of Empires in Nebuchadnezzar's Dream

Empire	Dates	Prophetic Symbol	Significance
Babylonian Empire	605 BCE – 539 BCE	Head of Gold	King Nebuchadnezzar's own empire, the height of Babylon's influence, known for luxury and power but destined to be overthrown by a stronger kingdom.
Medo-Persian Empire	539 BCE – 331 BCE	Chest and Arms of Silver	Known for its **bureaucratic system**, it conquered Babylon and was a major power in the

			ancient world.
Greek Empire	331 BCE – 146 BCE	Belly and Thighs of Bronze	Spread of **Greek culture and philosophy** throughout the world, including the rise of **Alexander the Great**, influencing many areas of Western thought.
Roman Empire	27 BCE – 476 CE	Legs of Iron	Strongest and longest-lasting empire of ancient history, known for **military dominance**, legal innovations, and control of vast territories, including Israel.
Divided Kingdoms	Post-476 CE to present	Feet of Iron and Clay	Represents the **fractured nature of modern global politics**, alliances, and the weakened unity of world powers, seen in post-Roman kingdoms and modern nations.

Appendix D: Key Eschatological Texts Across Religious Traditions

Religious Tradition	Key Prophetic Texts	Core Eschatological Themes
Christianity	Book of **Revelation, Daniel 7, Matthew 24**	**Second Coming of Christ**, final judgment, establishment of the **Kingdom of God**, battle of **Armageddon**, resurrection of the dead, **New Heaven and New Earth**.
Judaism	**Isaiah 11, Ezekiel 38-39, Daniel 9**	**Messianic Age**, restoration of Israel, rebuilding of the **Third Temple**, ultimate peace, defeat of **Gog and Magog**, resurrection, judgment, and eternal rule of God.
Islam	**Surah Al-Kahf (18:99), Hadith on Mahdi**	The rise of **Dajjal** (the Antichrist), the coming of the **Mahdi**, return of **Isa (Jesus)**, final battle, resurrection, and establishment of the **Divine Kingdom**.

Zoroastrianism	Yashts, Zand-i Vohuman Yasht	The coming of the **Saoshyant** (Savior), defeat of evil forces, resurrection of the dead, final purification of the world, and the renewal of creation in eternal peace.

Appendix E: Key Figures and Movements Influenced by Prophecy

Figure/Movement	Influence of Prophecy
Christian Zionism	Belief in the prophetic role of **Israel** in the end times motivates **political support** for Israel and advocacy for **Jewish control** over **Jerusalem** and the **Temple Mount**.
Premillennial Dispensationalism	Focus on the **Rapture**, the **Tribulation**, and the **Millennial reign** of Christ shapes evangelical activism, particularly regarding **moral issues** and **Middle Eastern politics**.
Islamic Eschatology Movements	**Shia** and **Sunni movements** anticipating the **Mahdi** and **Isa (Jesus)** have influenced **political ideologies**, especially concerning global conflicts and justice movements.
Progressive Christian Movements	Inspired by the vision of the **New Jerusalem**, these movements focus on **social justice**, **racial equality**,

	environmental **stewardship**, and **peacebuilding** as reflections of **God's kingdom**.

Appendix F: Glossary of Key Eschatological Terms

Term	Definition
Armageddon	The final battle between the forces of **good and evil**, as prophesied in the **Book of Revelation** (16:16), often associated with **global conflict** in the Middle East.
Antichrist	In **Christian eschatology**, the figure who will arise during the **end times** to oppose Christ, often linked to themes of **deception**, **global power**, and **persecution**.
Mahdi	In **Islamic eschatology**, the messianic figure who will appear before the **Day of Judgment** to restore justice and defeat **Dajjal** (the Antichrist).
Dajjal	The **Islamic Antichrist** figure who will spread **deception** and **evil** before being defeated by **Isa (Jesus)** and the **Mahdi** in the end times.
Rapture	In **Christian theology**, the event where believers are taken up to heaven prior to the **Tribulation**, often associated with **premillennial dispensationalism**.

New Jerusalem	The prophesied eternal city described in **Revelation 21**, symbolizing the **renewed creation** where **God dwells** with His people after the final judgment.